# Coat of Many Colours

Dedication

This book is dedicated to Pastor (Mrs) Folu Abeboye
for her compassion to the poor, oppressed,
distressed and the needy

# *Coat of Many Colours*

The Origin, Growth, Distinctiveness and
Contributions of Black Majority Churches
to British Christianity

Copyright © 2012

All rights reserved. No part of this publication may be reproduced or transmitted in any form or by any means, electronic or mechanical including photocopying, recording or any information storage or retrieval system, without prior permission in writing from the publisher.

First published in the United Kingdom in 2012
by Wisdom Summit

ISBN 978-0-9561800-1-8

Produced by
The Choir Press, Gloucester

# Contents

| | |
|---|---|
| Commendations | *Page* vii |
| Foreword | xi |
| Acknowledgements | xiii |
| Abbreviations | xv |

| | |
|---|---|
| **Chapter One:** Introduction | 1 |
|    Methodology | 3 |
|    Scope and Division of The Work | 4 |

| | |
|---|---|
| **Chapter Two:** The Origin of Black Churches in Great Britain | 7 |
|    Introduction | 7 |
|    Black Antecedents in Britain | 8 |
|    The Origin of Black Churches in Britain | 19 |
|    Black Christian Heritage – Pre-*Windrush* Era | 33 |
|    *Windrush* and The Black Church Movement in Britain | 39 |
|    Summary | 48 |

| | |
|---|---|
| **Chapter Three:** The Numerical Growth of Black Majority Churches in Great Britain Since the 1950s | 49 |
|    Introduction | 49 |
|    Growth Dynamics: Push and Pull Leverages | 50 |
|    Distinctive Growth Phases of Black-led Churches | 83 |
|    Health Check: Real or Apparent Growth | 99 |
|    Summary | 111 |

| | |
|---|---|
| **Chapter Four:** The Distinctive Theological and Practical Features of Black-led Churches in Great Britain | 113 |
|    Introduction | 113 |
|    Denominational Strands of Black-led Churches | 114 |
|    Black-led Churches and Traditional Pentecostalism | 118 |
|    Distinctions Between Oneness and Trinitarian Pentecostal Doctrine | 122 |

Coat of Many Colours: Theologies of Black Majority
    Churches in Britain      127
The American Black Theology Features in Black Majority
    Churches in Britain      149
Summary      153

**Chapter Five:** The Contributions of Black Majority Churches and their Members to British Christianity      154
    Introduction      154
    Church Growth and Resonance in Inner Cities of Britain      155
    Social, Economic and Political Relevance      160
    Black Majority Churches and "Labelling Theory"      176
    Political Activism of Black Majority Churches in Britain      184
    Faith Communities: State and Social Public Policy in Britain      189
    Summary      196

**Chapter Six:** Applying the Lessons of History      197
    Introduction      197
    Retrospect: Looking Back      198
    Repositioning: Learning the Lessons      205
    Resourcing: Maximizing the Future      222
    Summary      228

**Chapter Seven:** Conclusion      230
    Migration, Diaspora and Religious Identity      234
    Uniqueness of the Black Majority Church Praxis      240
    Raising the Stakes: Black Majority Churches' Social Capital      242
    Missionary Challenges      246

Notes      251
Bibliography      285
Index      306

# Commendations

This is a fine study on the history and significance of African and African Caribbean Pentecostalism in Britain today. The author writes from the inside of the movement with alacrity and insight, and this book will surely need to be consulted by anyone wanting to understand British Black Churches in future.

Allan Anderson<br>
Professor of Global Pentecostalism<br>
School of Philosophy, Theology and Religion<br>
University of Birmingham<br>
Birmingham

*Coat of Many Colours* adds the much needed spices to the rich historiography of African and 'Black Majority' Churches in Britain. The popularity of the discourse on the shift in the centre of gravity of Christianity from the North to the South sometimes obscures the ongoing revitalization of Christianity in the Northern hemisphere. This book provides the needed caution in understanding how and to what extent immigrant religious communities, such as African and African-Caribbean Christianities in Britain, are contributing to the re-energizing and re-empowering of Christianity in Britain but also repositioning World Christianities. It is a must-read for all interested in the reconfiguration of Christianity in our modern cosmos.

Dr. Afe Adogame<br>
Centre for the Study of World Christianity<br>
The University of Edinburgh<br>
New College, Mound Place<br>
Edinburgh, UK

This book has succeeded in adding a new chapter to the history of Black majority Churches in Britain. Babatunde in this decisive work also gives valuable insight to the role of the black people in the emergence of British Pentecostalism.

*Coat of Many Colours*' uniqueness is profound as Babatunde Adedibu has not only documented the historical antecedents dating from the origin of modern black churches in Britain to 1907 and the relevance of these churches. He also passionately argues that the missiological agenda of Black Churches in Britain needs urgent assessment. He writes perceptively and in a critical manner which depicts a heart yearning for change and a passion for these churches to maximise their potentials comes across very strongly.

*Coat of Many Colours* is a great resource material for Black Church leaders in Britain. Babatunde's effort is not only commendable, it is a book that every one of Britain's Black Church leaders and those who want to understand Black Majority Churches, should read.

Pastor Agu Irukwu<br>
Jesus House, London

*Coat of Many Colours* is a detailed and comprehensive study of churches of African and Caribbean background in the United Kingdom. It provides the reader for the first time a general overview of this increasingly influential strand of Christianity in the West. The author's personal involvement facilitates his combining an insider's insight with a more distanced description and analysis. Recommended reading for the one who wants to know more about the future of Christianity in Europe.

Mika Vähäkangas
Professor in Mission Studies and Ecumenics
Centre for Theology and Religious Studies
Lund University, Sweden

This book gives an unparalleled and comprehensive account of the growth of Black Church life in the UK from its earliest beginnings. In short, this is an insider's view of a modern and amazing movement of God in the UK. Anyone wanting to understand in detail the incredible black phenomenon which has happened in the last 50 years in Britain should read this volume. If you want a vibrant, up-to-date, knowledgeable overview of Black Church life today, this is second to none, and is highly recommended.

Dr Peter Brierley
Senior Lausanne Associate for Church Research
Editor, *UK Church Statistics, 2005–2015*
Director, Peter Brierley Consultancy
Former Director, Christian Research UK

I welcome this seminal work by Babatunde Adedibu. It makes a significant contribution to the body of knowledge of the urban explosion of Black Majority Churches in the United Kingdom. *Coat of Many Colours* is not only a compendium of historic facts but gives a critical appraisal of Britain's amazing Black Church Movement. If you are interested in the history, distinctiveness, challenges and the growth of Black Majority Churches in Britain, this publication is second to none. I commend this work to all.

Bishop Wilton Powell, OBE, FRSA
National Overseer
Church of God of Prophecy
United Kingdom

*Coat of Many Colours* is by far the most comprehensive description of African and Caribbean Church experience in the United Kingdom, well researched and focused on providing an insight not captured in any other publications or writings from previous church leaders and writers. This work is pathbreaking and provides those of us dedicated to Church-based community development and social action with the spiritual blessing and underpinning that is normally lacking from amongst the African and Caribbean Communities. Most importantly it also recognizes individuals, their sacrifices and how they overcame the discriminations of their time. There are many lessons to be learned today.

Rudi Page
CEO
RAFFA International Development Agency
United Kingdom

# Commendations

Babatunde Adedibu has added a new chapter to the historical antecedents of Britain's Black Majority Churches with the publication of *Coat of Many Colours*. Babatunde is quite perceptive, critical, identifying and prescribing solutions to some of the challenges of Britain's Black Majority Churches. *Coat of Many Colours* is thought provoking, engaging and futuristic. I commend this work to all and sundry.

Pastor Lloyds Ademola Adeleke
Senior Pastor, House of Praise
Camberwell, London

All over the globe, the Spirit of God is at work in bringing the Black church into the vanguard of spiritual and social leadership. This is a prophetic book which should act as a reference and guide towards the emerging Kingdom. Its pages reflect missio dei; God on a mission, shaping and transforming a people for His purpose and Glory. In the coming days, the significance of this writing will become more striking as the Lord builds and brings cultures and colours together for the healing and restoration of broken communities and nations. Read this book and pray. Study the chapters and cry. Digest its contents and act. I hope that this book helps to change your perspective motivating you to help knit God's coat of many colours for mankind.

Dr Jonathan Oloyede
Global Day of Prayer, London

The presence of the African Majority Churches in the West is critical for the future of Christianity. Understanding their life, witness and role is of tremendous significance and Babatunde Adedibu has made an invaluable contribution to this debate. I am more than happy to commend his work to all who have an interest in this area.

Dr Martin Robinson
Principal
Springdale College
Birmingham

We underestimate at our peril the impact of Black Majority Churches on the Church landscape across Great Britain. This work not only looks back – reflecting on the historic contribution of Black Majority Churches – but looks to the future, as to how the life, health and vitality of these churches might have maximum impact on the years to come. Senior students of the Church in the United Kingdom will regard this as an important contribution to better understanding the diversity of God's people in this nation.

Steve Clifford
General Director
Evangelical Alliance UK

The expansion of Black-led Churches and Southern Christianity has become a significant feature of Christian life in metropolitan and urban England over the past half century. We have benefited greatly from those theologians and commentators within that community (and from the historic denominations) who have helped us to understand both the gifts being offered by these communities of Christians and the challenges facing them. The literature is diverse and rich – Robert Beckford, Anthony Reddie, Michael Jagessar, Joe Aldred and Mark Sturge have all made significant contributions. To their ranks must now be added Babatunde Adedibu. The significance of his research is threefold. First, he writes as part of the African Diaspora, and he offers new and not uncritical insights into the dynamics of African (and especially Nigerian) Christianity. Second, his historical researches provide a significantly longer perspective on the history of Black Pentecostalism in England – now confidently dated back to the early twentieth century. Third, he writes as a missiologist who is passionately convinced that the future of what might loosely be called the Black Pentecostal Movement lies in mission to indigenous English society. That is both a profound challenge and an exciting agenda. If it is to make headway, this book will need careful reading, and its lessons must be assimilated by all who are part of God's mission in England.

Dr David Cornick<br>
General Secretary<br>
Churches Together in England

*Coat of Many Colours* has succeeded in bringing into focus the historical antecedents of the first Black Church in Britain established in 1907. The uniqueness of *Coat of Many Colours* is not only in its rich historical research but it also offers distinctive missiological narratives of the challenges and prospects of Black Majority Churches in Britain. With 1.9% of Britain's population being Africans and Carribeans, Babatunde gives a critical appraisal of the "triumphant mode" of the success of these churches which is yet to translate to conversion amongst the Caucasion population. This book is highly commendable and is a major contribution to Black British Theology.

Dr David-Sola Oludoyi<br>
Senior Pastor<br>
Royal Connections, UK

I strongly recommend this book to all Christians interested or even concerned about church growth in the UK. It is very informative on the subject of church growth and an encouragement to all believers praying for a revival in our nation. It also comes as a challenge to what we might wrongly refer to as *white-led* churches. The author has diligently researched the history, growth and ongoing development of what he describes as *black-led* congregations. However he shows great awareness of the problems facing what in effect are often multi-racial and diversely ethnic groups of believers, and offers meaningful help to those numerous groups of churches reviewed in this book.

Rev. Prof. Dr Colin Warner<br>
Faculty Member and Internal Examiner for the<br>
Greenwich School of Theology<br>
External Examiner for Middlesex University<br>
Registered Tutor with Chester University

# Foreword

~

The supreme irony of the much-vaunted growth of the Black Church Movement in Britain is that it occurs precisely at the moment when Christian church membership and attendance in Britain have been in decline. Attendance in Britain's historic churches has been falling particularly since the Second World War, to its current low of some 6% of the population (Peter Brierley). Conversely, from a near standing start in the *Windrush* era, the Black Church Movement has experienced tremendous growth, mainly through migration and biological growth among people of Caribbean and African heritages. There are resonances here with the story of Joseph in Egypt, with a God-inspired plan for food in a time of famine (Genesis).

The growth of the Black Church Movement however, needs to be studied and better understood; not least because the concentration of African and Caribbean people in major conurbations can give a misleading impression of a presence bloated by this phenomenon. The 2001 Census cited the size of the British African heritage population at 0.9%, and the Caribbean at 1% which means that however plenteous these may appear in London, Birmingham, Manchester, Bristol etc., there is the overwhelming majority of 98% of the British population outside of that. There is a great risk of not seeing the wood for the trees!

Indeed, I argue that the Black Church Movement now faces a challenge of spiritual maturity. Growing into maturity implies the ability to care for or minister to oneself and others. Glorying in growth among 2% of the British population should not be a lasting preoccupation for the community itself or onlooking well-wishers. The Black Church Movement in Britain has to ask itself, why has God placed this leaven in this dough? It cannot exist for its own satisfaction or glory, but to benefit the whole. And in this regard the Black Church Movement is challenged to move beyond the embryonic to maturity, which given the state of the dough is a matter of some urgency.

This work argues that British Black Majority Churches have not risen to the missionary challenge of the British community. This is self-evidently true. However, this can either be a millstone around the neck of the still fledgling Black Church Movement or a cause to pause, take breath, and resolve to grapple with, having come the kingdom "for such a time as this" (Esther). Sixty years since the *Windrush* landing in 1948 that so symbolizes the rise of the Black Church Movement, is not a long time in church history, and so there need not be guilt at such qualified failure to reach beyond the Black Church Movement's natural constituency. But time is short, the Lord is at hand, and we have no time to waste in getting on with the missional task of ministry to the British community, not just the African and Caribbean heritage bit of it. The vibrancy, commitment, love for God and God's mission to the world are not exclusive to, but are distinctive features of, the Black Church Movement in Britain. And the country awaits the dawn of a mature ecclesiology and missiology inherent in British Black Christianity that delivers a message of hope found in the Gospel of Jesus Christ.

Dr Adedibu does well to remind the Black Church Movement of where it has come from, the struggles it has been through, the significant contributions it has made already to British life, and most especially its missiological raison d'être. As Britain becomes what is now described as a "super diverse" society, particularly in terms of a polyglot of ethnicities, faiths, cultures and nationalities (Runnymede Trust), the Black Church Movement will need to work both harder and smarter, emboldened by the Holy Spirit, to be the messenger of the Good News of the Gospel of Jesus Christ to the people among whom God has placed it.

Bishop Dr Joe Aldred<br>
Secretary<br>
Minority Ethnic Christian Affairs<br>
Churches Together in England

# Acknowledgements

There are a number of people who assisted in making this publication a reality and I am grateful to all of them. Firstly, my gratitude to the King of Kings and the Lord of Lords who is the source of my inspiration and accomplishments. I am particularly grateful to Dr Martin Robinson who instilled in me the art of critical theological reflection as a mentee.

This publication is the adaptation of my doctoral thesis submitted to the North-West University, South Africa and as such I wish to acknowledge the contributions of Professor Colin Warner, my promoter, and Professor Derrick Mashau, my co-promoter, for their guidance and critique of the thesis at various stages of the research.

I am indebted to the General Overseer of the Redeemed Christian Church of God, Pastor E.A. Adeboye, for his fatherly disposition and assistance in my life. I am also grateful to Pastors Agu Irukwu, Andrew Adeleke, Kola Bamigbade, Leke Sanusi, Janet Adedipe and Modupe Afolabi, of the Redeemed Christian Church of God, United Kingdom, for the privilege of serving the organization as the Research and Policy Officer. Several of my colleagues who kept me in step with various stages of the book include Seyi Oke, Sade Oshewa, Nike Ishola, Tolu Kasali, Akinfisoye Babatunde, Wiliams Erinle, Emmanuel Okolie, Yinka Oduwole, Giberline Mbah and Rayo Tinubu.

Dr David-Sola Oludoyi: your love, kindness and encouragement even in the most challenging phase of my Christian experience is exemplary, touching and profound. People whose shadow falls over much ground in this work are numerous students that I have instructed in various theological colleges in Britain whose quest for answers to the perceived challenges of Black Majority Churches in Britain prompted me severally to publish this work.

Grateful thanks also to Desmond Cartwright, the official historian of Elim Pentecostal, Great Britain, for sharing with me the historical antecedents of Black Majority Churches in Britain, and Professor David

Killingray for his assistance. Rev. Weeks, the church historian of the Apostolic Church, Great Britain, added a unique dimension to my research findings and conclusions on Thomas Brem-Wilson. Dr Iain MacRobert, thank you for your suggestions during the writing of this book.

The achievements of the forerunners of Black British Theology in the likes of Dr Emmanuel Lamptey, Robert Beckford, Anthony Reddie, Michael Jeggassar and Joe Aldred created significant leverage for my generation to build on. Your commitment and assertions on black British theology are not only unique but you have all charted a new course and generations after you shall call you blessed.

My gratitude to the following people for their contributions to this research: Dr David Muir, Rev. Yemi Adedeji, Pastors Richard and Adejoke Odejayi, Shola Ajani and a host of others too numerous to mention. The contributions of Dr Richard Burgess, Dr Daniel Akhazemea and Dr Hugh Osgood to this work cannot be overemphasized.

I'd like to thank my editor, Fiona Thornton and Miles Bailey and his colleagues at The Choir Press for their work to make this publication a reality.

Finally, thanks to my wife, Jadesola. Your unflinching faith in my potential and your love over the years cannot but be appreciated. Emmanuel and Theophilous: your sacrifices and appreciation of my theological commitments are well appreciated.

*Chapter One*

# Introduction

∼

This study was motivated – one might even say necessitated – by the extraordinary growth of Black Churches in Great Britain over the last six decades. The urban explosion of Black Majority Churches in Britain constitutes something of a paradox in the context of official statistics that point to a decline in church attendance generally over the same period.[1] It is my intention not only to investigate the validity and possible reasons for such an apparent dichotomy, but also to provide the basis for any future reflection on the "new" and significant era in the history of Black Majority Churches[2] in Britain, especially in respect of their origin, growth, distinctiveness and contribution to British Christianity. Thus far, such a study has not been adequately or appropriately made available.

Historically, the seeds of what was to become the current phenomenon of Black Churches in this country arrived aboard the SS *Empire Windrush* at Tilbury Docks on 22 June 1948. Over four hundred Jamaicans had responded to a newspaper advertisement in their homeland inviting interested parties to make a new life for themselves as part of a British government initiative to meet the labour shortfall that had resulted from the effects of the Second World War. Those who came brought their skills, their hopes and their work ethic; perhaps more significantly, they also brought a faith that was common to many, but unique to them in its mode of expression.[3]

From such humble beginnings, it was estimated that by 1962 there were almost eighty congregations representing a wide array of groups of West Indian Pentecostal or "Holiness" churches in Britain.[4] The rapid growth of these churches was so pronounced that within two years of Malcolm Calley's initial study, the number had risen to just under four hundred.[5] By the 1980s, there were over 2,500 such congregations representing around 160 denominational groups, their aggregate membership estimated to constitute approximately 13% of the total Afro-Caribbean population in Britain.[6] It would seem that this rate of increase has not diminished in recent years, as evidenced by the following telling observation from the Archbishop of Canterbury, Dr Rowan Williams, in 2005: "This is having a big impact on our major cities, where the black majority churches are growing fast ... People from ethnic minorities are also bringing new life and energy into churches from established denominations such as the Church of England. This is one of the reasons why the Anglican Diocese of London, for example, is now growing steadily."[7]

It has been estimated that there are currently in excess of five hundred thousand black Christians in Britain.[8] There have been a number of notable attempts to rationalize and categorize this growth and its associated features, some with less convincing arguments than others. Aldred's treatise *Respect: Understanding Caribbean British Christianity*, made a significant contribution by emphasizing the need for a shift in emphasis from liberation theology praxis to "theology of respect" amongst black British scholars. Aldred's focus, which was mainly Caribbean, commensurately limited the scope of the work but it is a benchmark publication on black British theology. A major shortcoming of Mark Sturge's contribution,[9] for example, has been his isolationist approach that largely fails to consider the history of Black Churches in Britain as his study did not take into consideration certain historical antecedents of Black Churches in Britain and the context of their specific contribution to British Christianity has significantly changed since his publication. Sturge failed to engage various publications of Black British Theologians which could have given his work broad spectrum appeal to scholars. David Killingray and Joel Edwards, on the other hand, have produced an anthology of the presence of black people in Britain since 1500 in terms that that – by their own admission – pays scant regard to the history of Black Churches in this country during the second half of the twentieth century.[10]

Stephen Hunt employed a different strategy altogether. He investigated one of the fastest-growing Black Church set-ups in Britain, Jesus House, a parish of the Redeemed Christian Church of God (RCCG). His research disclosed that a large proportion of the RCCG's membership in this country is of Yoruba extraction. This research provided the platform for his own later exploration of the role of RCCG congregations in a contemporary Western context.[11] Hunt concluded that the RCCG brand of Pentecostalism is unique in addressing the needs of black ethnic minorities, though the narrowness of his study commensurately limits the scope of its value in the larger context of our focus.

## METHODOLOGY

The focus of previous publications undertaken by other scholars is altogether inadequate for one reason or another, either because it does not appropriately address the issues of concern that are the focus of this study or because it provides an inaccurate representation of the whole. The central question of this study, therefore, is: "How may one determine the current status of Black Churches in Great Britain in the context of their origin, growth, distinctiveness and contribution to Christianity there?" The questions that naturally arise from this problem are: What seeds were sown by the pioneers of Black Churches in Britain that strategically influenced all that followed? What have been the major contributory factors towards the subsequent growth of Black Churches in Britain since the 1950s? What are the distinctive theological and practical features of Black Churches in Britain? What lessons can be learned from the above findings in relation to maximizing the potential of Black Churches in Britain today? The aim of this study is to evaluate the current status of Black Majority Churches in Great Britain in the context of their origin, growth, distinctiveness and contribution to Christianity. The interrelationship of the objectives of this work is reflected in the aims, which are fivefold: firstly to reflect upon the historical account of the pioneers of Black Majority Churches in Britain; secondly to identify the major contributory factors towards the subsequent growth of Black Majority Churches in Britain since the 1950s; thirdly, to assess the distinctive theological and practical features of Black Majority Churches in Britain; fourthly to examine the above findings in order to learn how the potential of Black Majority Churches in Britain today might be maximized; and finally to evaluate the contributions of Black Majority Churches to Christianity in Britain since the 1950s.

The central theoretical argument of this study is that the emergence and development of Black Majority Churches since the 1950s, especially in view of their distinctive features, has contributed significantly towards a new era in the history of Christianity in Great Britain.

The aim and objectives – as identified above – will be approached from a broad framework that is decidedly within the Black British Pentecostal Church tradition, though measures were taken to ensure that my findings do not give cause for unwarranted allegations of unnecessary bias. Thus I am concerned to utilize the relevant historical literature available on the subject in conjunction with relevant secondary sources using histographic methods. The selection of sources is motivated by historiographical interests in relation to central theoretical argument.

The historiographical method utilised in this study provides an opportunity to acquire a rich understanding of situations and the context in which they exist. Knowing the background to any situation or to any issue enhances comprehension and improves perception to see what is important and what is not. In the words of Elton, "historical knowledge gives solidity to the understanding of the present".[12] During the course of the historical rigour I exercised integrity regarding present evidence, avoiding fixed ideas and using a wide-ranging set of sources, thorough criticism of sources used, and rationally objective arguments.

It is imperative to note that there is no general consensus as to precisely how history should be researched and written.[13] Marwick buttresses this by saying that history is an ill-defined line of work.[14] Marwick further posits that the term historiography may be attained not for the treatise of past events themselves but rather a personal subjective interpretation of events by historians. It is in the light of this assertion that I consider historic opinions in the subject matter under consideration just as important as reports and other hard evidence.

I evaluated the liturgical practices, preaching styles, common ethos and generally accepted doctrinal statements frequently associated with major strands of Black Majority Churches in Britain mostly through primary and secondary sources and as a participant observer. This facilitated very good understanding of the theologies and doctrinal persuasion of Black Majority Churches which is more of "doing" rather than creedal based. I considered the fluidity of the African and Caribbean cosmology in the expression of the faith of Africans and Caribbeans to cope with their daily exigencies. A wide range of documents were used which included church brochures, directories, annual reports, magazines and church bulletins. Secondary texts utilised include doctoral theses.[15] The long essays provided the opportunity to engage different facets of Black Church life in Britain due to the fact that few scholars have actually researched Black Majority Churches. In addition to these theses, two postgraduate theses[16] and publications in various sociological, theological and Pentecostal Journals were utilised.[17] This present study further contributes to the emerging publications on Black Majority Churches in Britain.

## SCOPE AND DIVISION OF THE WORK

The focus of this study is the use of historiography and sociological approaches to provide a basis for the evaluation of the origin, growth and distinctiveness of Black Majority Churches and their contributions to

British Christianity. This study has succeeded in effectively dating the origin of Black Churches in Britain to 1906 in consonance with previous assertions of MacRobert[18] but also ascertained the nature of the first Black Church in modern Britain as a multicultural church and with very strong ecumenical ties linked to the emergence of British Pentecostalism at Sunderland.[19] It is apt to assert that this study is not a theological treatise on Black Majority Churches but a historical and sociological exposé on African and Caribbean Diasporic Pentecostal churches in Britain spanning over a hundred years. It is pertinent to acknowledge the contributions of Walter Hollenwenger, Emmanuel Lamptey, Robert Beckford, Anthony Reddie, Michael Jagessar, Joe Aldred, David Muir and Mark Sturge to British black theology. But since the focus of this study revolves around the Pentecostal prism of African and Caribbean Diasporic churches in Britain, the distinctive nature of the scope of this work is imperative. Beckford has provided a distinctive paradigm on political theology for black British theology. This is reflected in his canon[20] and media programmes that have consistently in the last ten years focused on various structural inequalities in Britain. One of the unique features of Beckford's postulations is the challenge to Eurocentric theologians to accept the Theological Liberation Praxis as a legitimate form of hermeneutics. Mark Sturge's and Joe Aldred's contributions were mainly historical and sociological treatises on Black Majority Churches.[21] Aldred essentially chronicled an aspect of the diversity of the Black Church which is the British Caribbean Christianity. The succinct appeal and understanding of the Caribbean cosmology, especially his Jamaican roots, became a reference point in extolling the religious consciousness of Caribbeans. Granted, he was quite emphatic in his assessment of the social and racial injustices of the *Windrush* era but he clamoured for a paradigm shift from the American Liberation Theology semantics with a definite agenda for the future – remembering the past as part of the history of Black British Churches but with much enthusiasm to face the future.

The uniqueness of this research in relation to previous scholarship on Black Majority Churches is that it is written from a missiological perspective. Various studies on the expansion of Pentecostalism[22] generally are on the increase but there is a dearth of missiological work on Black Majority Churches in Britain. This study captures the emergence of the Black Church in Britain from its infancy as the "black man's church" to the silent years of late 1929 when the historical antecedents of the first Black Church was almost blurred through affiliation to White Pentecostal denominations, to the second phase through the ministry of Reverend Daniel Ekarte in Liverpool in 1938, the *Windrush* religious awakening, the African

Independent Churches' emergence in the 1950s, the emergence of African Pentecostal Churches and finally the Neo-African Pentecostal dispensation. The uniqueness of this research is not only in the historical narratives of Black Majority Churches' origin, growth and their distinctiveness. The study also reconstructed the history of Britain's Black Majority Churches from their origins necessitating a critique of the sociological and missiological inadequacies in relation to the future of these churches. This study is not without its limitations: the burgeoning 4,000[23] Black Majority Churches in Britain cannot be sampled in their entirety due to a dearth of data and research limitations of manpower, finances and time frame. In the light of this, this study's focus is reflective of the evaluation of common doctrinal subscription amongst Black Majority Churches.

The book is made up of seven chapters. The first chapter provides the basis of the research in relation to previous research efforts, the aims and objectives and the historical context of the study. Chapter Two gives a definite historical overview of Blacks in Britain as far back as the twelfth century and their associated challenges which culminated in the emergence of Black Churches in Britain. Chapter Three explores the reasons for the proliferation of Black Majority Churches in Britain. The uniqueness of this section is the distinctive growth phases of these churches especially in the last sixty years. Chapter Four examines the distinctive theological praxis of Black Majority Churches. Black Church theology is not uniform, but its diverse strands, like Oneness beliefs, are described and compared with Trinitarian Pentecostal doctrine, collectively with their vital strengths and weaknesses. The vitality of these churches and their theological subscriptions has endeared the churches to their members akin to a similar resonance in global Pentecostalism. Chapter Five gives vivid insight into the contributions of Black Majority Churches and their members to British Christianity, showing their concern in assisting those who are not well off in innumerable ways, often with the dynamic support of relevant local authorities. This chapter further explores the implications of the social initiatives of these churches in relation to the future of Black Majority Churches. Chapter Six of the study provides a panoramic view of Black Majority Churches in critiquing their journey of faith retrospectively, repositioning and resourcing for the future of these churches, while Chapter Seven is the final chapter and conclusion of the study.

*Chapter Two*

# The Origin of Black Churches in Great Britain

∼

### INTRODUCTION

The history of Black Majority Churches, Black-led or Black Churches in Britain cannot be divorced from the black historical antecedents in Britain. Britain of today is a multi-ethnic and multicultural country as a result of over five hundred years of assimilation of various nationalities, and this has made Britain a unique country whose inhabitants display diverse socio-cultural and economic integration.

Postmodern Britain is incomparable to the Britain of any other era in history and owes its present composition to a multiplicity of factors which include historical antecedents of Roman occupation, the slave trade, Commonwealth ties, globalization, and economic and forced migration, which has contributed significantly to the emergence of African and Caribbean communities in Diaspora throughout the Western world. The term "black" within the context of this work refers to those of African and Caribbean origin and descent within the Pentecostal prism.

The intrigues and emancipation of Africans and Caribbeans as slaves who rode on the crest of ethnocentrism and religious bigotry of the slave masters eventually became an avenue that contributed to the demise of the slave trade as some slaves sought their freedom on the platform of conversion to the Christian faith and the ordinance of baptism which the slaves thought was "absolute decree" for their emancipation.

By the mid-eighteenth century various alliances, relationships and community cohesion were evident amongst Blacks, expressed in art, entertainment and literary works, but an organized form of religion amongst Blacks was identified in the nineteenth century, according to Iain MacRobert.[1] He noted the existence of a Black Pentecostal Church in London around 1907, but according to a Sureway International Christian Ministries publication[2] the first Black-led Church was started by Bro. Thomas Kwow Brem-Wilson and Bro. Newlands in 1906. The history of

Black Churches is inextricably linked with the history of the British Pentecostalism of the nineteenth century which had its roots in the Azusa Street revival of 1906. The nineteenth century marked the turning point in black history as Blacks migrated into Britain for further studies and professional fulfilment thereby changing public perception that Blacks were associated with inferior status while playing an active part in the socio-economic life of Britain. The *Windrush* era provided the backdrop for the migration of Caribbeans, Africans and Asians, which accentuated the re-emergence, growth, and proliferation of Black Churches in Britain over time. The proliferation of Black Churches in Britain has heralded a new era in British church history.

## BLACK ANTECEDENTS IN BRITAIN

### *Genesis of Black Antecedents in Britain*

The history of black people has always been part of British history. The historical antecedents of Blacks in Britain has been traced to AD 193–211, when around 500 North African soldiers were stationed at the Roman military garrison at the Fort of Aballava on Hadrian's Wall in Cumbria[3] but the invasion by the Anglo-Saxons saw the demise of black people during the fifth and sixth centuries according to Williams.[4] These facts strongly repudiate the misconception that the presence of Blacks in Britain was a result of the slave trade.

Archaeological evidence of Africans, probably legionaries and their relatives, buried at York and the remains of a young African girl aged around fourteen years buried at Norfolk during Medieval times are strong reminders that Africans had found their way into Britain earlier than many might have conceived.[5]

The presence of black people was noted in various parts of Britain at diverse times, for instance in Scotland the marauding activities of the Vikings in Morocco and the subsequent captivity and forced migration of the captured Blacks was the genesis of Blacks in Scotland.[6] The sixteenth century heralded Blacks in royal service in the court of King Henry IV of Scotland; he attached a small group of Africans to his court. Blacks became a common feature in the social life of the Scots as they featured prominently in the tournament of the black knight and some of the black ladies were part of the Scottish Queen's attendants. Those who enjoyed fringe benefits as royal messengers or slaves included two black ladies at the Scottish court on whom the King spent seven pounds or ten French crowns as a new year gift, while "Black Elene" was given five French crowns in 1512.[7]

Blacks in the Middle Ages in Britain had roles not only as servants and slaves but they were prominent in the entertainment life of British people. Kings Henry VII and VIII employed a black trumpeter as did the courts of Elizabeth and James I, whose wife, Anne of Denmark, was painted accompanied by her black maidservant.[8]

In view of the providence afforded the Blacks in the late sixteenth century amongst the nobles as servants, white ladies disguised themselves as black, a common feature amongst ladies in waiting in the Court of Queen Elizabeth during theatrical performance. This was a social reconstruction of changes within the British cultural landscape and created a vivid connectedness to the roles that Blacks were identified with in Britain. Such theatrical plays, even when Blacks were represented or involved, were mostly woven around the Eurocentric notion of the superiority of Whites over Blacks.

The emergence of competitiveness between the British and the Portuguese, who had enjoyed the gains from the slave trade for over a century, was preceded in 1555 by the visit of five Africans from the coastal town of Shama in present-day Ghana with the assistance of John Lok, son of a prominent London merchant and alderman.[9] The status of the men in question could not be ascertained, as there exist two schools of thought; the first assumes they were kidnapped slaves, while Shyllon[10] says they were sent to Britain to learn English, so that on their return to Africa they would be a "helpe to Englishmen as interpreters". From Shyllon's perspective it can be inferred that the "Shammarians" might be domestic slaves of an African king that were lent to the British slave masters as a publicity stunt to disabuse the mind of the average British subject about the "dark continent of Africa" and the negative stereotypes about Africans while at the same time making a public presentation of the magnitude of the economic loss to would-be British merchants and slave merchants and economic gains that the Portuguese had enjoyed from Africa.

The visibility of "Blackmoores" within the realm of England was an issue of concern, as Queen Elizabeth wrote on 11 July 1596 in an open letter to the Lord Mayor of London and his aldermen that "those kinds of people should be deported".[11] This event instigated the deportation of Blacks in British history as "Blackmoores" were traded by Her Majesty to the Spanish and Portuguese slave dealers in lieu of 89 British citizens that were to be repatriated after serving their prison terms. Her Majesty noted the "reasonableness of the offer" to get rid of the Blacks in her realm, and it was indeed a brisk, shrewd business deal and a good end to black visibility as the "Blackmoores" were "bartered" for the repatriated British citizens.[12]

The aftermath of the initial successes of the first deportation of Blacks might have been the catalyst for the Elizabethan proclamation of 1601 as the Queen empowered Casper van Sanden to arrest and discharge Blacks from her kingdom as a result of economic challenges and because they were heathens that had no understanding of the Gospel and Christ! This certainly was a perversion of history on the part of the monarch as Africans and Africa had rich Christian traditions in biblical times prior to the Dark Ages[13] as the Christian faith was in Egypt by the middle of the first century. However, the concept of Africa as a historical and ancestral land of black culture "does not play a prominent role in either the Old Testament or the New Testament".[14]

The Elizabethan proclamation of 1601 was the royal seal that inferred that the Christian faith supported ethnocentrism; this indeed might have created late allusions to the Christian faith as being supportive of slave trade and racism. It was rather amazing that the pharisaic attitude of the Queen's proclamation of 1601 was grossly incompatible with the Great Commission of Jesus, as Christianizing the Africans was not an issue in comparison to the economic preservation alluded to in her "absolute decree".

The genesis of the slave trade in Britain cannot be told with clarity. Shyllon quoting Beckwith suggested that the first black slaves arrived in Britain in 1440 while other sources suggest dates as late as 1553.[15] However, John Hawkins pioneered the first British slavery expedition in 1555.

The success of the British Atlantic slave trade rode on the crest of the British "sweet tooth" for sugar and rum as huge numbers of slaves were required in sugar cane plantations in the Caribbean and America. Blacks were thus indispensable to the prosperous British economy according to Malachy Postlethwayth, who said: "if we have no Negroes, we can have no sugars, Tobaccos, Rice, Rum and ... consequently, the publick revenue, arising from the Importation-Produce, must be annihilated: And will this not turn many hundreds of thousands of British Manufacturers a Begging....".[16] It was not surprising that the state declared that the slave trade was beneficial to an "infinite extent".

It is often said of Liverpool in the late nineteenth century that "every brick in the city had been cemented by slave's blood".[17] The obvious drive for wealth by slave merchants cannot be over-emphasized as Blacks became indispensable for the making of "brick" even though it was against their wishes as wealth created was utilised to finance the capitalist economy and the industrial revolution, as merchant Joshua Gee wrote in 1779: "the supplying our plantations with Negroes is that of extraordinary advantage to us, that the planting of Sugar and Tobacco, and carrying on trade there could not be supported without them, which Plantations... are the great cause of the increase of the riches of the kingdom... All this great Increase of the riches of our Treasure proceeds chiefly from the Labour of Negroes in the plantations."[18] Bristol, Liverpool, London and other smaller ports like Chester, Glasgow, Whitehaven, Lancaster and Lyme Regis were slave ports that facilitated the transatlantic slave trade before it ended in 1807.

The massive exploitation of the black slaves through transportation to America also had its ripple effects on emigration to Britain from America, as many returned as domestic servants, seamen and labourers. This eventually led to a socio-economic crisis amongst Blacks in London as many could not afford the basic necessities of life, and some resorted to crime and prostitution. The prevailing moral ineptitude and poverty of the Blacks were common problems in the public domain as the West Indian lobby cartel utilised these to perpetuate their negrophobic campaign. Notable amongst such antagonists of black emancipation were Edward Long and William Beckford.

### Retributive Effects of Slavery in the British Social Landscape

By the mid-1780s it was noted that "great numbers of Blacks and people of colour, many of them refugees from America and others who have by land or sea been in his Majesty's service, were from severity of the season in great distress", according to a memorial of Henry Smeathman dated 17 May 1785.[19] The social demand was quite enormous as philanthropist and government aid was grossly inadequate, and there was contention within British Government circles as to whether the black population should be moved out of Britain.

The allusions to the social menace of some Blacks became stereotypes, but these completely ignored the fact that the functionalities of Blacks in terms of their potential was determined by the permissive will of the slave masters, as the ideology of slavery was holistic. It was "a deliberate system of cultural and psychological genocide. Every connection with the past was to be obliterated and the slaves were so thoroughly dehumanized and brainwashed that they would forget that he or she had been anything other than Nigger John or Nigger Mandy created by God, as early catechisms taught, 'to make a crop'".[20]

Plutocratic ideology also entailed the suppression of the giftedness of

Blacks. Any form of social expression was outlawed, as it was perceived it might foster social and community cohesion amongst the Blacks which might have led to rebellion. This giftedness included music, but the brilliance and giftedness of emancipated slaves was later celebrated in Britain.

This era witnessed the emergence of Samuel Coleridge Taylor, an accomplished black musician in his day. Coleridge Taylor was a product of the Royal College of Music London by the age of 15; Edward Elgar, Britain's leading composer, described Coleridge as the cleverest fellow amongst the young men in his day as his ingenuity was attested to with the production of *African Romances,* a setting of Paul Laurence Dunbar's poems. He was an accomplished producer and professor of music.

George Bridgetower, a friend to Beethoven, was a black music prodigy who showed extraordinary musical talent and made his professional debut in Paris at the age of nine when he played a violin concerto by the Italian composer Giovanni Giornovichi; his benefactor was the Prince of Wales who arranged for him to be taught theory of music. He eventually became the first violinist in the Prince of Wales' private orchestra for over a decade. He was a graduate of music from Cambridge University where he obtained the Bachelor of Arts. Beethoven described him as "a very able virtuoso and an absolute master of the instrument".[21]

The blanket ban on expression of giftedness inevitably created an identity crisis and social exclusion. The natural tendency of the untrained mind is to revolt against the moral code that perpetuates such ideology, and this was a major factor for slaves like Bill Richmond, a boxer who owned a gymnasium in London, John Baptist, who received his MD at Edinburgh and some other Blacks who re-orientated themselves and excelled in their endeavours.

The apparent condemnatory disposition of most commentators on the slave trade about the British slave merchants is a bit naïve, as Africans were actively involved in the arrest, detention and sale of their colleagues to Europeans. Before their passage to American colonies there was often a period of "seasoning" in which slaves were sold and conditioned to a life of servitude and deprivation with a high mortality rate. Slaves were routinely subjected to physical, psychological and sexual abuse.

Blacks became a common feature in the various parts of Britain but the greatest concentration was in London: many, mostly women, were employed as domestic servants, but poverty and misfortune made some become ladies of easy virtue. The recruitment policy of most slave dealers, favouring the procurement of male slaves over women (on account of the rigours of transportation, work demands on plantations and the seasoning effects) eventually had its knock-on effect on the social scene, as there was acute population disparity between black males and black women. The obvious results were the inevitable relational ties between black men and white women.

The publication in 1556 of *A summarie of the Antiquities, and wonders of the worlde*, an ancient folklore of Elder Pliny (AD 23–79) which featured misconceptions about Blacks' socio-cultural lives, had prepared the breeding ground for one of the worst negrophobic campaigns in Britain in the eighteenth century. This campaign, kindled by common law relationships, took the form of publications on white racial supremacy. Edward Long, a negrophobic activist, noted that "the lower women in England are remarkable [remarkably] fond of the blacks, for reasons too brutal to mention; they would connect themselves with horses and asses, if the laws permitted them"[22] but historical accounts negate his perspective: black males were associated with the nobles of their day, for example, there was scandal concerning the Duchess of Queensbury and her black servant, Scoubise.[23] Francis Barber was said to have had an exceptional experience amongst his contemporaries as he was once pursued by a lady haymaker from Lincolnshire to London.[24] Antagonism to such relationships came from anti-Abolitionists, especially from the pens of those West Indians who were involved in economic exploitation of Blacks rather than promoting their dignity, respect and civility.[25] Edward Long's treatise on black male and white female relationships was based on fear of miscegenation. His fears were grossly unfounded and unrealistic, but, ironically, his argument was not based on the inter-racial relationships between black men and white females but on an age-long prejudice about eugenics.[26]

The English propertied class employed African domestic servants who were protected and encouraged by their white masters to establish their families and homes. This facilitated the enhancement of historical data, as records of birth, marriages, baptism and death have contributed to the contemporary validation of Blacks' historical antecedents. Artistic seventeenth-century paintings of landed families give glimpses of the black servants tucked away in the corner in family settings and this culminated in the social bonding of some of these Blacks with their masters who returned to England's American colonies as government officials or military personnel. Some of these Blacks were beneficiaries of their masters' kindness that granted them "liberty", but this was an exception rather than a rule, as many slaves had to pay their way to be emancipated.[27] Pockets of individual paintings of black servants and notable black achievers were a common feature of the artistic world in Britain in the eighteenth century.

By the mid-eighteenth century, there was evidence of cohesion, solidarity and mutual help among black people in Britain, expressed in arts, entertainment, journalism and literary works, as many began to write about their experiences as slaves.[28]

### The Abolition of Slavery Recipe for Inclusiveness of Blacks in Britain

The ineptitude of the British judiciary dating back to 1569 was the "cracking noise" that was not heard until almost two centuries later as English law failed to recognize the status of a slave, but in 1667 in *Butts and Penny* it was held again that the British law recognize the status of slaves on the ground of being chattels. The legal disputations on slave status continued as Justice John Holt quashed earlier judgments that slavery is not a status recognized by the law of England. The British judiciary was enmeshed in legal arguments for over a century, trying to determine the rights of the slave master and the traditional British values of liberty.[29]

The attitude exhibited by the slave masters was one of indignation. Leading Abolitionists were Christians, with leading proponents from the Quakers (whose members ironically profited from the slave trade), Anglican evangelicals, Baptists and Methodists. There was not only legal disputation about the slaves being chattels that slave owners had rights over, but there was also contention over the Christianization of the slaves. Barbadian planters had earlier vehemently opposed the Christianization of slaves, maintaining their economic exploitation and avarice. The apparent apprehension was that baptism was synonymous with freedom for the slaves. In 1729 the English Attorney General and Solicitor General asserted that "a slave by coming from the West Indies, either with or without his master's property or right in him is not thereby determined or varied and baptism doth not bestow freedom on him, or make any alteration in his temporal condition in these kingdoms".[30]

Despite the ruling, Blacks embarked on a relentless campaign of emancipation, asserting that Christianization or marriage conferred freedom on the Blacks. The apparent adherence of Blacks to this view must have been due to the Spanish slave code which recognized some elements of dignity by acknowledging their spirituality,[31] a complete departure from the "protestant [British] slavery" which was a denial and destruction of the humanity of black people. The black slaves were inevitably property over which their masters had absolute authority.

The Church of England never taught the doctrine that black people should not be baptized, as the 1662 Book of Common Prayer was inclusive of the Blacks as potential candidates for baptism. The preface to the book explains: "An office for the Baptism of such as are of Riper Years … by growth of Anabaptism is now become necessary and may always be useful for baptising of Natives [sic] in our plantation."[32] Records indicate that as far back as 1660 Charles II instructed the church on conversion, baptism and Christian instruction with respect to Blacks.[33] The church never affirmed that baptism conferred freedom on Blacks but recognized their spirituality. However, on account of greed and avarice, black humanity was adjured as non-existent by the ruling class. The climax of the church apathy towards truth was the proclamation made by Thomas Sherlock, the Bishop of Bangor, Salisbury and London in 1727 that "Christianity and the embracing of the Gospel does not make the least difference in civil property".[34] This was greeted with a lot of enthusiasm by the plutocratic class.

This era also witnessed the massive churning out of various perspectives on the biblical position on slavery, which made Blacks ambivalent about the Bible. For instance, systemic articulation was piloted by Thornton Springfellow copiously citing the Old and New Testaments in his postulations. He made reference to Exodus 12:44, 45 and Job 3:11, 13, 17–19 as the basis of having slaves within the context of the New World in relation to the Old Testament worldview. Springfellow argued that Abraham, Isaac, Jacob, Joseph and Job had slaves. Commenting on Genesis 24:35 he states that "here, servants are enumerated with silver and gold as part of the patrimony. And, reader, bear it in mind: as if to rebuke the doctrine of Abolition, servants are not only inventoried as property, but as property which God had given to Abraham."[35] Springfellow's hermeneutics on slavery involved using Jacob's and Isaac's having slaves that were propertied as a model for the justification of slavery. He also posited that God endorsed slavery through the Decalogue on Mount Sinai. It is pertinent to note that Springfellow's hermeneutics were not borne with any scholarly insight, as his assertions were a product of flawed exegesis, taking out of context the various scriptures cited.

Such unscholarly articulations provided a basis to articulate the perpetuation of the subjugation of the Blacks. It became a transatlantic phenomenon to use the Christian faith as a basis for exploitation and dehumanization of the Blacks. Up to the eighteenth century very few Blacks were baptized but amazingly by the turn of the eighteenth century there were evidences of baptism in church registers oftentimes at birth rather than as adults in Britain. This was a form of Imperialism due to the perceived advantages that Christianity might give to Blacks. The rise in baptismal records was not in relation to conversion but acceptance of white supremacy. The perversion of values culminated in cultural alienation by the Blacks: a point of reference is the Caribbean experience as noted by Kortright who asserted that:

> under a dominant policy which stressed their natural inferiority and the inconsequential nature of their basic cultural heritage Caribbean people became mutually contemptuous. They began to assume that anything foreign and white was good enough. People became institutionally and systematically alienated from their own inherent characteristics and their own cultural endowments (race, colour, language, belief systems, relationships, preferences, entertainment and leisure, work schedules, family mores, aspirations) and also from their rightful access to the corridors of power, social mobility, and participatory citizenship.[36]

Interestingly, very few Blacks that were devout to the Christian faith made a lasting public impression. Equiano and Ignatius Sancho are examples. Equiano wrote in his autobiography, "the Bible was my only companion and comfort; I prized it much, with many thanks to God that I could read it for myself, and was not left to be tossed about or led by man's many devices and notions".[37] Black spirituality in Britain became more prominent in the late eighteenth century, as it became the precursor for the initial arguments against slavery and the slave trade.

The cruelty and inhumane treatment accorded Blacks generated much sympathy from some white professionals; notable amongst such was Granville Sharp, a barrister who took up black advocacy as a matter of principle, maintaining that Blacks are not chattels and should not be treated as such. Granville Sharp's commitment to putting the plight of Blacks in proper perspective was greatly enhanced by his clout with friends who included William Wilberforce, and his brother, William Sharp, an eminent surgeon at St Bartholomew's Hospital who was instrumental in the admission of Jonathan Strong after his altercation with David Lisle, a lawyer and slave master in 1765.[38]

The prevailing events within the black community had fostered community cohesion and solidarity as Granville became one of the prominent "Gamaliels" for the black cause, which included the likes of Dr Mayo, James Ramsay and William Roscoe. The relationship had a symbiotic effect on the Blacks and Granville Sharp who was fast becoming a legal icon on black aspirations for dignity and honour in collaboration with the black elitists through literary contributions that highlighted their experiences in the hands of the slave master. The partnership of Granville Sharp and black emancipation groups generated a lot of publicity. An example is the case of the slave ship *Zong* in 1781: over 131 slaves were thrown overboard in a fraudulent attempt for insurance claims, as they asserted the legal argument was not morality but that of "chattels". Granville Sharp did not secure a conviction but there was enormous public interest in the case.[39]

The movement for abolition of the slave trade came to its climax in 1787 through the efforts of the Society for Effecting the Abolition of the Slave Trade, with William Wilberforce as a prominent voice in parliament. The Abolitionist endeavour in the House of Commons was described as "the damnable doctrine of Wilberforce and his hypocritical allies"[40] but Wilberforce perceived the anti-slavery movement as a divine initiative "for such a time as this".[41] The cause of the Abolitionist was further strengthened by black radicals such as William Davidson, son of Jamaica's Attorney General, an excellent tradesman and of active Christian inclination, a former Wesleyan Sunday school teacher, who was beheaded with four of his white comrades, Arthur Thistle, John Brunt, James Ings and Richard Tidd on 1 May 1820 with the active connivance of the state's *agent provocateur* George Edwards. Davidson and his colleagues were convicted of treason by the jury and the judge. This was the last decapitation in British history.[42]

The parliamentarians made a series of reforms but many perceived that slavery should continue within defined boundaries, mainly because of the economic exploitation of Blacks in West Indian plantations. Amongst those who denounced the slave trade were evangelical Christians Charles Wesley and John Newton, a former slave trader turned preacher, who was remorseful of his misdeeds as a slave trader.[43] Abolition was achieved in 1807, while policy for the amelioration of the slave trade in 1825 and the slave uprisings in Barbados, 1816, Demerara, 1823 and Jamaica, 1831, were obvious signs for the liberation of Blacks as slaves in Britain. Although the transatlantic slavery trade ended over two centuries ago, the twin features of slavery and colonial imprints are echoed in black ecclesiology in the form of "African retention and missionary retention". This has culminated in what Beckford has called the "bewitchment" of black Christianity.[44] The colonial reminiscences have been replicated by the way in which many Africans have contextualized Christianity. This has led to the emergence of creolized Christianity, which at best is the fusion of African Traditional Religion and Christianity. Beckford consistently repudiates the overt and covert influences of Eurocentric theology which further heighten the deceit of missionary theology that espouses white supremacy over Blacks.

### A New Paradigm in the Migration Pattern of Blacks to Britain

A new paradigm emerged in the twentieth century with the end of forced migration, which was a transatlantic phenomenon. A voluntary migration pattern emerged in the quest for economic and intellectual development within British society. The migratory pattern was greatly influenced by imperialist ties, as most of the migrants were already integrated into the British socio-economic system.

The intellectual capabilities of Blacks in Britain were evident in the twentieth century with increasing numbers of Blacks from West Africa and the Caribbean migrating for intellectual development and business opportunities in Britain. Black prominence was not only visible in religious circles, as the Blacks began to make inroads in the political terrain. The active involvement of Blacks in community initiatives and political initiatives paid off as Britain's first Black Mayor according to the American Negro Year Book 1914 founded by Monroe Work that "Mr Allen Glaisyer Minns, a col'd [coloured] man from West Indies was elected Mayor of the Borough of Thetford, Norfolk." Allan Glaisyer Minns was elected to the town Council of Thetford in 1903 and served a two-year term as mayor from 1904.

Dr. Allan Glaisyer Minns was the youngest son of John Minns (1811–1863) and Ophella (nee Bunch 1917–1902) and was born on October 19th 1858. He was educated at Nassau Grammar School and Guy's Hospital London. Dr Allan Minns was registered with the British Medical Association on 14th February 1884. He was also the President of the Horticultural society according to extract from Norfolk and Suffolk in *East Anglia, Contemporary Biographies*, W.T. Pike (1911).

Until recently John Richard Archer was thought to be the first black Mayor in Britain who was elected Major of Battersea in 1913. Archer's educational antecedents were largely unknown but he was a member of the Pan-African Association in 1900, had glowing political antecedents, and was well known for his fierce criticism of spiritualism in his public speeches. He was elected as a Progressive (Liberal) Councillor for the Latchmere ward in 1906. He was particularly interested in health and welfare issues and served on many of the Council's committees as well as the Wandsworth Board of Guardians. His political prominence nationally was visible when he supported Sharpurji Saklatvala, the Indian Communist, to become MP for Battersea North in 1922. Archer was involved in the formation of the new Battersea Labour Party in 1926 and was elected Deputy Leader of the Labour Group in 1931.

From the preceding therefore, the "Cross event" of the experiences of

Africans and Caribbeans during the transatlantic slave trade, *inter alia*, played a major role in establishing the right conditions for the future of Christianity in Britain and in particular the contributions of her black community to the Christian faith. The conversion of black people to the Christian faith during the period under review is the compelling evidence that God was surely shaping the history of Christianity in Britain. In this publication I take the view that God is not a figment of human imagination, and I believe that the history of black people cannot be written without reference to divine revelation. Revelation is not something that we can acquire by ourselves but God's self-revelation is about the revelation of "divine hiddenness" or "mystery". It is the revelation of mysteries that often results in spiritual transformation (John 1:1–13).

By implication therefore, the emancipation of those who were once slaves should be seen as a typology of engagement with the state and a form of political theology. It is rather ironical that Africans and Caribbeans that were denigrated in various phases of British history would eventually receive special revelations to become pioneers and leaders of Black-led Churches. The history of Africans and Caribbeans in Britain also reveals how and why they overcame those who stymied their efforts to gain ascendancy in various areas of their endeavours. This is why the history of black antecedents in Britain is relevant to the present study.

## THE ORIGIN OF BLACK CHURCHES IN BRITAIN

### *The Azusa Street Movement: Precursor to British Pentecostalism*

The transatlantic slave trade had reverberating effects on Blacks in Diaspora and their spiritual experiences, as the process of acculturation was not without its challenges for the Africans and Caribbeans. Acculturation brought about the emergence of an eclectic form of spirituality amongst Africans and Caribbeans during the slavery period as many of the slaves engaged in fusions of Western Christianity and the African Traditional Primal Religions. This was the basis of the emergence of a distinctive Black Christianity in the New World. Raboteau noted that the emergent Black Christianity was unique in comparison with Western Christianity and the African Traditional Primal Religions, as he was of the opinion that a major hallmark of Africans in Diaspora was the fluidity of their religious identity in the New World: "one of the most durable and adaptable constituents of the slave's culture, linking African past with the American present, was his religion".[45]

The merged African religious consciousness in the New World was preserved as a result of many factors: "oral tradition from generation to generation, symbolism, narratives, myths, legends and folktales, riddles, songs, proverbs and other aphorisms, enacted in ritual and drama, danced and sung, beaten out in the rhythms and tones of talking drums, the swaying of bodies and the stamping of feet".[46] The prevailing distinctive worship style in most Black Majority Churches or Black-led Churches is rooted in the African Traditional Primal antecedents. This was a common feature in the American meeting revival of the eighteenth and nineteenth centuries. Washington asserted that "Slaves tended to express religious emotion in certain patterned types of bodily movement influenced by the African heritage of Dance."[47] This is a common feature in most Black Churches not only in America but is prevalent in most Black-led Churches in Britain today.

The genesis of what can be referred to as the third realm of British Christianity is the emergence, growth and proliferation of Black-led Churches or Black Majority Churches in Britain, which offers a valid alternative orthodoxy to Anglicanism and other historic churches which constitute the second realm of British church history with the exclusion of the Catholic Church which was the basis of the extrapolation of the various movements that have emerged since the Lutheran movement.

The Pentecostal movement has its origin in the Judaic-Christian church which started on the day of Pentecost, at Jerusalem in AD 33. The biblical phenomenon of glossolalia has been experienced by diverse people and generations and has been known through the globe without cessation since the day of Pentecost. Vinson Synan observed that "many cases of glossolalia have been recorded throughout Church history".[48] This further lends credence to Demos Shakarian's assertion of the existence of various evidences of Pentecostal manifestations in some churches in different parts of Europe and in the Western Hemisphere.[49] From Europe to the West Indies (Jamaica, Barbados) to Canada and America, there are records that document the continued experience of receiving the Holy Ghost and glossolalia. An overview of the American movement will definitely facilitate a better understanding of the interplay of the forces that dominated the Azusa movement which eventually culminated in the emergence of British Pentecostalism.

The twentieth century witnessed one of the greatest events in human history with the re-emergence of the Pentecostal movement in America. Allan Anderson asserts that this movement is the "largest numerical force in World Christianity after the Roman Catholic Church".[50] The rapid growth of the Pentecostal phenomenon is unprecedented in Church history, as within one hundred years of its emergence it has attained global status not only in terms of numerical power but has also brought about revitalization of the Christian faith in Asia, Latin America, North America and Africa, especially Nigeria, which is fast becoming the hub of reverse mission to the Western world. The global membership strength of these churches has been estimated by Barrett and Johnson to be over 523 million Pentecostals/Charismatics.[51]

The genesis of the greatest church movement in history after Catholicism is traceable to the Holiness Movement which was a product of Wesleyan Methodism. The Wesleyan Holiness movement in the United States became the precursor to the twentieth-century Pentecostal movement as common features of Pentecostalism were distinctive features of the preceding Holiness movement: divine healing, revivalism, biblical literalism, rejection of ecclesiasticism, emotionalism, Arminian soteriology and ethical rigours which were components of John Wesley's teachings on the "second work of Grace". The Holiness movement made inroads into many Protestant denominations during the revival of 1857–58 especially in the northern parts of the United States. There was a strong emphasis on holiness in various churches, but this was short lived as a result of industrialization and secularization in the western parts of the United States in comparison to the churches in the northern parts of the United States. The effects of the secular culture amongst the middle class gradually polarized the Holiness movement, and discontent reared its head amongst white and black Christians as some of the members insisted on ascetic forms of life, and religious experiences in the form of charismata were desired and encouraged.

The gradual dissent amongst the Holiness movement by the beginning of the twentieth century led to a mass exodus from various denominations of the Holiness movement. This happened partly as a result of formalized religious creeds which curtailed religious emotionalism and ecstasy, and a "new" theological polemic emerged with strong emphasis on glossolalia as the "second" blessing. The adherents of the Holiness movement around this time were centred on the concept of worldwide revival associated with the pre-millennial second advent of Christ. Indeed there were "pockets" of revival, as in Wales, pioneered by Evan Roberts and in Australia, under Reuben Torrey.

The American Pentecostal movement emerged on 1 January 1901, as a result of Charles Fox Parham, a Holiness teacher and Methodist preacher, and his experiential approach towards the theology of the Baptism of the Holy Spirit. Parham was greatly influenced by John Wesley's Methodism and Irwin's "fire-baptism", that is, that a sanctification experience should be followed by Baptism of the Holy Spirit and fire. The first recipient of the Holy Spirit with evidence of glossolalia at Parham's Bethel Bible College in Topeka, Kansas was Agnes Ozman. The experience ignited a new dispensation in church history as the pulse of the experience was felt globally. The mystery of the Bethel Bible College on 1 January 1901 was not only in charisma, but also there was an amusing side to it: Charles Parham, who laid hands on the first recipient, did not have the experience of glossolalia until 3 January 1901, when he received the Baptism of the Holy Spirit with evidence of glossolalia.[52]

The media coverage of this distinct phenomenon in America was pronounced, but Parham disbanded the glossolalic group and laid strong emphasis on the doctrine of divine healing before pioneering a college in Houston, Texas, in 1905. He was a proponent of xenoglossia. Parham was discredited in late 1906 as a result of his theological postulations on unity and segregation, and for a variety of other reasons and allegations, in the movement he pioneered.

The social landscape and prevalent racial discrimination in America prevented William Seymour, the son of a freed slave, from being part of Parham's student body as he listened to Parham's lecture through an "open door" at Parham's Bible College in Houston. Seymour was gradually being prepared at the far "back of the desert" as early as 1900, when he was in transit from Indianapolis, where he joined the Methodist Episcopal Church, an inter-racial Methodist Church, rather than attending the nearby, homogenous Negro, Bethel African Methodist Episcopal Church. His work as a waiter blurred the lines of racial prejudice, as the working environment necessitated social interaction. Between 1900 and 1905 Seymour was influenced by Martin Wells Knapp, who also fostered inter-racial cohesion like William Seymour. The spiritual thirst and fervour of the young man from Louisiana was insatiable as he joined the inter-racial group Evening Light, where he was ordained after recovery from bouts of chicken pox that culminated in partial blindness which affected one of his eyes.

The move from Houston to Los Angeles at the invitation of the Santa Fe Mission to pastor the church marked the turning point in the career of William Seymour. Los Angeles was more tolerant to inter-racial relations and the impact of the Welsh revival had created a climate of expectancy of spiritual revival and the anomic migrant population was made up of popular Christian sects.

William Seymour was noted for his preaching on salvation, divine healing, parousia and glossolalia as the initial evidence of Baptism of the Holy Spirit. The Los Angeles movement started in a similar way to that of Charles Parham's movement. The laying of hands on the recipient of the Baptism of the Spirit and the later outpouring of the Holy Spirit on the preachers with the sign of glossolalia were experiences that these two men had in common, apart from certain doctrinal congruencies such as teachings on divine healing and sanctification, but Seymour strongly repudiated Parham's teachings on segregation.

The Los Angeles spiritual climate changed on 9 April 1906, as William Seymour laid hands on Edward Lee, praying that he might receive the Baptism of the Holy Spirit with the sign of glossolalia. Seymour narrated the reception of glossolalia at 214 Bonnie Brae Street to a crowded house made up of men who held menial occupations. Because of the media publicity and reported accounts of healings, testimonies and deliverance, the movement moved to 312 Azusa Street, where Seymour set up an egalitarian seating arrangement to affirm the equality of Whites and Blacks, who sat on improvised wooden planks in a circle with the pulpit and altar in the middle.

William Seymour's spirituality was a product of the holistic worldview of his progenitors characterized by oral narrative theology and liturgy, strong community cohesion, affirmation in spirit possession and the importance of dance and rhythms in worship. The Azusa movement rose above racial segregation and the leadership of the Pentecostal movement became an international phenomenon as people travelled from the entire Western world to America to have a glimpse of the Pentecostal experience. The racial integration and inclusiveness in these meetings was a departure from the prevailing social and cultural norm in America at that time of Jim Crow laws, and people from ethnic minorities discovered "the sense of dignity and community denied them in the larger urban culture".[53] The negative press review of the "strange phenomenon" helped publicize this revival.[54]

### British Pentecostalism: The Darkroom for the Emergence of Black Churches

The Pentecostal movement migrated into Britain as a result of the "American connection" through the ministry of Thomas Barratt who was born in England in 1862 into an ardent Methodist family. Thomas Barratt was bilingual as his parents migrated to Norway when he was a child; this enabled him to preach in English and Norwegian. In pursuit of his ecclesiastical commitment at a Methodist Episcopal Church in Norway, Thomas Barratt travelled to the United States to raise funds for the city Mission to the poor in Oslo which was not successful. The first Azusa Street magazine, *The Apostolic Faith*, became the first point of contact for Thomas Barratt and the Azusa movement as he later exchanged correspondence with the movement. Allan Anderson notes that "Barratt was baptized in the Holy Spirit in an African American congregation".[55] The revitalized Methodist Episcopal preacher's "new" experience was celebrated as he journeyed to Liverpool with other Azusa missionaries going to Africa, including Samuel and Ardella Mead on their way to Angola and Lucy Farrow en route to Liberia. The changes in the theology of Thomas Barratt on the Baptism of the Holy Spirit with evidence of glossolalia led to his expulsion from the Methodist Church. He founded independent Pentecostal churches (*Pinsebevgelsen*) which have grown to be the largest independent Pentecostal churches in Norway. Filadelfia Church in Oslo, where Barratt was the pastor, became the Azusa of Europe as various ministers visited, including Alexander Boddy, vicar of All Saints, Monkwearmouth, Sunderland, who became the first Anglican Pentecostal/Charismatic whilst still maintaining his ecumenist orientations.

**Sunderland, the British Pentecost**
Alexander Boddy's (1854–1930) father was an Anglican clergyman; he was a lawyer and practised for a few years before entering into the ministry through the influence of the Keswick movement. He was a protégé of Bishop Joseph Barber Lightfoot, a theologian and Bishop of Durham. Bishop Lightfoot was instrumental in his posting to the Anglican Parish at Monkwearmouth, Sunderland, in the north-east of England, to revitalize the local church that was on the verge of collapse due to gross incompetence and pastoral inadequacies of the former vicar.[56] The church was revitalized under the leadership of Alexander Boddy and a faithful few who held prayer meetings for the revival of Sunderland in the vestry of the church. The reverberating news from Azusa and the unfolding events in Norway in the ministry of Thomas Barratt were all precursors to the genesis of the Sunderland movement. Alexander Boddy's pilgrimage to Oslo in March 1907 was the launching pad for Sunderland as one of the "Pentecostal cities" like Azusa, Oslo and also Hamburg.

The Sunderland meetings held by Thomas Barratt in September and October 1907 at the invitation of Boddy were attended mainly by leaders and workers responsible for small missions, seeking renewal in their ministries. Many of them were laymen; very few of them belonged to the main denominations; few if any were prominent church leaders. The initial gathering was devoid of eminent personalities in comparison to previous spiritual movements in Britain in the eighteenth century.

Sunderland was not only the launching pad of modern Pentecostalism in Britain but also the "darkroom" for the prominence of the first Black-led Church in Britain. Robinson opined that it was the attention of the secular press[57] to the claims of glossolalia that created focus to many Christians on the possibility of experiencing a new encounter with the Holy Spirit beyond the Keswick teachings but an experiential opportunity (glossolalia) manifested in their domain (Britain) after more than thirty years of the Keswick Conventions.

The resultant effect of the Azusa revival and the birth of "British Pentecostalism" was given impetus by the preceding Holiness movement and the gains of the Welsh revival of 1904, as both movements were breeding grounds for most of the active proponents of British Pentecostalism.[58] There were various associated myths with respect to the history of the Pentecostal movement in Britain, as some schools of thought were inclined to affirm that speaking in tongues was a major feature of the Welsh revival. A notable proponent of this school of thought was Vinson Synan when he declared that: "Tongues were also prevalent in the Welsh Revival of 1904 . . . It is quite probable that Bartleman and Smale were aware of this aspect of the Welsh revival when they began their efforts to duplicate it in Los Angeles"[59] but this has been refuted by G. Williams who noted that: "So far, I have found no explicit reference to glossolalia in any first hand report, either in Welsh or in English, dealing with that eventful period."[60] Desmond Cartwright, the official historian of Elim Pentecostal Church Great Britain, says of such an assertion that "at best it was crypt amnesia!" as he explains further that "I have had some correspondence with Vinson and others. They have misread the account of the Yorkshire paper (I have a copy and that is not what it says)."[61] Cartwright, a Welshman, attributed the misconceptions of the Yorkshire paper to "people who heard religious Welsh" in childhood "now [in public worship] using it again in the presence of a reporter who did not understand Welsh". He was of the opinion that the reported glossolalia was after the end of the Welsh Revival around 1907 while the main part of the revival was over in 1905. The Pentecostal emergence had profited from the seeds sown during the Welsh Revival as major proponents of the Pentecostal movement in Britain had their roots from the Welsh Revival.[62]

There were obvious similarities in media coverage of the Azusa revival and the Sunderland conference led by Barratt in 1907 as secular media focus reinforced the gains of Keswick teachings of almost thirty years after about the experiential nature of the Baptism of the Holy Spirit as evidence of glossolalia.

*Thomas Brem-Wilson – The First Black Church Pastor in Modern Britain*

The British Pentecostal movement heralded the prominence of the first modern Black pastor in Britain as a result of the gains of the Barratt meetings. Donald Gee, in *Pentecost*, the official voice of the Pentecostal world movement, gave this synopsis of the founding days of the oldest Pentecostal church, Sumner Chapel:

> In 1906 two coloured ministers opened an assembly in Sumner Lane Peckham, and returned from Sunderland in 1907 baptised in the Holy Ghost. It was stigmatised as the "Black Man's Church." Led by Brother Wilson until his death in 1929, it was pastored by Bro. James, and Bro. P. [Peter] Van der Woude, until the present Pastor [as at the date of this publication], C. [Charles] Corston, took over in 1940.[63]

History was made during the Sunderland meeting in 1907, as one of the seventeen people[64] who were baptized in the Spirit with evidence of glossolalia was a Ghanaian businessman named Thomas Brem-Wilson from Dixcove, born in 1855[65] to a wealthy family. Thomas Brem-Wilson was a school master of a missionary school in Ghana prior to his migration to Britain in 1901. The actual age of Brem-Wilson could not be ascertained as he was aged 39 years when he married Miss Esther Cantor which contradicts the birth date (1855) from Iain MacRobert's perspective. It is quite intriguing to say the least that Pastor Brem-Wilson had a dark side to his ministerial credentials. He was formerly married to Hagar Brem, before his marriage to Esther Cantor, a "Jewish stage artiste" whose father was Philip Cantor, a sponge merchant, aged 25 years on 11 July 1906 at Fulham registry.[66] Bro. Brem-Wilson was resident on 21 St Oswald's Street, Fulham in 1906 while the bride was living at 239 Shaftsbury Avenue, West End. The obvious source of his wealth was family wealth, as he was a general merchant like his father, Thomas Birch Wilson. According to Killingray,

> [Brem-Wilson did] not marry her [Esther Cantor] in a Christian ceremony, which, as a member of the Dowie Zion Chapel in the Euston Road, would have been the usual course of action for a Christian. They had six children, of whom three survived to adulthood. The marriage was tempestuous and it is known, from newspaper reports [*Asburton Guardian*, 19 November 1920] that in 1920 Ettie [Esther] sued Brem-Wilson for assault. By 1923 the marriage had effectively ended and Ettie withdrew from the married home.[67]

Divorce in Britain used to cost a fortune; prior to the Divorce and Matrimonial Causes Act of 1857 divorces could only be obtained through a cumbersome legal procedure. The 1857 Act allowed moderately wealthy men to divorce their wives but there was no mutual consensus for divorce before 1923. The dark side of Brem-Wilson never found its way into the public domain but his diaries have revealed he was a man living in two worlds as the dark side of his private life was a pain he concealed from the public. Thomas Brem-Wilson was noted to have been an admirer of Alexander Dowie and actually visited Zion City with a bussiness proposition for him, according to Killingray who has been privileged to have his personal diaries.

There exist divergent historical accounts of the year of establishment of the first Black Pentecostal Church. Gee's perspective[68] and the centenary publication of Sureway International Christian Ministries[69] both asserted that the church began in 1906 while Iain MacRobert[70] and Cartwright[71] opined that the church started around 1907. Thomas Kwow[72] or Kwaw[73] Wilson was a man of tremendous spirituality as exemplified in one of the proceedings of the Sunderland meetings according to the *Sunderland Daily Echo and Shipping Gazette* of 4 October 1907:

> By about 8.30 something like a hundred were present. Suddenly a dark gentleman started a revival hymn, which was taken up with vigour by the congregation. The hymn ended, the dark gentleman began in fervid tones to ask that the Spirit of Christ might enter the hall. While so engaged he burst into loud sounds and instantly the bulk of those present broke into exclamations. Hallelujah! Hallelujah! Was shouted from all parts of the building. The excitement was intense.[74]

His spiritual fervours were quite distinctive, probably as a result of his leadership responsibility, as it was ascertained that in 1906 he had started the first "black man's church". Sumner Road Chapel was in transit from its founding days within Peckham Borough until 1920 as a result of tenancy and socio-religious constraints. Pastor Thomas Brem-Wilson's church started at the site of the Blind Factory in Peckham through the initiative of the Surrey Association for the General Welfare of the Blind, established in 1857. The church later relocated to Rye Lane where they met under the railway arch for a year, then to White Hart Square in Kennington for another year before relocation to Walworth Road where the church was given the pejorative name the "black man's church" with complaints that their meetings were too noisy; this must have been a result of the emotionalism associated with Pentecostal meetings as it was experienced at Azusa Street meetings. The church operated from the "red light district" of Castle Buildings in Mansion Street, Camberwell for a while before moving to Elder Street which was the operational base of the church for four years and finally acquired the former Primitive Methodist Church on Sumner Road in 1920 according to the centenary anniversary brochure of Sureway International Christian Ministries.[75]

Bro. Brem-Wilson's church was well known not only amongst the Pentecostal visionaries of his day but also amongst leaders of historic denominations, as he was visited by Alexander Boddy, vicar of All Saints, Monkwearmouth, Sunderland, accompanied by Cecil Polhill. The church must have witnessed so many charismata as it was reported that, "T. Brem-Wilson is now having a great time of Blessing at Bethel Hall, Camberwell. The power and presence of God has been manifest in recent meetings".[76] Sumner Chapel, also known as Peckham Assembly, hosted the first Apostolic Church Convention in London. This was held in June 1923, supported by "groups in Peckham, Dulwich, Hammersmith and Farringdon Street, Ludgate Circus. The speakers were Pastors D.P. Williams, A. Turnbull [publicly ordained as prophet by the laying of hands at the New Year Convention in Glasgow in 1923], F. Hodges, H.V. Chanter, W.J. Williams and W.A.C. Rowe."[77]

The Apostolic Church Conference held at Peckham Assembly (Sumner Chapel) which featured in the July edition of *Riches of Grace*,[78] the British Apostolic Church magazine edited by D. Williams. He noted that "the power of God was greatly manifested in the salvation of precious souls, and a good many were baptized unto the Holy Ghost". Brem-Wilson was photographed along with some of the Apostolic Church officers during the annual 1923 convention. There is a dearth of information on the exact time Sumner Chapel became an affiliate of the Apostolic Church, but Bro. Brem-Wilson was listed as the Overseer of Peckham Assembly in the official directory of the Apostolic Church of Britain published in the July edition of *Riches of Grace* magazine.[79] Peckham Assembly was the hub of the united monthly meetings of Apostolic Church assemblies from Hammersmith, Dulwich, Peckham and the City assemblies, according to the testimony of L. Charlton in the December edition of *Riches of Grace*.[80] Peckham Assembly became an affiliate of Assemblies of God of Great Britain and Ireland on 1 May 1939, according to Sureway International Christian Ministries. The Church was received into fellowship with 30 other assemblies recognized by the General Presbytery in 1939 during the annual Presbytery Conference of Assemblies of God held at Weston-super-Mare with 150 presbyters in attendance and J. Viden as the pastor.[81]

The obvious enculturation that brought about the pejorative label of Bro. Brem-Wilson's church is similar to the Azusa Street movement which was the approximation of the African American Christian tradition which had evolved since days of slavery in the South. Similar expressive worship was prevalent in Bro. Brem-Wilson's church. This involved shouting and dancing, as expressed by members of the Azusa movement, which was not only a feature of Appalachian Whites or Southern black Americans but a demonstration of fluidity of culture in religious worship.

Sumner Road Chapel, as the first Black Pentecostal Church, appears to have undergone various phases of growth following its establishment in 1906. After the demise of Pastor Brem-Wilson in 1929, there seems to be a void in the leadership of the church from 1929 to 1941, according to the centenary anniversary brochure of Sureway International Christian Ministries (formerly Sumner Chapel). Donald Gee[82] provided insight to the leadership of the church from 1929 to 1940. He asserted that the church was "then pastored by Bro James[83] and Bro P. Van der Woude until Pastor C. Corston took over in 1940" but the centenary publication of Sureway International Christian Ministries states that Rev. C. Corston's leadership commenced in 1942. This instance of inadequate historiography is probably due to the shortcomings of oral transmission in which valuable historical information could be omitted or forgotten.

After the death of Pastor Brem-Wilson, the church leadership dynamics changed as white ministers took the helm of its affairs (Rev. C. Corston 1942–1952, Rev. Golding 1952–1960; Rev. Lewis 1960–1962, Rev. Ronald Eske 1962–2007). Affiliations with the Apostolic Church and Assemblies of God might have constituted the blurring of the historical antecedents of the church as the first Black Pentecostal Church in Britain. The historical antecedents of the emergence of Black Churches seem to have been misconceived as many sociologists and commentators have always attributed the emergence of Black Churches in Britain to social deprivation theory in relation to the West Indies migrations of 1948, the 1950s and 1960s, but this was due to the lack of historical facts, as Britain's first Black Church evolved not as a result of racism but a mission initiative.

The church did experience racism from the prevailing British urban culture as the label given to the church was a pejorative term not born out of sociological considerations but like the Azusa movement the members of Bro. Brem-Wilson's ethnic minorities might have discovered "the sense of dignity and community denied them in the larger urban culture".[84] The first Black-led Church in Britain was not born out of social discontent. This fact repudiates Anderson's perspective that African Pentecostalism emanated out of radical racial discontent.[85] Anderson's assertions are much more appropriate for the description of the re-emergence of Black Churches in Britain in the 1950s and 1960s. Roswith Gerloff also notes that there were traces of indigenous African Christian faith in Hornsey in the 1930s.[86]

There seems to be a dearth of information on the first Black-led Church in Britain, except for a very few insights about Bro. Brem-Wilson, the leader of the Church, concerning his spirituality, Christian virtue, passion and commitment to the Christian faith.[87] Brem-Wilson wrote an article entitled "The Palm" in the November edition of *Riches of Grace*.[88] His literary prowess and use of imagery in relation to his topic could not but be appreciated. The article has all the features of the present-day Black Majority Church hermeneutics characterized by literalism and imagery. His African roots were demonstrated in this article, as he wrote extensively about the growth and distinctiveness of the palm tree as a tropical plant in relation to Christian maturity. Bro. Brem-Wilson was noted to have paid off the debt of the first edition of the first British Pentecostal Magazine, *Confidence*, published in 1908 by Boddy at the cost of £13, which was the equivalent of five weeks' wages for a working man.[89]

Desmond Cartwright's article[90] on the historical antecedents of the Pentecostal Movement and Black Churches is a commendable effort but is inadequately referenced. It gives a unique perspective on the historical antecedents of Black-led Churches in the United Kingdom. Most scholars and writers have affirmed that migration from the West Indies in the 1950s heralded the emergence of Black Churches in Britain, but this was obviously due to lack of consideration of some historical facts by these authors. Brem-Wilson led the "black man's church" on Sumner Road, Peckham, until his death on Good Friday, April 1929,[91] though Killingray[92] says that Brem-Wilson died on 29 March 1929 aged 62 years of acute bronchitis and influenza while his last known address was 3 Bridges Cottages, Penrose Street, Walworth, Southwark.

Bro. Brem-Wilson's church was a multicultural church, as amongst his associate ministers was a Dutch man known as Peter van der Woude (1895–1978), who was converted in the church on 23 October 1921. He was ordained as an Assistant Pastor in 1929, and migrated to Holland in 1934[93] after the death of Brem-Wilson.[94] Peter Van der Woude was among the second generation of Dutch Pentecostals which included Piet Klaver (1890–1970) and Nico Vetter (1890–1945). Van der Woude was pivotal in the initiation of Pentecostalism in Rotterdam under the auspices of the Assembly of God (Gemeente Gods).

Peter van der Woude most likely formed his transnational relationship with ministers under Brem-Wilson's leadership. This was replicated in van der Woude's evangelistic ties with British evangelists which led to the establishment of a number of church outposts in Rotterdam. Peter van der Woude reignited the memories of first generation Pentecostal preacher

Gerrit Roelof Polman (1868–1932) through a Pentecostal periodical under the name *Spade Regen*, which was the name used by Polman in his heyday. The publication was continued under a new name, *Volle Evangelie Koerier*.[95]

Sumner Chapel, the first Black-led African Church in modern Britain was inclusive and had distinctive similarities with William Seymour's movement in terms of elimination of racial barriers and a strong sense of oneness of the members and the prevalence of charismata amongst the members. This inevitably created an "ideal community" in contrast to the prevailing "larger urban community" that was distinctively racial and divisive.

The church on Summer Road underwent refurbishment in 1950 under Rev. C. Corston and another hall was added to it. The old Primitive Methodist Church property on Sumner Road that accommodated the first Black-led Pentecostal Assembly in Britain was sold to the New Testament Church of God (Annapolis) in 2003 after over eighty years of usage by the church established by Bro. Brem-Wilson. Sumner Chapel is now known as Sureway International Christian Ministries, still an affiliate of Assemblies of God with affiliates in eight countries and two churches in the United Kingdom. The Church is situated on 1 Higgs Industrial Estate, Herne Hill, London. The leadership of the church is now vested in the hands of Stephen Armah, a Ghanaian.

*Second Phase of Black-led Churches in Britain – the Daniel Ekarte Model*

Most scholars' and writers' accounts of the historical antecedents of Britain's Black-led Churches have not considered sufficiently all of the relevant historical influences as most asserted that Black Churches emerged in Britain during the *Windrush* migration of the 1950s and 1960s. However, the social and religious landscape of Liverpool was revitalized by the social and pastoral efforts of Pastor Daniel Ekarte (1890s–1964), a Nigerian. There exist two schools of thought about the birth date of Daniel Ekarte. Sturge notes that Ekarte's date of birth as indicated on his Seaman's Identity Service Certificate was 1 January 1904, but Sturge observes that Sherwood refutes this assertion as she posits that the early 1890s may be more appropriate.[96]

Ekarte arrived in Liverpool in 1915 from Calabar, in the southern part of Nigeria. He was impacted from childhood by the Christian faith through the ministry of Mary Slessor, a Scottish missionary among the Okoyong people in Calabar, Nigeria, who campaigned tirelessly against the stigmatization and the killing of twins amongst Calabar people.

Reminiscing about his acquaintance with Mary Slessor, Ekarte said that "on her missionary tour she was again the guest at Dr. Wilkie's (my master). I shall make no mistake about this 'holy' woman this time. I had not long to wait, she saw me, and our friendship began there and then. Her personality was of great interest to me. I decided I must go and live and learn of Jesus, Son of God, who was crucified for our sin, and to learn the Lord's Prayer."[97] Despite Ekarte's Christian background and passion, he backslid on arrival in Britain, as his perception of England as the "land of angels" proved far removed from the Christian values of the Christian missionaries he was acquainted with while in Nigeria. Ekarte's re-conversion memoirs note his recommitment to the Christian faith after seven years of depravity; he fellowshipped with other Africans at the mission hall at 4 Hardy Street, Liverpool.[98] This scenario further repudiates the assertions that Black-led Churches emanated during the *Windrush* era.

Although without any theological training and not educationally articulate, Ekarte was a controversial figure and a community leader who founded the African Churches Mission in 1931 in the working-class and multi-ethnic district of Toxteth. Ekarte's ministry focus was to meet the religious aspirations of Africans as he preached to his African colleagues and other Blacks in Liverpool. Although the ACM lacked adequate financial support, it was not a haphazard operation.

Wilson, in his article, "Racism and Private Assistance: The Support of West Indian and African Missions in Liverpool", highlights the subtle and organized racial discrimination experienced by Blacks in Liverpool after the First World War despite the fact that there was no legal segregation in the community. Wilson notes:

> Regrettably, many of these agencies possessed and expounded a racist, paternalistic ideology which viewed blacks as a problem. Blacks were seen as a people of naturally inferior ability and morals who needed special aid in order to survive in a foreign, white, and competitive society. These agencies believed their approach to providing desperately needed services for indigent blacks was beneficial.[99]

Ekarte was recognized widely not only for his Christian beliefs but also as an ardent campaigner for racial and economic equality of Africans with their white counterparts. Wilson opined that Ekarte was "especially active in lobbying for better working conditions and higher pay for African seamen who worked for the Elder Dempster Shipping Company. African seamen usually performed the same work as English seamen but there was a substantial differential in their wages."[100] Various organizations including the League of Coloured People, led by Dr Harold Moody, acknowledged the contributions of Ekarte to the cause of Blacks in Liverpool and he was commended at the Pan-African Congress held at Manchester in 1945.[101]

One of the lasting legacies of Ekarte was his commitment to addressing the social challenges of "brown babies" in Liverpool in the post-war era. The stringent military rules and racial undertones created a distinctive social challenge as the English girls found the charm, charisma and socializing etiquettes of the black American soldiers irresistible. Because of ethnocentrism and prejudice against the black American GIs, many of the soldiers were refused approval to marry the English girls by the military. This situation led to the abandonment of "brown babies". Pastor Ekarte's social action was holistic, as he met the spiritual, physical and psychological needs of the children through church activities.

## BLACK CHRISTIAN HERITAGE – PRE-*WINDRUSH* ERA

### Black Heroes of Faith in Britain

History has shown that as early as 1565 Blacks in Britain were baptized and later buried, as the first recorded baptism was that of "John the Blackmoor" and his burial is also listed as "John a Blackmoor" on 23 May 1566.[102]

Black Christian Heritage in Britain during the slave era was a product of the approximation of the Christian faith, not necessarily as a matter of absolute conviction of the Blacks but as Christianization and baptism were misconstrued by many of the slaves as a "means to an end" of their emancipation from the clutches of slavery. As such, some of the so-called conversions may not have been genuine. But it is important to realize that "God uses the foolish things of this world to confront the wise" as Paul asserted in his first letter to the church at Corinth. Escape from the clutches of slavery inherently brought about the genuine conversion of some of the slaves to the Christian faith. In his autobiography entitled *The Life Of Olaudah Equiano, Or Gustavus Vassa, The African,* Olaudah Equiano gave an account of his conversion on a voyage to Spain, when he saw "the bright beams of light" and was born again.[103] He was baptized in 1759. It seems there was a prevalence of allusions to theophanic experience by slaves as they seemed to resign their fate to faith in the Divine.

James Albert Ukawsaw Gronniosaw, a slave from Northern Nigeria, was converted through the reading of Richard Baxter's text "A Call to the Unconverted", a gift from his master Theodorus Frelinghuysen. The conversions of Gronniosaw and of other Blacks were providential, as most of the slaves were heathens. Gronniosaw's renunciation of worldly riches was probably circumstantial – subsequent economic challenges reflected his spirituality but cannot be perceived as monasticism in any form.[104]

Scipio Africanus, named after the Roman General who invaded Africa in 204 BC, was noted in 1739 to attend evangelical meetings in London while he was a servant of the Seward Family. This was a novel phase in black history as Blacks began to be involved in the evangelical cause and it eventually heralded the birth of Methodism in Britain. Because of the dearth of historical records on Scipio Africanus, his contributions to the evangelical movement cannot be ascertained. Tragically, the contributions of many other Blacks in the sixteenth and seventeenth centuries might also have been lost.

The middle of the sixteenth century witnessed the ordination of a black minister. According to *The Gentleman's Magazine* in 1765 it was reported that "at the ordination of priest and deacons at the chapel royal at St James by Hon and Rev. Dr Keppel, Bishop of Exeter, a Black was ordained, whose devout behaviour attracted the notice of the whole congregation".[105] The gentleman in question was Philip Quaque, who was the first African to be ordained as a priest in the Church of England. He was a Ghanaian and came to England at the age of thirteen in 1754 to be educated on a scholarship from the Society for the Propagation of the Gospel with Thomas Caboro and William Cudjo. Fryer clarifies the identity of the ordained candidate as he states that "in 1765 Philip Quaque was twice ordained: first as deacon, by the bishop of Exeter in the St James Palace chapel royal; two months later as a priest, by the bishop of London in the same chapel". After his marriage to Catherine Blunt he was appointed "missionary Catechist and School master to the Negroes on the Gold Coast [Ghana] in Africa at a salary of £50 a year".[106] Though Philip Quaque's ministry afterwards was not particularly successful on account of many factors beyond the consideration of this publication, his ordination deconstructs the age-long conception that Blacks in eighteenth-century Britain were slaves, subjugated and grossly insignificant in the scheme of things.

The gradual involvement of Blacks in public preaching in Britain was given further impetus in the early nineteenth century by their involvement in open-air preaching. John Jea, according to Killingray and Edwards[107] was a Nigerian born in 1773 in the Old Calabar, kidnapped at the age of two, sold and enslaved in America. He was a self-taught man at fifteen years old and was a Christian as well as a seaman. John Jea was a Methodist and a pacifist; he referred to himself as the African Preacher in his autobiography. He was an itinerant preacher in various towns in Britain and

Ireland, including Southampton, Portsmouth and "Limerick to Cork" as noted by Killingray and Edwards. The faith of the Christian activist might have been boosted as a result of his past experiences as a slave, but above all he was a committed preacher. As a writer he published *A Collection of Hymns* in 1816.

Some of the slaves, by the peculiarity of their circumstances, became seamen or servants, and some travelled widely on account of the vagaries associated with being attached to the lifestyle and occupation of their masters. The literacy level of the black Christians was on the increase in the eighteenth century, as some of them were taught how to read and write by their masters, while others were adjured not to read, in order to entrap them perpetually in slavery. Indeed, as Ignatius Sancho learnt, "ignorance was the best security for obedience".[108] But providence opened the door of literacy as Sancho was taught by the Duke and Duchess of Montague, who left him a legacy of £70 and an annuity of £30. Ignatius Sancho was a staunch Anglican but was known to have had leanings towards Methodism. He was probably a preacher, as he asserted in a letter that he wrote to Jack Wingrave that "I had done some preaching".[109]

### Public Engagement of Black Heroes of Faith

Ignatius Sancho was a man immersed in the use of irony in his letters. He chided the "divide and rule" policies of the slave masters as they provided ammunition for their African collaborators to maim, capture and ensure continued trafficking of Africans to American colonies while simultaneously feeding the ego and flesh of the Africans with strong liquor. The vividness of the irony utilised mostly in his letters was his continual reference to the Protestant faith of the slave masters as he affirmed the essence of the Christian ethos to be justice, dignity, fellowship and charity, which negates the ethics of slavery. The brilliance and the intellectual capacity exercised by Ignatius Sancho demonstrated the potential that African Christians possessed in the eighteenth century. However, very little is known about him except for his letters, referred to in Joseph Jekyll's brief biography of him. In the last two decades contemporary scholars like Vincent Carreta and Paul Edwards have explored Sancho's life story with increasing frequency and critical sophistication.

Quobna Ottobah Cugoano, a Ghanaian, joined the list of black Christian contributors to the Abolitionist movement through the publication of their autobiographies and correspondence to their friends. His was the first Abolitionist publication in English by an African. It was published in 1787.

He was a man deeply convinced that the Christian faith would bring about evangelization of the heathen. He berated the Protestant Church's involvement in slavery:

> Were the iniquitous laws in support of it, and the whole of that oppression and injustice abolished, and the righteous laws of Christianity, equity, justice and humanity established in the room thereof, multitudes of nations would flock to the standard of truth, and instead of revolting away, they would count it their greatest happiness to be under the protection and jurisdiction of a righteous government.[110]

His argument was centred not only on the injustice of the slave trade, but also the potential results of refraining from such barbaric acts: honour and fame would be brought to the British Empire as a result of the establishment of dignity, love and truth, which are generally accepted as virtues amongst people irrespective of creed, colour, race or gender. The continued subjugation of the black community in total ignorance was perceived to be a great disservice to a Protestant nation that prided itself as a Christian nation.

The literary skills of black Christians were not gracious to the contentious issues of the slave trade. The autobiography of Olaudah Equiano, apprehended as a slave with his sister at the age of 10, was a huge literary success and was utilised tremendously as a portrayal of the ills and deprecatory nature of the slave trade. From this publication Equiano also profited financially, and he became an itinerant campaigner, Christian speaker and successful black figure in Britain, travelling as far as Birmingham, Sheffield, Bristol, Hull, Devizes, Belfast and Dublin.

Black Christians were becoming visible in public service and the ethnic challenges of their day. Olaudah Equiano's Christian background and pious disposition for the cohesion and inclusiveness of the Blacks in Britain contributed to the effort to resettle Blacks to Sierra Leone. He was employed in 1786 by the Navy Commissioners as commissary in charge of stores for the resettlement programme, but this position was short-lived. He was sacked for opening up a Pandora's Box that revealed protracted organizational flaws and corruption of officials involved in the scheme. The public enquiry instituted by the commissioners acknowledged the integrity of Equiano in the scheme, with a public apology, and he was adequately compensated.

Black Christians were very proactive in British church life by the mid-eighteenth century, as some of them became evangelists to their native countries for the propagation of the Gospel, while others of them continued with their commitment to social equality and an inclusive community. Robert Wedderburn, a Jamaican, kept watch over British society; he was known as a social critic who had Unitarian leanings and was revolutionary in his postulations rather than reformatory. He had a strong dislike for the endorsement of slavery by the state because of the government's corruption; he was a pioneer for press freedom and was incarcerated twice by the government for blasphemy; he was a man of deep Christian conviction, often drawing parallels of Christ's life with his own life to justify his radical postures.[111]

By the late eighteenth century Blacks were becoming more visible in ecclesiastical positions in Britain. Reverend Peter Sanford became the first black preacher in Birmingham. He was not an African but an American, but his appointment heralded a new era in black Christian history in Britain. Missionaries were trained, equipped and employed to serve in their native countries and some of them had more remarkable successes than their white counterparts, as they engaged the worldview of the natives, which was not alien to them, and eliminated the cultural barrier as they contextualized the Gospel in their language, which facilitated effective communication. The success of some of the black missionaries was pronounced not only in clerical duties but also in biblical translation. Bishop Ajayi Crowther translated the Bible into the Yoruba language, spoken by one of the three major tribes in Nigeria. In the midst of the unfolding missionary zeal amongst Blacks the Christian faith was also spreading its literary prowess as Celestine Edwards from Dominica obtained a degree in theology, and was appointed the editor of *Christian Lux* from 1893–1895. He was the first black man to edit a white-owned newspaper.

Theophilus Scholes, a Jamaican medical doctor, was a missionary to Congo and an avowed antagonist of the white supremacy ideology, who opposed colonialism and racial prejudice. He vehemently criticized the killing of black people in the United States, drawing on the similarities of the Armenian savagery in the Ottoman Empire. He was quite vociferous on the abuse and low remuneration of women involved in the construction of roads in Jamaica. The thrust of Scholes' argument was that the messianic Gospel, as espoused by the Church of England, was irreconcilable with the prevalent oppressive posture of white Christians over black Christians, because the Christian Gospel is about justice and the equality and dignity of its adherents. He was of the opinion that "in theory the Ethiopian does not receive Christian protection. But the church fails to carry her theory fully out into practice. And this is especially true of the protestant section of the Church. If the church had fully recognised the Ethiopian as a man and a brother, politics and literature would have done likewise, for in this respect at least they would reflect the action of the Church".[112]

The social landscape was changing in Britain in the nineteenth century as black Christian professionals settled in, amongst whom was Dr Harold Moody. He was born in Jamaica but came to Britain in 1908 as a student at Kings College Hospital in London where he specialized in ophthalmics. Moody's resolute determination to succeed as a medical doctor, despite racial discrimination against him on the issue of employment in government hospitals, culminated in his setting up private practice at Peckham in February 1913. One of the greatest achievements of Dr Harold Moody was the establishment of the League of Coloured Peoples with the assistance of Dr Charles Wesley, an Afro-American professor of history. The League of Coloured Peoples emerged at a meeting held at the Central YMCA, Tottenham Court Road, London, on 13 March 1933. The founding members included Dr Belfield Clark, Sgt George Roberts, Samson Morris, Robert Adams and Desmond Buckle. Harold Moody's protest against racial intolerance culminated in an apology from BBC News for a presenter's use of the word "nigger" while on air. Harold Moody was a great public speaker who took "enormous pains over each lecture and offer[ed] his manuscript to God" and was an evangelical Christian with a passionate love for children. He was appointed to the Colonial Missionary Society's Board in 1921 and was President of London Christian Endeavour.[113]

Dr Harold Moody was instrumental in the elimination of the colour bar in the British Armed Forces. He was committed to equal opportunities irrespective of race and his son, Captain Arundel Moody, was the first black commissioned officer in the British Army. He not only fostered community cohesion amongst Blacks, but also promoted an inclusive community. Some of Moody's contemporaries in the medical vocation included Ernest Goffe who played in a cricket team with the author A.A. Milne, Ivan Shirley and H.E. Bond.

Dr John Alcindor was Trinidad-born and was a graduate of the University of Edinburgh in 1899. He was one of the 37 delegates to the Pan-African Congress meeting held in Westminster, London, which included Samuel Coleridge Taylor, John Archer and Dadabhai Naoroji, and was active in Catholic charities. He was a General Practitioner with researches on cancer, tuberculosis and influenza published in the *British Medical Journal.*

The social landscape of Liverpool was greatly transformed by the controversial preacher Daniel Ekarte, through his community initiative of care for the needy and the homeless. His work was greatly recognized by the local authorities and he became a community leader of the coloured people. Pastor Ekarte was an enigma: he stood up for the black cause in Britain but showed moral ineptitude, as he was alleged to have had an amorous relationship with his housekeeper, but rebuffed calls for repentance of his misdemeanour. His success plummeted as a result of racial prejudice, financial constraints and his moral inconsistency.

Black Christians also made remarkable inroads in sports. Arthur Wharton, a Ghanaian who came to England to train as a Methodist Missionary, was an outstanding athlete. He was a former world record holder of ten seconds in the 100 metres and was the first black professional footballer; he played for Preston North End football club but suffered racial challenges. He died in 1930 as a penniless alcoholic, his only possessions being a Bible and some pictures.

Black Christian heritage in Britain is important socially and ecclesiastically, as much was achieved by many black Christians. Their accomplishments and challenges have contributed significantly to British church history, since some of the black Christians worked with the established denominations for over a century prior to the *Windrush* era of 1948.

## *WINDRUSH* AND THE BLACK CHURCH MOVEMENT IN BRITAIN

### *The Third Stream of Black-led Churches in Britain*

The contemporary Black Church Movement in Britain owes it genesis to the landing of the troopship SS *Empire Windrush* on 22 June 1948 at Tilbury with 417 migrants, the majority of whom were from Jamaica, while others were from several Caribbean countries including Trinidad, Guyana and Bermuda.[114] This heralded a new era in the immigration history of Britain due to the influx of migrants from the Caribbean and the New Commonwealth. The Caribbean migration to Britain in the 1950s was an integral part of wider migration from Asia and Africa. The migration was in response to the decline in the fortunes of the British economy as a result of the numerous effects of the Second World War on the various sectors of the British economy; these were quite pronounced amongst the semi-skilled sectors.

Paradoxically, amongst the migrants were artisans, students, musicians, artistes, ex-servicemen and a Guyanese judge. The average age of the migrants was 27 years 4 months, with the eldest being Margaret Campbell, sixty-three years old, and the youngest thirteen-year-old Vincent Reid. None of the migrants had any ecclesiastical or pastoral training to take up leadership responsibility, but they came with their faith and culture.[115]

The West Indies migration of 1948 was the genesis of a "brain drain" from the Caribbean economy as the cream of the labour force migrated to Britain; 24% of the migrants had management or professional training, 46% were skilled workers, 5% were semi-skilled and only 13% were unskilled manual workers.[116] The obvious implication was that many migrants found the prospect of the Caribbean economy experiencing resurgence a dream in comparison to the British economy that was on the verge of industrialization and rejuvenation after the devastating effects of the Second World War.

The Caribbean migration to Britain was due to a multiplicity of push and pull factors. The Caribbean economy was at the lowest ebb in its history, with the hurricane disaster of 1944. The Caribbean in 1900 had been described as "one of the most socially and economically unstable places in an unstable world".[117] The natural propensity was for the Caribbeans to embark on the journey to the "mother country" which was at the same period experiencing industrial revolution and restructuring. The ideology of "Britannia rules" which formed the basis of life in all British colonies, where Britain was adjured to be the land of decency, economic prosperity, civilization and loyalty to the Queen, with the Union Jack as a symbol of her sovereignty over the colonies, was further perpetuated in the educational system, as instruction was structured around British ethnocentricity. Baron Baker, the Jamaican who made sure the government of Britain assisted the migrants for governmental support, said: "We were taught at school that we were descended from the primitive and the uncivilized and ungodly until the British arrived and carried us out of the Wilderness."[118] The orientation of the Caribbean migrants inevitably was that Britain had a "messianic" status, and as citizens of her colonies they saw themselves intrinsically linked with their destination as they sought opportunities with hopes of cultural acceptance and economic advancement.

The euphoria of "mother country" withered as soon as they arrived in Britain. They were faced with disappointment and disillusion as their expectations as British citizens fizzled out. The migrants had to accept "the rejects" of the British: "We get the job the white man does not want, the room the white man does not want to live in, the woman he throws out."[119] The *Windrush* migrants had high expectations of life in Britain but this was far from reality. This might have been a product of years of systemic, ethnocentric indoctrination. Rex and More discovered that "a central theme was the brainwashing of West Indians at home about Britain. They had been told about the Queen and the Parliament, but no-one had told them there was a colour bar. They had thought they could get a flat where they chose and that Frank could get a job like any other carpenter."[120]

Racism was not limited to employment opportunities but was an ideology that was evident in the social, economic, religious and cultural life in Britain in the 1950s. In their search for accommodation many migrants were greeted with boards that read, "Rooms for Let – Sorry No Coloured, No Irish, No Dogs". This led to the evolution of cohesive community amongst early black migrants and the fluidity of the Caribbean culture emerged in Britain with the commencement of the "Pardner Hand", a traditional saving scheme that creates economic leverage for the members to raise capital for personal projects.

The arrival of the migrants in Britain caused a divisive public outcry, especially from the mass media, that the recruitment drive should be forestalled, but pivotal to parliament's resolution of this outcry was its stress on the potential economic benefits to Britain and the role of the Caribbean as a British colony. The imperialist ideology, with its assumptions of ethnocentrism and black inferiority, were the prism through which colonial migrants were received and perceived by the community, but the West Indians never envisaged being strangers who were inferior to the British. As products of the slave trade and of British colonization they identified culturally with Britain, and believed they were kinsmen with the British; in fact they were British.[121]

This era marked the emergence of "fables" about the migrants and the social consequences that Britain would experience on the arrival of the immigrants from the Commonwealth, but the *Birmingham Christian News* of September 1961 noted that "the Minister of Health says there is no reason to think that, to any large extent, immigrants from the Commonwealth bring disease into this country, or constitute a danger to public health". The government agencies and the officials tried as much as possible to reassure the public that adequate arrangements had been made for the migrants and that as Commonwealth citizens they had the right to migrate to Britain. According to the Colonial Secretary, "These people have British passports, and they must be allowed to land ... There's nothing to worry about, because they won't last one winter in England."[122] This was probably a diversionary tactic, making it seem that the issue at stake was the legality of the migration and not permanent residency in Britain.

The arrival of the migrants aboard the *Empire Windrush* in 1948 heralded a new phase in British immigration and Christian history. It can only be evaluated retrospectively in relation to the growth of Black-led Churches in Britain today. The early migrants came not only with their skills but also with their faith and socio-cultural beliefs. The new wave of migration was further accentuated in late 1948 with the arrival in Liverpool of the *Orbital* with 180 migrants from the Caribbean, while in November 1948, 39 Jamaicans, of which 50% were females, arrived via the *Reina del Pacifico*. In the summer of 1949 *Georgic* brought 253 West Indians to Britain, 45 of them female. The trend continued into the 1950s and early 1960s, but this was curtailed by the Commonwealth Immigration Act of 1962. Prior to this, thousands of men and women migrated to England as a result of the invitation from the early migrants who had decided to make the "mother country" their permanent residence, not only improving their own economic conditions, as the wages and new lease of life in England were quite irresistible, but also contributing to the ailing British economy.

### Dysfunctional Assimilation in Britain – Black-led Church Thrives

The *Windrush* era heralded a turning point in Black Church history in Britain, as it consolidated the gains of past efforts of black independent church leaders and black Christians who served the historic churches as evangelists, missionaries and inner-city social workers in nineteenth-century Britain. Amongst such black Christians were notable social critics and professionals who excelled in the midst of the challenges of racial barriers. Concrete evidence of the organized religious activity was the existence of a Black Pentecostal Independent Church in London since the early twentieth century.

To say that the *Windrush* migrants were predominantly economic migrants would constitute a farce. Motivations for migration were peculiar to individual migrants, and included peer pressure, parental influence and educational pursuits, together with economic and missiological reasons.[123] The ecclesiastical landscape of Britain in the 1950s and 1960s proved unattractive to the Caribbean migrants as many of them were members of the denominational churches in the Caribbean. In the mid-twentieth century it was noted that 31% of churchgoers in the Caribbean were Church of England, 29% were Wesleyan Methodist and 17% were Baptists[124] but they soon realized that the churches in the "mother country" were quite unwelcoming and insulated along racial undertones, as many churches shut the door of fellowship to the migrants. Few historic churches welcomed the migrants, who began to realize that they were alien to the "commonwealth of the saints"; their gifts, potentials and skills were ignored as they "identified without belonging" to the denominational churches.

An exception was the Congregational Church led by Clifford and Monica Hill at Tottenham in the 1960s. This was a multicultural church of over 1,000 members. Significant percentages of the members were West Indians and Africans. The success of Monica and Clifford Hill's church was that they facilitated the assimilation of the migrants through job searches and accommodation. This led to various racial and social backlashes as the couple were called "Nigger lovers".[125] Clifford and Monica's experiences further authenticate the fact that religious commitment is associated with anxiety status, especially for those who, in Diaspora, are in the process of assimilation on account of various socio-economic constraints.

The indigenous liturgy, spontaneity and enculturation of the Caribbean mode of worship was absent in the worship services of British historic churches and as such there was culture shock, but the defining line for an alternative to the staid, cold worship of the denominational churches was racism, as the communicant card that was expected to be accepted in church was declined by historic churches just as the British passport failed to enhance their integration into the community. Ironically it was believed by the migrants that English churches ought to be the first place where integration and assimilation would occur.[126] The basis for such an orientation by the West Indian migrants was this assumption:

> [They had] inherited their culture from the British and shared similar cultural values, beliefs and behaviours exhibited in the same institutional forms, i.e., Christianity and churches. After all, hadn't it been English missionaries who had brought Christianity to the West Indies? Secondly, beyond the work shift, church activities provided a space for social interaction where favourable contact between migrants and their hosts would win in the field of race relations.[127]

However, the much-vaunted claim of universal brotherhood of the Christian faith was not experienced in most mainline historic churches. This situation resulted in "black flight" as Blacks were not integrated into the ecclesiastical ranks in historic churches and did not attend or participate in services.[128] Both the laity and the synods manifested an appalling gap between their public policy of benevolence and equality and a private policy of antipathy and racism.[129] It was felt either that Blacks were heathens who had to be converted[130] or that religious expression is not a forum for racial and social integration.[131]

According to MacRobert, racism in the historic churches and white Pentecostal churches in Britain was not the only factor that led to the emergence of the Black-led Churches in Britain.[132] Dissatisfied black members of the historic churches teamed up with members of the Pentecostal and Holiness members in Diaspora as the seeds of the Holiness movement were already planted in Jamaica: "60% of Jamaicans were already members of a Christian church or group" according to the *Daily Mirror* of 8 September 1958.

Ira Brooks, an ex-Anglican, writes from her experience of racism in the "cold" reception she received in a Gloucester church: "Even those who had entrusted themselves into the fellowship of the established religious institutions of the country began to sense an environment of growing coldness. With the natural human desire for fellowship and acceptance, most of the immigrants discarded their old religious differences and in their need for consolidation accepted the Pentecostal message."[133]

Within the African and West Indian conception, church was perceived as a community, and involvement with the historic churches then, even if accepted, was perceived as alienation from the traditional black Christian communal community; this perception led to the emergence of homogenous communities of Blacks and Whites on the basis of religious persuasion, while the economic matrix was the melting point for limited social interaction. The encounter of the Caribbean migrants with British historic churches was characterized by a distinctive sense of loss of the wider African-Caribbean oral and social context. The migrants lost a real sense of community, a wide united family not bereft of the wisdom of old people and a religion which was part of a living culture.

The inadequacy of the British denominational churches was the leverage that attracted the black migrants to the Pentecostal churches, where most of the migrants had the opportunity to participate in church life, and experience community and authentic faith such as many had experienced in the Caribbean. Some British historic denominations made heroic efforts to accommodate the *Windrush* migrants, but to posit that racism was the only basis for the emergence of Black Churches implies that Black Churches evolved by default.[134] On the contrary, Black Churches evolved to meet distinctive spiritual, cultural and social needs of Africans and Caribbeans in Diaspora.

The magazine *Pentecost*, edited by Donald Gee, contained an interesting item culled from the American *Church of God Evangel* under the heading, JAMAICANS IN ENGLAND: "There are a great number of Jamaican emigrants in England. They find it difficult to feel at home in the more conservative type of Pentecostal service to which the British people are accustomed, so they have started their own meeting and God is blessing them."[135] This was a subtle rebuttal of the relative deprivation theory to which Hill[136] has attributed the emergence of Black-led Churches, i.e., that it was due to racial rejection and discrimination suffered from white churchgoers and clergy in historic churches. The negative impact of racism on the black communities in Britain was asserted by Howard:

> [Racism has] influenced British and African-Caribbean communities just as it has affected other areas of Black experience in this country. It is a major reason for the establishment and growth of the Black-led Churches, and it is the root of under-representation of Africans and Caribbeans in Historic churches. It has shaped and is still shaping Black Theology.[137]

West Indian Christians were integrated into some of the Pentecostal churches but many craved the Caribbean brand of Christianity.

The distinctive socio-cultural values and apparent racial prejudice experienced by the *Windrush* migrants reinforced their spirituality and missionary zeal in the mother country, for instance Oliver Lyseight in 1953, in conjunction with G.S. Peddie and H.G. Brown, founded a "Church of God Mission" amongst the growing number of black migrants in Wolverhampton and within three years the membership was forty in the West Midlands, Manchester and London.

Black Churches in the pioneering days in Britain were quite unique in comparison to the white historic churches, which were perceived by Blacks as unloving, powerless and staid. There were other sociological and psychological roles that Black Churches served in the days of their emergence. The emerging Black Churches thus became a community where the dignity, solidarity and faith of those in Diaspora were celebrated and their psychotherapeutic needs met. Warmth and brotherhood flourished amongst the members of the Black Churches as the initial cultural and social alienation was eliminated.

To most migrants in the 1950s, Britain was a mission field, on account of the perceived moral decadence and the cold complacency of the historic churches. Therefore, missionaries from the Caribbean were willing to extend their denominational frontiers, and this marked the turning point in the establishment of various denominations. Oliver Lyseight reminisced about the origin of the New Testament Church of God in the 1950s when he said:

> People were coming into the Country and when they come, some of them have friends and the friends, if they don't even go to church, would know where we are. And they would tell them that so and so is at such and such a place, and sometimes they take them themselves. Sometimes we don't know them personally from home, but they come from Jamaica and they are from the New Testament Church of God and so they come to [the] service and we all pull together.[138]

The emergence of the New Testament Church of God heralded Britain as an American mission field, as the churches established had international recognition and the Pentecostal Gospel, which has been described in the words of Dempster *et al.* as "a religion made to travel",[139] fostered a sense of community, integration and recognition amongst the migrants. The influx of American denominations to the "British mission field" contributed immensely to the proliferation of Black Churches, but according to Mohabir[140] it had negative consequences on black unity in Britain.

The missionary zeal of Americans in expanding their denominational frontiers eventually led to various acts of contempt, disloyalty and desire for autonomy amongst the Blacks in Diaspora as a result of the recognition and associated benefits from the American churches. Donald Gee, a prominent figure in the Assemblies of God in Britain, was very critical of the American invasion of Britain as a mission field. Writing under the pseudonym *"Circumspect"* in *Redemption Tidings* of 6 January 1956, he came out with a stinging article entitled "Foreign Subsidies" on the invasion of the British Isles by American churches.

The changing religious landscape of the 1950s due to the growth of Black-led Churches was part of the agenda of the British Pentecostal Fellowship at their annual meetings of 1956 and 1957, when the leadership of the Pentecostal churches affirmed the inclusiveness of their denomination, many arguing that there was no colour bar to fellowship.

The apparent composition of the emerging Black Churches in the 1950s was distinctively homogenous and as such the descriptive expression "Black Churches" emerged in the British religious landscape and was used until recently, when the leadership of the defunct African and Caribbean Evangelical Alliance under the leadership of Mark Sturge renounced the label on account of its various misconceptions and inadequacies, and adopted the expressions "Black Majority Churches" in preference to Black-led or Black Churches.[141] The word "black" is better thought of as a signifier rather than a derogatory label, but based on the law of first mention, it was indeed pejorative as utilised in 1911 to describe the first Black Pentecostal Church in Britain.

### *The Black Church Movement in Britain*

The expression "Black Church Movement in Britain" owes its existence to Roswith Gerloff with reference to the phenomenal growth of Black Churches. Gerloff describes Black Churches as mushrooming, gaining strength and rapidly attracting more widespread attention as they function within the social political arena as well as in the Black/White Church scene.[142] Gerloff's assertion is a reflection of the foundation and growth of a wide array of denominations among immigrant settlements in the 1950s, many of which started as house groups or family prayer meetings that resulted from initial acts of racism from white denominational churches and palpable resistance from the general public in Britain on their arrival. The proliferation of Black Churches has been a subject of interest, curiosity and research amongst sociologists, statisticians, governmental agencies and researchers who have tried to evaluate the basis of the phenomenon and its active role in socio-economic, political and cultural life of the migrants and in the creation of a climate of community cohesion in policy formulation and implementation in Britain.[143]

The growth phases of Black Churches in Britain have been delineated by various researchers, and the obvious peculiarities of such phases identified.[144] The last two decades have witnessed the emergence of "New Pentecostal Black Churches" which is almost a global phenomenon from West Africa. These churches are of a different genre, with distinctive doctrinal statements, ethos and practices which are almost identical with older Caribbean and African churches that have stagnated or declined. Most of these New Pentecostal churches have been noted to have emerged during the late 1980s and 1990s in the United Kingdom as a result of the increase in the population of economic migrants and the student population who desired their "home" brand of Christian faith.

The magnitude of the impact of Black Churches is observable in the Christian research findings that describe Black-led Churches as propping up national church attendance, with London as a prime example. The findings of Tear Fund, a Christian international aid and development agency working globally to end poverty and injustice, in research conducted in the United Kingdom, indicated that 48% of black people attend church regularly; three times the rate of the white community.[145]

Statistical figures have indicated that there may be about 400 different denominations and independent churches, 4,000 focal congregations,[146] and increasingly Black Churches in Britain have been identified as vital in the implementation of multicultural policies of the state. Rex and Tomlinson assert that a church can therefore act as a "black self-help group which can interface with ethnic social work and policies in a positive way".[147] Black-led Churches in Britain act in this capacity by providing identity and a social point of engagement to reach the ethnic minorities and contribute to social integration of their local communities.

The legitimacy and recognition of these churches gives credibility to Black Majority Churches. It is based not on their theological persuasions which enable them to engage in social work, but their street credibility is the greatest leverage. The seeds for the proliferation and consolidation of Black Majority Churches in Britain today were sown in the pre-*Windrush* era through the pain of racism, missionary zeal, unemployment and poverty, but today many Black Churches have a visible presence in the political, socio-economic and religious life of Britain. The acorn sown in the midst of economic adventure and missionary zeal covered with faith and providence is now an oak tree blossoming and fruitful in Britain.

## SUMMARY

To discover the antecedents of Black Churches in Britain we have to reflect on the historical records which indicate that there were black Christians in Britain as far back as 1500. There was an upsurge of black populations in the sixteenth, seventeenth and eighteenth centuries as a result of the transatlantic slave trade, though most were Christianized as a result of their escape from the clutches of slavery. Some had a "Damascus experience" which was reflected in their Christian values, vocational attainments and successes. The earliest black Christians in Britain served within the historic denominational churches as evangelists, missionaries and preachers, mostly to their home countries.

The influx of migrants after the abolition of the slave trade in Britain changed the social and professional spectrum of black Christians as they became change agents and accomplished professionals. The twentieth century was a remarkable century in global Christianity as Charles Parham and later William Seymour became active proponents of glossolalia which later impacted Britain. The home of Pentecostalism in Britain, Sunderland, through the ministry of the English-born Norwegian Methodist minister, Thomas Barratt, and his meetings of 1907, was one of the visible launching pads for the first modern Black Pastor in Britain. Bro. Thomas Brem-Wilson, a businessman from Ghana and the pastor of the first Black Church in Britain, received the Baptism of the Holy Spirit with evidence of glossolalia. The church had a very dynamic partnership with historic churches and Brem-Wilson was noted for his spirituality.

The *Windrush* era ushered in a new era in British church history with the expansion, rather than foundation and proliferation, of Black Churches in Britain, which has contributed to a re-awakening of spirituality in Britain and the social integration of black Christian groups.

*Chapter Three*

# The Numerical Growth of Black Majority Churches in Great Britain Since the 1950s[1]

∽

### INTRODUCTION

Black Majority Churches are the fastest-growing and are among the largest churches in the United Kingdom, and substantial numbers of these churches are Pentecostal. It is estimated that there are over 4,000 congregations and a membership of one million, the majority of them in urban cities as a result of the growth of these churches from the 1950s to 2008.[2] The growth of these Black Majority Churches is a new phenomenon that has ushered in a distinctive era in British church history.

The growth and proliferation of Black Majority Churches in Britain is a reflection of the tenacity of the faith and consistency of African and Caribbean Diaspora pioneers of Black Majority Churches during the *Windrush* era. The *Windrush* era undoubtedly resulted in the emergence of a second wave of Black Churches in Britain. Migration from the West Indies to post-war Britain was necessitated by manpower shortages in certain sectors of the British economy and a multiplicity of other factors.

Various anthropologists and sociologists have adduced various perspectives for the proliferation and growth of Black Churches in Britain.[3] Most of them firmly assert that many emerged as a result of social deprivation and a re-socialization response to assimilation as the magnitude of racism experienced by the migrants was not only a social challenge but a monstrous experience that pervaded their economic, social and spiritual interests. The growth of these churches over time has gradually given most of the churches a global identity, as these denominations or churches are continually exporting their brand of denominationalism into the Western world through their missiological agenda to re-Christianize secularized Europe as they engage in reverse missions.

The growth of Black Majority Churches in Britain has been phenomenal since the 1950s; they have attained a status of recognition amongst historic denominations, faith leaders and policy formulators. This is a departure from the anthropological and sociological researchers' perspective in the foundational stages of these churches when they were viewed with so much scepticism.

## GROWTH DYNAMICS: PUSH AND PULL LEVERAGES

The growth of Black Majority Churches is of a distinctive genre in the annals of church history in Britain. The growth phenomenon of Black Churches has been a major research focus over the last sixty years, but the apparent approach of most of these scholars has been a broad generalization of the pull and push factors. Historically the focus of most of the growth analysis had always been a panoramic perspective, but the growth pattern over time is a reflection of the distinctive eras in the history of Black Churches in Britain. The general consensus amongst scholars has been that social deprivation was the precursor for the proliferation of Black Churches during the *Windrush* era as Black Churches filled the obvious void created by the staid, historic churches with their deficiencies in racial and missiological understanding.

The historic denominations in the 1950s were already suffering congregational decline as a result of the devastating effects of the world wars and pastoral crisis. The declining fortunes of historic churches in the 1950s and 1960s in Britain have been treated from an isolationist perspective. The issue of faith and spirituality of the people had always been accessed within the immediate context of the challenges of historic churches in terms of decline in church attendance, growth and effects of secularization excluding preceding events in relation to the devastating effects of the First and Second World Wars on the British subjects (not Commonwealth subjects) which were reflected in their commitment to the Christian faith.

The effect of the First World War was not just to diminish manpower and resources for overseas mission, as the euphoria of Global Mission (a result of the Edinburgh Conference) died a natural death.[4] Much more seriously, the First World War made a profound impression on Christian Europe itself. The magnitude of the perils of two world wars might not be fully comprehended by most people who never witnessed the great extent of the sociological, psychological and environmental effects of war, especially on the civilian population. War is never pleasant, no matter the victor. The social and environmental consequences are not easy to obliterate, especially for those that are directly involved in the conflict. But for the first time in human history, war in the twentieth century touched and involved the civilian population in a way that earlier wars never had. The concept of total war, which entailed the holistic commitment of various countries' industrial, economic, political, social and military resources, ushered in a new paradigm in war history.

The impact of the First World War on the Christian faith was that the spirituality of some Christians was enhanced as their faith was strengthened, but some lost their faith during the conflict. While some of the returnees from the war denounced their faith, it brought some to a living faith and strengthened the faith of others, but it is also the case that many were completely sickened by what they saw and lost their faith completely. There was obvious complicity created by the involvement of bishops, archbishops and cardinals of Europe, who urged their compatriots to take up arms against the enemies of their respective countries, so that the Christian faith became a weapon of mobilization; the perception of war as having a divine mandate, and that God was on their side, was reinforced by the bishops and other church leaders.[5]

The combined effect of the two world wars contributed to the various movements of independence from imperial rule that emerged in many colonial lands. The tell-tale signs of a fractured imperialist domination began to emerge, suggesting that the various European empires would not survive for long after 1945. Change was definitely inevitable. The loss of empire not only changed life in the nations that won their independence, but the impact of such change also challenged the assumptions that Western nations had of their own worldview. The notion that empire had a civilizing mission came to a close and inevitably those same Western nations began to ask questions about the role of mission, which had become so inextricably connected to the enterprise of empire. The commercial enterprise of the British Empire, which effectively became the Commonwealth states, heralded a new era in British Christianity through the emergence and proliferation of Black Churches.

The proponents of the social deprivation theory assert that racism and rejection from mainstream historic churches, experienced by first- and second-generation migrants from the Caribbean and Africa in the 1950s, 1960s and 1970s, was responsible for the emergence and growth of Black Churches in their founding days. This school of thought argues that the British historic churches shut the door of communion to their fellow communicants from the Caribbean and Africa as they presented themselves in various churches in the 1950s and 1960s. The general racial persuasions of British churches became a motivational factor for the rapid growth of Black Churches from the early 1960s.

The derogatory experiences of the early black Christian migrants from the Caribbean who were members of historic churches are well documented, not only by sociologists and anthropologists, but also through the gradual emergence of reflective writings from the experiential perspective of first-generation Caribbean migrants, articulated by the expression "*whe dem say* [what they say]?" and of second-generation Caribbeans and Africans who were raised in the midst of these challenges and were proponents of multiple Christian identities.[6]

The growth and proliferation of Black Churches in Britain can be described chronologically, taking into account the various socio-economic factors that culminated in the proliferation of these churches. The growth phases and the associated push and pull factors are discussed chronologically below, but it is important to state that the push and pull factors have dynamic interplay beyond each growth phase chronicled. The push and pull factors are considered under these broad sub-divisions: (a) The Foundation for Growth; (b) The *Windrush* Effect; (c) Emergence of Diaspora African Initiated Churches; (d) Neo-Pentecostal Churches' Growth Phase.

### *The Foundation for the Current Growth of Black Majority Churches*

The burgeoning Black Majority Churches today in Britain are a result of various historical events traceable to the Blacks' antecedents in Britain. The various factors included: (a) the "enforced transplanting of Africans" in Europe, which resulted in eclectic culture amongst Africans and Caribbeans due to the distortion of their traditional religious orientations in their purest form; (b) post-slavery migration and integration of Blacks into the socio-economic activities in Britain; (c) the educational aspirations of the bourgeois African/Caribbean class; and (d) the multifaceted impact of economic Diasporans.

The incredible religiosity of Blacks is traceable to their African ancestry, as articulated by John Mbiti, who asserts that: "... Africans are notoriously religious. To be without religion amounts to a self-excommunication from the entire life of society, and Africans ... do not know how to exist without religion."[7] The culmination of the inherent African traditional religiousness amongst Blacks found its expression through the Christian faith as some were converted, baptized and became active Christians in Diaspora as far back as the fifteenth century. The emergence of British Pentecostalism precipitated by the American and global renaissance of

Baptism of the Holy Spirit and glossolalia in 1907 was witnessed by Bro. Thomas Brem-Wilson who started Sumner Chapel in 1906. Sumner Chapel provided a dynamic model in black/white partnership in an era that was preceded by ethnocentric propaganda, racial intolerance and distinctive class structure. The foundation of the present gains of black evangelicals today in Britain are traceable to Bro. Brem-Wilson's ministry as he was actively involved with Cecil Polhill, Alexander Boddy and their ecumenical/Pentecostal aspirations.

Evangelicals of his day had great respect for his ministry and he was visited by Alexander Boddy and Cecil Polhill in London. The founding days of the Black Church were devoid of any "organized" church planting (the establishment of new churches) by the pioneers, as it was perceived to be an exception for a black man to pastor a church in England in 1906. Church planting has become the hub of Black Majority Churches in Britain, with London having over 900 different Pentecostal denominations today. London is noted for being the administrative and economic heartbeat of Britain and has been the host of most ethnic minorities from as far back as the seventeenth century to the present day.[8] Similar church planting by Nigerian Pastor Daniel Ekarte in Liverpool, a major slave trade port during the transatlantic slave trade, was typical of the urban explosion of Black Churches in Britain.

The obvious inherent sociological explanation as adduced by Miller and Yamamori that Pentecostalism "often attracts people who are suffering from what sociologists refer to as anomie"[9] is apt if the migration pattern of the Pentecostal churches is a local migratory pattern, but the uniqueness of the Black-led Churches was that adherents suffered from "transnational anomie". This is the impact of the social, economic and political challenges as a result of migration from undeveloped economies to developing economies. Pastor Daniel Ekarte (1930s–1966) was motivated by a sense of divine call to preach the Gospel, but his social action on behalf of the "brown babies" galvanized his ministry into the limelight in Britain. Thus the pattern for urban colonization by Black Churches was pioneered by Bro. Thomas Brem-Wilson and Pastor Daniel Ekarte. The social action of Ekarte was not directed towards the Blacks but assisted in solving a serious communal and racially motivated alienation of children of English girls and American GIs after the Second World War. This action demonstrates a holistic Christian worldview as exemplified by Jesus in his Sermon on the Mount.

That the urban model of church planting by Ekarte and Brem-Wilson has widely, consciously or circumstantially been adopted by most Black

Majority Churches in subsequent phases of growth is attributable to socio-economic and immigration antecedents. The urban model was also a major feature in the gradual emergence of the American denomination, Pentecostal Assemblies of the World, as "cities [in the USA, such as Baltimore and New York] became the central focus of independent Black Apostolic churches".[10] A major feature of the Ekarte church model was that it was intricately linked with the social deprivation model induced as a result of racism and prejudice, but this attracted a lot of public and state commendation. A similar paradigm, with the exception of the causative problem of racism, is utilised by the Church of God of Prophecy, with the Nehemiah Housing Project in Birmingham.

Pastor Brem-Wilson and Daniel Ekarte's antecedents in church planting heralded the reverse mission approach, the potential of which is now being explored by Black Majority Churches in Britain. A similar paradigm is observed in the New Testament when Blacks engaged in cross-cultural missions. The conversion of Apollos of Alexandria in Acts 18:24–28, who later engaged in a reverse mission to the people of Corinth, is one example.[11] This further attests to the existence of the Christian faith in Egypt as far back as the middle of the first century CE.[12]

## The Windrush – Push and Pull Factors

The resilience of the faith of some West Indian migrants during the *Windrush* era starting from 1948 contributed significantly to the proliferation of Black Majority Churches in Britain today. The journey to Britain was in response to a manpower shortage in Britain as a result of post-war economic dynamics in the booming industrial sector in Britain. The push factor of West Indian migration to the motherland was also traceable to the American congressional decision to limit migration from the West Indies to America and the declining fortunes of the West Indian economy, which was predominantly an agrarian economy built around subsistence agriculture. There were complex reasons for the economic decline of the Caribbean, for instance Jamaica's economy was worsened by the divesting of the gains of slavery from the local economy by absentee slave merchants. This was further compounded by the collapse of the plantation economy. A British Labour MP noted various brochures' description of Jamaica as a "tropical paradise"; however, he was of the opinion that "it would be truer to describe it as a tropical slum".[13]

The economic climate was chaotic and became a breeding ground for massive unemployment, filth, deplorable health conditions and poor housing facilities. The causes and effects of the economic strangulation of

Jamaica were succinctly laid on active players of the colonial masters' capitalist exploitation of the nation.

This view is antithetical to Booth's imperialist–colonial historiography in her thesis which neglected the impact of racism on the Blacks in British church history.[14] To the Caribbean migrants of the 1950s and 1960s, escape from the clutches of national hunger and deprivation to the "mother country" was the only respite even if the intention of most of the migrants was to go for just a few years before returning to the West Indies. Britain, however, eventually became home to many.

The British passports and the communicant cards of the West Indian Christians were two inseparable identities rejected by the British public, which was hostile to the social-cum-economic integration of migrants, while the historic denominations fostered an age-long racial and ethnocentric disposition to maintain a homogenous community of worshippers. This eventually led to the emergence of large communities of Blacks in urban areas in London, Birmingham, Wolverhampton, Leeds, Manchester and Liverpool, especially in the inner-city areas. These industrial cities became the launching pad for the proliferation of Black Churches.

The snobbery and rejection by historic churches of denominational affiliations resonated in the hearts of Caribbean Diasporans as they were confronted with the paradox of the racial brand of Christianity in Britain; they felt estranged and isolated even when welcome, as colour became a dividing line in the pew. Not only was the culture shock racially motivated, but the Caribbean Diasporans were alienated from the British worship style despite the familiarity of the liturgy and hymns to the migrants. The worship sessions were devoid of a palpable sense of joy and celebration of the faith as Christ was celebrated with so much sobriety that many migrants perceived such gatherings as dull, uninviting, unattractive, staid and devoid of their familiar cultural trappings. The church was expected to be a beacon of hope, assimilation and inclusiveness by the early Christian migrants of the *Windrush* era, but they were shocked as they were ignored, patronized and asked not to preach or return to the churches because their continued presence might offend the parishioners.[15]

The pain and misery of the early migrants were compounded by their sudden translation from the agrarian economy of the Caribbean to a burgeoning industrial development characterized by individualization – a far cry from the collectivism and communal lifestyle in the Caribbean and Africa in the 1950s and 1960s. The rude awakening of the industrial revolution of Britain staring at the migrants who were raised within a rural, agrarian economy, and the attendant social and economic constraints associated with industrialization, were contributory factors to the overwhelming culture shock experienced by the migrants. The culture shock and rejection were turned into motivation for the emergence of a sense of community, brotherhood and a respectability amongst brethren; the Black Churches met the spiritual, emotional, social and even economic needs of *Windrush* migrants in a hostile environment.

These Black Churches became sanctuaries where the physically and emotionally broken found healing. The alienation of the migrants through racism and rejection boomeranged as the migrants were unable to accept involvement with British institutions. To the Caribbean and African Diasporans, the Black Churches were holistic and fostered a sense of community and support, in contrast to British historic churches.[16] Calley posited that the effect of racial discrimination was two-fold as the migrant suffered from discrimination "neurosis" which provided a basis for shunning British society and becoming overly reliant on the resources of the migrant community, but she further asserted that in the absence of racism and rejection, Black Churches will still emerge along ethnic boundaries as the churches provide a therapeutic and religious sanctuary as a result of the strains of social integration.[17]

The British historic churches of the 1950s and 1960s failed to hold allegiance with the migrants who were established Christians from the Caribbean. As a result the early black Christians withdrew from these churches. The expectations of the *Windrush* migrants were very high because of their colonial and cultural affiliations to Britain. They were disillusioned with the racist and moral decadence which resulted in deliberate avoidance of historic denominations by the West Indian migrants. This created natural reminiscences of their identity and colonial affinity and led to them querying the past social and economic exploitation of their nation.

The rejection of the British churches by the early West Indian migrants was not a rejection of their Christian faith but replacement therapy to cope with their disillusionment, disappointment and apathy towards a culture that was not receptive to their aspirations. The process of acculturation was hardened on account of racial undertones which polarized the process of re-socialization of the migrants. The culture shock must have had negative psychological effects on the migrants. This created an era of racially induced Ethiopianism amongst the Caribbean Christians.

A major compensatory growth factor of Black-led Churches during the *Windrush* era was that the early migrants held on to their social and cultural values: a major feature was collectivism. The prevailing trend in the West

Indian migration of the 1960s was the growing number of women and children arriving to join their menfolk as soon as they had settled, saved sufficient passage money and had accommodation in Britain. Because of their family ties, family loyalties and social and economic stability, the first migrants in each family became role models, guides to life in Britain, and the immediate source of re-socialization of their kith and kin. This had positive effects on the growth of the emerging Black-led Churches. Marriages amongst the early migrants were also compensatory growth factors of Black Churches. The majority of the migrants in the 1950s and 1960s were men and women in their reproductive years, as indicated in Robert Mills' survey of Jamaican migrants from 1953–55.[18] The average age of migrants was just over 30 years and 75% of both sexes were in the 20–39 age group.

This survey was a broad generalization of the immigration age brackets from the West Indies but it was asserted by Hill in a survey of six major historic denominations that 4% of the people living in Britain attended church, in contrast with the church attendance of migrants from the West Indies, of which 75% were church attendees.[19] The evolving social re-orientation, culture shock, pharisaic disposition of the historic denominations and licentious opportunities were obvious factors that enticed most West Indians away from the Christian faith on their arrival in Britain. This depicts the impact of the fluidity of the host culture on the assimilation process of the migrants, which often leads to alienation of their religious-cum-cultural orientations in comparison to life before migration in their respective countries. The migrants were thus confronted with the effects of secularization in British cities in contrast with the agrarian economy of the West Indies. Parsons is of the opinion that the significant drop in church attendance by migrants in the 1950s has a wider implication: the shift from historic churches to Black-led Churches is suggestive of the dynamic relationship between African-Caribbean identity and religion which heralded a distinctive phase in British church life.[20]

The post-migration effects on African-Caribbean migrants in their Christian commitments in the British context should not be viewed in isolation, as the obvious distinctive feature of the migrants was the intensity and visible presence in Britain of economic missionaries – those gainfully employed and serving their denominational organizations. Parsons further posits that the percentage decrease in the commitment of the migrants in the 1950s has no significant impact, as the growth of the Black-led Churches was unprecedented.[21] The drop certainly might have hitherto been associated with the effects of secularization of the mother country and the tragedy of the drop in the commitment might be seen as the loss to the historic denominations, but eventually there was the emergence and proliferation of Black Churches in Britain. The leaders of the Black-led Church of the 1950s became the modern-day Gideon army.

The genesis of reverse mission in Britain in the early 1950s and 1960s gradually led to the growth of Black Churches in Britain as missionaries from the West Indies migrated to Britain. The hubs of reverse mission in relation to the growth of Black Churches were the quest for the preservation of scattered flocks amongst the West Indian Diasporans[22] and the "Divine" missiological agenda of people like Philip Mohabir. Mohabir was a Hindu and rural school teacher who obeyed the "Macedonian call" to become a missionary to Britain.[23] His misconception of Britain as a utopian Christian home of the saints was replaced with empathy, passion and commitment in his missionary endeavour in Britain. Denominationalism was not a general feature of some of the "new missionaries" engaged in radical proclamation of the Christian faith in the midst of the declining influence of Christianity in Britain, which was fast becoming an amoral community.

The gains of such evangelistic commitment were not limited to converts amongst the black communities, as depicted by the ministry of Philip Mohabir.[24] There were mainline denominations that partnered some of this pioneering mission with missionaries in Britain as they made available their infrastructures for the use of the missionaries. The cooperative effort of black and white Christians was quite complementary to Mohabir's missionary effort, as a couple of pastors from Gresham Road and Stockwell Baptist Church lectured at Mohabir's evening meetings. The evangelistic fervour and prevalence of charismata in most of the evangelistic prayer meetings gradually attracted other migrants and Whites and they metamorphosed into networks of prayer groups in almost all immigrant settlements. Some of these groups opted for school halls and unused church halls, and developed into congregations.

The dynamism of the African and Caribbean Christians in Diaspora and their commitment to overcome initial economic challenges and assimilation into Britain were not only pivotal to the emergence of Black Churches but also contributed significantly to the growth of Black Churches in Britain. It is to the credit of the migrants' industry and initiative that they created economic leverage, as many were dissatisfied with the inherent economic strangulation experienced on arrival in Britain. Many saved, acquired mortgages, purchased homes and established various business initiatives. The economic leverage was not personalized by the migrants, as many of the migrants were financially committed to the emerging congregations, being financial stakeholders in their churches.

## Denominationalism

Denominationalism became a major contribution to the growth of Black-led Churches in Britain as far back as the 1950s. The era of denominationalism that eventually became prevalent in the 1960s amongst Black Churches was not without disaffection amongst some of the missionaries who had no denominational credentials, especially by some of the early West Indian missionaries in Britain. The proliferation of denominationalism by the West Indian churches was described as a "sad departure from the Spirit, and from the love which we [Mohabir and his friends] started; our initial idea was not to have denominational barriers, island barriers, or colour barriers erected. We felt we were in the forefront to create a new thing – a church that was alive, integrated, multi-racial, multicultural, diverse but yet united; a church that would not reflect a peculiar brand of doctrine."[25] Mohabir's idealist fellowship is suspect, as the natural inclination of human beings is not only in meeting economic or pastoral needs but the opportunity to make choices in the midst of competing needs.

Denominationalist leaders were quite ecstatic and persuasive in the bid to establish their denominations in the mother country. Some of their members were perceived to be pilgrims in Diaspora, and this perception necessitated a unifying umbrella for the perpetuation of their denomination as Britain became a mission field. The impact of denominationalism was significant amongst Black-led Churches in the 1960s and almost all prominent African-Caribbean churches became denominationally affiliated.

Roswith Gerloff's perspective on the genesis of denominationalism amongst Black-led Churches from the *Windrush* era notes that the Church of God in Christ was the first to be established, during the first Pentecostal conference in London in 1952, while the New Testament Church of God, now led by Bishop Brown, and the Church of God of Prophecy simultaneously followed.[26] She notes that later the Rehoboth Church of God in Christ inevitably became a mission field for American denominationalism, but the spread of denominationalism was not only limited to American influence on Black Churches in Britain in the 1960s. It also included denominational loyalties, as the migrants were encouraged by denominational leaders from the West Indies to hoist the flag of their denomination on the mission field of Britain. The history of Black-led Churches' denominational affiliation is traceable to the first Black Church established by Thomas Brem-Wilson in 1906. Thomas Brem-Wilson's Church, Peckham Assembly, was affiliated initially with the Apostolic Church, UK, but was accepted into the fellowship of the Assemblies of God on 1 May 1939.

The spread of denominationalism amongst West Indian migrant churches was born out of a spasmodic approach to church planting modulated by the perceived needs of the migrants to maintain their spiritual fervour in the midst of the effects of moral and social permissiveness of Britain in the 1950s and 1960s. This era marked transnational migration of preachers into Britain. Arnold notes the establishment of the London branch of the NTCG in 1955: James Tomlin of the New Testament Church of God at Bombay, Manchester, Jamaica, arrived in Britain and "wrote back to a friend and minister in Jamaica urging him to come to England to start a Church. He rented a small hall in preparation of the arrival of his friend, and in October that same year, Reverend S.U. Thompson, leaving his wife and young family in Jamaica, arrived in London."[27] This was after the establishment of the churches in Wolverhampton and Handsworth under the leadership of Oliver Lyseight.

The only prerequisite for the spasmodic church planting of the West Indian churches then was the presence of Diaspora believers, often initiated through the prayer meetings at various homes but at times in unconventional venues. For example, "F.F. Poyser, a young minister from Jamaica, gathered six other believers in a kitchen of an immigrant home off Granville Road, Sheffield, and laid the foundation for what has now [then] become the third largest church in the nation [within the New Testament Church of God circuits in Britain as at the time of the assertion]."[28] The passion, zeal and commitment of the West Indian Christians at times were quite unconventional in evangelism and church planting.

The inherent growth of Black-led Churches as a result of denominationalism was not without a detrimental effect on the unity of the emerging migrants' community. Denominationalism amongst African and Caribbean church leaders trying to meet the spiritual and socio-cultural diversity of the migrants in various urban and industrial areas of Britain provided a catchment focus for Black-led Churches on account of the high concentration of Blacks in urban cities. The 1960s era saw re-alignment of Black Churches by the forces of denominationalism as dependencies were fostered.

The effect of the polarization of relationships and the right to freedom of worship created a dynamic reoccurrence of "fission and fusions" amongst Black-led Churches after the 1960s "according to the efficiency of leadership, degree of participation, personality conflicts, class distinctions, [and] geographical (islands!) or national loyalties and the racial, moral or financial policies of North American headquarters".[29] The overriding influence of American denominationalism on Black-led Churches in the

British Isles coincided with the 1962 Race Relations Act. The effect cut across the board amongst Black-led Churches and led to dissociation, realignment and new affiliations, as many Black-led Churches bore resemblances to their black American antecedents. It was an era noted for the diverse convergence of identities as indigenization of the black Diaspora churches emerged, such as Bethel Apostolic Church.

The leadership and administrative machinery of the American denominational churches provided the much-needed leverage for the Black-led Churches to function maximally in Britain with full accreditation, strict doctrinal statements and good economic support. The success of American denominations in spreading the frontiers of their denominationalism was attributable to the indigenization of their missiological approach in the West Indies prior to the *Windrush* dispensation. The indigenization of the West Indian Churches later became the opportunity to transfer the "home grown churches which had lent to the poor and underprivileged a sense of spiritual belonging, indigenous leadership, a functioning organization and a feeling of being in harmony with genuine Biblical theology".[30] The triumph of the pioneers of the second stream of Black-led Churches in Britain as a result of the *Windrush* migrants was an American affirmation in the indigenization approach in church planting.

The apparent condemnatory notion that denominationalism and other extraneous factors contributed to the declining fortunes of the historic church should be assessed with caution. Denominationalism can lead to a state of complacency and inaction on the part of the leadership, and this state, due to past historical achievements, might impair the missional focus of the church.

The second generation of the *Windrush* migrants, mostly the West Indian youth, provided more dynamism to the growth of Black Churches. They became proactive through the influence of Rastafarianism as they challenged the colonial "Thatcherism" of the Christian faith in lieu of African consciousness and agitation for enculturation of spiritual symbolism in worship and liturgy. Racism was adjured as a factor in the economic strata that most migrants were identified within, as most were below the middle economic class. The contributory social upheaval of the 1980 race riots facilitated more dynamic and resilient Black-led Churches as many developed into functional organizations committed to improving the socio-economic conditions, cultural identities and the spirituality of their faith communities. They also served as springboards for the promotion of community cohesion and enlightenment of the larger community polarized along race and spiritual persuasions. This era marked the genesis of social action from

Black Churches in collaboration with state agencies in addressing various socio-cultural and religious diversities in various communities in most urban areas of Britain.

The emerging Black-led Churches attracted many migrants from the Caribbean or the United States who were Christians, and members of the historic denominations joined the emerging Pentecostal churches because of the racially induced socio-economic constraints. This was in consonance with the view of Harvey Cox, one of the foremost religious researchers of the twentieth century. He asserted that Pentecostalism would mark "the reshaping of religion in the twenty-first century". The doctrinal persuasion of the Black-led Churches in Britain was within the framework of the emerging global Pentecostal phenomenon which Harvey Cox described as "primal spirituality" which is hinged on a tripartite model of spirituality: (a) primal speech, exemplified by glossolalia, "another voice, a language of the heart"; (b) primal piety, found in the renaissance of the Lucan account of "trance, vision, healing, dreams, dance and other classic religious expressions"; and (c) primal hope, which he described as "Pentecostalism's millennial outlook... that a radical new age is about to dawn".[31]

These aspects were prevalent in the emerging Black-led Churches in Britain in the 1950s and still are today. Cox saw glossolalia as a deconstructive experience: not a humanistic mechanism but a spiritual response to "ecstasy deficit in our contemporary world".[32] He further posited that Pentecostalism, to which most of the Black-led Churches in the *Windrush* era subscribed, was "closer to the most sublime forms of mysticism than are the more respectable denominations that sometimes look down on it".[33] The tripartite hubs of Cox's "primal spirituality" were typical of the African and Caribbean cosmology as their spirituality had always had the element of supernaturalism exemplified in it. It is apt to note that Cox further affirmed that "ecstatic utterance goes beyond even this lofty, classical mystical insight. It is something with particular relevance to our own searching but sceptical generation. Not only is the ultimate mystery indescribable and its way unsearchable..."[34]

The worldview of Africans is such that it sees spiritual interpretations, explanations and guidance in every problem of life. Pentecostal inspirational manifestations have gone a long way in satisfying these desires in African Christianity. For example, prior to the advent of Christianity, Africans consulted Ifa oracles to ascertain daily, occupational and family exigencies: whether it would be safe to embark on a journey, get married to a woman from a particular family background, take a risky step, determine the destiny of a new child, and so on. The Black-led Churches' worldview, hinged on the Pentecostal prism, appealed to the sensibilities of the migrants. Connectedness is created as an alternative to African Traditional Primal Religion, though this might have led to the fusion of the Pentecostal worldview and the African Traditional Primal Religion which constitutes syncretism. While the intention of Black-led Churches in Britain from the 1950s until now is biblical, their theology is also shaped by local concerns and contexts.

This is in keeping with Hollenweger's observation that all theology is culturally conditioned.[35] This view is further supported by Africa's illustrious authority on Pentecostalism, Ogbu Kalu, as he posited that the failures of the colonial masters that are culturally and anthropologically liberating became the gains of Africans in their distinctive worldview. According to Kalu:

> A significant aspect of the nineteenth century was that as missionaries sowed the seed of the gospel, Africans appropriated it from a primal, charismatic world-view and read the translated scriptures in that light. Indigenous agencies recovered the spiritual resources of the gospel and challenged missionary Christianity to be fully biblical. This set the stage for the decolonization process that followed the world wars. New forces such as the implosion of the state challenged the heritage of African Christianity; and the collapse of the dictatorial states and attendant poverty probed the tensile strength of the churches' stewardship. Inexplicably, charismatic and Pentecostal spirituality resurfaced to provide the energy for growth and sustainability in the midst of hostile circumstances.[36]

This assertion is a fitting testimony to the tenacity, faith and persuasion of the West Indian migrants of the 1950s and 1960s in Britain.

Subscription to primal hope was not only viewed from the eschatological millennial perspective but also in relation to their experiential perspective in terms of the socio-economic challenges of assimilation into the British community. The understanding of the cosmos of Black Majority Churches in Britain is exemplified by their thought and attitudes. This has influenced the shaping of their sacred space and time; for instance the Yoruba traditional aphorism "Aiye loja, Orun nile" (the world is a marketplace, the spirit world is home) is typified by the worldview of the Celestial Church of Christ.[37] The obvious inference is that the existential and transcendental theology of most Black Majority Churches in Britain is at one and the same time a component of society, while distinctive from each other.

The inherent Pentecostal orientation of Black-led Churches as far back as the 1950s and 1960s has led to a distinctive Pentecostal hermeneutics of warm experientialism and pious affection. The development of a relevant theology in Black-led Churches started as far back as the 1950s. Harvey noted that "the Black[-led] Church in Britain is in the process of developing a relevant theology which embraces their dual heritage as a people of African [or Caribbean] descent and as Christians".[38] This was quite evident in the music and worship of the early West Indian migrants as they longed to encounter the Spirit of God in an emotional, existential experience characterized by a fervent devotion to Gospel music and songs that were typical of the prevailing socio-economic difficulties of their times, such as "Rock of Ages" and "Amazing Grace". Religion to the Blacks is a lens through which adjustment to immediate challenges is perceived and this is replicated in their worship and liturgy. This provides a psychotherapeutic effect and expresses a worldview according to which God's love to the members of the faith community is undeniable; the experiential acknowledgement becomes a default mechanism to cope with the strangulating effects of the wider community in terms of racial, social and economic challenges.

### The African Initiated Churches' Growth Phase – Push and Pull Factors

The growth of Black-led Churches in Britain was given greater impetus with the transplanting of the home-grown African Initiated Churches (AICs), as a result of the migration of West Africans, especially Nigerians, Ghanaians and Sierra Leonians, for further studies in Britain. The emergence of the first Cherubim and Seraphim Church, London is quite instructive as S.A. Abidoye and fourteen other members, without any ecclesiastical commission from Cherubim and Seraphim, Nigeria, established the Church in London.[39] Similar commitment to religious affirmations and migration is seen in the paradigm of the Jewish community in Diaspora in which the Torah and synagogue were transported from local identity to transnational identity. There exist divergent perspectives amongst scholars as well as religious practitioners about the appropriate nomenclature to describe African Initiated Churches: synonyms such as Enculturation, Indigenization, Contextualization, Africanization or African theology are utilised to describe the search for an "authentic African expression of Christianity".[40]

The diversities of various cultural orientations of Africans culminated in the emergence of distinctive African Indigenous Churches such as the Church of the Lord (Aladura). "Aladura" in Yoruba means "owners of prayer", "Prayer Fellowship" or "The Praying People". Aladura, according to Oshun,[41] is generic: he identified three broad classes of Aladura as: (a) Typical Aladura; (b) Aladura Apostolic; and (c) Aladura Atypical. Aladura's emphasis is on power in praying and belief in faith healing and various elements associated with Pentecostalism. Healing meetings and miracle services were a common feature of the African Initiated Churches amongst African students in Diaspora as many appropriated the opportunity of practising their faith within their indigenous and cultural prism in Britain. Such African churches include Cherubim and Seraphim, Celestial Church of Christ, Divine Prayer Society or the Church of Universal Prayer Fellowship, and the Musama Disco Christo Church of Christ (Army of the Church of Christ [MDCC]) which was founded on 19 October 1922 by prophet Joseph Appiah, a Ghahian and former Methodist Cathechist. MDCC is quite Afrocentric, distinct from any Western or American influence; its theology is a fusion of Judaism and Africanization. One of the church elders in London is the grandson of the founder, Rev. Jerisdan Hartna Jehu-Appiah, a PhD holder in theology from the University of Birmingham and the first full-time pastor posted from Ghana to the United Kingdom in 1979.

Jenkins provides a broad-spectrum and balanced overview of the diverse attempts of inculturation and syncretic practices not only synonymous with the African Independent Church but within the Roman Catholic Church. He notes that "the Roman Catholic archbishop of Bloemfontein, South Africa, not only suggested that Christians might be permitted to honour their ancestors through blood libations, but that a ritual sacrifice of sheep or cows might be incorporated into the Mass".[42] This raises the issue of permissible boundary delineation of inculturation that places some of the African Initiated Churches beyond a Eurocentric Christian worldview.

The home grown Aladura churches movement, according to some scholars, was motivated by the desire to make missionary Protestantism relevant to the practical needs of the cultural milieu from which it evolved. The Aladura church's ability to replicate itself in Britain cannot be divorced from the fact that religious persuasion is inextricably linked with cultural identity. The spread of the Aladura churches from Nigeria in Britain created the cultural context for the Diasporans in Britain to replicate their home-grown church through the influx of migrants from Nigeria and other African countries.[43] The Aladura worldview is characterized by vibrant worship sessions and the appropriation of elements of the African Traditional Religion worldview such as belief in spiritual powers, angels, mystical forces and spiritual healing. Various scholars have described some of these churches as blending cultic materials with Christianity,[44] synthesizing the Yoruba worldview with Christianity[45] or as a form of "syncretism"[46] or "pagan features" or tendencies and "occultism".[47] The membership of the Aladura movement is almost homogenous and mainly of the Yoruba extraction rather than those who do not share this cosmological underpinning from Nigeria, and as such the initial success of the movement depended on its adaptability as the movement "adapted Christianity to the primal [Yoruba] religious worldview".[48]

The Africanization of Christianity, according to Meyer,[49] is not a new phase; she asserts that "Africanization, understood as appropriation of Christianity at the grassroots level, has been an integral component of the spread of missionary Christianity from the outset." This "Africanization from below" came about through processes of both translation into the vernacular[50] and the diabolization of Ewe religion (and its construction as "heathendom"), thereby merging nineteenth-century popular missionary Christianity and local religious practices and ideas. Meyer's assertion reflects the origin of syncretism within the African Initiated Churches which is still replicated in some Black-led Churches in Britain. She further asserts the fusion of the African Traditional Primal Religion along with accessible Christian doctrine. For instance, she opines that:

> Old gods and spirits, and also witchcraft, continued to exist as Christian demons under the auspices of the devil. Hence in addition to investigating African ideas about God or the positive convergence of African and Christian notions, I argued for the need of scholars to consider the negative incorporation of the spiritual entities in African religious traditions into the image of the Christian devil as part of the local appropriations. In this way, the "old" and forbidden, from which Christians were required to distance themselves, remained available, albeit in a new form.[51]

It is quite obvious that the dualism identified by Meyer has contributed to the growth of Black-led Churches in Britain, although some Africans' fusion of the Christian faith with traditional African religious practices has led to a deprecatory use of the term "syncretism" employed by mainline denominations, so as to designate African Initiated Church Christian understandings as impure and deviant.

The growth of the African Initiated Churches in Britain rode on the crest of the pneumatic (Spirit-led) community that claims to interact with the supernatural to bring about divine solutions to almost all human problems inclusive of fertility, bewitchment, fear and poverty that often

Pentecostals are perceived as not able to handle. The independent African Churches have a holistic view of spirituality as they provide spiritual, financial and psychological support to their members. The churches have become substitutes of an ideal community in lieu of the larger community perceived as grossly racist and subversive to their economic, social and spiritual aspirations.

It has been noted that most African Initiated Churches have similar theological leanings to Pentecostal churches as they stress the importance of the Holy Spirit, often divergent to biblical doctrines, and provide room for prophetism, dreams, speaking in tongues, prayer, healing, fervent affirmation of angelic supernaturalism and deliverance from evil spirits.[52] This invariably creates a thin line of distinction between AICs and Pentecostalism and this has contributed to the upsurge of AICs in Britain. Harris, in her anthropological study of Cherubim and Seraphim Church in London, affirms this as she notes that Aladura churches, like the Pentecostal churches, are still engaged in the "ubiquitous Yoruba search for spiritual power" and regard the Spirit as the "ultimate source of worldly success".[53]

Many AICs straddled the typological divide and recast themselves as Pentecostal churches, as many of the AICs affirm the gifts of charisma.[54] In the course of this research it was observed that some AICs have re-evolved and emerged as Pentecostal denominations in Britain, abandoning the highly Afrocentric theological persuasions shaped by African Traditional Primal Religion. For example, Celestial Church of Christ, Unity Parish, an African Initiated Church located in Chatterham Place, London, established in October 1994, evolved as a Pentecostal church in 2008 and is now known as Christ Royal International Church. Sturge observed similar resonance amongst some Unitarian churches in Britain like Christian Life Centre, led by Bishop Malcolm Wayne, which has almost pitched its tent close to the Trinitarians; he also notes that Bishop T.D. Jakes has abandoned the Oneness ideals next to the Trinitarians for broad-spectrum appeal.[55]

Oshun, using the Aladura Churches as a model of African Initiated Churches in Britain, noted that there exists a dynamic relationship between the immigration of Africans and West Indians and the establishment of various African Initiated Churches.[56] He further asserted that other compensatory growth factors to the Aladura model in Britain include: (a) strong evangelistic drive complimented by a sense of divine call to engage in reverse mission in Britain; (b) the effect of the racial climate in Britain of the 1950s and 1960s on Commonwealth citizens; (c) the resonance of racism in almost all sectors of the British economy; (d) a dearth of adequate pastoral care for migrants, resulting in rejection and marginalization. Oshun refutes Terence Booth's attempt[57] to defend the official imperial–colonial views, arguing that Booth's apologetics fail to consider the impact of the imperial actions on the Africans and Caribbeans.

Ludwig[58] in contrast with Oshun noted that the proliferation of Cherubim and Seraphim in Britain was based on seven identified factors. Ludwig's seven propositions for the emergence of Cherubim and Seraphim in Britain give a broader perspective inclusive of the migration perspective. The seven propositions include the openness of the church to ecumenism and ecumenical challenge; the fluidity of schism within the church hierarchy; inherent replication of leadership structure from Nigeria; and transferred membership.

A major articulation of Ludwig is the diversity of "non-Western Christianity" exemplified by the differences in the African and Caribbean cosmologies amongst the Nigerian (Yoruba) and West Indian brethren of Birmingham Cherubim and Seraphim on the doctrine of angels. The obvious differences, though doctrinal, also support the notion that African theology is contextual, experiential and diverse. From the experiential perspective as an African church leader, some AICs have evolved as a result of irreconcilable doctrinal persuasions but often the underlying motives are associated with schism and leadership tussles. This is not peculiar to either AICs or Black Majority Churches but is a general feature of many social movements.

### The Neo-Pentecostals from West Africa – Push and Pull Factors

The general classification of the emerging new Black Churches in Britain has been considered a herculean task because of the fact that historically the new Black Churches have their roots in Classical Pentecostalism in Africa. According to Hunt, the "westernizing dimensions and culture affirming nature" of the new Black Churches in the West "radically depart from the earlier black Pentecostal churches and are sufficiently different again from the white middle-class Renewal movement".[59] Hunt was of the opinion that the proliferation of Neo-Pentecostalism in Britain amongst the new Black Churches is inextricably linked with limited social deprivation. This in my opinion is correct but cannot be compared with the experiences of the West Indians in Britain during the 1950s and 1960s with racism so pronounced. But nevertheless the classical Pentecostal orientation of "world rejecting" and puritan roots[60] is repudiated by the new Black

Churches as most are "world accommodating", with strong American influence of the prosperity gospel[61] but are rooted often in African cosmologies. The proliferation of these new Black Churches in Britain according to Hunt is due "to their new strategies of survival and the restructuring of personal and collective relationships against a backdrop of severe economic decline. Contemporary black Pentecostalism in the West must be understood within this broader West African environment." [62]

The emergence of distinctive New Pentecostal Churches from West Africa in the late 1970s, 1980s and 1990s heralded a turning point in the proliferation of Black Churches. Hunt opined that these churches' "practices and ethos ... in many respects mark them out from the well established black Pentecostal Churches".[63] He was of the opinion that the new Pentecostal Black Churches especially from Nigeria offered optimism for the future of Black Pentecostalism in Britain "at a time when the 'classical' Pentecostal churches (including those of the older Caribbean and African tradition) and the predominantly white middle-class independent and denominational charismatic churches have generally stagnated or declined". The emergence of such churches was not on the fringes of theological or doctrinal separatism from Black Churches that had been in existence since the 1950s, but their social composition marks them out in such a way as to challenge long-accepted sociological frameworks regarding the origins and functions of these churches. The prolific growth rate of the New Pentecostal Churches from West Africa in Britain which constitute the third stream of growth dynamics in Black-led Churches is a research niche not yet adequately explored in comparison with the profound interest shown in their remarkable growth in West Africa.[64]

The peculiarity of the growth of Pentecostal Churches from Africa, especially West Africa, has generated global interest, as most of the churches are translating their local identities to a transnational phenomenon. It has been affirmed by some scholars that Nigeria, Africa's most populous nation, has been the home of Pentecostalism since the late 1990s.[65] Pentecostalism has experienced spectacular growth in Nigeria with a diverse proliferation of churches, notably in cities. This growth has carved out a distinctive Nigerian Christianity. Examples are churches such as Deeper Life Bible Church, pioneered by William Kumuyi in 1973, a former Lecturer of Mathematics at the College of Education, University of Lagos, with its headquarters at Ayobo, Lagos, and over 6,000 branches across Nigeria[66] and Winners Temple (Living Faith Ministries) pioneered by Bishop David Oyedepo, which has opened the largest church auditorium in the world, Faith Tabernacle, with a seating capacity of 50,400 worshippers at Otta, Ogun State. The success of these churches is not limited to the Nigerian Pentecostal scene but they are replicating their identity in the global space with the Redeemed Christian Church of God led by Pastor E.A. Adeboye, a PhD holder in Mathematics from the University of Lagos, which is the fastest-growing church in Africa. It has over 20,000 parishes in more than 140 nations in five continents according to Pastor Adeboye, speaking during the Festival of Life workers' rally of the church on 26 October 2010 held at the Excel Centre, Docklands, London. Wagner and Joseph noted that the Nigerian brand of Pentecostalism cuts across frontiers and is a veritable "export commodity to Africa, Europe and the United States, as the biggest churches in Tanzania, Ghana, Zimbabwe, Jamaica are led by Nigerians".[67]

Similar trends are replicated in England with Kingsway International Christian Centre led by Matthew Ashomolowo, a former minister with Foursquare Church, Nigeria and Britain, who started the church in the 1980s. Today it has over 12,000 members and several satellite churches. The Embassy of God, led by Sunday Adelaja, started in 1993, and has over 25,000 members. It is an exception to the transnational phenomenon of African churches in Europe, as 99% of its members are citizens of Ukraine.[68] The global proliferation of Pentecostalism through which Pentecostal missionaries serve a "reverse mission" to the Western world from Asia, Africa and the Caribbean is due to the capacity to transcend numerous cultures with an alternative view associated with a belief system characterized by miracles and esotericism. This is further precipitated by the ability of the New Pentecostal Churches in Britain in the 1980s and 1990s to acculturate themselves to localized traditions across Britain. Such "pliability" is often experiential and appeals to a sense of community during periods of rapid social and economic change as most of the proponents of Pentecostalism in Britain are Africans or Caribbeans in Diaspora. This further affirms that amongst Diasporans during the processes of assimilation, religion becomes a means of identification, survival, community and collective identity to the host culture, while the new community's birth by religious ascription functions to recreate the local identities and spiritual subscription that governs their worldview.

The emergence of the New Black Pentecostal Churches from Nigeria has a supernatural dimension as Joe Olaiya noted: "the current revival in the nation of Nigeria comes in fulfillment of the promise of God to raise up a mighty army that will take the gospel far beyond the boundaries of nation".[69] Such optimism of divine initiative is suspect amongst some

Christian leaders as the much-vaunted revival centres on humanism with strong subscriptions to materialism, but despite the pessimism, Neo-Pentecostal movements from Nigeria are already replicating local identities into a global phenomenon as Pentecostalism is Nigeria's best gift to the world in the twenty-first century in terms of social mobility.

The Redeemed Christian Church of God (RCCG) epitomizes the growth, influence and potential of the new Neo-Pentecostal Churches in Britain. The church is the largest and perhaps the most successful in terms of church plant and membership strength. In 1985, the RCCG "planted" its earliest church in Britain with just four people at the first service with the General Overseer, Pastor E.A. Adeboye in attendance.[70] According to Sturge RCCG now [as at 2005] has over five hundred parishes of varying sizes in the United Kingdom and a membership somewhere in the region of 18,000,[71] while Hunt noted that the membership strength of the church was over 250,000.[72] Sturge and Hunt's membership figures for the RCCGUK are grossly under- and over-estimated. However, the current membership of the RCCG in the United Kingdom is estimated to be over 80,200 according to the Parish Liaison Officer of the RCCGUK, Sade Williams. RCCG now has over 600 parishes in the United Kingdom.

Hunt's perspective is grossly unrealistic and unsubstantiated and is a product of the isolationist approach of his research: he used Jesus House, one of the RCCG network of churches in the United Kingdom (comprising 436 parishes), which is inappropriate, because, though the doctrinal tenets are the same, leadership and growth dynamics are quite unique to each local church. Sixty-four percent of the parishes of RCCG are located in London and the West and East of Midlands, but they also have a sizeable representation in a number of Britain's larger urban areas. The RCCG has planted churches in 68% of cities of the United Kingdom.[73] It is pertinent to note that the West Indian Churches simultaneously started a renewal process as the second-generation migrants began to pioneer new churches as a result of divine call and a contemporary mission: amongst such are Bishop Francis of Ruach Ministries, which has a membership strength of over 5,000 and has been instrumental in various social action initiatives in the United Kingdom.

John Francis was ordained as a Bishop of Ruach ministries on Sunday 7 June 1998. He is a recipient of the British Gospel Association's (BGA) Award, "Contribution to Gospel Music" and "Gospel TV Series of the Year" as co-presenter of the UK's pioneering Gospel TV programme, "People Get Ready!" Bishop Malcolm Wayne, the founder and Bishop of Christian Life City is an enigma due to the various social, community and entrepreneur initiatives of his church in the community. His pastoral work started on 1 May 1988 at Jubilee Scout Hall in Woodford Green with nine people in attendance at the first service. The church presently has a membership of over 3,000.

The obvious growth of the Redeemed Christian Church of God in Britain, which is perhaps one of the most successful Neo-Pentecostal churches in Britain, is a result of push and pull factors. The church policy on church planting – within five minutes' driving distance in developed countries – can be ascribed to the proliferation of the "model" parishes in Britain in sharp contrast to the "classical" parishes in the founding days of the church in Nigeria. Beneath this policy lies the profiting of the Church from the mobility of its elite members: because of the elimination of clericalism in most Black Churches, the laity is adequately mobilized, and as such, most Black-led Churches are participatory. The governing rule for such economic migrant members of the church is to start an RCCG Church "away from home but still at home". The inherent mobilization structure is created by the parent body in Nigeria through the "brand orientation" of RCCG members who were undergraduates through the Redeemed Christian Fellowship, which leads to further sustenance on their graduation to Redeemed Christian Corpers' Fellowship.

The underlying principle is doctrinal and denominational branding that eventually culminates in membership of Christ Redeemers Friends Universal, which aims to evangelize those in the top echelons of society. Some of the membership of Black Majority Churches in Britain, such as the RCCG, have grown over the years through the influence and impact of their denominational strategies on mobilization for growth through social and occupational mobility. This is in consonance with the observations of Miller and Yamamori that the multifaceted deprivation theory (including Karl Marx's "opiate" perception, Sigmund Freud's escapist theory and Emile Durkheim's primitive postulations of social order) is only "helpful in the explanation of growth of Pentecostalism [Black Majority Churches in Britain]" in comparison to the *Windrush* era, in which the social deprivation was a major influence.[74]

The Black Majority Churches in the last two decades are attracting affluent and educated people, a departure from the global and British historical antecedents of the emergence of Pentecostalism. The elimination of clericalism in most Black-led Churches places a strong emphasis on a universal priesthood of believers, leading to mentoring and discipleship, as the laity is effectively mobilized into the church life. The subscription of Pentecostals globally to the doctrine of a priesthood of believers, which eliminates the distinction between the clergy and laity, has contributed significantly to the growth of Black Churches in the United Kingdom. In contrast, this has had a negative impact on their missional agenda, as most of these churches shun formal pastoral and missiological training, and this has contributed significantly to their anti-intellectualism until recently.

The clarion call to end the apathy of Black Majority Church leaders to formal theological or missiological training is reflected in Beckford's denunciation of the trend as a major flaw that has allowed the continued bewitchment of Blacks in their mission agenda through colonial influences.[75] The lack of formal theological training seems to be a reoccurring feature of Pentecostals globally, as Saayman noted that the "Spirit speaks equally to all believers regardless of gender, education, or social status, and so each Pentecostal believer is potentially a minister and missionary".[76] Anderson's observations about Pentecostals generally are applicable to Black Majority Churches in Britain: on account of their pragmatic commitment to evangelism and church planting, most are seemingly unconcerned with socio-political context. This raises a fundamental question of the *modus operandi* of these churches within their local context, but the exception to this quiet disposition only emanates when social or governmental policies affect these churches, such as challenges in acquisition of planning permission, immigration and changes in charitable laws.[77]

Most Black-led Churches are still very much passive in terms of political action. Anderson further identified that the influence of the "tent-making" ministry in missionary endeavours of Pentecostals has had a positive impact on the inculturation of these Black-led Churches in comparison to orthodox churches in Britain.[78] It is imperative to assert that the process of this mobilization cannot be immediately evaluated in terms of missional significance and extending the denominational frontiers of these churches. Immigration into the United Kingdom in the 1980s from African countries, notably Nigeria and Ghana, ushered in a distinctive phase in the immigration history of Britain, creating new socio-economic challenges as a result of the deregulation by the International Monetary Fund (IMF) of economies of debtor nations. This was a World Bank programme aimed at streamlining the economies of debtor nations, especially Third World countries, so as to borrow, leading to further indebtedness of the borrowing nations fraught with fiscal inadequacies.

The new migrants were not only economic migrants but came with their faith, as did the West Indian migrants of the 1950s and 1960s. Etan-Adollo noted the growth of the Black Churches during the era of

"Thatcherism" which was marked by steep economic policies and promises characterized by "global love for free-market economic policy tools of privatization, deregulation, liberalization and commercialization without adequate provision for policy shortcomings such as inequality, arrival of immigrants and refugees, [and] weakening of the welfare system . . .".[79] He further asserted Harvey Cox's position that the euphoria of 312 Azusa Street emanated from an era experiencing downward economic challenges. This presents a similar remodelling of the earlier pioneers of Caribbean churches in the 1950s and 1960s as both dispensations had similar socio- and race-related factors. Later migrants built on the success of earlier migrants in terms of acculturation and a better understanding of the African and Caribbean brand of Christianity in British church history.

The apparent alienation, pain, segregation and misconceptions in the 1950s and 1960s became leverage for the Black Churches in the 1980s and 1990s as in the words of Joseph "you meant it for evil but God meant it for good". But it is pertinent to note that the use of the Joseph model in Genesis 37–50 might be grossly inappropriate, as the context of the experiences in terms of the precursor of their captivity was their sinfulness. According to Birch,[80] Old Testament prophets held the view that "exile was God's judgment on Israel's own arrogance, injustice and unfaithfulness". But this approach cannot serve as a generic basis for the understanding of the interplay of divine involvement in the Israelites' narratives as this contradicts the revelation of God to Abraham about the captivity of his descendants (Gen 13:15).

The British economic situation, burgeoning as a result of the new wave of industrialization, was akin to the Egyptian prosperous economy that accommodated three million economic migrants. The Caribbean migrants not only had economic aspirations but also came to Britain with their socio-cultural-cum-religious orientations. The Israelites' religious persuasions led to a distinctive location – Goshen – to accommodate their idiosyncrasies in terms of their occupations (shepherding, for example, was detestable to the Egyptians' religious and socio-cultural practices (Gen 42:32)). The indigenous Egyptian community were unperturbed, unlike the British community in the 1950s and 1960s which was obstructive to the Caribbean migrants' settlement in their midst. The phenomenal growth of Black Majority Churches is comparable to the explosive growth of Pentecostal and Charismatic movements in Korea as Harvey Cox states: "for any religion to grow in today's world it must possess two capabilities: it must be able to include and transform at least certain elements of pre-existing religions which still retain a strong grip on the cultural subconscious".[81]

The likes of Brixton, Mosside, Wolverhampton and Handsworth became the Goshen of British Black Church pioneers who moved into deprived inner-city ghettos that had experienced "white flight" on account of the socio-economic conditions of the communities. The apparent success being replicated over the years by Black Churches is linked to the fact that the churches are mostly planted in urban areas where the migrant population is very high. For instance, London, the south-east in particular, has the highest concentration of ethnic minorities, especially in Lambeth and Southwark Borough.[82] The era of denominationalism heralded the emergence of Black-led Churches along nationality lines as compared with the early stages of the emergence of the churches. The strategy of the proliferation was not to engage in reverse mission but to create a homogenous church to meet the sociological and spiritual needs of the community.

Fragmentation has contributed significantly to the numerical growth of Black Majority Churches. A major reason for the proliferation of these churches has been their fissiparous nature which is generally a global trait of the Pentecostal movement. Schism is a common occurrence amongst Britain's Black Majority Churches. Various churches have emerged as a result of schism, often as a result of high-handed authoritarian leadership, insecurity of leadership, poor management skills, moral ineptitude and other extraneous factors. From my experience as a minister in a Black Majority Church in Britain, I have heard of several churches that emerged because of irreconcilable differences amongst members, ministers and leadership. The most common trend is the sense of insecurity of some Black-led Church leaders in regard to their associate minister. John Wilson's sociological model of religious schism is a point of reference to gain insight into the current trends of schism in various African and Caribbean churches in Britain.[83] Wilson's theory is based on Neil Smelser's Theory of Collective Behaviour which was a model derived from the studies of social movements. Wilson opined that some types of organizational structure can lead to fragmentation. Schism is more likely to occur when an organization ranges between highly centralized organization and decentralized, but it is instructive to note that the organizational and leadership culture has proved vital in creating balance in any organizational structure.

A major feature of Wilson's concept is that strain is a cornerstone of his model. The apparent means of identifying strain in a religious group is what is considered to be deviation from the norms and values of the organization. A major schism pattern reoccurring amongst Black Majority

Churches in Britain is the "blockage of mobility among laity and exclusion from the position of power".[84] The scandal of the infamous Pastor Douglas Goodman, convicted of moral ineptitude and financial impropriety, was not only due to his moral and financial misdemeanours but also to strain within the leadership structure of the church. This was asserted in the prosecution of Goodman, as Yemi Adedeji noted: "They [some church elders] wanted to be more responsibly involved, particularly in finances... He [Douglas Goodman] knew some elders who wanted a power based position within the church which they didn't have."[85]

The irony of the schism is that the active participants exhibit a "closed valve" mentality, to the detriment of the Christian faith. The British missiologist, Lesslie Newbigin, observes that when schism occurs "something essential to the true being of the church is lost",[86] which most times is detrimental to the faith, as this leads to sectarianism. Churches are polarized along personality divides, insulating the missional effort of the church, slowing down church growth and suffering from "social flight" as the sphere of influence of the church begs to be excused; thus the integrity of the church suffers.

The tragedy of schism amongst Black Majority Churches is the apparent false claim of justification for contemptuous insinuation and acrimony in the relationship of the parties concerned; this depicts the level of human depravity that supposedly ought to have been dealt with as a Christian. Time, resources and a great deal of effort that could have been constructively used in the furtherance of gospel is dissipated in the public domain over trivialities, personal mistrust and schism.

Steve Bruce's perspective suggests that the effects of schism amongst African and Caribbean churches in Britain should be significant, as he argues that "sectarianism hastens secularization by weakening the dominant religious tradition and driving religion out of the public domain",[87] but it seems the Black Majority Churches are exceptions to Bruce's postulation, as many churches are still evolving. This suggests further research: the dynamics of sectarianism, Black-led Churches, secularization and growth are potential topics yet to be explored.

Luther Gerlach and Virgina H. Hine observe that "organizational unity is functional in a steady state social institution designed to maintain social stability and the status quo. Segmentation and 'internecine dog fighting' are functional in a social institution designed for rapid growth and the implementation of social change."[88] The doctrinal and theological differences amongst church leaders in Black-led Churches are the products of personal conflict dysfunction. The challenge of doctrinal and theological disputation is a general feature of most religious movements, the Black-led Churches inclusive.

Personal conflict and schism has contributed to the growth of Black Churches in Britain, as new churches are started, and as evangelization and proselytization are enhanced. According to Gerlach and Hine, an internal safety mechanism is created by decentralized structures (such as are represented in the Pentecostal structures) as the effect of misdemeanour can be greatly minimized if each functional unit is independent rather than decapitating the whole organization.[89] This survival mechanism thrives on the fluid nature of Black Pentecostalism in Britain that is connected by a multifaceted and casual array of interactions.

Schism is a universal phenomenon that can occur in any social movement when the core fundamental values are challenged or when leadership inadequacies are noticed by adherents or ecclesiastical leaders. The Anglican Communion, through the Archbishop of Canterbury, Rowan Williams, has desperately tried to forge a unified front and avoid the imminent collapse of the Communion along the North–South dichotomy regarding the ordination of gay bishops. The ongoing impasse within the Anglican Communion is a reaction to a perceived change in the "doctrinal status quo" of the Anglican Communion on the issue of human sexuality. Henry Orombi, the Archbishop of Uganda, whose diocese comprises nine million adherents, stated that "there is a tradition on human sexuality that was passed to us by the apostles, and if we're an apostolic church how come the Episcopal Church claims they are better than St. Paul? Why do they turn their back on the faith their grandparents brought to us?"[90]

Significant percentages of the Black Majority Churches in Britain have adopted an egalitarian attitude to females in comparison with conservative Pentecostals who are gender-biased, viewing women as restricted to certain responsibilities and unable to serve in a pastoral capacity. The egalitarian ethos of some of the Black-led Churches today is a product of renewal and revitalization and represents a shift from the classical Pentecostalism more akin to the pietistic movement. The Redeemed Christian Church of God historically was rooted in classical Pentecostalism.

Roy Wallis characterized such churches as a "world-rejecting religious movement"[91] but Ukah opined that the RCCG is now "world-accommodating", a by-product of "situational theology".[92] The church has been transformed under the leadership of Pastor E.A. Adeboye from "pauperism" to a global missionary player. The church was noted to have had gender bias against women and this might have contributed to the slow growth of the church, as eight years after its inception the church had only one hundred attendees at the 1960 convention.[93] The revitalization heralded by the incumbent leadership of the church in the person of Pastor E.A. Adeboye led to gender bias being addressed to some extent, but it is pertinent to note that there exists no female representation in the governing council of the church.

The change in the leadership of the Redeemed Christian Church of God after the demise of the founder and General Suprintendent Rev. Josiah Akindayomi heralded a distinctive phase in the structure and theology of the church. Pastor Adeboye initiated policies and restructuring that his predecessor never attempted. For instance, Adeboye addressed the patriarchal organizational structure of the RCCG through the appointment of his wife (Pastor Mrs Folu Adeboye) and the wife of late General Superintendent Pastor Josiah Akindayomi of the RCCG, late Pastor Esther Akindayomi, as "Mothers in Israel". Adeboye's theological perception entails gender equality, as he also started ordination of female pastors in the RCCG. The use of the title "Mother in Israel" is consistent with the Aladura's ecclesiastical nomenclature from which the RCCG has its roots.[94]

The implication of this androcentric structure might be a progressive journey to gender equality within the RCCG and some other Black Majority Churches in Britain in the non-distant future. The paradigm shift within the RCCG is a reflection of changes within the global Pentecostal landscape,[95] Latin America[96] and Italy.[97] Gerontocratic and patriarchal structures of some Black Majority Churches in Britain might have to be dismantled in their organizational structures regardless of gender to create equal opportunities in the ministry. This process of eliminating these structures to create an inclusive and broad-spectrum utilization of potentials of people amongst Pentecostals irrespective of gender, race or social class, as enabled by the empowerment of the Holy Spirit, is referred to as the "Pentecostal theology of liberation". This school of thought is in conformity with the Pauline epistle to the church in Ephesus concerning ministry gifts, as the essence of the five-fold ministry is the equipping of the saints in order to do the work of the ministry (Eph 4:11–13).

Black Majority Churches in Britain vary widely in the extent of formal authority and leadership opportunities given to women. This variety is modulated, according to Toulis, by the "denominational mediation of a theological position of absolute male dominance".[98] Toulis further observes that in the New Testament Church of God, gender conciliation is accomplished on realistic and symbolic levels, but this has not eliminated male supremacy, which is probably perceived as a tradition, as female dominance is at odds with and pathologized by the dominant gender order.⁹⁹ However, this is also replicated in the Executive Council of the Redeemed Christian Church of God, United Kingdom, made up of Agu Irukwu, Kolawole Bamigbade and Andrew Adeleke. Similar gender supremacy is also a feature of the North American arm of the RCCG as all the executive members are male. It seems there is a covert gender supremacy not only within the New Testament Church of God but in most Black Majority Churches in Britain, which retain elements of male supremacy in their leadership structure.

It is pertinent to acknowledge the fact that the RCCGUK has succeeded significantly within the RCCG global brand to be inclusive, as a woman Modupe Afolabi, currently serves as the Administrator of the RCCGUK Central Office, the regulatory body of the church. Modupe Afolabi also serves as the Secretary to the RCCGUK Executive Council. A similar leadership position is held by Rev. (Mrs) Nezlin Sterling, the International General Secretary of the New Testament Assembly, UK.

A distinctive feature of Black-led Churches that has contributed significantly to the urban explosion of these churches is the distinctive functionality of the Black Majority Churches' theology. The contextualized theology of Black Majority Churches has brought about the dynamic functionality of these churches in terms of relevance to the prevailing socio-economic-cum-religious identity of their members. Black Majority Churches' theology thrives on a 'tripod' model in which the three elements are (a) the Bible and Christian practice; (b) African traditions and religious conviction; and (c) the current socio-political context.¹⁰⁰ These churches differ slightly in some aspects of doctrinal inclination but their functional orientations are always similar, as the churches resonate with the pragmatic and power-oriented nature of African spirituality.

Jehu Hanciles, in his research findings on why Blacks worship in Black Churches in America, observes that 74.3% of those interviewed were attracted because of the exuberant worship which is predicated on a participatory mode, while 64% were in the churches as a result of the "solid preaching"; 55.9% stated that their spiritual needs were being met, while 53% were members of Black-led Churches because of the leadership of their pastors and 52% because of the members' care for each other.¹⁰¹ Hanciles' research elucidates the myriad of internal dynamics that have contributed to the continued cultural captivity of Black-led Churches in the United States. He opines that these churches are "overwhelmingly products of West African Pentecostalism" with covert American charismatic influences. Hanciles' assertion seems to reflect a transatlantic phenomenon, as similar trends exist amongst Black-led Churches in Britain.

Burgess[102] concurs with Comaroff,[103] Meyer[104] and Maxwell[105] that one of the major sources of generating funds for evangelism and church planting of Black Majority Churches is their entrepreneurial initiative. Ukah repudiates this opinion as he notes that "prosperity churches from Africa are profit making enterprises" rather than public institutions established for the common good of the members and the community.[106] Burgess further articulates that some RCCG Parishes in Britain, like Jesus House and Trinity Chapel are exceptions to the rule. This is because the prosperity teaching is expected to bring about personal and socio-economic transformation which is replicated in "socio-economic mobility utilised in the financing of evangelistic and social welfare initiative".[107]

The social action of the Black Churches has a supernatural dimension, as many of them posit it as a type of Abraham that is "blessed and is to be a blessing to others".[108] The social ministries emanating from these Black-led Churches are not only empowering to their immediate religious context but also to the wider British community. The effect of the changing paradigm in some of the Black-led Churches has been acknowledged by state agencies and public figures like Prince Charles.

The social engagement of some of the Black Churches is providing a new paradigm that reflects the dynamic growth of Black Churches, as some of these churches' relevance and complementary services to state agencies, articulated as far back as the 1990s, are attracting new adherents who hitherto might have been at the fringes of "identifying but not belonging". Black Majority Churches' social engagement initiatives have made significant contributions to urban and inner-city renewal, often in working with various governmental agencies, and this has been the case since the late 1980s.[109] This era marked the genesis of a "social theology and social gospel within their traditional evangelical and Pentecostal theology".[110]

The gradual integration of faith communities might have been a product of reflective practice resulting from their poor record of achievement in urban regeneration, but because of the Black Majority Churches' holistic approach to spirituality and communal orientation, they offer an alternative model for social engagement and a complementary effort to the state approaches. This has culminated in a charge that the leadership of some of the Black Majority Churches is involved in aggressive church planting, by which they seek to increase the membership base,[111] financial commitment of the members and the acquisition of property.

The inter-related dynamics of church planting, increase in membership, financial commitment and a permanent or conducive place of worship are the four pillars of social engagement of Black Majority Churches in

Britain. These are facilitated by the repertoire of fiscal and human resources that some of these churches have generated over the years. This approach of social engagement which was a latter initiative by the Caribbean church is incomparable to the pace of the new Neo-Pentecostal Churches in Britain. The New Testament Church of God's social and political engagements are well documented at the national level in Britain.[112]

The Caribbean initiatives of social action in terms of multiplicity cannot be compared with the apparent trajectory of new Neo-Pentecostal Churches like the RCCG in Britain. This apparent disparity might be a reflection of changes in statutory and regulatory functions of the Charity Commission. The recently introduced regulation on charitable status is the public benefit test of the Charity Commission, introduced by the 2006 Charities Act, which places responsibility on charities in England and Wales to provide documentary evidence that they are benefiting the local community.[113] This might be responsible for the multiple social actions by New Pentecostal Churches in Britain to continue to enjoy the patronage of the state for the generous compensatory financial gain of 28 pence for every one pound contributed by a tax payer through the Gift Aid Scheme. The charitable status of most of the Black Majority Churches contributes significantly to economic well being of these churches through charitable business rate and gift aid scheme.

This might suggest that the inherent social action initiatives of some of these churches are by default. Black Majority Churches in the mould of Glory House, New Wine, Ruach Ministries, New Testament Church of God and the Church of God of Prophecy have illustrious antecedents of social action in Britain. Some of these churches have indeed engaged in a structural critique of social issues; they are not only prescribing but are developing systemic processes to social challenges.[114]

The emergence of the transnational phenomenon of the status of some Black Majority Churches has facilitated the branding of their churches all over Europe, Britain included. Their proliferation has been facilitated by both financial and human resources that are redeployed from Africa. Anna Quass, in her transnational research on Nigerian Pentecostal Churches, quoted a pastor of the RCCG, Germany, in her presentation at the Transnational Pentecostal Conference at Birmingham in 2009, saying that the basis of the establishment of the church is found in transatlantic financial support. Anna was informed by an RCCG pastor in Germany during her field work that, "Ireland branch [an RCCG parish] to us [the church plant in Germany] they are like father ... When we wanted to start, some money they gave to us, we bought some instruments, we bought most of the things we needed, maybe the first rent, they helped us paying. So in any time we always have relation together. And the same thing happens to all the Redeemed over."[115] This is quite important as the flow of financial and administrative support is incomparable to the affiliation of Caribbean churches of the 1960s as American denominations. A similar trend has been identified by Adogame in North America, where salaries of RCCG pastors were being paid from Nigerian churches.[116]

This constitutes a distinctive change in the reverse flow of resources from Third World countries to the West and America, and raises the question of moral judgement regarding the huge capital outlay from these Third World countries that are classified as poor nations. But this in itself counteracts the notion of Dele Olowo on the concept of transnationalism in the context of the proliferation of these churches in the West, as the basis of his postulation was mainly economic migration.[117] Adogame[118] and Ogbu Kalu,[119] however, opined that religion constitutes a major factor in migration.

The preaching of many Black-led Church pastors is quite powerful, relevant and urgent to the aspirations of their members. Nobel laureate winner for literature, Chinua Achebe illustrates in his novel *Things Fall Apart* the impact of black preaching on an Igbo convert (Igbos are a tribe in the eastern part of Nigeria and were the focus of the secession bid in the 1966 Nigerian civil war).[120] He stated that "it was not the mad logic of Trinity that captivated him. He did not understand it. It was the poetry of the new religion, something felt in the marrow ... He felt relief within as the hymn poured into his parched soul. The words of the hymn were like drops of frozen rain melting on the dry palate of the panting earth." This metaphor paints a vivid picture of the obvious exuberance and emotionalism that is appropriated by members of the Black-led Churches. Though Black-led Churches' hermeneutics derive their theology from the Bible, they often have a "bumper sticker" or "literalist experientialism" approach in their exegesis as many passages are utilised out of historical context.[121]

This uncritical hermeneutic is generally synonymous with Pentecostalism, as Gifford noted that African Pentecostals make their theology relevant within their context.[122] The spasmodic fusions of scriptural passages by the preachers of Black-led Churches are at times a reflection of their predetermined expository line of thought to their congregants. Asamoah-Gyadu suggests that this "proof-texting" approach can result in "truncated, if not erroneous, views on theological issues" but the relevance of the preaching with respect to the socio-economic life of most black worshippers cannot be overemphasized.[123] In the midst of the flourishing housing sector in England in the early 2000s, the Senior Pastor of Kingsway International Christian Centre, Pastor Matthew Ashimolowo, focused on creation of wealth. Although he is not a qualified financial adviser, he offered financial and investment advice which was a fusion of a biblical worldview and the workings of the British financial industries to his congregation through his sermons, books and CDs. Pastor Ashimolowo in such teachings and seminars always issued a disclaimer notice that exonerated him from any liability as a result of such teachings. This era marked a turning point in black activism in financial and investment opportunities in Britain.

The relevance of the preaching of most black pastors reflects the understanding of the local context of the needs of their congregants and some, such as Mountain of Fire and Miracles and The Christ Apostolic Church, are deeply rooted in the African cosmology. Some of these Black Majority Churches like Mountain of Fire and Miracles have been identified with a "do it yourself" model. Adogame observes that this DIY approach "serves as a source of spiritual empowerment to the laity in the acquisition and retention of spiritual power, and plays down the interlocutory role of the clergy as the bridge between members and the spiritual entities".[124] This approach eliminates the barrier of clericalism and eventually births dynamism amongst the lay members – a sense of empowerment and spiritual authority – minimizing the continued patronage of the clergy for exorcism. The resultant effect is the appropriation of the existing pool of resources, creating a sense of spiritual responsibility and a fulfilling of the biblical mandate of the ministry gift for the equipping of the saints.

## DISTINCTIVE GROWTH PHASES OF BLACK-LED CHURCHES

The antecedents of the growth phases of Black Majority Churches in Britain has been chronicled in the last sixty years by various scholars, mostly second-generation Caribbean Diasporans[125] and German missiologist Roswith Gerloff.[126] The apparent distinction amongst these scholars in their articulations is that Edwards and Sturge worked in chronological order from 1950 and 1948 respectively. The obvious growth phase identified by Roswith Gerloff and Joel Edwards was from 1950 to 1998, while Aldred and Sturge in their assessment of the growth phases reflected the developments after 1988, as the scope of their classification was from 1948 to 2004. Because of the multiplicity of factors relating to changes in the growth phenomenon of the Black Churches in Britain, it becomes imperative that these changes are assessed, and this study aims to contribute significantly to this process.

It is apt to note that previous scholars' attempts at articulating distinctive growth phases of Black Majority Churches are not true reflections of the historical antecedents of Black-led Churches in Britain. Gerloff, Edwards, Aldred and Sturge all focused on the *Windrush* era as the genesis of Black Majority Churches, though Gerloff[127] noted that Iain MacRobert opined the existence of the first Black Pentecostal Church in London two years after the Azusa revival (1908), but Donald Gee,[128] in *Pentecost* magazine, stated that the first Black Pentecostal Church in Britain started in 1906. The obvious historical inadequacies of these writers is depicted by their chronological perspectives: Edwards, Gerloff, Aldred and Sturge all refer to the *Windrush* era, and they all use synonymous phrases such as "The early mission",[129] "The inception of the Afro-Caribbean Church",[130] "Initiation"[131] and "The scattered church".[132] Sturge's treatise noted the existence of a Black Church in Liverpool, pioneered by Daniel Ekarte, as far back as 1931, but he was very restrictive in his chronology, suggesting that the distinctive phase of growth of Black Majority Churches was from 1948.

### *The Genesis (1906–45)*

The current proliferation and growth of Black Majority Churches in Britain is the product of the gains of two distinctive eras in the history of Black Majority Churches in Britain. There exist incontestable historical antecedents in the roles of Africa and Africans to Christianity as far back as biblical times. The global renaissance was accentuated by the Azusa movement which became a centrifugal force for the spread of global Pentecostalism as a result of William Seymour's corrective theology in comparison to the racist teachings of Charles Parham. The First Black Pentecostal Church in modern Britain was already in existence prior to British Pentecostalism's prominence in 1907. The first Black-led Church, led by Bro. Brem-Wilson, was a typology of the William Seymour Azusa movement as the local identity that evolved over time was similar to the Pentecostal phenomenon characterized by glossolalia and charismata. Ireson, a protégé of Brem-Wilson, noted that Sumner Road Chapel was also known as the "House of God". He further affirmed that Thomas Brem-Wilson was "a powerful evangelist and being black, was somewhat of an attraction in those days, when one saw few coloured folk in London".[133]

It is posited that Ireson was more fascinated by Brem-Wilson's ministry and not his race as he was a member of Sumner Road Chapel as far back as 1923 until early 1926.[134] The hosting of the 1923 annual conference of the Apostolic Church of Britain at Sumner Chapel, Peckham, was a memorable experience for the members of Brem-Wilson's church. Ireson was particularly impressed with the opportunity of fellowship with the leadership of the Apostolic Church. The Life President of the Apostolic Church and editor of *Riches of Grace* magazine of the church, fondly called Dan Williams by Brem-Wilson, was in attendance. Other Apostolic church dignitaries included W.A.C. Rowe, Frank Hodges, W. Jones Williams, H.V. Chanter and Andrew Turnbull.[135]

The heterogeneous nature of Brem-Wilson's congregation demystified the Eurocentric misconceptions of Blacks, as Ireson's and Van der Woude's ministries were honed under his leadership. The racial divide that was preceded by strong ethnocentric orientations in the wider community in the nineteenth century was unexplainable with the emergence of the heterogeneous composition of Brem-Wilson's congregation. This was the precursor to the inter-cultural relationship that evolved in Bro. Brem-Wilson's ministry. Sumner Chapel, Peckham can be judged as being in the league of the Azusa Street revival, as some members of the church were missionaries to other countries. For example, Van der Woude made contributions to Dutch Pentecostalism and Cecil Ireson was a missionary to Australia, New Zealand and China.[136]

Despite being faced with a dysfunctional relationship with his wife, Brem-Wilson was quite succinct in the defence of his faith and church. The *Ashburton Guardian* of 19 November 1920 reported that Brem-Wilson was charged for assault at Lambeth Police Court along with four elders of his congregation. When asked by the presiding judge what sort of sect he presided over, Brem-Wilson said: "We are not protestants and we are not Catholics. We are Christians within the meaning of the Word as it is written." This is a familiar position of Pentecostals globally because of their subscription to the inerrancy of the word of God, to experience and to pneuma-centrism. In the assault case instituted by Esther, Brem-Wilson's wife, she noted the pneuma-centric emphasis of Brem-Wilson's church. When she was asked by the court what her husband's sect called themselves, she replied "They called themselves Holy Ghost people inspired by God."[137] The case was dismissed by the court because of Esther Brem-Wilson's lack of discretion in visiting Sumner Chapel against the directive of her husband to request more money than the four pence Brem-Wilson had given her. Brem-Wilson was given the benefit of the doubt with respect to the appropriateness of force used to put his wife outside the church. The case was sensational probably because of interracial marriage and also because Brem-Wilson's vocation attracted a lot of attention from a courtroom full of women.

The effect of the dysfunctional family life of Brem-Wilson on Sumner Chapel as Britain's first Black Pentecostal Church cannot be evaluated precisely because of lack of credible evidence. However, Brem-Wilson's ministry commitment was impressive, as he preached as an evangelist in Leominster and a host of other cities in the United Kingdom. The death of Brem-Wilson on 29 March 1929 heralded a new era in the history of Sumner Chapel. This created a blurring of historical antecedents and recognition of the church due to change of leadership as successive leaders of the church were Whites.

Fryer's historiography of Blacks in Britain gives vivid insight into the emergence and continued influx of Blacks into Britain as far back as Roman times.[138] Because of the transatlantic slave trade, Blacks were noted to have been concentrated around slave ports such as London, Bristol and Liverpool. The incredible religious nature of Blacks was noted by Sherwood as black people used to hold fellowship at the Coloured Men's Religious Institute at 4 Hardy Street in Liverpool in the early twentieth century.[139] The social and moral wantonness was far from the idealist indoctrination of the super Christian nation of Britain painted by British missionaries, but Mary Slessor was an exception as she warned Ekarte that adventure to Britain would result in an illusionary experience of Christianity.[140]

The emergence of the African Churches Mission (ACM) in Toxteth, led by Pastor Daniel Ekarte in 1931, changed the socio-cultural and political landscape of Liverpool. A distinctive feature of the Ekarte model was that it heralded urban social action and reverse mission. Daniel Ekarte's fight against racial inequalities is well articulated by Wilson in his article titled "Racism and Private Assistance: The Support of West Indian and African Missions in Liverpool, England During the Interwar Years".[141] The subtle nature of institutional racism was experienced by Daniel Ekarte's organization, the ACM, and also by the Association of West Indian Mission (AWIM) led by Reverend Earnest Adkins, a white preacher. Adkins was succeeded in 1932 by J.G. Lawson from Sierra Leone, but most of the clientele of AWIM were second-generation Blacks that were born in Liverpool. Although Wilson observed that both organizations' services to black communities were affected by inadequate funding, AWIM was favoured because of Adkins' distorted views about the challenges of the black community in Liverpool. Wilson noted that Adkins, in his correspondence to John Harris, a former missionary to Congo, was an advocate of segregation of black and white Christians in Rhodesia (now Zimbabwe) and South Africa as an avenue to preserve traditional African values.[142]

Adkins inadvertently became a supporter of John Harris's racial ideology, which led to systematic funding of AWIM through Harris's sphere of influence, while Ekarte's funding application was never considered. Harris was described as a "benevolent paternalist" from the old school by Paul Rich:

> Adkins rarely advocated or suggested that blacks whom he served were capable of personal growth, not to mention deserving racial, economic, or social equality. For the most part Adkins' intentions were well meaning and in accordance with Victorian paternalism, but, from a humanistic perspective, he failed to grasp the intensity of the frustration felt by those blacks who had lived in Liverpool for many years.[143]

Despite the frustrations from government social agencies in strangulating Ekarte's efforts for social and economic equality of Blacks in Liverpool, institutional racism was his Waterloo. His vociferous campaign for parity of black seamen's wages with those of their white colleagues was one of his numerous contributions to equality. Despite the effects of institutional racism on the part of the government agencies in Liverpool, Ekarte sourced funding from Africa for the orphanage: the "mission received occasional support from Africa" according to the *Liverpool Daily Post* of 8 July 1931.[144] Ekarte's model of a Black Church heralded a unique holistic approach to social initiative which has been replicated in subsequent years by Black Majority Churches.[145] The social initiatives of Black Majority Churches now are partly a reflection of their regulatory responsibility as required by the Charity Commission and partly a fulfilling of a holistic Christian worldview. The demise of the social action of the African Churches Mission was partly a result of racism and other personal misdemeanours of Ekarte. This succinctly shows that racism is more of an ideological orientation that often evolves as a product of re-socialization by migrants in a new community, rather than that the host community being ethnocentric.

### *The* Windrush *Effect Growth Phase (1948–55)*

The economic and utopian concepts of mother country were quite pivotal to the emergence of the second wave of growth of Black-led Churches in Britain. Most West Indian countries, especially Jamaica, have a culture of migration but it is pertinent to note that social mobility is no longer limited to economic factors and religion had always been a significant factor in migration. The distinctive migration culture of Jamaicans is a product of the agrarian economy which cannot sustain the economic aspirations of the country. The arrival of the *Windrush* migrants was the genesis of racially induced Ethiopianism, a result of the social and religious ostracization of the new migrants: their "Britishness" was rejected, and their membership of the historic churches of the West Indies was not recognized by the British Churches.

The *Windrush* migrants came not only with their skills but their culture and faith. This era witnessed the emergence of Black-led Churches typical of the African Initiated Churches. The churches which emerged within the time frame under consideration were representative of a distinctively "Caribbean" Pentecostal brand of Christianity. The ambiguity of the generic phase "African Pentecostal Churches" was clarified in Anderson's study on African Initiated Churches in South Africa. Anderson noted first "Pentecostal mission churches", those churches originating from predominantly white Pente-costal missions (the majority of whose members are Blacks); secondly, younger African Initiated Pentecostal or charismatic churches, not very different from Pentecostal mission churches, but founded and governed by Blacks and independent of white control; and thirdly, the vast majority of AICs in Southern Africa related to the Pentecostal churches, including the so-called "Zionist" and "Apostolic" churches, quite different in some respects from the first two groups, and called "Pentecostal-type churches".[146]

The British Black-led Churches during 1948–55 were dominated by the Pentecostal mission churches and the African Pentecostal mission in line with Anderson's categorization but with the exception of the Zionist Church. The obvious dissimilarity with the South African categorization by Anderson was that racial Ethiopianism was wholly a Caribbean initiative. This was reflected in the regrouping of the Diaspora's members of the Pentecostal churches from the Caribbean in the mould of The New Testament Church of God (NTCG). The social and religious racial inertia experienced by the early migrants were the catalyst for the decision of the migrants to preserve their faith, although it would be grossly untenable to label all British churches racist as some of the Jamaican church leaders preached in some Pentecostal churches.[147]

To assert that racism was the only basis for the emergence of Black-led Churches would amount to distortion of the historical facts. Black Churches evolved in Britain to meet the distinctive socio-cultural and religious needs of the black community. This era marked the genesis and growth of the Caribbean brand of Christianity characterized by evangelistic zeal, communal orientation, and oral liturgy. The first service of the NTCG was held in September 1953 at the YMCA hall, Waterloo Road, Wolverhampton, under the direction of the first General Overseer of the Church, Oliver Lyseight, and H.D. Brown. Regional alliance amongst various prayer teams and Blacks was a major feature of this growth phase as the emerging churches provided a "world within the world" and a sanctuary free from social and racial acrimony. The emergence of the churches was devoid of any church planting strategy but arose from the needs of various migrant populations in urban industrial areas of Britain.

The social deprivation theory opined that religion became a default mechanism for survival in a new community but beyond the survivalist's postulations is the inherent holistic and experiential quest to practise the Christian faith within their cultural milieu. This invariably created the underlying distinctiveness as the emerging church was willing to disengage from the Western stereotype of Christianity. This growth phase was more successful than previous growth eras on account of the consistent migration pattern from the West Indies to Britain, an identical pattern of settlement into urban, industrial cities due to job opportunities, and cultural affinity to the early migrants similar to the "Genesis" era highlighted previously.

### *The Denominational Growth Phase (1955–66)*

The second wave of growth is intricately linked to the denominational growth phase. As such, there exists a dynamic overlap of various distinguishing hallmarks of the preceding era. The World Pentecostal Conference of 1952 heralded denominationalism in the second wave of growth of Black-led Churches. Britain became a mission field as American denominations infiltrated the emerging Black-led Churches but this had a boomerang effect on the unity of Black-led Churches.[148] This culminated in schism and competition amongst the Blacks as the Black-led Churches sought to be "conservative and escapist".[149] The Church of God, now the New Testament Church of God, was the first Black-led Church during the *Windrush* era to be affiliated with an American church and almost at once the Church of God of Prophecy followed.

The emerging African and Caribbean churches between 1953 and 1960 almost all had foreign dependencies from American denominations that provided institutional, ecclesiastical and administrative support that was hitherto not available to the Black-led Churches in Britain. Oliver Lyseight clarified that the NTCG was not able to get financial support from the mother church in the United States until the 1970s, despite requests for assistance.[150] The ingenuity of the pioneering leaders of the African Caribbean churches was a result of unflinching commitment to the propagation of the Gospel and the financial commitment of their members who ironically were in the lower economic income strata. The success of the American invasion of the emerging Black-led Churches was predicated on the indigenization approach that was utilised in the West Indies. This provided leverage and credibility for the Americans in the British mission field for creating the Caribbean home brand Christian faith in Britain. These churches included the Church of God of Prophecy, the New Testament Church of God, the Rehoboth Church of God in Christ Jesus Apostolic, the Church of Our Lord Jesus Christ of the Apostolic Faith and the Pilgrim Wesleyan Church. The emerging Black Churches under this dispensation gradually became polarized according to nationalities and diverse theological orientations.

The apparent lack of theological adequacies was made up for by the appropriation of the doctrine of "priesthood of believers", as the "testimony of an illiterate man can be as liberating as the sermon from the preacher".[151] The inherent effect of home-grown ministers provided the initial pastoral oversight for the fledging Black-led denominations.

### *The Proliferation Phase (1966–75)*

The various crossover events of denominationalism amongst the Black-led Churches' leadership culminated in fusion and fission which was the genesis of the proliferation of Black-led Churches in Britain. The growth dynamic was given further impetus by the influence of Nigerians and Ghanaians who pioneered African Independent Churches in Britain in the late 1960s. The influx of West African (Nigerian and Ghanaian) students was prior to the granting of independence to the two nations in 1960 and 1958 respectively. The general relaxation in the immigration regulations of Britain to allow former British colonists to have residency rights was a major boost to the migration of West Africans to Britain.

A major contributory factor to the influx of students into Britain was the British educational system inherited by Nigerians and Ghanaians, who could read and write English. The influence of Britain on Nigeria and Ghana was holistic, as all economic transactions were in British pounds, and likewise the imperial measurement system was the rule. The natural inclination of most students was to study in Britain, as they were already acquainted with the British educational and financial systems. The explosion of Aladura churches in Britain had a divine imperative; a good parallel is "the value of Jewish Diaspora to the spread of the Christian faith in the Roman world of the early church".[152] The healing, prophetic and distinctive cultural relevance of the African Independent Churches to the socio-religious worldview of Nigerians and Ghanaians accounted for the emergence of African Independent Churches like the Celestial Church of Christ started by Bilewu Oshoffa in Port Novo, Benin Republic, the Cherubim and Seraphim Society, the Christ Apostolic Church, the Church of the Lord Aladura, and others.

The consumer orientation that pervades the mindset of some Black-led Churches has contributed (and is still contributing) significantly to transfer growth, and was evident in the 1960s in the evolving Black-led Churches. This era witnessed much "shopping around"[153] by the migrants as churches became polarized along the lines of nationalities and personality dysfunctions amongst the leadership of the emerging Black-led Churches. During this era many sought churches where their cultural, religious and doctrinal needs could be met amongst the multiplicity of Black Churches.

The influence of American denominations on the mission field of the British Isles proved quite overwhelming as many independent churches came into existence. The British Isles were Americanized as leadership accolades and titles synonymous with the Americans featured in the organizational structure of the Black-led denominations. The proliferation also benefited from Ethiopianism as some West Indian churches registered as independent churches.[154] Social action initiatives amongst some British churches in the mould of Bethel Apostolic Church were started in order to cross racial and religious barriers. Gerloff noted that two-thirds of the population of stable Black-led Churches at the time of her publication had started during this phase of growth.[155]

Sturge observed the effects of the initial separation of family units by the early *Windrush* migrants as siblings were not able to cope with the lifestyle of the commitments of their parents to their jobs, and commitments to and nurturing of their children.[156] This resulted in diverse educational and sociological challenges which were eventually reflected in the social interaction of the second-generation migrants.

By the early 1970s the second generation of the *Windrush* era were grossly dissatisfied with the racial inequalities in British public life. The majority of these youngsters found the faith of their fathers was not a true reflection of being able to confront and challenge the inherent perceived social and educational inequalities. Though most of them were now British, they clamoured for the dignity of their cultural ideology. Rastafarianism became a default mechanism to satisfy the ideological deficiencies that the second-generation migrants perceived the burgeoning Black-led Churches could not offer. The relevance of the church was queried as they wanted a reflective, tenacious faith that not only served the feudal British ideologies but an egalitarian Christian faith that spoke against the social, religious and educational inadequacies of their age.

The multiple identities of the second-generation *Windrush* migrants ultimately shaped the next phase of Black-led Churches in Britain, highlighting fundamental social and cultural relevance to a generation seeking to address their cultural ideology, whilst at the same time asserting their rights and privileges as British citizens, yet maintaining their Christian values apart from the perceived apathy of the first-generation migrants. Because of the fluidity of culture, the second-generation migrants began to query some doctrinal persuasions of their churches. For instance, the doctrine of exclusivity was strongly upheld by the Church of God of Prophecy. It was adopted in 1906 and was not reversed until 1994. The exclusivity doctrine depended on the assumption that the Church of God of Prophecy was the one true church that descended from the apostles and to which other denominations would return before the rapture. But the Apostolic Church of Great Britain also had such a doctrinal persuasion.[157] The gradual demise of such doctrinal error came in the wake of hermeneutical and theological polemics of the second-generation migrants who had always challenged the world-rejecting posture of the church on the use of adornments such as jewellery, earrings and rings. The Church of God of Prophecy's revitalization has led to disaffection and litigation amongst the members and the leadership.[158]

The emerging polarization of social and intellectual outlook between *Windrush* migrants and their second and third generations necessitated a paradigm shift in teaching and preaching. This gradually culminated in the spread of denominational colleges in the mould of Overstone College of the New Testament Church of God (NTCG), the Central Bible Institute, Sheffield, Shiloh United Bible College, Croydon, South London Christian College of Jubilee Christian Church led by Dr Femi Olowo and the RCCG's denominational College, Christ Redeemer Christian College.

### *The Revitalizing Phase (1975–85)*

Gerloff's and Sturge's perspectives on this growth phase amongst Black-led Churches are superficially antithetical to each other.[159] This is exemplified in the subtitles of their chronology: "Restless church" (Sturge) and "Stabilization" (Gerloff). The obvious disparity in the perspectives of the two writers has a converging point as both writers acknowledge that this phase heralded social theology amongst Black-led Churches. The *laissez faire* disposition of Black Churches towards social theology, community issues and human rights was abandoned, and the development of a relevant and functional church, beyond their theological and religious persuasions, took place.

The obvious challenge posed by the second-generation migrants stifled the exclusivity doctrine of some Black-led Churches and their inactivity in regard to the social and racial challenges of their time. This dispensation in the Black-led Churches might perhaps be described as the "Jah renaissance generation" as many teenagers became more Afrocentric in their religious persuasions, extolling African culture through the teachings of Rastafarianism. The second-generation migrants had a penchant for reggae music due to their search for identity and acceptance. The first-generation West Indian Christian migrants in Britain detested Rastafarianism, as it was perceived to be anti-Christian.

Robert Beckford, the foremost black British theologian, has heralded his canon of black theology as he has articulated Bob Marley as a liberation theologian.[160] The influence of reggae music in Beckford's theological assertions depicts the cultural dynamics that second-generation *Windrush* migrants encountered in the midst of white Christianity as practised by their parents.

The social actions of Black-led Churches during this era demonstrated the potentials of Black Church leadership. The churches started moving towards being missional, as the focus shifted from the gathering of the saints (the church) to the community. The pharisaic disposition which had ignored the community challenges and youth crisis was gradually reversed as the church became the neighbour of the community (Lk 10:29). Gerloff asserted that this era marked the genesis of interdenominational, interracial and intercultural partnership.[161] The commencement of this development brought about a climate of acceptance amongst the British Council of Churches. Gerloff identified various parachurch organizations such as the Afro West Indian United Council of Churches (AWUCOC) established in 1976.

The proliferation of parachurch organizations was a subtle indictment of the systemic failure of the International Ministerial Council of Great Britain (IMCGB), which had wider geographical appeal. Aldred opined that the demise of the association was inextricably linked to its appellation as a ministerial council that had a broad scope but could not be translated to its target audience, as "influential Caribbean British and other Black-led Churches" could not find a niche in the organization.[162] The irony of the proliferation of parachurch organizations as identified by Aldred was that disunity was a major contributory factor to the demise or ineffectiveness of these organizations.[163]

The plethora of parachurch organizations began to become a distinctive phenomenon, for example associations like the Council of African and Afro Caribbean Churches (CAACC), which was established by Most Reverend Father Olu Abiola in 1977. He noted the overt influence that might be asserted by international bodies on African Independent Churches as a reason for their complacent disposition to the evolving parachurch organizations, as "they fear[ed] others might want to influence and change their beliefs and practices".[164]

Philip Mohabir was pivotal to the emergence of the West Indian Evangelical Alliance (WIEA) which later metamorphosed into the African Caribbean Evangelical Alliance (ACEA). He had a pioneering role in building bridges among Pentecostals and Charismatics, being a voice for the West Indian and English communities, developing leadership and fostering unity between black and white Christian communities. ACEA built on Mohabir's foundation as it enjoyed large patronage from many Black Majority Churches in its early stages; this was due to the support of the UK Evangelical Alliance.[165]

The success of Black Majority Churches must be seen in the strength of character of the leadership of the associations and functionalities which have been successfully articulated through the media and the celebration of African and Caribbean values of the Christian faith, although Aldred observed that ACEA is more Eurocentric than Afrocentric in its identity as a result of the influence of the Evangelical Alliance as its financier.[166] He further identified in his discourses with various people involved that the "AWUCOC was primarily concerned with black and white ecumenism, WIEA/ACEA's primary goal was black/white ecumenism and IMCGB was thought to be about ministerial accreditation, where it was recognised at all".[167]

The inherent fusion of ACEA (black and white ecumenism) might be responsible for the apathy of some Black Majority Church leaders towards ACEA as not being a true reflection of Africans' and Caribbeans' distinctive theology. The intriguing irony of such a polemic is that it is has no biblical antecedents, as the atoning sacrifice of Christ was neither the exclusive right of Jews nor Gentiles but a sacrifice that has universal appeal.

A major test case for the leadership of ACEA was the investigation of the Kingsway International Christian Centre (KICC) led by Pastor Matthew Ashimolowo by the Charity Commission of England and Wales in 2002. Some Black-led Church leaders perceived that the association was a toothless bulldog that could not pull its weight in support of the single largest congregation in Britain. Though the Evangelical Alliance and African Caribbean Evangelical Alliance made representations, this was perceived by some African pastors as grossly inadequate considering the significance and impact of KICC in the history of British Black Pentecostalism as the single largest church in England.

The apathy of most leaders of Black Majority Churches to ACEA eventually culminated in the demise of the organization on 27 March 2009 on account of lack of funds. The situation depicts a dearth of organizational planning, a systemic failure and lack of collective responsibilities of Black Majority Church leaders towards the organization that purportedly claims to champion the cause of Black Majority Churches. Andrew Adeleke noted that the demise of ACEA might constitute a typology of the dearth of Judges in Israel after the death of Joshua, which had serious social and religious consequences for the nation of Israel. This retrospective view certainly considers what might have happened but not what could have been done to address the situation.[168]

### The Diverse Church Phase (1985–95)

The use of this title for this sub-section is due to my agreement with Sturge's view of the history of events that happened during this phase.[169] However, he made the broad sweeping assertion that the church was "not declining"; this view is myopic with respect to various West Indian churches pioneered in the 1950s and 1960s, as Aldred in his thesis asserted that the Church of God of Prophecy experienced a decline in membership.[170] Numerical growth is only one of several indices of growth; amongst the Black Majority Church leadership structure (and from my personal experience as a minister within Black Majority Churches) growth is seen as a reflection of the church's spiritual state.

This era witnessed mass economic migration to Britain from African countries, especially Nigeria and Ghana, as a result of the strangulating effects of the local economies. The migration pattern of the 1980s was similar to the push factors during the *Windrush* era, as many of the migrants were already rooted in Pentecostalism and were eager to export the brand of their denomination to Britain. The African brand of Christianity was synonymous with the era of "church bombing"[171] due to the massive growth of the new African churches, mostly Neo-Pentecostals and Charismatics. The apparent "growth syndrome" of Black Majority Churches was that the hand of God had prepared repositories of expectant Africans in urban areas in Britain that wanted a distinct African brand of Christianity.

The health status of these churches is hard to evaluate, but the majority of the membership of Britain's Black Majority Churches are transferred growth as a result of emigration and local transfer. The economic success and professional accomplishments of some of the Africans were transferred to their financial and religious commitments to their various churches. Osgood traced the emergence of the array of Black Majority Churches that emerged, including Deeper Life Bible Church (1985) pioneered in Britain by Pastor Pre Ovia, Foursquare Gospel Church (1985) and New Covenant Church (1986).[172] New Covenant Church was pioneered in the United Kingdom by the late Pastor (later Bishop) Titus David, who was redeployed by Pastor Paul Jinadu to pioneer the denomination in London. Titus David eventually left New Convenant Church in 1988 because of leadership challenges, to start Christ Family Church. There was also the Redeemed Christian Church of God established in the United Kingdom in 1988. Pastor Matthew Ashimolowo, a bosom friend of the late Bishop Titus David, also left Foursquare Gospel Church, London in September 1992 with 300 members and rented a hall at Holloway Boys School, North London, to start Kingsway International Christian Centre. Further, there were Green Pastures (now Glory House) pioneered by Dr Albert Odulele, with the inaugural service held in March 1993 at 78 Capworth Street, Leyton, London, and New Wine Church (1993), which was started as Upper Room Fellowship in Greenwich, London, by Dr Pastor Tayo Adeyemi.

The emerging pneumatic community of Africans was more interested in experiential knowledge than in intellectual development and the proliferation of theological and Bible colleges, which lack formal accreditation, as many of the leaders argued that theology is pneuma-centric. This is a reflection of the age-long misconception by some Pentecostals that there is no meeting point between pneuma-centric theology and academic theology, but this misconception has proved fatal to black theology. This myth has been disproved by the likes of Robert Beckford, Anthony Reddie, Virginia Beecher, Michael Jagessar and a host of other black British theologians who have maintained balance between the rigours of academia and their church commitments.

The huge potential within the Black Majority Churches is evident in the many musicians and artistes that dominated the British Black Gospel scene in the latter part of the twentieth century and the early twenty-first, such as Noel Robinson, Bazil Meade (the founder and leader of London Community Gospel Choir), Joe Edwards (former Director of Evangelical Alliance, UK), and Bishop John Francis (the multi-talented leader of Ruach Ministries). Noel Robinson's influence on the British Black Gospel artistes and producers has facilitated a new wave of creativity and acceptance even with the British Broadcasting Corporation.

The success story of Karen Gibson (the founder of the Kingdom Choir) cannot but be acknowledged, as Smith noted that Noel Robinson recommended Gibson to become the resident tutor of BBC programme Radio Train.[173] One of the choir group mentored by Noel Robinson described the Kingdom Choir as "a choir of quality and excellence with a heart of worship that was created to usher in the Kingdom of heaven".[174] Sturge traced the genesis of the contemporary Black Gospel popularity to the Heavenly Hope group led by Joseph Pitt and Bazil Meade.[175] Joel Edwards and Joseph Pitt were members of the band Kainos who enjoyed wide acceptance amongst white Christians such as those who attended the Greenbelt Festivals.

Sturge's further classification of the Black Majority Churches into revitalized and recognized phases reflects the dynamism of the renewal of individual Black Churches.[176] The classification is not a product of the internal renewal of most Black Majority Churches. In view of the fissiparous nature of Black Majority Churches, new churches will always emerge from the fringes through religious and doctrinal differences, or extraneous or organizational mitosis. This reflects the effort of the leadership of the Black Majority Churches' flagship in the mould of ACEA, articulating a holistic perspective to Black Majority Churches and a vantage position to influence policy decision-making processes in Britain. The larger than life image of ACEA suffered an irreparable loss on 27 March 2009, as ACEA Chair of Trustees, the Reverend Pedro Okoro said:

> ACEA has dedicated the past 25 years to providing a unique voice for African and Caribbean churches in the UK, so this has been a very painful decision. Operations are now suspended pending a planned review and consultation with our constituency as to how we can best continue to respond to the Black Church's need for representation. The patrons and trustees are committed to ensuring that the views of members of the Black Majority Churches continue to be heard and the trustees will continue to meet to explore an appropriate way forward for the organisation.

The sudden demise of ACEA seems to reflect a systemic disease that has continually plagued almost all Black parachurch organizations that have evolved in Britain with a definite agenda to articulate the interests and aspirations of African and Caribbean Christians. It is ironic that the Evangelical Alliance had provided funding for ACEA since the rebranding after the death of Mohabir, the founding father of ACEA. The lack of organizational foresight and "colonial subsidies", which were a major feature of churches with denominational affiliation in Africa and the Caribbean, is replicated in the ACEA organizational structure. The lack of commitment of the members of ACEA could be a reflection of individualism which is prevalent in the Western world replicated in organizational leadership sewn together by such loose threads of relationship that the benefits can hardly be determined.

The appointment of Rev. Katei Kirby as the Chief Executive of ACEA, after Mark Sturge, heralded a period of public policy statements on a wide range of issues related to Black Majority Churches – issues such as the Religious Hatred Bill, and the criminalization of Black Churches over alleged cases of child abuse. The sudden demise of ACEA raises the question of the role of the constituent members of the Board of Trustees. Sturge, in an interview with *Christianity Today* (9 August 2005), criticized the Board for lack of financial commitment to ACEA, and cited this as an inhibitory factor and as the basis for his resignation. He expressed his frustrations as he said:

> Finances are very important. I don't think that my board responded to the challenge . . . Instead, the agenda placed on the table was something I was not prepared to work with. I am used to making bricks out of straw, but I felt we could not be expected to run a national organisation on these reduced resources. I decided it was time to stand down as I wasn't convinced that I'd be able to be as effective as I had been in the past.[177]

The purported claim of the Chair of the association to consult with their constituencies is best termed "Adam's escapism", a default mechanism to cope with obvious failure of the Board of Trustees' overt or covert inaction. This further authenticates the assertion of Aldred[178] that most leaders prefer a denominational agenda rather than the representative agenda of the African and Caribbean Christians. It is in the light of this that many of the purported claims of government fraternization and engagement might have been perceived as extolling the aspirations of ACEA's principal leadership with minimal benefits to members of the organization, although Arlington Trotman, who is the consultant appointed to review the activities ACEA, in his preliminary report highlighted the various achievements of the organisation in its 25 years of existence. It is pertinent to note, however, that such achievements are not even comparable with the attainments of some of the denominations affiliated to ACEA. Adeleke, a member of the Board of Trustees ACEA, was quite philosophical about the demise of organisation. Rhetorically he asked: Could it be that ACEA has outlived its usefulness to the Black-led Churches?[179] But he also opined that obviously there is a void created in articulating the voice of Black-led Churches in Britain. However, Obunge applauded the demise of ACEA, as he affirmed the Christocentric view of the believers that in Christ there is neither "Jew [white] nor Greek [black]".[180]

Irukwu opined that the concept of Black Churches or Black Majority is a transitionary issue, as these churches' nomenclature will change when the indigenous community become members of these churches and the overt emphasis on the racial divide will die a natural death.[181] Future growth delineation of Black Majority Churches will build on changes within the socio-organizational activism of these churches, as the foundation, growth and relevance of Black Majority Churches have been established. The obvious inherent challenge that is unaddressed by the leadership of most Black Majority Churches in Britain is the inability of the churches to attract the indigenous white community membership. The attraction of white membership to these churches will be a new paradigm in the history of Black Majority Churches in Britain.

## HEALTH CHECK: REAL OR APPARENT GROWTH

The health of Black-led Churches in Britain is often related to misconceptions about church growth. The general notion amongst some preachers, scholars and laity is that numerical growth of a church is synonymous with good health. The term "church growth" is used almost exclusively to mean numerical growth. If the numbers don't go up, the church is experiencing a "plateau", a buzzword for stagnation. If the numbers are going down it must be unhealthy and in a state of decline. It is in the light of this that blossoming and proliferation of the Black Majority Churches in Britain needs a health check, but it is important to note that a biblical perspective emphasizes both qualitative and numerical growth.

This places an onerous responsibility on the leadership of the Black Majority Churches to ensure that these churches are not just dotting the urban landscape of Britain, but have a holistic growth, as only a healthy body can be effective. The apostle Paul in 1 Corinthians 9:27 presents an ideal model of engagement in the race of life. Paul emphasizes the role of discipline in conditioning his body to run the race of life so as to have eternal recognition. This model is given a contemporary relevance by Stedman:"No athlete spends all his time running races or playing the game for which he is trained; he must also spend many hours keeping himself in shape and developing his skills to a high degree. So it is with the body of Christ. The work of the ministry will never be properly done by a weak and unhealthy church, torn with internal pains and wracked by spiritual diseases."[182]

This implies that there exists a positive correlation between the health of a church and its effectiveness in a given context. This issue has been addressed by various scholars, especially church growth exponents, including the progenitor of the church growth movement, Donald McGavran. Win Arn made significant contributions on the components of a healthy church, but the incumbent heir of the church growth movement, Peter C. Wagner, chronicled seven essential hallmarks of church growth in his book *Your Church Can Grow: Seven Vital Signs of a Healthy Church*. Similar contributions have been made by Rick Warren, Christian Schwarz, Mark Dever and Stephen Machia.[183] The diverse perspectives have contributed significantly to the ongoing discourse on church health but an identifiable shortcoming of these authors is not addressing the meaning of the concept of church health.

In the case of the Black Majority Churches in Britain there is a dearth of this assessment; this present work aims to contribute to this discourse through the lens of the American proponents of church health theory. The medical paradigm is helpful in the understanding of the health of Black Churches in Britain. This analogy is quite profound and relevant in assessing the growth of Black Churches. The context (church) that is being examined experiences much dynamism as a result of multitudes of factors. These factors can inhibit or enhance growth of churches. It is necessary to address obvious pathological signs of a diseased condition before a diagnosis of church health can be made. Chaney and Lewis noted that, "In medical terms a diagnosis is the determination of a disease by a comprehensive examination of a patient. Accurate diagnosis is the foundation of modern medicine. Proper treatment is only possible when the cause of the illness is known ... Comparable procedure is necessary to determine the growth of a church."[184] The obvious basis of the health check of churches according to Chaney and Lewis's model is the hexagonal diagnostic factors which are: (1) numerical growth; (2) the rate of growth; (3) the type of growth; (4) the location of growth occurring; (5) an adequate number of leaders; and (6) the efficient use of resources. The obvious imperative of this approach is that it be utilised in prognosis. If utilised in the evaluation of the health status of Black-led Churches in Britain, the emphasis of the approach is not holistic, as the focus is mainly on numerical assessment, but there exist a myriad of factors that can impair the health of a church, for example the sociological parameters and other extraneous factors are not considered.

A retrospective look at the American church growth movement might constitute a warning sign that Black Majority Churches and their leadership need to examine the health of their churches. The appraisal of the church growth movement with all its principles by the church researcher, George Barna, reached the shocking verdict that:

> Since 1980, there has been "no growth" in the proportion of the adult population that can be classified as "born again" Christians. The proportion of born again Christians has remained constant at 32%, despite the fact that churches and parachurch organizations have spent billions of dollars on evangelism. More than 10,000 hours of evangelistic television programming have been broadcast, in excess of 5,000 new Christian books have been published, and more than 1,000 radio stations carry Christian programming. Yet despite such widespread opportunities for exposure to the gospel, there has been no discernable growth in the size of the Christian body.[185]

There exists disparity in the prevailing scenario in Britain, as the subject under consideration is not all of the British Churches but a distinctive part of the British Church which seems to be blossoming in its proliferation. The absence of statistical figures in terms of the conversion and membership of all Black Majority Churches in Britain makes a proper evaluation of the nature of the growth and contributions to the Kingdom a daunting challenge. It is sufficient to note that Black Churches indeed have experienced numerical growth in terms of membership over the years. Hunt, writing in 2000, noted that membership of Jesus House, led by a law graduate of Warwick University, Agu Irukwu, was 1,700, but as at 2012, the membership is over 3,000.[186] Similar growth can be seen in the Redeemed Christian Church of God: as at 2002 it had 100 churches, mainly in London and the Midlands, but this has now increased to 660 in 2012. Kingsway International Christian Centre led by Pastor Matthew Ashimolowo had a membership of 5,000 members at the main church in 2002 but by 2009 had a 12,000-strong membership and several satellite churches in Britain.[187]

The older Caribbean Churches like the Church of God of Prophecy, however, experienced a decline in membership over time.[188] Some of the older West Indian Churches of the 1950s and 1960s are undergoing revitalization as some of the second and third generation of *Windrush* migrants' views about spirituality have been shaped by Anglo-American Pentecostalism. The latter is a noted extraneous source of new religious ideas, modes of organization, dress, style and general identity by which the young can turn away from structures dominated by the elderly. This is a reflection of the effects of cultural shift on the values and identity of consumers and its effects on the spirituality of people.

The identifiable growth portals for churches have been identified to be: (a) economic and forced migrants; (b) biological growth; (c) transferred growth; and (d) proselytization growth. Black Majority Churches in Britain have received much impetus from migration. Hunt observed that 96% of the membership of Jesus House was of African origin and 90% were Nigerians, but the dynamics of the Nigerian composition of this church is gradually changing: it was ascertained in the course of this research that the membership is still distinctively African with Nigerians constituting over significant percentage as ascertained during the course of writing this book but it is still distinctively African.[189] This is more of a generic situation in most Black Majority Churches in Britain, as the hope of re-Christianizing Britain is far from being a reality for now. The Black Majority Churches have not had significant followings amongst the host communities but are quite successful in evangelizing the Africans and the Caribbeans in Britain.[190] The basis of this is the lack of understanding of the worldview and cultural dynamics of the host communities which is a sharp departure from the African prism of ministry. It is worthy of note that very few Black Majority Churches are missional; they have not succeeded in attracting large numbers of white communities into their membership, although there are exceptions, such as the Lighthouse Fellowship at Liverpool, pastored by Tani Omideyi.

The preponderance of transfer growth which is a common feature of Black Majority Churches is a pathological sign of a disease condition best described as "Quitting to Reacquaint Syndrome" (QTRS), which is the mentality of Christians consumer shopping for an ideal church. The disease is almost endemic and bears resemblance to the mega churches that evolved in the wake of the American church growth movement of the 1970s which led to transferred growth in various congregations eager to reacquaint themselves with the saints in bigger, urban and marketing-oriented churches. QTRS is dubbed "sheep stealing" by William Chadwick. Astonishingly, William Chadwick was also a disciple of the church growth movement. He asserted that he wrote "from the perspective of an insider" which must have been a product of hindsight and the experiential mistakes of his ministry, as he noted the monstrous effects of transferred growth on other churches. He argues that "the shifting of saints from one church to another is killing individual ministries within the Church which has transformed ministry to an art form".[191]

The consumer mentality has found its way to church as Christians exercise their rights like consumers and "shop around", devoid of any commitment and sacrifice to a particular local church. In some Black Majority Churches, people are gradually ceasing from building age-long relationships that are a strong basis for a sense of community, as a result of schism, personal distrust and leadership ineptitude. In fact, in some African churches the rhetoric is "I am moving on". Transferred growth is cheap growth that has no emphasis on evangelism and discipleship, and this repudiates Christ's valedictory instructions (Mt 28:18–20). It is rather ironic that much of the vaunted claims of most Black Majority Churches are rooted in numerical numbers akin to the church growth movement in America that has been criticized for its inadequacies. As Warren stated, "You don't judge an army's strength by how many people sit in the mess hall. You judge an army on the basis of how many people are trained and active on the front line."[192]

The functionality of this perspective is that the missional objective of Christ's commission is cardinal to the health of a church. Transferred growth is unhealthy, as the objective of the church is to "rescue the sheep", not to steal them, though there are exceptions: in some cases "they [believers (sheep)] are rescued from a setting where false teaching and heresy occur. And some sheep need to be rescued from abusive church settings."[193] The proliferation of Black Churches in Britain has been a safe haven for the "rejects" of the 1960s, and today provides a valid alternative to the orthodox evangelicals' staid and unresponsive worship. The rise in eclectic culture in the West thus presents vast opportunities for transfer growth for churches in Britain through evangelism and conversion of sectarian members of such faith communities.

The proliferation of Black Churches in Britain was mostly a result of transferred growth from the historical denominations, as most of the West Indian migrants who pioneered the West Indian Churches in Britain during the *Windrush* era were from historic churches. Admittedly this implies there exist various functionalities to consider in analysing transferred growth in relation to the health of a church. Chadwick commented on historical churches: "We speak of the churched lost in 'historical' (i.e. historically evangelical but now unorthodox) Christian churches. Should we encourage those who become saved to leave these churches? ... The easy answer is of course we should!"[194] In response to the various models of church health enumerated above, Stephen Macchia developed a biblical model. He identified ten characteristics of a healthy church, namely: (1) God's empowering presence; (2) God-exalting worship; (3) spiritual disciplines; (4) a learning and growing community; (5) a commitment to loving and caring relationships; (6) servant leadership development; (7) an outward focus; (8) wise administration and accountability; (9) networking with the body of Christ; and (10) stewardship and generosity.[195]

The appropriateness of Stephen Macchia's perspective is reflected in its broad-spectrum approach that includes biblical, theological and sociological considerations. Black-led Churches based on this model in Britain are noted to affirm their theology from the Bible with much emphasis on supernaturalism and experiential spirituality.[196] These obvious features are in consonance with general Pentecostal orientation but with a distinctive cultural flavour. This theology, practised within a cultural context, does not in any way make African or Caribbean Pentecostalism subordinate to Global Pentecostalism. Sepulveda asserts that the cultural milieu cannot be divorced from understanding of the Gospel. He says, "we cannot grasp any meaning without the help of our precious cultural categories".[197] Though some of the Black-led Churches at times incorporate their pneumatology with their pre-Christian rites, in fact they can be syncretic. But Hollenweger observed that even Western mainline churches can fall into the error of syncretism.[198]

Walter Hollenweger further noted that the inherent "oral structures" of Pentecostalism, also a distinguishing feature of Black-led Churches in Britain, are responsible for its origin, similarly to how Christianity itself began. The oral structures, not any "particular Pentecostal doctrine", are the reason for its initial growth. The oral structures, according to Hollenweger, include oral liturgy, narrative theology and witness, reconciliatory and participant community, the inclusion of visions and dreams in worship, and understanding the relationship between body and mind revealed in healing by prayer and liturgical dance. These are also predominantly African cultural features, evident in the leadership of William Seymour, whose "spirituality was reflective of his African roots". These features have greatly contributed to the vitality of the Black Churches in Britain which are a replication of the conditions of the Azusa movement. For the Black-led Churches in Britain, the debate about the historic churches' foundation in relation to the Black-led Churches is not a chronological matter but a theological orientation. The historic churches represent the exaltation of clericalism and church traditions while Black-led Churches represent the "reconciling Pentecostal experience" and "a congregation where everybody is a potential contributor to the liturgy".[199]

The holistic nature of the worship, liturgy, preaching and music within Britain's Black-led Churches reflects spontaneity and enthusiasm, producing flexible oral liturgies learnt by rote by the Pentecostal congregation. The most important element of these liturgies is the active participation of every member in the congregation. The Pentecostal liturgy of Black-led Churches in Britain has social and revolutionary implications, in that it empowers marginalized people.

Black Majority Churches in Britain have a strong emphasis on the spiritual disciplines of prayer, fasting and worship. Sturge gives a detailed exposition of the biblical basis for Black Majority Churches' spiritual disciplines.[200] The overview is replete with various New Testament examples of the Early Church engagement in the spiritual disciplines of fasting, prayer and worship. Sturge highlights the various kinds of prayers that are vital to healthy Christian lives, such as: (a) Prayer of Unity (Acts 1:14; 2:1); (b) Prayer of Penitence (Ps 51, Nehemiah 1:6; James 5:13–18); (c) Identification Prayer (2 Chronicles 7:14–15); and (d) Warfare Prayer (Mt 17:18–21). One of the major distinguishing features of Black Majority Churches is the use of imprecatory prayers, and this is often a reflection of the African traditional worldview and proof-texting of scriptures. Prayer within the Black Majority Churches in Britain is spontaneous in comparison to the prayer disposition in White-led Churches or historic denominations; this, according to Wilkinson, is the aftermath of the "historical experience of God in oppression".[201]

Wilkinson's assertion is not a true reflection of the distinctiveness of Black Majority Churches' prayer meetings. Although imprecatory prayers might have historical relevance to the challenges of Africans and Caribbeans during the period of oppression, it is more of literalism in exegeting the scriptures. But often such imprecatory prayers are born out of a desperate and passionate desire for divine manifestations of their hearts' desires. The informal nature of prayers intermingled with proof-texting from various scriptures is quite prominent in prayer sessions; the reliance on prayer liturgy is not a common feature of Black Majority Churches in Britain. Various Black Majority Churches have structured spiritual disciplines that are observed for the vitality of their members.

From my experiential perspective as a minister and church leader within the Black Majority Churches, a major feature of most prayer meetings is "consumer religion". This is a brand of Christianity that is not mindful of the "Cross and of the prophetic vocation" of Christianity[202] and in which Christians have a naïve humanistic notion of prayer. God is there for the sake of human needs, and faith is a lever for manipulating God into showering blessings on human beings. Thus faith, and *ipso facto* God, have no essential value in themselves.[203] In this respect there seems to be a renewal movement amongst the leadership of Black Majority Churches, as some are beginning to emphasize the importance of the cross in the health and prosperity of their domain.

A typical example is the Global Day of Prayer in Britain led by Jonathan Oloyede, a graduate of medicine and a former pastor with Glory House, Plaistow, London who left in 2008 to start an "intentional multi-racial church" known as City Chapel situated at Newham. This is a typical example of moving beyond the confines of stereotypical misconceptions about prayer modulated by humanistic dispositions to a Christocentric approach. This form of renewal is not peculiar to the Global Day of Prayer but it is gradually being replicated at various levels of the church life of Black Majority Churches. This is a healthy sign for Black Churches as a broad-spectrum network potential is forged between various churches.

Even historic congregations like Holy Trinity Church, Brompton, have featured prominently in various exchange programmes with Jesus House, a parish of the RCCG, London.[204] Agu Irukwu since 2008 has featured as speaker at the leadership conference of Holy Trinity, Brompton. On 21 May 2010 over five thousand Christians came together at the HMV Hammersmith Apollo, at a gathering organized by Holy Trinity, Brompton, Jesus House and Hillsong, to celebrate Pentecost. After the success of that event, all three churches – Jesus House, Hillsong and Holy Trinity, Brompton held Pentecost 2011 on 11 June 2011 at the O2 Arena, the former Millenium Dome, with the theme "Life in the Spirit". It was estimated that the event attracted about 17,000 people from a variety of churches in the UK on this historic night!

The Redeemed Christian Church of God, United Kingdom, has actively been at the forefront of holding an all-night prayer meeting tagged Festival of Life; this has being declared to be the largest gathering of believers in the United Kingdom for prayers. Held on 27 November 2010, it was attended by 40,000 people. The evangelistic drive of the RCCG is reflected in the partnership with British evangelicals through the HOPE 2008 leadership team. The thrust of the partnership is to foster unity of the Christian faith while seeking avenues to evangelize Britain. Representatives of the HOPE 2008 leadership team and some RCCG pastors were prayed for by Pastor (Mrs) Folu Adeboye during the Festival of Life programme of April 2010.

A major fault line amongst Black Majority Churches is moral and financial accountability.[205] This is fast becoming an unhealthy scar on the vibrant and enduring Christian movement in British church history. There are various moral failures and financial misdemeanours that have plagued the leadership of some Black Majority Churches in the last decades. The infamous saga of Pastor Douglas Goodman, a former bus driver with

London Transport, is a point of reference. Goodman was indicted after a two-year investigation by the Charity Commission of Victory Christian Centre, formerly the second biggest Pentecostal Church in Britain; it registered debts of £200,000 despite having an income of £3.5 million at its peak.

The probe found evidence of "misconduct and mismanagement", including "significant unauthorized salary payments and other benefits provided to the pastor and his wife as well as a number of trustees" according to an article by Richard Edwards published in the *Evening Standard* on 7 September 2004. The article was entitled: *Scandal in Second Biggest Penteostal Church in Britain*. The Charity Commission report unveiled the circumvention of managerial checks and balances of the governance of the charity as Pastor Goodman and his wife Erica profited from the funds of the charity. The climax of the demise of the Victory Church was the conviction of Pastor Douglas and his sentencing at the Old Bailey to three and a half years in jail for assault on a 19-year-old woman, attempted indecent assault on a 26-year-old woman and perverting the course of justice. However, it is important to note that sexual and financial ineptitude resists "colour mapping", as the likes of Jimmy Swaggart, Jim Bakker, Bishop Michael Reid, Ted Haggard and Jesse Jackson were brought to the canvas by the lure of sexual sin. The conquest for the soul of Christians by Satan is that of a spiritual warfare that is not modulated by colour, profession or status but by systemic, cosmic and sustained attacks, as Paul noted in Ephesians 6:12.

Sturge, in an interview with *Christianity Today*, 9 June 2005, further asserted this perspective as he noted:

> Douglas Goodman did not do what he did because he was an independent pastor or because he was black. He did what he did because the evidence suggests he delighted in sinning, he took pleasure from sinning and that is a sin that could befall anyone. When I was at theological college I was told that 12% of us would sleep with our secretaries. That fact didn't come from the black church. That's a white middle class institution reflecting on itself ... There is the law of the land, which governs how charities and companies operate and what is acceptable behaviour. We've also got the ultimate sanction available to us, which is Scripture and its examples and demands.[206]

It seems that a pattern prevalent in some Black Majority Churches is the authoritarian leadership style of founders of these churches with a strong disregard for statutory regulatory bodies. The adulations and encomiums on some of the "successful" preachers is rooted in the African culture of celebrating success: not to do so is unacceptable, but to overdo it is sinful.

This was a major flaw noted by Simmidele Adedeji in an interview with *Sunday Times* correspondent Nicola Woolcock on 7 May 2004. She noted that, "Pastor Douglas and his family were icons. They were like pop stars. He was idolised. Women would shift their loyalty from God to the man and it became an obsession. Girls would throw themselves at him. His services were electric. He was the star." This is a reflection of the distortion of the message of the cross to unconscious idolatry as the focus of such adulations is the recipient of God's grace and gifting but not the giver of the gifts and grace.

The administrative takeover of the London-based Kingsway International Christian Centre (KICC) was initiated by the Charity Commission of England and Wales in 2002 and was widely publicised by the British media. This was another benchmark case that caused a lot of panic amongst Black Majority Church leaders in Britain as the opinion amongst Black Church leaders was that if KICC should go under the hammer of the Charity Commision of England and Wales, then no Black Majority Church was immune. The takeover was later reversed after the report submitted by the accounting firm KPMG (the government-appointed administrator), although the Charity Commission noted that there was "serious misconduct and mismanagement" according to Ruth Gledhill of Timesonline of the 20th of October 2005.

The report noted that Pastor Matthew Ashimolowo, the founder of the Kingsway International Christian Centre, and his family lived rent-free in a house owned by the charity. It was also reported that he used the charity's credit card to buy a £12,000 timeshare in Florida and ran a commercial business from church premises. Among benefits he received was a £120,000 birthday party, of which £80,000 went on a Mercedes. However, the Charity Commission in the course of various consultations with Evangelical Alliance, African Caribbean Evangelical Alliance and leaders of Black Majority Churches proposed a new governing document specially aimed at churches. Hugh Osgood in his thesis gives very detailed insight to the KICC saga. His exhaustive research on the subject is quite objective while highlighting the role played by Evangelical Alliance (EA), Britain, African Caribbean Evangelical Alliance (ACEA), the British media and Charity Commission during the incident.

It is imperative to assert that the organizational and leadership strength of the KICC should be commended. Despite the media frenzy and backlash on Pastor Matthew Ashimolowo, the church is still making a significant impact in Britain as the largest single congregation. The KICC recently relocated from its former premises in Hackney, East London, to make way for the London 2012 Olympic development. Services are currently held in a temporary home at Hoe Street, Walthamstow, while the management committee searches for a suitable site to create a new, purpose-built church and conference centre complex. The most successful trading year for the KICC recently was 2008 according to the audited company accounts submitted to the Charity Commission, which reveal that the organization made a profit of £4.9m. The 2008 company accounts also showed that £9.5m was raised through tithes and offerings donated by the members. The influence and financial muscle of the KICC amongst Black Majority Churches in Britain cannot be underestimated.

In spite of the growth and contributions of the KICC to community development in Britain, the church is yet to find a permanent place of worship due to non- issuance of planning permission for their new church, offices and community complex at Beam Reach by Thames Gateway Development Corporation. The decision is not only shocking but seems surprising in view of the broad consultations of the church and its commitment to the community development of Beam Reach. Ironically a new mosque has been proposed near East Ham Station which would be able to accommodate 40,000 people with the option of being extended to accommodate 70,000 people. It is pertinent to ask whether there are sinister motives behind the refusal of planning permission to the KICC while other faiths' planning permissions are granted despite Britain being a Protestant nation by law!

It seems there is no end in sight to the plethora of vices amongst the leadership of some Black Majority Churches, for example, the self-appointed Bishop Gilbert Deya's "miracle baby" scandal. This added another dimension of supernaturalism to the despicable acts of fraud which also resonated in Britain's Channel 4 television programme *Dispatches* episode entitled "Britain's Witch Children" shown on 26 July 2010. *Dispatches* went undercover to record some African churches in the UK, where evangelical pastors perpetuate a strong belief in witchcraft (this is a reflection of the animistic background that some of the preachers might have been raised in, and inadequate theological training) and found that some of the pastors requested money to carry out exorcisms. The Evangelical community and the Minority Ethnic Affairs Office of Churches Together in England in a joint communiqué issued to the press responded promptly to the *Dispatches* programme.

Steve Clifford, General Director of the Evangelical Alliance, said: "We are taking every step within our power to ensure exploitative practices conducted by a small minority of unaffiliated pastors are entirely stamped out and a higher expectation of accountability is firmly established. We remain extremely disappointed that Dispatches implied such abusive behaviour is being committed by more than a very small minority."[207]

Dr Joe Aldred, Secretary of Minority Ethnic Christian Affairs for Churches Together in England said: "In light of recent evidence shown in Dispatches we jointly re-affirm our whole-hearted commitment to ensure excellent child protection standards are upheld within all UK churches. This should be delivered in the form of increased education and registration at the ISA [Independent Safeguarding Authority] and all other appropriate regulatory and ecumenical agencies. CCPAS [Churches Child Protection Agency Services] have already made huge strides in training up to 5,000 African church leaders in optimum standards of child protection over the last few years alone."[208] The prompt response of the two leaders was apt in terms of damage limitation to their constituencies but the issue also raises fundamental questions on the investigative etiquette of *Dispatches* as the two constituencies were not given the opportunity to express their views on such practices.

Britain's Black Church Movement and the Evangelical community were further awoken to a rude shock with the conviction of Dr Albert Odulele, the Senior Pastor of Glory House, Plaistow, East London at Woolwich Crown Court on 31 March 2011. His conviction was for indecent assault of a minor and sexually assaulting another pastor; he was jailed for eight months and six months respectively, to run concurrently, and put on the sex offenders' register for five years. Dr Albert Odulele's conviction raises fundamental questions with respect to accountability and moral rectitude of some Black Majority Church leaders in Britain.

The coincidence of Dr Albert Odulele's conviction shortly before the out-of-court settlement of Bishop Eddie Long, the Atlanta-based mega church leader, with four young men who accused him of sexual coercion in 2010, further reiterates the nature of the challenges faced by "men of God" globally. Perhaps the "high horse" spiritual ride of independent ministers has contributed to a lack of circles of accountability. The perceived inabilities of the leaders of these churches to identify and seek assistance outside their faith communities to address their sexual and family dysfunctions have contributed to the emerging show of shame globally.

The Irish Catholic Church in 2009 was under the world spotlight when the submission of a nine-year investigation found that Catholic priests and nuns had for decades terrorized thousands of boys and girls in the Irish Republic, while government inspectors failed to stop the chronic beatings, rape and humiliation. The high court judge Sean Ryan unveiled the 2,600 page report of Ireland's commission into child abuse on 29 May 2009, which drew on testimony from thousands of former inmates and officials from more than 250 church-run institutions. It is apt to submit, based on the diversities of the occurrence of the moral ineptitude of priests, vicars, pastors or bishops, that they are at best men and women who are still struggling with moral failings and need a support mechanism within their primary constituencies along with a personal commitment to a life of piety in a consumer-driven and sexualised world.

However, it should be noted that there are many Black Majority Churches in Britain, some of which include the KICC, Christ Faith Tabernacle, Ruach Ministries, New Wine Church, New Covenant Church and the RCCG, which are conscious of the need to be financially accountable, partly because this is a condition for maintaining charitable status, and partly to balance the dualism of their world-accommodating ideology of prosperity while simultaneously maintaining their strong holiness ethic which discourages the acquisition of money through dishonest ways.[209] Balancing this dualism seems to be very challenging for most Black Majority Churches. From the foregoing, it is clear that the Black Majority Church in Britain is still a growing body that is gradually revitalizing itself in various areas, but the obvious shortcoming that has affected the credibility of the movement is accountability and the containment of some extreme cultural practices which are the product of the syncretism existing in the theological leanings of some of the Black Majority Churches.

## SUMMARY

The numerical growth of Black Majority Churches in Britain in the last five decades in Britain has moved them from the fringes of obscurity to the limelight. The growth phases of Black Majority Churches have been chronicled by various scholars, and it is pertinent to note that the phases identified overlap. The urban church planting model was pioneered by Bro. Brem-Wilson in 1906 in London and Pastor Daniel Ekarte in 1934 in Liverpool.

The growth of these churches in urban cities was greatly accentuated during the *Windrush* dispensation, with the emergence of West Indian Churches, some of which were affiliated to some American denominations, African Independent Churches and Neo-Pentecostals in the 1980s. There were diverse push and pull factors that have shaped the proliferation and growth of these churches in Britain and ushered in a new paradigm in British church history. The shift in the centre of gravity of reverse mission from the West to Africa, especially Nigeria, has heralded Nigeria and some countries in West Africa as missionary-sending nations to the West and America.

The Black Majority Churches' health check is a new phenomenon in Britain compared with Black Churches in America. Various models reflecting diverse health parameters have been developed over time to determine the health of churches. A major shortcoming of a majority of the churches is the over-reliance on sociological and numerical parameters. A major feature of the growth of some Black Majority Churches in Britain is the fact that transferred growth is a common feature and has been responsible for the homogenous groups in most Black Majority Churches.

The Black Majority Churches are still in a dynamic stage of growth, and the potentials of some of these churches are gradually being celebrated within Britain on account of their social theology. The worship and oral liturgy of the Black Majority Churches have contributed to the increasing dynamism of these churches. As vibrant as Black Majority Churches are, the movement is also synonymous with acute lack of accountability and the ineptitude of some of its leaders. The recent indictments of leaders of some flagship Black Majority Churches are signs of a diseased condition, but evaluating this in the light of the history of the Christian faith in the twenty-first century, it seems that leadership and accountability are two Achilles heels of the Church generally.

*Chapter Four*

# The Distinctive Theological and Practical Features of Black-led Churches in Great Britain

∽

### INTRODUCTION

The proliferation of Black-led Churches in Britain, especially in the late twentieth/early twenty-first centuries, has heralded a renaissance of anthropological, sociological and theological research into the distinctiveness of these churches. The uniqueness of these churches, though broadly referred to as Black-led or Black Majority Churches, is their heterogeneous composition in terms of their denominational and their doctrinal subscription. This heterogeneity has contributed to the shaping of the theologies and leitmotifs of these churches. The apparent influence of liberation theology – a product of the influence of James Cone's fusion of Martin Luther King's and Malcolm X's "theologies" of social equality and social injustice in relation to the egalitarian status of Blacks in America and the repudiation of colonialism – cannot be over-emphasized. Though there exist diverse denominational strands amongst the Black-led Churches, the intriguing and challenging feature of these churches is the absence of generalized theologies common to all the Black-led denominations in Britain. There exist, however, points of convergence on various doctrinal ideals such as prayer, the strong affirmation of literalism in biblical exegesis, works of the Holy Spirit and power evangelism.

A major feature of the Black-led Churches is that most of the theologies of these churches are not necessarily systemic but reflective of the African and Caribbean emancipatory theology which is more of "doing" than written, existential, contextual and experiential. This reinforces the fact that theology is contextually conditioned;[1] the understanding of the conditioned theology of Black Churches in Britain has brought into focus common theological themes of African and Caribbean Christians. This section examines the broad-spectrum theologies of the major denominational strands of Black-led Churches in Britain, the distinction between Oneness Pentecostals and Trinitarian Pentecostals, and the common theological features prevalent amongst most Black-led Churches in Britain.

### DENOMINATIONAL STRANDS OF BLACK-LED CHURCHES

The various denominational strands of Britain's Black-led Churches are a result of a multiplicity of factors including theological orientation, the contextual emergence of these churches and revitalization within these faith communities over time. Theology is dynamic, functional and contextual, as noted by Graham *et al.*[2] According to Gerloff, the Black Majority Churches in Britain exhibit diverse "theological traditions of African and Afro-Caribbean/North American descent",[3] but since this assertion there has been a rapid diversity and influx of more dynamic African Initiated Churches, some classified as Neo-Pentecostal with theological and ecclesiological orientations similar to classical Pentecostal ideals. The Black Majority Churches in Britain are no longer in search of identity but have emerged with a distinctive theological orientation that is reflective of Cone's liberationist or emancipatory theology ideals constructed around the African and Caribbean cosmologies. The heterogeneity of the churches re-defined by Sturge[4] as Black Majority Churches is only relevant in terms of sociological reference, but the composition of their theologies is unique within the context of their cultural praxis.

For instance, Aldred[5] explores the thematic emergence of British Caribbean Christianity and the need to understand its multiple identities, while Reid-Salmon explores the Caribbean Diaspora Church from a transatlantic viewpoint.[6] The likes of Ogbu Kalu[7] and Paul Gifford[8] give a concise historiography and emphasize the thematic uniqueness of African Christianity. Gifford's effort gives a synopsis of the emergence and functionalities of African Churches and their public engagements in Ghana, Uganda and Zambia, but a major weakness of his effort is that, apart from Ghana, the countries investigated in the book are not at the forefront of the ongoing revitalization of Christianity in Africa. Indeed much of his writing, as suggested by the title, was meant to be wholly Afrocentric, but some of his illustrations were steeped with Eurocentric comparisons with the accomplishment and attainments of historic denominations in the countries he investigated. Gifford's effort could have reflected a broad-spectrum appeal but was commensurately limited as Nigeria, which seems to be the hub of the revitalization of Christianity, was not considered.

Gifford also failed to take into consideration the multi-facated diversity of African Pentecostalism. This inevitably resulted in sweeping generalizations in his assessment of African Christianity, ignoring the historical and cultural nuances associated with African religion.

The liberationist and distinctive theological persuasions of the likes of Emmanuel Lartey, Anthony Reddie, Michael N. Jagessar, Robert Beckford and Joe Aldred, who are progenitors of black theology in Britain, have consistently moulded the current Caribbean and African Pentecostal ideals within the ecumenical and independent churches in Britain. These churches are the products of acculturation, cross-fertilization and a synthesis of theological praxis of North American Pentecostalism and the West Indian Pentecostal churches of the 1950s and 1960s. A new paradigm is evolving in relation to black theological studies in Britain through Robert Beckford's theology of de-colonization, with its approach to the reversal of institutional and systemic postulations of Eurocentric views on theology. His book *Jesus is Dread* is indeed the authentic expression of his theology, reflecting his multiple identities as Jamaican and British, and the influence of Rastafarian music (reggae) and contextualizing, within the Caribbean cosmology, its inherent potential to theologize.

### *The Theory of Bewitchment (Beckford)*

The inherent "bewitchment" of African theology, Beckford asserts, had contributed to the perpetuation of the slavery and colonialism of Africans through the inherent anti-intellectualism of Blacks.[9] The Eurocentric missionary perspective has continually enslaved Blacks and their theology. Beckford's articulation of "bewitchment" gives a reverse perspective from the African Traditional Primal Religion to a de-colonized ideal, which gives a new perspective to the political theology of Blacks in Britain. His enculturation of the concept into wider African and Caribbean modes of "Zombie and Cannibal" is a reflection of the African cosmology which Beckford uses as a typology of European bewitchment themes. A major oversight of Beckford's postulation was that the continued retention of colonial influences on African and Caribbean theology after the demise of the slave trade in these continents was partly due to multi-faceted reasons such as the continued conspiracy of Africans to esteem Eurocentrism in preference to Africanization and failure of African and Caribbean Christians to renew their minds on their ecclesiology in relation to political and social injustice. The continued reflective ascriptions of the aftermath of the colonial injustices to the colonial states ought to have caught up with the likes of Beckford but it seems that he is an exception and not the rule for the generality of Africans and Caribbeans involved.

The process of renewal presents a holistic typology, distinctive to the Africans and Caribbeans, of nonconformity to the prevailing bewitchment and slavery mentality of the colonial masters, just as Paul advocated in Romans 12:1–2 that the Roman Christians' lifestyle, behaviour or worldview should not be modulated by the Roman worldview. The failure of renewal is purely a matter of the collective responsibility of the Diaspora generations of Africans and Caribbeans in Britain. Beckford uses the Gerasene model of Mark 5:1–15; he opines that demonic possession, resulting in mental colonization and resonance of zombie behavioural manifestations, suddenly came to an end by reason of Jesus' intervention. This view is further strengthened when we consider Jesus' ministry: Luke asserts in Acts 10:38 that Jesus healed, delivered and restored. The Gerasene model utilised by Beckford fails to view the broader aftermath of the intervention of Jesus. Slavery and colonialism have been terminated in Africa and the Caribbean, although there exists diverse economic slavery that has brought about the emergence of the "fair trade" slogan to African and Caribbean produce. Beckford's role and contributions in sensitizing the British black communities to the effects and implications of the economic policies of Western nations, the World Bank and the international Monetary Fund is replete with deep soul-searching historical, economic and cultural media research. Documentaries broadcast by Channel 4 which include such episodes as "The Great African Scandal" (September 2007), "Empire Pays Back" (August 2005) and "Britain's Slave Trade" (1999), highlight elements of the re-colonization of Africans and Caribbeans.

The former demoniac (Gerasene) was no longer a product of the past, but undeniably the wastage, and the mental and economic colonization of the past could not be atoned for; nevertheless, his renewal was quite astonishing to his community. The age-long self-subscription and apathy coupled with obvious anti-intellectualism and ineptitude shown by Blacks in Britain has contributed to the process of continued mass "bewitchment" of Black Christianity. The Gerasene model, as it were, never had a post-demoniac syndrome, but most Diasporan Africans and Caribbeans have failed to define the authenticity and the uniqueness of their identity as Beckford (*Jesus is Dread*) and Aldred have defined theirs through the approximation of their "Britishness", Caribbean roots and intellectualism.[10]

Beckford's third hub of bewitchment, as depicted by the bicentenary celebration of the Abolition of Slavery at Westminster Abbey in 2008, is the continued influence of colonialism and slavery. Mr Agbetu's pan-

Africanist stance and call for restitution, the desecration of the sacrifices of black ancestors during slavery, and the "zombification" effect of liturgical processes as accentuated by the Westminster scenario, call for a rethink on the political theology agenda of Blacks in Britain. Beckford's recipe of exorcism in itself might constitute a distinctive paradigm to black theology as most Blacks have shown conditioned reflexes to mastery and superiority of Western Christianity. This might constitute a reversal of Hollenweger's rebuttal of Western Christianity in intercultural theology in which Black-led Churches are now claiming superiority over Western Christianity. The voices of the Black Majority Churches provide opportunities for intercultural studies but a sense of superiority over Western Christianity shows "how conditioned, parochial or ideologically captive of our own theology [the Black Majority Church] is".[11] The emerging paradigm is paradoxical. Black Majority Churches in Britain are as guilty as Western Christianity, previously celebrated and accepted, in a Eurocentric way, as the custodian of the Christian faith. African and Caribbean theologies have brought about a shift in thinking whereby any theology outside the context of the West is considered at best inauthentic and hermeneutically flawed. Beckford gives a clarion call to black Christians to "think deeply and courageously to develop new ways of mirroring the egalitarian, counter-cultural values of the Kingdom and seeking out ways of making these resources the basis for social transformation. That is, if your church believes in the equality of all before God, be they men or women, Caribbean or African, young and old."[12] Beckford's recipe is a perspective which might usher in a renewal amongst Black-led Churches in Britain.

Beckford's unique articulation is not only from a scholarly perspective but a product and approximation of his experience as a second-generation Diasporan who witnessed the dynamic tension between the Old and New Identity amongst the second-generation Caribbeans from the *Windrush* era. Beckford has always been an advocate for political engagement of Black Churches to accompany its emphasis on mission and social engagement. The political power of Black Churches is yet to be maximized as it seems to be still in latent mode, but "the example of increasing success within the United Kingdom of Black Christianity offers a model and hope to the rest of Europe of what is possible even from a skeptical and humble beginning".[13]

## BLACK-LED CHURCHES AND TRADITIONAL PENTECOSTALISM

The Black Majority Churches in Britain are unique despite emerging within diverse contexts, but demonstrate convergence on various doctrinal positions and religious practices which are similar to those of the European Pentecostal Churches like Elim Pentecostal Church and Assemblies of God in terms of "modes of worship, degrees of participation, styles of leadership, doctrines, understanding of 'holiness' and racial inclusiveness or exclusiveness".[14] Hollenweger observed that Pentecostals are noted for "oral liturgy, narativity of theology and witness, maximum participation at all levels of reflection, prayer and decision-making and therefore a form of community which is reconciliatory; an understanding of the body/mind: the most striking application of this insight is the ministry of healing by prayer".[15] These features are common within most Black Majority Churches in Britain.

MacRobert also noted that features like periodic hand clapping, congregational participation in the sermon, the experiential pneuma-centric focus in the services and baptism by immersion are generic Pentecostal practices, some of which are synonymous with the African Traditional Primal Religious practices.[16] These generic features are core sociological and behavioural traits of early Pentecostalism; the current growth and proliferation of African Pentecostalism explains its significance to Africans. MacRobert noted that 80% of the membership of Black Majority Churches are Pentecostals.[17] This percentage might have increased in the wake of theological and ecclesiological renewals amongst some African "Spiritual" churches as well as the meteoric growth of Black Majority Churches, which is estimated at about four thousand churches in Britain today.[18] Some of these Black Majority Churches, like the Church of God of Prophecy, have undergone revitalization. The process of revitalization has generated diverse strains within some of these churches, resulting, for example, in litigation, as is the case with the Church of God of Prophecy on doctrinal (exclusivity) and exegetical issues.[19]

Gerloff's *Plea for Black Theologies* (1992) gives insight into the denominational strands amongst Black Majority Churches in Britain. She identifies eleven categories of denominational strands amongst Black Churches in Britain but the scope of this research is within the Black Majority Churches Pentecostal group which she identified as "Holiness Churches; Trinitarian Pentecostals of the two-stage and three-stage crisis; Oneness (Apostolic) Pentecostals; Revival (Healing) Pentecostals".[20] She observed the effect of racism by the American Assemblies of God as a major inhibitor to the spread of the AOG two-stage-crisis experience amongst the West Indian churches of the 1960s. The three-stage Trinitarian Pentecostals have significant adherents in Britain, with over 600 churches, including three of the largest Pentecostal Churches in Britain, namely the Redeemed Christian Church of God, New Testament Church of God and Church of God of Prophecy. MacRobert, however, noted that the Church of God of Prophecy once rejected the term Pentecostal because of the assumption that the church emerged on the day of Pentecost, which was antithetical to the teachings of the Church of God of Prophecy at the time.[21]

The New Testament Church of God, the Church of God of Prophecy, the Apostolic Church of Jesus Christ, the Wesleyan Holiness Church and the African Methodist Episcopal Church were all denominations with international affiliations.[22] Prominent Charismatic and Pentecostal churches in the United Kingdom include the Redeemed Christian Church of God, Glory House, Faith Tabernacle, Ruach Ministries and Victory Christian Centre. Victory Christian Centre was taken over by Pastor Douglas Goodman in a former dance hall in Kilburn, North London in 1996, but foreclosed by the Charity Commission of England and Wales on 18 December 2002 on account of mismanagement and misconduct. The church has now re-emerged as Victory to Victory, started by Erica Goodman after the foreclosure. Victory to Victory is now led by Pastor Douglas Goodman on his release from prison.

Kingsway International Christian Centre and the other churches mentioned above were African and Caribbean Independent Churches that emerged in Britain in the late 1980s and early 1990s with strong charismatic and Trinitarian Pentecostal ideals. There exists a general consensus amongst scholars that the majority of the Black Majority Churches in Britain are Trinitarian Pentecostals.[23] There seems to be a trend amongst Black Majority Churches, akin to the American model, of couples pastoring a church together.

### Oneness Pentecostalism amongst Black Majority Churches in Britain

The Oneness Pentecostals within Britain's Black Majority Churches are intricately linked with the American Oneness theology, which has its roots in the "New Issue" polemics. This can be traced back to the pre-emergence of Pentecostalism, according to David K. Bernard, in his book *Oneness and Trinity: A.D. 100–300*, where he stated that the teachings of Praxeas, Noetus, Sabellius and others lay behind the theological postulation of the movement.[24] Bernard identified various distinctions between contemporary Oneness Pentecostal beliefs and primordial Modalistic Monarch-ianism. The contemporary renaissance of Oneness two-stage Pentecostalism is inextricably linked with the doctrinal disputations which occurred within the American Assemblies of God, which further led to the split of the church in 1916.

Prior to 1908, Pentecostals generally affirmed the three-stage soteriology, but the genesis of the doctrinal disputation was traced by Brumback[25] to William H. Durham, who taught soteriology with two-stage conversions and Spirit Baptism. Carl Brumback, the historian of the all-white Assemblies of God, described the emergence of the disputations as a "distressing error which almost ruined the work of God"[26] but Gerloff also noted that James Richardson, the historian of Black Apostolic denominations in the United States, viewed it as essentially an "extension of the Pentecostal Church".[27] The doctrinal landscape of the early Pentecostals was given further impetus by the experience of John G. Scheppe, as he listened to an exposition given by Canadian Pentecostal leader Robert McAlister on Acts 2:38 and baptism in the "name of Jesus". Thrilled by the insight and revelations during an all-night prayer meeting at a campsite meeting in Arroyo Seco, California in 1913, he began to share his experiences with other attendees, according to John Ankerberg and John Weldon.[28]

According to Anderson, the newly formed Assemblies of God was almost "consumed" with the controversy, as the church asserted the Trinitarian position in 1916 with the exit of "156 ministers from Assemblies of God (AG) including Ewart and Haywood [the only prominent black member; this later had a far-reaching effect on AG as the racial dimension was added to the 'New Issue' schism] as they were barred from fellowship".[29] This led to the emergence of splinter groups which later re-aligned in 1945 to form the United Pentecostal Church, Inc. Anderson states that "by the end of the 1920s three of every five Pentecostals had adopted the finished work view of sanctification" but he observes that "the finished work movement proved far more attractive to Whites than Blacks".[30]

David Edwin Harrell in his critique of white sects and black men opined that ethnic and communal views of Pentecostals were influenced by class stratification rather than theological presuppositions; he observed that racial integration often occurred in the poorest "sects" (denominations) like the Church of God and the Church of God of Prophecy (USA) in which the social stratification is either rich or poor with no middle-class focus.[31] It is imperative to note that a similar trend was adduced by

Anderson in his book *Vision of the Disinherited*, where he identified the strangeness of the industrialized economy compared to the familiar agrarian economy of most migrants from the Caribbean as a beacon of attraction to Pentecostalism as the migrants suffered from "status anxiety".[32] The escapism from the social deprivation amongst the Blacks became the attraction to Oneness theology; as Anderson noted, this was also evident in the social origin of Pentecostalism.[33]

The attraction to Oneness theology by the Blacks was more of a racial and cultural protest as they were apolitical and as such their commitment became a default mechanism to cope with prevailing social-cultural challenges which were expressed by their religious ideology. A similar perspective is expressed by Mickey Crews in his study of Church of God, Cleveland, as he posited that the populist movement and Church of God emerged amongst farmers with similar socio-economic status.[34]

The growth of the Oneness Pentecostal movement is traceable to the inadequacies of Trinitarian Pentecostals to articulate their Trinitarian doctrinal persuasion. The proselytization of the splinter group was aggressive, as noted by David Reed in Burgess *et al.*, but I think that the doctrinal divide reflected a racial dichotomy and the prevailing racial and ethnocentric ideology prevalent in America at the time.[35] As Mitchell posited, the ability of the Oneness Pentecostal movement to acculturate itself with the "Blacks and urban North America" was the catalyst for its missionary success "up in the hills" of Jamaica and other Caribbean islands.[36] Consequently, the West Indian Churches in Britain constitute the majority of the churches that affirm Oneness Pentecostal ideals. The missionary endeavours of British Oneness Pentecostals have replicated Oneness theology in Africa, India and Pakistan.

Peter Brierley gives an overview of the membership and congregation of Oneness Apostolic Churches in England as 256 churches with a membership of 15,435 in 2010.[37] The Oneness Apostolic churches seems to enjoy marginal growth in terms of numbers of churches and membership as in 2005, there were 205 churches and membership of 13,145.[38] However, in a previous research conducted by Gerloff citing Peter Brierley, it was asserted that there were over 200 congregations and membership of 21,000 in Britain. Gerloff further noted that Oneness Pentecostals in the United Kingdom "formed approximately one third of black Pentecostalism".[39]

The increase in growth might be due to multiple reasons which might include the continued relevance of the churches' social action and liberationist disposition as the churches acculturated themselves with the socially deprived Black Diasporans in the 1970s, 1980s and 1990s. The social theology of the Oneness Pentecostals in Britain in the 1980s and 1990s fostered ecumenical fraternization, community initiatives and "social responsibilities".[40] The words "Apostolic", "Bibleway" or "Shiloh" are synonymous with almost all Oneness Pentecostals.[41] Oneness Pentecostals in Britain include Pentecostal Assemblies of the World (the oldest in Britain), the Church of our Lord Jesus Christ (Apostolic), First United Church of Jesus Christ (Apostolic), Mount Zion Pentecostal Church (Apostolic), Rehoboth Emmanuel Church of Jesus Christ (Apostolic) and Shiloh United Church of Christ, according to MacRobert.[42]

### Black-led Churches: Two- and Three-Stage Pentecostalism

The membership of three-stage Pentecostals in Britain today is difficult to ascertain. There are multiple reasons for this, such as the proliferation of these churches, schisms, and the lack of any up-to-date database. These churches subscribe to the original three-stage teachings of Charles Parham and William Seymour. MacRobert observed that the dissimilarity between most Pentecostals and three-stage Pentecostals is that two-stage Pentecostals "agreed on the nature of and necessity for justification", but the three-stage Pentecostals teach that a second crisis experience is necessary and that the penitent may be "instantaneously sanctified".[43] Some of the three-stage Pentecostals in Britain include the New Testament Church of God, Church of God of Prophecy, The United Church of God, The Church of God Fellowship, Calvary Resurrected Church of God and the African Methodist Episcopal Zion Church.[44]

## DISTINCTIONS BETWEEN ONENESS AND TRINITARIAN PENTECOSTAL DOCTRINE

The doctrinal differences between the Oneness Pentecostal and Trinitarian Pentecostal doctrine amongst Britain's Black Majority Churches are reflective of the inherent theological influence of the American denominational positions that were taken with missionary zeal to the West Indies in the founding days of the Trinitarian Pentecostal movement which was the precursor for the spread of Oneness theology amongst Black Majority Churches in Britain in the 1950s, 1960s and 1970s. However, MacRobert in his thesis observed the existence of certain incongruities amongst some Oneness Pentecostals which emerged from three-stage Pentecostal antecedents.[45]

The Oneness Pentecostal and Trinitarian Pentecostal theologies amongst Britain's Black Majority Churches have identical features, with the exception of three irreconcilable theological and doctrinal assertions.[46] The theological distinctives of Oneness Pentecostals are modalistic and repudiate the doctrine of Trinity, baptism using the name of Jesus and Sanctification.

### Doctrine of Trinity

The doctrine of Trinity has been completely rejected by various denominations and sectarian groups, including the Jehovah's Witnesses, The Way International and the Church of God International. The doctrine of Trinity, according to Oneness apologists, was a product of the approximations of the pagan Greco-Roman traditions and is unbiblical, as the word "trinity" was never utilised in the scripture and as such is pagan in its historicity and usage.[47] The concept of Trinity, according to Boyd, had its origin in pagan civilizations who believed in "triadic deities" (tritheism), which were the three most distinguished gods at the top of a pyramid of other lesser gods, similar to polytheism.

According to Oneness Pentecostal apologist David K. Bernard, the author of *Oneness of God*,

> We believe that Trinitarianism is not a biblical doctrine and that it contradicts the Bible in many ways. The scriptures do not teach a trinity of persons. The doctrine of trinity uses terminology not used in the scripture. It teaches and emphasizes plurality in Godhead while the Bible emphasizes Oneness of God. It detracts from the fullness of Jesus Christ's deity. It contradicts many specific verses of the scripture. It is not logical. No one can understand or explain it rationally, not even those who advocate it. In short Trinitarianism is a doctrine that does not belong to Christianity.[48]

Bernard's apology gives a broad-spectrum representation of the Oneness position on Trinity; he further posits that Trinitarian theology leads to "Tritheism"[49] but this misconception is fraught with exegetical mistranslations. The central fault line of Oneness theology as observed by Bowman is the modern misunderstanding of the word "persons" with respect to the distinctions within the Trinity (Father, Son and Holy Spirit).[50] More correctly, the word "persons" implies that each member of the Trinity is absolutely autonomous with respect to others, to the point of being dissimilar with others, according to Milne.[51] The Greek and Latin etymology of the word used for "person" (*prosopon, persona*) contradicts the contemporary thought line, as *prosopon* does not ascribe individualism to the Trinity. However, Prestige, a patristic scholar, noted that the term originally meant "face" until in the fifth century its meaning changed to "representative" or "type".[52] Prestige further posits that the concept of

Trinity is supposedly predicated on the Christian doctrine of *perichoresis* which repudiates Tritheism, as all of God is present in each "person".[53]

Prestige identified differences in the interpretation of "persons" in the Greek and Latin perspectives, as he notes that, "Augustine was neither alarmed nor surprised to find that the Greeks interpreted the Trinity differently from the Latins."[54] He noted that Augustine asserted that "for the sake of describing things ineffable, that we may be able in some way to express what we are in no way able to express fully, our Greek friends have spoken of one essence and three substances, but the Latins of one essence or substance and three persons". Augustine's conclusion on the doctrine of Trinity was that the modalities of the finite are not able to understand the infinite, as such a doctrine is beyond human comprehension, and he concluded that it was a mystery.

Karl Barth's articulation on *perichoresis* was the genesis of the various theological discourses in the twentieth century. He was of the view that there must be a process of demystifying Augustine's perception, as he said "all rational wrestling with this mystery, the more serious it is, can lead only to its fresh and authentic interpretation and manifestation as mystery".[55] Though Barth was criticized for his modalist disposition, he refuted this as he subscribed to the distinctiveness of the three persons of the Trinity.[56] Contemporary scholars in the mould of Thomas Torrance[57] and Colin Gunton[58] have used the *perichoresis* model to depict the interrelatedness of the cosmos in relation to the functionalities of the persons in the Trinity.

Trinitarians opine that the word "person" is connotative of the difference that exists in one eternal God. The relationship between the three distinctions is identified in the use of three eternal and Divine Persons, who are exemplified in the New Testament: the Incarnation of Jesus (John 3:16; Gal 4:14; 1Jn 4:9) and the Dispensation of Grace in which the Father and Son send the Holy Spirit (John 14:26; 15:26; 16:7; Gal 4:6). The functional relationship between the Father and Son is depicted in Matt 11:25; 36:39 and John 17, while the Son also addresses the Holy Spirit as another (John 14:16–17, 25–26; 16:5–15) whose function is to glorify the Son (John 16:14) with a similar objective by the Son to the Father (John 17:1–4).

Trinitarians argue that for the identified functionalities it is implicit that the Father, Son and Spirit are more than the one person who is operating in the various functions. The use of the personal pronoun, such as "He" instead of "it", for each function and "another" in place of a "thing"[59] further asserts the Trinitarian position. There exists a general consensus amongst Trinitarian apologists that the concept of "Persons" has obvious functional disadvantages, but there is no other word that has been agreed as a better synonym despite the limitations and misconceptions associated with it.[60]

John Calvin expressed relational ties between the Persons of the Trinity:

> Scripture sets forth a distinction of the Father from the Word and of the Word from the Spirit. Yet the greatness of the mystery warns us how much reverence and sobriety we ought to use in investigating this. And that passage in Gregory of Nazianzus vastly delights me: "I cannot think on the one without quickly being encircled by the splendor of the three; nor can I discern the three without being straightway carried back to the one." Let us not, then, be led to imagine a trinity of persons that keeps our thoughts distracted and does not at once lead them back to that unity. Indeed, the words "Father," "Son," and "Spirit" imply a real distinction – let no one think that these titles, whereby God is variously designated from his works, are empty – but a distinction, not a division.[61]

The general Oneness claim of non-biblical heritage of the word Trinity is true, but Oneness theology makes use of non-biblical words to describe its theology. Similar polemics also exist in some sectarian organizations like Jehovah's Witnesses.[62]

### *Baptism in Jesus' Name*

The genesis of the current disputations of the triadic baptism model and the "Jesus' name" perspective of Oneness apologists was in 1913. Prior to this, both models were effectively used to administer baptism by early Pentecostals, including Charles Parham, who shifted ground four times on his theology by using the "triadic formulae", Dowie's model (triple immersion) and simple baptismal approach of Jesus' name.[63]

The pre-baptismal preaching of Canadian Robert McAlister in a camp meeting near Los Angeles culminated in the emergence of baptism as a divisive issue, as he concluded his homily by asserting, "The Apostles invariably baptized their converts once in the name of Jesus Christ; the words Father, Son and Holy Ghost were never used in Christian Baptism".[64] This was further accentuated by G. Sheppe during the camp meeting and the "Canadian triad" in the form of Thomas Haywood (a multi-gifted man who was known as an evangelist, editor and hymn writer), G.A. Chambers and McAlister, particularly in the Assemblies of God. Another major advocate of Oneness was evangelist Frank Ewert, whose ministry was impacted by McAlister, and which contributed to his affirmation of

Oneness theology. The schism of "New Issues" within Assemblies of God was the open door for Oneness apologists to leave the Assemblies of God in 1916.

The simple baptismal model of Jesus' name based on Matthew 28:19 thus became a contentious issue amongst Oneness apologists and Pentecostals as they stressed that the command was to baptize in his name and not in the Trinity. Jesus' name baptism apologists further substantiate their view by citing the apostolic generation that copiously baptized in the name of Jesus (Acts 2:38; 8:16; 19:5) and not plurality of titles, but it is important to note, with Boyd, that there was no general consensus in the baptismal formula of the Apostles in the book of Acts, as Acts 2:38 has "on [epi] the name of Jesus Christ"; Acts 8:16 and 19:5 have "into [eis] the name of the Lord Jesus"; and in Acts 10:48, as Luke wrote, believers were baptized "in [en] the name of the Lord", with variation in some texts that read "Jesus Christ" and others "Jesus".[65]

MacRobert stated that "fundamentalists cannot admit to the contradictions and their view of inspiration ruled out any consideration of textual, literary or form criticism although paradoxically, this anomaly is explained away by using artifice vaguely akin to linguistic criticism" as the triadic baptismal formula needs to be clarified with reference to water baptism in the books of Acts and Pauline Epistles.[66] Bernard, a Oneness theology apologist, disputes that Jesus is not the name of the Father, Son and Holy Spirit, but salvation is predicated on absolute performance of baptism in His name – but this will contradict the overall witness of the New Testament as Jesus recognized the distinctiveness of the Father, Son and Holy Spirit.[67] As such it seems impossible to affirm that Jesus was in some way referring to Himself as all three in Matthew 28:19.[68] The resonance of water baptism using the simple formula of Oneness theology has "rapidly developed into an understanding of the Godhead which was in direct conflict with the crude, simplistic and anthropomorphic understanding of the Trinity which most of the two-stage Pentecostals adhered to".[69]

The "name of" according to the Greek, Semitic and rabbinical cultural milieu of the first century has multiple meanings, which creates ambiguity of interpretation. The underlying historical-cum-cultural context of the usage is defined by Beasley-Murray.[70] For instance, Matthew 10:40–42 speaks of receiving a prophet "in the name of" a prophet, a righteous man "in the name of" a righteous man, etc., clearly meaning to receive such a one because of who they were and not by simply receiving them with the words "I greet you in the name of a prophet". Another point of reference is in rabbinical literature: it is a common sight to read phrases in which pagan slaves were expected to receive a baptism "in the name of slavery" (understood to mean "being immersed into") under the authority of a Jewish family. Similarly Samaritans circumcise "in the name of Mount Gerizim". Because of the historical/cultural context of the phrase "in the name of", Beasley-Murray thus posits that in the context of Matthew 28:19 it might originally mean "in the authority of" or "for the sake of" the Father, Son and Holy Spirit. The same can also be said of the book of Acts when it speaks of baptism being administered "in Jesus' name".[71]

### Trifocal Soteriology Model

The trifocal salvation model is the third distinctive doctrine of Oneness Pentecostals. The principal soteriological text is found in Acts 2:38: "Men and brethren, what shall we do? Then Peter said unto them, 'Repent and be baptized every one of you in the name of Jesus Christ for the remissions of sins, and you shall receive the gift of the Holy Ghost.'"

Peter's words are the basis of the Oneness theology of the triad pathway to salvation, as it is required that anyone who is saved must have repented of his or her sins, been baptized in Jesus' name and been filled with Spirit with evidence of glossolalia. The largest Oneness Pentecostal Assemblies of the world define the basis of the membership of the church on the three religious experiences, namely baptism in water in Jesus' name, being filled with the Holy Ghost and the experience of glossolalia. The trifocal soteriological order of Oneness Pentecostal theology has generated diverse doctrinal and theological discourses on the appropriateness of such assertions, though Oneness Pentecostals do not ascribe to glossolalia any salvific value. However, individuals who have received the Holy Spirit will be saved and exhibit the gift of tongues.

## COAT OF MANY COLOURS: THEOLOGIES OF BLACK MAJORITY CHURCHES IN BRITAIN

The heterogeneity of Black Majority Churches in Britain in terms of sociology, nationalities, denominational affiliations and religious observance are replicated also in the diversity of their theologies and doctrinal persuasions. There are several attempts by various scholars to chronicle the emergence of theologies of the Caribbeans and Africans. Reid-Salmon gives a graphic basis for his treatise on emancipation theology of the Caribbeans as inclusive and exclusive of liberation theology. He opines that, "Caribbean theology engages the Caribbean experience as it relates to local and universal struggle for emancipation to constitute one of the theological foundations of the Diaspora church."[72] This is predicated on the historical antecedents and the diverse social-cultural alienation experienced by African-Americans during the transatlantic slave trade, akin to the British context chronicled by Aldred, which is an authentic expression of the Christian faith but not a reactional theological response to Eurocentric or Western theology.[73] The convergence between Caribbean and African theology is reflected in the retention of African cosmology during the Christianization of the Caribbeans by European missionaries, as Philip Curtin observes: "Since the whites were not anxious to force Europeanisation further than was necessary for plantation work, the slaves were left to educate their own children. Consequently, there developed a new culture, compounded of the diverse African and European elements."[74]

Similar colonial imperialism is replicated amongst the Africans; as has been observed, the political motivation of colonialism was behind mission in Africa. This has resulted in the emergence of an African Christianity with a distinctive African flavour that incorporates the African Christian experiences and identity. This opens up a distinctive paradigm alien to Eurocentric Christians but a unique experience of the story of salvation by Blacks. This has created dynamic faith which is practical and existential. Black Churches' theologies in Britain have become a type of Noah's Ark to ride over the floods of racism, social deprivation and assimilation challenges which have gradually alienated the churches towards cultural captivity, contradictory to the Macedonian mandate of re-Christianization of Britain espoused by most Black-led Churches.

Relevant here is not only the convergence of the African and Caribbean theology but also their inclusion of liberation theological ideals. This approach is based on decolonization theology that takes "experience as a starting point". The broad denominational distinctions highlighted in the preceding sections cannot suffice as the basis to derive generalized theologies of Black Majority Churches in Britain, as even within the Trinitarians there are diverse church doctrinal persuasions that to an evangelical theologian might constitute a sectarian feature. Some of the Black Majority Churches in Britain that have international affiliations are reflective of the doctrinal positions of their wider national or international affiliations. The theologies of most Black Majority Churches are a reflection of the inherent denominational affiliations that they subscribe to, but Sturge observes that there seem not to be any misconceptions that the doctrinal persuasions of Black Majority Churches are antithetical to the historic churches.[75]

This, however, is unsubstantiated. It suffices to note that there seem to be elements of extremism or exegetical inadequacies on some doctrinal positions within some churches, as it was with the Church of God of Prophecy in Britain on the doctrine of exclusivity, as observed by Aldred, but this was an issue of "crossover syndrome" with the denominational affiliation from the headquarters of the church in America.[76] It is imperative to assert that though there are elements of syncretism in the doctrinal persuasion of some Black Churches, the problem is not peculiar to Black Majority Churches but a general feature in the history of the church at large.

Chigor Chike, in his book *African Christianity in Britain*, examined the "Diasporal effect" in relation to some biblical doctrines as espoused by African Pentecostals in Africa and Diaspora. He noted that there seem to be arising dissimilarities between the Diasporan Africans and African preachers as a result of the fluidity of the Western culture, as elements of rationalization are expressed by the Diasporans. A major flaw of his treatise is the broad generalization of his submission, as there exist diverse exegetical and ecclesiological traditions in various doctrines amongst Pentecostals inclusive of African and Caribbean Pentecostals. The over-reliance on reviews of books of African preachers by Chike is not in its entirety a true reflection of African theology; it is not systemic theology but more of "doing". Warrington's effort to give concise treatment to Pentecostal theology was from a European perspective, as his main objective was "to focus on a Pentecostal theology which is defined by distinctive elements of Pentecostal belief and praxis but especially by an under girding Pentecostal philosophy".[77]

His exploration was centred on the Western model, as the focus of his writing was on North Atlantic Pentecostalism. This is not an encompassing work in terms of global Pentecostalism, as most of his sources and works cited were predominantly Western. Warrington's treatise failed to reflect adequately the shift in the growth of Pentecostalism from North America to the Global South with the very prolific growth rate in Asia and Africa as he mentioned few African churches, but the work is quite relevant within the Western context. The late illustrious African Pentecostalism writer, Ogbu Kalu, in the book *African Pentecostalism: An Introduction* gave a well articulated overview of the history, socio-political elements and theological probables that have honed African Pentecostalism. He was of the opinion that African Pentecostalism was the product of contextualization of the Gospel by Africans, and that "the effort has been made to retell the story of African Pentecostalism by paying attention to space, time, themes, and various scholarly discourses. The overarching conceptual scheme indicates that African Pentecostalism emerged from African indigenous and cultural responses to the gospel message."[78] Because of the defining colouration of Black Majority Churches which is primed by the African and Caribbean praxis, it seems the inherent inter-relatedness of African Pentecostal challenges as noted by Kalu is inevitable amongst Black Majority Churches in Britain.

The modification of Kalu's concern with the words in brackets is my submission which is an appropriate avenue to give an overview of the principal theologies of Black Majority Churches in Britain. Kalu asked:

> How do Pentecostal [Black Majority Churches'] theologies [in Britain] connect the conception of salvation with issues of contemporary significance like poverty, wealth, prosperity, health, healing and the reconstruction of daily life? Is African [African and Caribbean] Pentecostalism a genre of fundamentalism? Finally, how do Pentecostals [Black Majority Churches in Britain] read and preach the Bible and claim the enduring, archaic power of its oral nature?[79]

This prescription in its entirety will inevitably be outside the immediate scope of this study, as it is inclusive of public engagement theology, whereas my treatise is on the distinctive theological praxis amongst Black Majority Churches. From my perspective as a member and minister in one of Britain's Black Majority Churches, I agree with MacRobert that Black Pentecostal (Black Majority Churches') theology is more than "statements of doctrine, ethics and values". It is more of an experiential faith as people seek to have "ongoing encounters of the divine to confirm their faith, and the ultimate truths which banish anxiety are conveyed in symbol, story, song and liturgical motor behaviour to the unconscious".[80]

The copious statements of faith of most Black-led Churches are a reflection of the North American influences, as theology to most Black-led Churches in Britain is seeing and experiencing God in every facet of their life. *Black Theology in Britain*, edited by Reddie and Jagessar, gives a thematic perspective of black theologies in Britain which depends on comparative analysis with the American black theology. The uniqueness of their treatise is that its focus is thematic rather than taking a historiographical perspective which is overly dependent on the American black theology.[81] This should not be accepted as a demerit but a deliberate thematic feature of their work, which gives a concise comparative account of British black theologies in relation to American black theologies. The obvious inference is the convergence of certain features of both theologies which might hitherto have been glossed over. This work, rather than being restrictive, provides broad-spectrum and incisive comparisons of transatlantic black theologies.

### Hallmarks of Black Majority Churches' Theologies

The inherent heterogeneity of Black Majority Churches in Britain make it a herculean task to succinctly harmonize their theologies, but Robert Beckford noted that the hallmarks of Black Pentecostalism in Britain are expressed in three unique theological categories, which are: the experience of God, a vibrant spirituality and empowering worship.[82] This further reignites the observation of Hollenweger that theology is contextually conditioned, but he was of the opinion that no expression of the Christian faith can be adjured as the best *modus operandi*: this, in Hollenweger's perspective, will assist in intercultural theology.[83] The shift from North American Pentecostalism to the Global South and the resonance of the replication of the growth of Black Majority Churches in Britain will significantly contribute to the renewal process of black theology and its "catholicity".[84] The multiplicity of the variation within the Black Majority Churches thus creates multiple theological traditions amongst these churches, but there exist elements of convergence on some theological issues.

### The Use of the Bible Amongst Black Majority Churches in Britain

A principal feature of African Christianity identified by various scholars has been the strong affirmation of the Bible.[85] John Mbiti, an African scholar, articulated this explicitly as he noted that "the Bible is making indelible marks on the religious scene in Africa. It is read widely, it is expounded from pulpits, street corners, market places, on radio and television, as well as a wide range of publications."[86] The Bible thus is the epicentre of African Christianity. This is true not only in terms of expression and affirmation, but economic space is also gradually becoming Christianized. As observed by Anderson: "small businesses in cities [in Nigeria and Ghana] proclaim its influence: 'In the name of Jesus Enterprises', 'To God be the Glory Computers', 'Hands of God Beauty Salon', 'El Shaddai Fast Foods', 'God is Able Cold Store'".[87]

The Christianization of economic space by Africans observed by Anderson is a variation of the theophanic biblical narratives which the business owners affirm as an imprecatory and defining model to enhance their economic initiatives and a seal of divine endorsement. He also noted that every social space has a signage of a church, a fellowship or a Christian slogan. Even stickers on bumpers of automobiles display such slogans as "With Jesus I Always Win" and "Your Success Is Determined By Your Faith".[88] The biblical influence on Africans is almost a transnational phenomenon, as Burgess similarly noted that the Old Kent Road in London is replete with the signage of Black Majority Churches such as the Holy Ghost Zone, Winners Temple, New Covenant Church, Holy Ghost Arena, Foursquare Gospel Church, Inspiration House and Victory House.[89]

The gradual "biblicafication"[90] signage of these Black Majority Churches on the Old Kent Road competes favourably with other service providers; they might be an unconscious attempt by these churches to blur the secular and religious space divide on one of London's longest roads and reposition themselves within the framework of laying claim to divine ownership of economic, secular and social space based on the psalmist's assertion that "the earth is the Lord's, and the fullness thereof; the world, and they that dwell therein" (Ps 24:1).

Various convention themes include "Overcomers Conference", "Let God Arise", "Taking Your Territories", "Winds of Change", "Preparing for Greatness" and "The Regenerated Man", which are features of Health and Wealth ideologies which intricately link "material success and spiritual success",[91] especially in the south-east of London which has the highest percentage of African migrants. Ironically, however, such neighbourhoods are "wracked by poverty, gang violence [including gun crime], substandard education, and pervasive drug and alcohol abuse".[92]

Chike was of the opinion that there exists a positive correlation with the use of many quotations from the Bible amongst African Christians and African Diasporan Christians in Britain, but opined that there exist variations in their biblical worldview which might be attributable to socio-political differences in the British context and the use of human reason in theological discourse.[93] Chike failed, however, to explore the changes within the British cultural paradigm that have brought about the variation in the expression of the faith of African and Caribbean Diasporans in Britain as a result of assimilation. The scope of his book was Afrocentric, and inevitably failed to reflect the entire constituencies of Black Majority Churches, as the Caribbean perspective was not considered. Most Black Majority Church members are selectively assimilated into the British culture, as they continue to maintain their cultural identity with a strong desire to worship in ethnic churches, are educated, and often speak English with distinctive African or Caribbean accents – a common feature amongst the first generation but almost non-existent among the second generation, who are linguistically acculturated.

The process of the changes within the British cultural paradigm as a result of late modernity or postmodernity invariably has divergent effects on second-generation Diaspora Africans who are members of Black Majority Churches, and this resonates on their faith and identity.[94] The effects of globalization and the consequential effects of changes as a result of migration of Diasporans of African and Caribbean descent in Britain ushers in a new socio-cultural paradigm alien to their former socio-cultural orientations, and in trying to interpret these changes members of the Black Majority Churches turn to those "sections of the Bible that portray Jews and, later, Christians trying to exist and survive under the shadow of dominant empires and cultures, often far from their homeland".[95] A typical example is Leke Sanusi's 2006 publication, *Take it by Force: How to Possess your Possession*, an exposition of the Jewish liberation from Egypt as a typology for Christians to go far in life. He was able to draw a lot of allegories from the scripture: his exegesis was more of liberation theology and literary interpretation. Sanusi cited the testimony of an immigrant who was given a four-year leave to remain in the United Kingdom by the Home Office, but according to Sanusi the lady prayed, fasted and had the conviction that she was entitled to indefinite leave, which he claimed was granted to her.[96]

Humanism constitutes a major emphasis in the subjective interpretation of the scriptures amongst the Black Majority Churches in Britain. Most Black Majority Church members want to see the Bible as relevant to their ongoing challenges such as assimilation, immigration, poverty, social justice and racism, and it is for this reason that proof-texting often brings about contemporary relevance to the preaching of Britain's Black Majority Church leaders.

There seems to be a strong veneration for the Old Testament by most preachers within the Black Majority Churches in Britain. A survey of the most-favoured texts amongst African Diasporans, as observed by Chike, is similar to that observed in African Christianity generally.[97] Among Old Testament books, Genesis is the most often cited, with Exodus and Isaiah. The wisdom books have great appeal amongst Black Majority Churches in Britain. From my experience as a church leader with the Black Majority Churches, the use of wisdom books, Exodus and Isaiah, is quite pronounced amongst the first-generation Nigerians in Britain, but the second and third generations might not be comfortable with every minute example of moral or social etiquette in the book of Proverbs.

Achebe illustrated the familiarity of Africans with proverbs and this has resonance in the strong affirmation that most Africans find in the

Book of Proverbs. He observed that "proverbs to Africans [are] the spice by which Africans chew kola".[98] For instance, according to the Yoruba, the second largest tribe in Nigeria, an adage says, "Lékèélékèé òyé ẹyin dúdú; funfun ni won ńyé ẹyin won" ("Cattle egrets never lay black eggs; only white eggs do they lay"), which, within the Yoruba context, implies that only certain types of behaviour are suitable for people in certain positions.

The use of proverbs within the African and Caribbean cultural context was normative, and most Africans and Caribbeans can identify well with the wisdom books. Moreover, "the oral literature of the African people is their unwritten Bible. This religious wisdom is found in the African idioms, wise sayings, legends, myths, stories, proverbs and oral history."[99] Waske's assertion has enjoyed the endorsement of the Catholic faith, as Majioga noted that a modern Catholic Bible commentary finds "no contradiction between biblical wisdom and African wisdom since both are based on human experience and inspired by God".[100]

Biblical interpretation amongst Africans is deemed to be of high significance. The ongoing Anglican Communion "schism" on the ordination of gay priests has further given African Christianity the platform to articulate their strong adherence to their "fundamentalist" ideals on the inerrancy of the scriptures as Akinola, the former leader of Anglican Communion in Nigeria, asserted that "In this Church [Anglican Communion, Nigeria] we teach about the total depravity of man and his absolute need for salvation through faith in Jesus the Christ. For us, therefore, adherence to scripture is not only paramount, it is also non-negotiable. In matters of faith and practice, scripture provides sufficient warrant for what is considered right and what is judged to be wrong."[101] This has invariably led to the Global South Christianity being labelled as "fundamentalist". Wright regards fundamentalist interpretation of the scripture as "literalist and wooden".[102] From the Western perspective Pentecostalism "was the synthesis of late nineteenth century fundamentalist, dispensational and holiness theology".[103]

The World Christian Fundamentals Association dis-fellowshipped Pentecostals in 1928.[104] However, the hermeneutical style of Pentecostalism was shaped by absolute commitment to literalism and inerrancy of the scriptures and as such they are considered to be hyper fundamentalists. This is similar to the branding of the Nigerian Anglican Communion on the ongoing theological schism on the ordination of gays as priests due to their (the Nigerian Synod's) subscription to inerrancy of the scripture.

## The Distinctive Theological and Practical Features of Black-led Churches 135

Wright, quoting Gabriel Fackre, gives vivid insight into the notion of fundamentalist engagement of the scripture. Fackre noted:

> Fundamentalist evangelicals [Pentecostals] hold unswerving to "biblical inerrancy", the belief that the biblical text, being inspired by God, participates in the quality of divine life to the extent that it is without "errors" of any type. The Bible is not only theologically true therefore, but literally true at every point on whatever subject it deals with, whether nature, history or doctrine. By mutual comparison, certain statements can be seen to be metaphorical in force, for instance, because "God is Spirit" anthropomorphic references to God are not taken literally. But the Bible can never be subjected to criticism from points outside itself, for instance modern science or understandings of history, since this would be to surrender its authority to earthly authorities, thereby denying its supremacy.[105]

This view might be the basis for the "higher than life" sacredness attached to the Bible by Pentecostals globally, Black Majority Churches in Britain inclusive; this has contributed to the retention of what they consider to be the core doctrine of the Gospels.

A result of the increasing influence of Africans on the global theological discourse on the authority of the Bible in lieu of the relativized Global North was the abdication of the conservative membership of the Lutheran Church who were placed under the head of the Lutheran Church in Kenya, as the ripple effect of the Anglican Communion became an issue amongst the Lutheran faithful. Bishop Walter Obare Omwanza denounced the Lutheran leadership for their relativity and abdication of biblical truth for the acceptance of a "secular, intolerant bureaucratic fundamentalism inimical to the word of God and familiar from various church struggles against totalitarian ideologies of the 21st century".[106] But Jenkins noted that this sort of disputation is a common occurrence in international conferences and also North American religious communities with large immigrant populations. Various scholars have made similar observations with respect to Jenkins' assertion from Asia and North America on the distinctive theological divide in immigrant populations globally.[107]

The North and South Global biblical interpretation has a thin line of distinctiveness in terms of geographical divide because of the fact that there exist diverse denominations within the two areas that express conservative and literary interpretations of the scripture, especially the charismatic and Pentecostal expressions of the Christian faith. The fascinating theological orientations across the global landscape, Britain inclusive, have inevitably brought about the understanding of various theological traditions within the ecumenicals in Britain. For instance, Churches Together in Britain, an Ecumenical Initiative, has created the Minority Ethnic Christian Affairs Unit led by Bishop Joe Aldred, a Bishop of Church of God of Prophecy, in order to engage the theologies of ethnic minority churches in the UK, but there exists the paradox that ethnic or minority churches have changed the British Christian historical landscape while the historic churches are declining in membership. Even where growth is experienced amongst the historic denominations it is a by-product of migration from Asia, Africa and Eastern Europe.[108]

### *Black Majority Churches' Hermeneutics*

The last three decades have heralded various perspectives with respect to many aspects of Pentecostalism ranging from the shift of global Christianity from North America to the Global South, the pneuma-centric polemics, social theology and Pentecostal hermeneutics. There seems to be a general consensus amongst scholars on the distinctive nature of Pentecostal hermeneutics due to the experiential nature of Pentecostal theology.[109] The Barthian school of thought nullified the experiential perspective of Pentecostals, claiming that man cannot know God through experience because of the fact that the divine cannot be subjected to an experience! Moltmann, however, taking a stance that was a complete departure from the Barthian school of thought, asserted that "God's revelation is always the revelation of God to others and is therefore a making-itself-experienced through others."[110] The uniqueness of the Black Majority Churches, like the global Pentecostal family, is that some experiences cannot be reduced to abstract theology. Moltmann further posits that "theology of revelation is church theology, a theology for pastors and priests. The theology of experience is pre-eminently lay theology."[111]

However, in spite of the heterogeneous composition of Black Majority Churches, which is akin to the heterogeneous nature of classical North American Pentecostalism, the unifying bridge is the common Pentecostal ethos rather than a unifying creedal or liturgical subscription. The Christian "Holy writ" has become an inseparable mark of spirituality amongst African and Caribbean Diasporans, and has been almost a transatlantic phenomenon as far back as the seventeenth century. Black Christian faith rode on the crest of black experiences and a multifaceted dialectic relationship with the reading and interpretation of the scripture. This has brought about the emergence of various scholarly interests in the experiential interpretation of the scripture by the Black Churches globally.[112] The process of re-contextualization in the light of the cultural and socio-political paradigm prevalent in Britain has facilitated black Christians to cope with various racial and institutional challenges in the light of scriptures that had similar features or experiences. Reddie opined that the influence of James Cone's text, *God of the Oppressed*, cannot be overemphasized;[113] this has further been complemented by black theologians as the Bible has been given a further impetus and prioritization in their theological method. However, he noted that black scholars from "alternate schools of thought have critiqued the normativity of utilising Christian notions of revelation and self reverential modality of biblical witness as non-foundational ground for talking about liberation. The editors of the text, nonetheless, recognize and affirm the basis for talking about liberation." There needs to be a realization amongst Western Bible interpreters that Black-Majority Churches will not part with the prioritization of the Bible in their theological discourses. The expression of the Christian faith is not only modulated by the inherent historical and critical exegesis of the scripture but also the cultural contexts of the reader in relation to an existential appeal that the divine is intricately involved with the Black Majority Church members "here and now" and not with an historical narrative. This seems to be the point of convergence with American black theologian James Cone in retrospect on the slave era and the black Christian experience:

> Through the experience of Black slaves, [black Christians] encountered the theological significance of Jesus' death: through the crucifixion Jesus makes an unqualified identification with the poor and the helpless and takes their pain upon himself. If Jesus was not alone in his suffering, they were not alone in their slavery. Jesus was with them! He was God's Black slave who had come to put an end to human bondage. Herein lies the meaning of the resurrection ... Through Jesus' death, God has conquered death's power over his people.[114]

The obvious inference is that the Gospels and the Old Testament often have inherent similarities with experiences of Blacks and as such the Bible is not perceived as an historical book about the nation of Israel but a living testimony in relation to its applicability to the prevailing experiences of black Christians within the British cultural milieu.

Beckford's articulation on Liberation Theological Praxis (LTP) and Rasta hermeneutics urges reflective practices in order to authenticate and reinforce the hermeneutics of Black Majority Churches in Britain which take "into serious consideration liberation, praxis, revelation and history".[115] Beckford's distinctive LTP hermeneutic has more broad-spectrum appeal than previous models proposed by various scholars, as he observed that "the action-reflection method prioritizes creative transformation of the social context through action – it would be consistent to suggest that action must be reflected upon through theo-cultural analysis and through theological reflection – what the Bible has to say about a given situation. This is a dynamic process that results in more action." Beckford in Jaggessar and Reddie further highlighted the distinctiveness of his model in comparison to Cone's assertions:

> Whereas for Cone, the primary concern was for the elimination of racism, other black theologians have suggested alternative starting points ... Similarly, other theologians have made class and sexuality other existential starting points. What this means for me is that the experience of being black in England is a legitimate starting point for theological inquiry. Because Blackness is multiple, this multi-dimensional approach to experience means that liberation strategies will not all be the same because experience is not singular.[116]

He reinforced his perspective that there exists a dynamic relationship that needs to be explored apart from the ideological disparities such as "racism, social injustices, oppression within the Biblical text that must be explored. I [Beckford] must also enable a dialogue between analysis and scripture in order to discern African centred and theo-cultural themes within the scripture."[117]

Hence there exists a dual interaction in Beckford's[118] assertion between analysis and the interpretation of the scriptures. Beckford further authenticates that theology and theologians, especially Eurocentric theologians, should consider black experiences as a valid tool for doing theology amongst Britain's Black Majority Churches with strong emphasis on literalism. The position of those who criticize this aspect of Black Majority Churches is that scripture should be utilised to interpret experience, but it should be noted that there is no such thing as totally objective and impersonal exegesis. The scripture is approached by Black Majority Church members, as any other document or piece of communication, with various pre-understandings, and these presuppositions are intricately linked to previous experiences which might include the understanding and interpretation of the scripture. Thus often there is an unconscious trajectory in finding similar resonance in their personal lives akin to some biblical narratives or characters, especially in the Old Testament. Personal experiences do add a distinctive dimension to how members of Black Majority Churches read and interpret the scripture.

However, this hermeneutic postulation is yet to gain wider acceptance amongst most evangelicals, as they view the hermeneutics of most Black Majority Churches as suspect. This suspicion is further compounded by some Eurocentric Pentecostals in the mould of Gordon Fee, himself a former Pentecostal, referring to Pentecostals in general:

> their attitude towards Scripture regularly has included a general disregard for scientific exegesis and careful thought out hermeneutics. In fact, hermeneutics has simply not been a Pentecostal thing. Scripture is the Word of God and is to be obeyed. In place of scientific hermeneutics there developed a kind of pragmatic hermeneutics – obey what should be taken literally; spiritualize, allegorize or devotionalize the rest.[119]

Inasmuch as there might be excesses and misinterpretation amongst most Pentecostals globally, Black Majority Churches in Britain inclusive, this challenge is not peculiar to Pentecostals or Black Majority Churches. It does not suffice to disregard the pre-understanding or prior structure of experience, as no one can "claim an Archimedean vantage point from which to peer at truth".[120]

In a similar vein it has been noted by various scholars that most Pentecostals are guilty of proof-texting without due consideration for the context and historical-critical analysis of texts, but this is an easy trap for any Christian to fall into.[121] However, this does not imply that any rigorous application of "scientific hermeneutics" suddenly sweeps away foundation stones of Pentecostal doctrine. In recent years there has been much exegesis from the pens of Black Majority Church leaders rigorously defending the theologies of Black Majority Churches in Britain,[122] but this is a reflection of a global renaissance amongst Pentecostal scholars as "dead intellectualism" which "stifles the Spirit-filled life"[123] in the founding days of Pentecostalism is gradually fading away with the articulations of the theological polemics of Pentecostals by various scholars.[124]

Black Majority Church members have been noted to utilize the literalist approach in their hermeneutics, which has led to selective reading of the scripture and "truncated, if not erroneous, views on theological issues" with a strong emphasis on familiar scripture, ideas or prejudice without due consideration for the context of the passage.[125] Ukah opined that such an approach constitutes a "bumper sticker" approach,[126] but Jenkins noted that it is a "little bit more than bumper slogans".[127] But I wish to posit that such an approach is born out of predetermined exegesis with the sole objective of applying the scripture to their immediate challenges, which is a departure from the prevailing Western status quo hermeneutics. Kalu called it "bumper sticker" or "experiential literalism" where "[p]ersonal and corporate experiences are interwoven into the hermeneutical task".[128] A commentator noted that this is a common feature amongst African Initiated Churches in Africa as the members "read the Bible contextually so that it might address their daily needs, problems and concerns the way their traditional religion did before the arrival of Christianity and the Bible".[129]

Thus Pentecostalism offers a replacement paradigm for Africans to cope with challenges of assimilation in the wake of globalization and migration. However, this provides an alternative, valid theological paradigm and "fundamental challenges to what has been going on within the dominant tradition in the name of 'theology'".[130] The "pliability" of Pentecostalism through the literal practices became a coping mechanism with immediate life challenges. Suffice to note however, that Reddie and Jagessar noted that Blacks have always opened the "closed door of hermeneutical circle of alleged Scriptural authority" by reading against the text[131] – this has always been reflective of juxtaposing of the divine in the experiences of black Christians as Olaudah Equiano did during the slavery era.[132]

Hyacinth Sweeney made a significant contribution to the use of the Bible as a tool for the development and liberation of women by drawing from four approaches as a feminist theologian: the Recuperative Approach; the Suspicion Approach; the Postmodernist Approach; and the Survivalist Approach.[133] It is expedient to note that her postulations were basically a reflection on the inherent androcentric Jewish culture that relegates women to the background, which has parallels with the traditional African androcentric culture, but she urged a critical evaluation of contributions of women during biblical times which will invariably facilitate the growth of the faith of women. She also made use of the liberation perspective of Professor Weems as she rejects scriptures that dehumanize and "misogynize women".

### *Role of the Holy Spirit in the Use of the Bible Amongst Black Majority Churches*

The proliferation of Black Majority Churches in Britain around the turn of the twenty-first century is an indication that the Black Majority Churches have overcome various institutional and socio-cultural challenges through affirming dependence on the Holy Spirit.

These Churches' position on the role of the Holy Spirit in the reading and interpretation of the scripture is generally akin to the global Pentecostal ideals. Reformers prior to the emergence of Pentecostalism understood the "elucidation of the Spirit" in reading the Bible, but

Pentecostals have a wider perception of the influence of the Holy Spirit. Black Majority Churches in Britain share similar pneumatic epistemology with the global Pentecostal ideals. This often takes place where believers or preachers, while reading the scriptures, "hear from the Lord" – the preacher is acting *ex spiritu* rather than *ex officio*.[134] The paramount expectation is that there should always be a constant interaction of the divine with the reader; the expectation is succinctly described as "a touch of the power of God in Jesus [in Black Majority Church parlance, "the Holy Spirit told me"] descriptive of the experience which Pentecostals [Black Majority Churches] consider essential, valid and authentic".[135]

This has constituted the basis of criticism amongst some scholars in the mould of MacArthur, who noted that even Charismatics (Pentecostals) can "misinterpret Scripture as they simply open their Bibles and 'let the Holy Spirit tell them what it means.' That attitude has led many into error."[136] This in itself is a product of gross negligence on the part of any preacher; it is failure to engage with the text, and over-reliance on the supernatural empowerment; it is a sign of personal ineptitude of some preachers. It might sound shocking, but from my experience, it is common to listen to some Black Majority Church leaders at times jokingly noting such ineptitude by using the text in Psalm 81:10, "open your mouth wide and I will fill it".

This type of criticism is valid, but many Pentecostals (Black Majority Churches) will not want to accept the reductionist hermeneutic which revolves round grammatico-historical exegesis to the exclusion of pneuma-centric exegesis. In fact, amongst the Black Majority Churches most are averse to scholarly exposition of the Bible; they concur with Ervin that "it is a word for which there are no categories endemic to human understanding. It is a word for which, in fact, there is no hermeneutic unless and until the divine hermeneutics (the Holy Spirit) mediates an understanding",[137] but Cargal noted that this view is "docetic" and "naïve".[138] In the context of appropriation of the scripture, members of the Black Majority Churches not only read the text but also gain insight into new "revelations" to which the Spirit opens their understanding.[139] However, claims that "God has spoken outside or apart from the Bible" in the history of religions have brought about the emergence of various sectarian movements and cults; the plumb-line test is whether the extra-biblical revelation is in conformity with biblical doctrine. The pneuma-centric influence on Bible reading by most Pentecostal (Black Majority) Churches is that the historical divide between the writer and the reader is bridged by the Holy Spirit and maturity in life of the Spirit has a positive correlation with the ability to understand and experience biblical realities.[140]

Amongst Black Majority Churches there exists the "call and response" preaching model in which the preacher is the performer while his audience wittingly contributes to his performance with their responses.[141] It is thus a common feature of Black Majority Churches that there is a great sense of participation from the congregants with a dual model of communication in which the preacher expects response from others to determine whether his sermon has any immediate impact on them. Comments from the preacher include, "Can I have a witness in the house?", "Hello church", "Am I speaking to someone in the church?" and the congregation might respond, "Yes, ride on pastor", "Yes, there is a witness in the house", "Go on Pastor" or "Preach it Pastor". The apparent influence of the Holy Spirit is often seen in services in which there is usually a high expectation that the "Spirit will come down" as on the day of Pentecost.

The aftermath of this as identified by Sturge is the creation of a "worshipping Pastor who cannot rely merely on expository preaching or exegeting a text since he or she might be considered 'dead' or dry or to lack the anointing".[142] The paradox is that if the Spirit fails to move then the preacher has to "move the Spirit", often with prolonged worship to usher in the "move of the Spirit" in the service. This is an extreme situation, but it does demonstrate that, amongst Black Majority Churches, the supernatural phenomenon of Acts 2 is not just an historical narrative, but a daily expectation through the empowerment of the Holy Spirit. In world religions, especially the Christian faith, deception and extremism in supernatural claims are not new as they have an eschatological dimension (Mt 24:1; Tim 4:1–2). Pentecostals globally have been noted to teach doctrine from historical books and ignore didactic works. This is often displayed in the Pentecostal predilection for Luke/Acts; Dayton succinctly noted "a distinct hermeneutic, a distinctively Pentecostal manner of appropriating the scriptures. In contrast to magisterial Protestantism, which tends to read the New Testament through Pauline eyes, Pentecostalism [Black Majority Churches] reads the rest of the New Testament through Lukan eyes, especially with the lenses provided by the book of Acts."[143] But the proponents of this school of thought are opposed to the anti-supernatural hermeneutic in the reading of the book of Acts. It might seem overly exaggerated to claim that this criticism is a norm amongst the Black Majority Churches in Britain, as some recognize the distinctives in the structure, vocabulary and synthesis of Paul/Luke thereby building up their New Testament theology. The basis of the over-emphasis on the Luke/Acts paradigm amongst Black Majority Churches in Britain is in relation to the global Pentecostals which might be due to the missionary nature of the Pentecostal movement right from inception and a normative paradigm to preach the Gospels.

Penny succinctly describes the obsession of Pentecostalism with the Luke/Acts paradigm. Most Black Majority Churches in Britain understand that "Acts is more than History for the Pentecostal: it is a missionary work of the Holy Spirit in the church, concluding, not with chapter 28, but with the ongoing Spirit-empowered and Spirit-directed gospel preaching of today."[144] The role of the Holy Spirit is intricately linked with empowerment of the church and believers into mission. Amos Yong noted that the outpouring of the Holy Spirit in the narrative of Acts 2:4–11 never ameliorated other tongues but enabled an "eruption of a diversity of tongues. On one hand, there is the cacophony of tongues, yet on the other there is harmony of testimonies, each witnessing in their own way to God's deeds of power."[145] This distinctive phenomenon as it was experienced in the Early Church is a core value amongst the Black Majority Churches in Britain, as Jean-Jacques Suurmond observed: in Acts 2:4–11 there is "a new decisive change in the relationship between God and the world and thus also the relationship between human beings".[146]

However, there seems to be a great variation in the expression of glossolalia amongst Black Majority Churches in Britain. The diversity of tongues on the day of Pentecost brought about a plurality of tongues in which strangers were brought together, but in most Black Majority Churches it is perceived as a symbol not only of inclusiveness but also of exclusiveness with regard to those that are yet to experience the gift of speaking in tongues. However, pneuma-centrism has been identified as an "Achilles heel" amongst Black Majority Churches akin to the identified trend within global Pentecostalism. In the words of David Martin in *Pentecostalism: The World Their Parish*: "It is the availability of the Spirit which drives forward and vitalizes the evangelical movement but inevitably it leads to a clash of rival charismata. The result is schism and contention and in the subsequent abrasions quite a number retire hurt and disillusioned."[147] Schism contributes to the continued proliferation of Black Majority Churches in Britain. The schism occurs as nonconformist leaders break off to start their own churches.

Black Majority Churches in Britain are invariably faced with the challenge of being text- and Spirit-oriented, but ironically African Pentecostals have similar challenges. The obvious inter-relatedness of African Pentecostalism might be attributed to the fluidity of African Pentecostalism and transnational migration, as most members of the Black Majority Churches migrated to Britain, except the second and third generation Africans and Caribbeans. Kalu refuted the fundamentalist ascriptions either philosophically or hermeneutically about African [and Caribbean] Pentecostalism.[148] He noted the ambiguity of the term "fundamentalism", the fact that experiential and charismatic ideals are not generally accepted by "fundamentalists", and the continued global resonance of African Pentecostalism as a result of pneuma-centrism; the multiplicity of theologies and variations within the movement have brought about diversities of orientations that have defied and will continue to defy a generic labelling and the absence of any idealistic militancy in both the public and sacred sphere. The political ideology of Black Majority Churches in Britain is still nascent and devoid of overt political engagement.

### *Worship in Black Majority Churches in Britain*

Worship amongst Black Majority Churches in Britain offers a unique paradigm to the historic denominations in which worship is conducted according to a set liturgy. Although the liturgy is not written, there exists a formalized procedure amongst most Black Majority Churches in Britain. This includes praise and worship, prayers, reading from the Bible, testimony, preaching, dancing and clapping. These features are indeed reflective of the fluidity of the African/Caribbean culture in the expression of the Christian faith. The worship services are often "loud" and exuberant demonstrations of enthusiasm. In the course of this research, I came across a man who, though an evangelical Christian, described the worship of Black Majority Churches in the UK as "noisy and like a rock concert"! The observer failed to realize that there are various expressions of the Christian faith and often the cultural matrix of a church accounts for these.

Anderson presents a comparative insight into the probable reasons for the staid and unresponsive worship prevalent in most historic churches in Britain:

> No European can say that the free, exuberant Christianity is merely because it is a cultural trait of Africans to be enthusiastic, rhythmic and noisy. One has only to be at a premier league football match to see that Europeans can have the same enthusiasm! The problem is not the culture of the European masses; but it may have something to do with the culture of their churches – perhaps this is one reason why the masses are not attracted to them.[149]

Anderson's assertion cannot be dismissed: the ongoing renewal within the Anglican and Methodist churches has brought a bilateral relationship between these two historic denominations with the *Fresh Expressions* initiative – not only aimed toward contextualization of the Gospel but also changing the age-long historic worship style to informal gatherings, which is reflective of the changing paradigm within the ecumenical fold.

The worship services of Black Majority Churches in Britain are participatory and music is pivotal. Pentecostalism, including Black Majority Churches, has been noted for the narrativity and orality of its theology and liturgy. Thus in order to articulate the views of a religious group, it is appropriate to analyse not only what is documented but also what is done. The culture of a religious group is inclusive of doing rather than written dogma alone. The worship session opens with a short prayer at times said by the worship leader. The worship team's composition varies across the denominations, and depends upon the gifting and available resources within a local congregation. The worship teams are made up of musicians whose skills and accompaniments create the synergy that anchors the singers or worship leaders. The usual rhetoric from the lead singer includes statements such as "We are in the presence of the Lord, there is fullness of joy and pleasures at his right hand, Let somebody shout Hallelujah", "Come on! Someone in the house, give God Praise", "Praise Him in the Beauty of his Holiness", "Lift Him high, Come on!", "The dead cannot praise the Lord", "It is of the mercies of the Lord that you have not been consumed", "Make a joyful noise to Heaven", "Shout Hallelujah, Give God the praise". The expression succinctly and creatively brings about a reflective practice amongst the congregants, who move from a liminal position to engagement in the worship.

The objective of worship amongst Black Majority Churches, according to Miller, is to transpose that "profane world of everyday life into a sacred moment where one can touch God".[150] The art of leading worship in most Black Majority Churches entails personal piety, rehearsals and prayers, and the leader of the worship is responsible through the enablement of the Holy Spirit to lead people beyond mundane issues of the moment to a state of divine consciousness. One distinctive feature is the mild tempo worship songs which are one of the two streams of worship in most Black Majority Churches; the second stream is the more expressive, exuberant and often fast-paced danceable songs akin to contemporary hip-hop songs, which is the praise session.

As a preacher, lecturer and researcher within Black Majority Churches, I have noticed that there seem to be three worship styles within most Black

Majority Churches in Britain. The first category is the "laggards", characterized by traditionalism in the worship context. Their worship songs are very much akin to their traditional African/Caribbean cultural background: they are authentic and culturally meaningful, and facilitate limited or selective assimilation within the British culture. An example of such a church is Apata-Irapada, an ethnic church in the network of the Redeemed Christian Church of God, on Camberwell Road, London. One of the two services is conducted in the Yoruba language, one of the three principal languages in Nigeria, and translated into English. The musical instruments are a fusion of African and Western instruments. The role of the traditional African talking drum is quite evident, as indigenous Afrocentric myths and identities create enthusiastic pulsating and rhythmic dance steps amongst the enthusiastic congregants. The pastor, though he preaches in Yoruba, dresses in a suit, thus presenting a picture of fusion and of selective assimilation and cultural identity: a case of identifying with but not belonging to the host culture.

The majority of the members are often the old grandparents and some younger men who are steeped in the cultural trappings of the Yourba, creating a worship experience away from home. The members of the Yoruba Church of Apata-Irapada are the linguistically ostracized as they have limited social interactions except within their immediate cultural milieu – and the middle-aged who want a feel of the indigenous "classical church" ideology of the RCCG, as noted by Ukah in his thesis.[151] All this indigenization, directed towards meeting the worship aspirations of the very minute population, mainly Yorubas, is rather antithetical to the preaching of the good news to the members of the host culture. However, this type of ethnic church is meeting the social and religious needs of Diasporans who might not be able to worship outside their cultural enclave.

Music is cardinal to worship in Black Majority Churches in Britain; the songs are often reflective of African cosmology and seem to assist in the assimilation of the migrant population in Britain on account of the social and political context that most worshippers are living in. For instance:

> "Kilo le se Olorunmi, Ki lo lese, Eyin ti eda aye, ati orun, Kilo le lese Olorunmi Ki lo lese" ("What is it that you cannot do, my God? What is it that you cannot do? You are the creator of the Earth and Heaven, What is it that you cannot do, my God? What is it that you cannot do?")

This further reinforces the fact that it is not only in prayers that Yorubas seek to enjoy practical benefits, as noted by Peel, but also through songs which connect with the divine.[152] The obvious enthusiasm, clapping of hands, kneeling and fervency that is displayed by *Egbe Akorin* (the worship team) and the participatory mode of the congregants is suggestive of their affirmation that God will answer their petitions.

The second category is the "dual modal churches which are receptive and retentive": Black Majority Churches where the mode of worship is linguistically conditioned to the host culture. The worship is more reflective of the Black American Gospel songs but with a deep affection for the retention of their cultural identity or ethnic identity. The songs are often not different from African songs and these churches seem to be an avenue for wider social interaction and assimilation. Songs in these churches include songs such as:

> "Praise the Lord, O sing O sing, Praise the Lord,
> Praise his Holy name, Praise the Lord."

The inherent organizational ethos of these churches is shaped by the leadership ethos of the church. Most of the members of these types of churches were products of the first generation of Africans or Caribbeans in Britain who have linguistically acculturated but have retained elements of their cultural identity. The worship and instrumentation are mainly Western. These categories of worshippers are becoming retirees and there exists a palpable nostalgic desire to worship in their homeland while away from home. The influence of the host culture reverberates as the younger members of the churches crave a balance in songs to reflect contemporary trends. The inability of a former church in which I worked as an associate minister to adapt to these needs gradually led to the younger generation "voting with their feet" and leaving the church in droves due to a lack of contemporary balance in worship. A major feature in the worship sessions of most of these churches is the continued use of eulogy which is a typology of *Oriki* (praise) amongst the Yorubas.

Thomas Lindon states that, in *Oriki Orisa*, "the names, deeds and character of the *orisa* [deity] are proclaimed as an act of worship during festivals and other important occasions".[153] Burgess noted that "there is an element of elation in the act of worship itself" but he observed that Lindon suggests that *Oriki Orisa* should nevertheless be regarded as "efficacious prayer" as a means of moving the deity to grant the worshippers' petition. In articulating this perspective Burgess further cited Omosade Awolalu who gave the synopsis of the ideology of *Oriki Orisa* as "the idea is that when the praise names are given, or sung, the divinities will be moved to pay attention to the worshippers and thus heed their requests and wishes".[154] The distinctive typology of *Oriki Orisa* is found among Nigerian Pentecostal Churches in Britain as they call the various names of God.

In fact, Ukah noted elements of charismatization as personified by the Follow Your Leader (FYL) phenomenon in the Redeemed Christian Church of God as the General Overseer, Pastor E.A. Adeboye admonishes the congregants to "call God by his names, call him, he is the King of Kings, the Lord of Lords, the Ancient of Days, the mighty God, The soon coming King, my Redeemer, my Saviour, the giver of Life..."[155] The style of worship resonates with the *Oriki Orisa* model and has a similar underlying principle. This has further been clarified in numerous sermons of Pastor Adeboye that eulogizing God through worship "will move God to answer your petition" just the way his mother used to call her husband by his *Oriki* (eulogy) whenever she wanted something from him.

The growth of Pentecostalism globally has been noted to be a product of missiological initiatives and the ability to acculturate itself across various cultural frontiers. Though some of these churches' worship is gradually embracing British and American Gospel music, overtly it is more about miming the songs of Kirk Franklin, Mary Mary, Alvin Slaughter etc, as most of the churches' choirs lack originality in their songs. There are a few, however, such as the London Gospel Choir, Ruach Ministries and Noel Robinson who have made remarkable inroads in contemporary music. A notable artiste in recent years in Britain is Muyiwa Olanrewaju, an exceptional song writer/producer and radio presenter with Premier Radio who has being making waves across Britain and America since 2002 with his debut album *Restoration*.

The third stream of worship style amongst Black Majority Churches is the contemporary style of worship. The uniqueness of some of these groups of churches is their ability to contextualize their worship styles with affection for transatlantic features prevalent in American and British Gospel Songs. These churches include the KICC, Ruach Ministries, Jesus House, Glory House and House on the Rock. The worship teams are not just volunteers but often professional musicians in the employment of these churches who are sought-after international artistes, accomplished and highly creative.

## THE AMERICAN BLACK THEOLOGY FEATURES IN BLACK MAJORITY CHURCHES IN BRITAIN[156]

The influence of black American theology as a transatlantic phenomenon cannot be overemphasized, but black theology in Britain, unlike American black theology, is interdisciplinary.[157] The fluidity of Pentecostalism over the years has led the movement to be branded the "missionary movement" on account of its ability to infiltrate various cultures and still express itself. The Americanization of British Churches in the second phase of the history of Black Churches in Britain has contributed significantly to the retention not only of the American philosophy but also of elements of American spirituality. Further impetus and broader expressions of such influences have been enhanced as a result of globalization and transnationalism, as religion is now a factor in global mobility. The Health and Wealth Gospel is one of the religious exports of American spirituality globally; the dogma of the Prosperity Gospel is centred on positive thinking and a strong affirmation that God wants all believers to be materially wealthy.

Hunt observed that the American Prosperity Gospel has put down its footprint and been accepted as far as "Scandinavia, Eastern Europe, Africa, India, Latin America and the Pacific rim of Southeast Asia" – and Britain too in the wake of the proliferation of Black Majority Churches.[158] The ripple effects of transnational migration and globalization have created a steady and significant influence of American theology amongst Black Majority Churches in Britain, especially those of African descent. Burgess noted the significant influence of prosperity theology on some leading African churches that are now global entities, such as the Redeemed Christian Church of God, which has over 498 [RCCG has over 600 parishes as at the time of this publication] parishes in Britain,[159] and the Mountain of Fire and Miracles, popularly known for its denominational exploits of "deliverance par excellence", though Burgess observed that the "name it and claim it",[160] "name it, grab it theology", "confess it, possess it", "crass materialism" and "positive confession" have been under the scrutiny of African scholars in the mould of Ayegboyin[161] and Asamoah-Gyadu.[162] Hunt also noted that at Jesus House, the flagship of the RCCG in the United Kingdom, prosperity theology is work-related and a practical financial discipline. He posited that it is a variation of the American model.[163]

The apparent emergence and influence of American prosperity theology cannot be traced to a particular timeframe, but a major contributor to the experience-centred aspect of Christianity, such as came into being through the

Charismatic movement, was the experienced-based theology of Friedrich Schleiermacher. The second contributory factor to the American domination of the global space with Health and Wealth theology was the emergence and influence of the positive thinking philosophy by Norman Vincent Peale[164] while the third hub was the influence of contemporary Western materialism.[165] The influence of the American prosperity theology paradigm was not in itself a new phenomenon to most Black Majority Churches, on account of the adverse socio-economic life of most Africans. When deprived of basic necessities of life such as education, food and nourishment, religious people are naturally inclined either to a doctrine which places less of a priority on the lack, or to one which suggests that the needs can be met.

Meyer noted the ambivalent relationship between money and power in Ghana,[166] and this also resonates among the Igbos and Yorubas in Nigeria,[167] but I concur with Ukah who asserted that "what accounts for the appeal of the prosperity doctrine is the cultural resonance which indigenous religious ideas offer but this does not account for its origin".[168] This contrasts with Ojo's perspective that prosperity theology has African roots,[169] although Beckford traced the history of the contemporary prosperity gospel to America.[170]

Sturge was quite liberal in his views on prosperity theology amongst Black Majority Churches in Britain; he asserted a holistic view of the scripture in relation to the poor, the disenfranchised, the downtrodden and the socially excluded, "but this is rather a farce as oftentimes the poor, the needy are continually 'fleeced' to part with their finances in order to 'reap their sowings'".[171]

Sturge wrote from an insider's perspective as a former General Secretary of the African Caribbean Evangelical Alliance in Britain, though he acknowledged various inherent abuses and misconceptions about prosperity theology. He was of the opinion that "it will be unreasonable to think of prosperity theology as being at the opposite end of the theological spectrum of Liberation theology" but he identified the distinction between the two as: (a) diverse responses to social, economic and political structures and (b) the fact that prosperity theology has a personal focus with capitalist ideology while liberation theology has an incarnational, transformational and communal focus. Miller and Yamamori also posit that Pentecostalism has "stepped into the vacuum created by the decline in Liberation theology".[172] Miller and Yamamori were of the opinion that liberation theology no longer appeals to the poor, as "the poor are opting for Pentecostalism". The apparent disparity might be a product of changes within the social structure in most Western countries.

There exists a discernible American influence in the theology of most African churches in administrative structure and faith practices. Most African Illustrious charismatic and Pentecostal leaders were devotees of American faith movement ideologies which permeated through their doctrinal and ministry practices.[173] The policy of subsidy to Africans was basically a form of imperialism whereby America's faith and prosperity theology was made accessible to aspiring young Africans in the mould of the late Bishop Benson Idahosa.[174] They enjoyed free books, theological training, funding, lavish receptions and foreign preaching engagements. This was a precursor of Africa's veritable export to the West as replicated by the prosperity theology of Black-led Churches in Britain[175]

However, Nigeria and Ghana have made a remarkable impact in the Africanization of prosperity theology through various religious resources and artefacts such as audio CDs, DVDs, books, etc. to African nations as well as spreading of denominational frontiers in Africa which have culminated in the reverse mission accentuated by the economic recession of the 1980s and 1990s leading to Diasporans in Britain.[176]

The teachings on prosperity amongst Black Majority Churches "follow a general pattern (a replication of the American prosperity theology that oftentimes has been Africanized in delivery and local context but the ethos is definitive and American)" according to Folarin.[177] Robert Booth wrote an article in the *Guardian* of 29 August 2008 entitled "Religion: Praise the Lord and pass the business plan as God embraces Mammon", on the International Gathering of Champions, an annual fiesta of transatlantic fraternization between Pastor Matthew Ashimolowo and the "leading lights" amongst the contemporary American Health and Wealth preachers. Ashimolowo indeed might be called the scion of Black Majority Churches' prosperity preachers in Britain.

Jenkins quoted an American journalist who observed the message of Ashimolowo's ministry as "a blend of Corinthians and Hallmark, gospel truth and pop psychology, rendered in the style of convention center motivational speech".[178] Ashimolowo has progressively in the last two decades churned out more books on Health and Wealth ideologies in Britain than any other Black Majority Church preacher. Some of his numerous publications include: *101 Answers to Money Problems, Volumes 1–4*, and *10 M's of Money and the Coming Wealth Transfer*. The copious influence of American prosperity is replete in his publications. Ashimolowo noted in *10 M's of Money* that "it is also having everything God promised in His covenant in Abraham. Remember God promised to bless Abraham."[179]

Copeland said, "after Adam's fall in the Garden, God needed an avenue back into the earth ... since man was the key figure in the fall, man had to be a key figure in the redemption, so God approached a man called Abram. He re-enacted with Abram what Satan had done with Adam ... God offered Abram a proposition and Abram bought it."[180] Copeland further espoused his view in his "classic" publication *Laws of Prosperity* that has attracted global patronage: "since God's covenant has been established and prosperity is a provision of the covenant, you need to realise that prosperity belongs to you now".[181] Cox, in his exploration of the American prosperity themes in the ministry of the late Kenneth Hagin, wrote, "through the crucifixion of Christ, Christians have inherited all the promises made to Abraham, and these include both spiritual and *material well being*".[182] Advocates of prosperity theology[183] across the Atlantic support their claim that it is the will of God that His children should have financial and entrepreneurial success by similar texts (Deut 8:18; 3 Jn 3:2; Mal 3:12; Mark 10:29–30; Ps 50:10; Haggai 2:8). These assertions are a product of literalism and an absolute negation of contextual, grammatical or historical exegesis, and are "highly subjective and arbitrary".[184]

One influence of the theological and biblical practices of American black theology amongst Black Majority Churches in Britain is the intrinsic adoption of the interrelatedness of prosperity theology and atonement: that both physical healing and financial prosperity have been provided for in the atonement. This idea makes much use of 2 Cor 8:9.[185] The repertoire of similarities in the American prosperity preachers and Black Majority Churches in Britain includes the doctrine's dependence on sowing and reaping, tithing, giving and "covenant seed". Sturge noted that prosperity theology has awakened the Churches' neglected doctrine but "unfortunately has become reactionary and dogmatic".[186] Perriman was quite succinct in his submission that American Health and Wealth ideology permeated to many Evangelical churches in Britain as some of the churches emulated the flamboyance of American prosperity preachers.[187] The influence of Morris Cerrullo on the mushrooming African Independent Churches was significant as Osgood noted that many of these pastors were actively supporting his ministry.[188] The media scrutiny and the indictment of Cerrullo Ministries by the Advertising Standards Authority over the ministry's aggressive "salesmanship" and extravagant claims were the Waterloo for the resignation of the Morris Cerrullo ministry from the Evangelical Alliance in the United Kingdom, although the veritable seed of prosperity had been sown to the mushrooming Black-led Churches. Interestingly media was and is still a significant vehicle for effective exportation of this ideology through various cable networks and Christian Channels such as God's Channel, Revival and Inspiration which mean that the teachings of Hagin, Copeland, Jerry Saville, Rod Parsely, Benny Hinn and others are readily accessible for private consumption. The proliferation of Black Majority Churches and the use of media has significantly been harnessed like the Americans by African and Caribbean pastors which has facilitated the prominence of the prosperity gospel in Britain.

## SUMMARY

The great heterogeneity amongst the Black Majority Churches in Britain has created diversities of theological leanings and faith appropriations. These have culminated in various latent expressions of the Christian faith amongst Black Majority Churches in Britain that often impact their doctrinal persuasions. The Trinitarian Pentecostal ideal seems to be replicating itself largely because of the influx of the African Pentecostal denominations in Britain in the 1980s and 1990s. The distinguishing features of the theological divide and the historical polemics of Oneness theology demonstrate that the influence of American theology is not a recent phenomenon in Black British Church history.

African and Caribbean theologies are replicated within the Black Majority Churches' ethos, as they are experiential, oral and narrative in consonance with features of global Pentecostalism. The salient features and idiosyncrasies of the various cultures have enhanced the enculturation of the Gospel; this is reflected in their experiential hermeneutics in which the Luke/Acts paradigm is not viewed only as an historical narrative but also as an experiential narrative with empowerment and missions as its motive. The Bible is the heart of the spirituality of Black Majority Churches, with a strong emphasis on literal interpretation and pneuma-centrism, though often this leads to excesses and misinterpretation – but this is not peculiar to global Pentecostalism or Black Majority Churches in Britain. Worship in these churches is noted to have various cultural resonances such as clapping, rhythmic dance steps, narratives and participatory acts.

The American black theology provides a paradigm to Black Majority Churches in Britain, especially with regard to the doctrine of prosperity theology, in which the American model is followed by most Black Majority Church leaders. This has brought about a process of Africanization of the American prosperity theology which has been greatly influenced by the power of positive confession, sowing, reaping and covenants.

*Chapter Five*

# The Contributions of Black Majority Churches and Their Members to British Christianity

～

## INTRODUCTION

The growth and proliferation of Black Majority Churches in Britain has led to a new epoch in the history of British Christianity. The obvious trajectory and importance of Black Majority Churches in Britain is acknowledged even amongst the historic denominations as well as the public officers in the United Kingdom.[1] The significance and relevance of the Black Majority Churches in Britain, now a multicultural and multi-ethnic nation so different from the Britain of Victorian times, is embodied in the fact that "10 percent of English churchgoers are black ... 44 percent in inner London".[2] The proliferation of Black Majority Churches in London is due to multiple factors which include the migration pattern of ethnic minorities towards identified cultural safety nets of their kith and kin, and the lure of the urban socio-economic indices, as London is the financial seat of Europe.

The pull and push factors which revolve round the socio-cultural and economic praxis have contributed significantly to the growth and resonance of Black Majority Churches in inner-city areas of Britain. It is apt to note that the proliferation of Black Majority Churches in London is significant in comparison to cities outside London, but the location of such churches is related to the migratory patterns of Africans and Caribbeans and the economic melting pots in Britain. This has led to a distinctive geographical spread of Black Churches in cities where Africans and Caribbeans have significant populations, and also to the emergence of ethnic or national churches. Black Majority Churches are in denial with regard to the latter point, as noted by Aldred with a few exceptions in the mould of Liverpool Lighthouse Fellowship.[3]

The last five decades in the history of Black Majority Churches in Britain have brought about changes from passive to active involvement of these churches in social, economic and political activism. The inertia preceding the shift in this paradigm was a by-product not only of reflective practice of some of these churches but also the circumstantial social and political insulation of the British policies that precipitated the changes. The political theology of most Black Majority Churches is still nascent, and some are still under the covert influence of imperialistic ideology, as noted by Beckford,[4] but this seems to be a work in progress, as some of these churches are no longer perceived as a coping mechanism for social deprivation but as stakeholders in their various communities, on account of their wide influence and their credibility.

The potential of faith communities has been identified by the state as a vehicle for community development and has been reflected in various social policies of the British government. However, there exist diverse ambiguities and irreconcilable challenges in the continued interaction of the faith communities and the state regarding social policies.

## CHURCH GROWTH AND RESONANCE IN INNER CITIES OF BRITAIN

The last five decades in Britain have ushered in much diversity amongst communities, a major feature of which is the growth and proliferation of Black Majority Churches. The REACH report of 2007 noted that "in 2001 the majority of the Black Caribbean (61 per cent) and Black African (79 per cent) populations lived in London. A further 15 per cent of Black Caribbeans lived in the West Midlands, particularly Birmingham."

The settlement patterns of these two majority ethnic minorities in Britain presents an interesting paradox, as instead of assimilation into the various British communities there have emerged ethnic minority communities in most inner-city areas in Britain because of socio-cultural affinities and the intra-migratory pattern of migrants. This might be a product of the re-enactment of eclectic cultural conurbations which does not foster assimilation into the host British culture. There is an historical resemblance to the current scenario in the history of migration to Britain. The emergence of the West Indian churches during the *Windrush* era was based on the same ideology, as churches evolved in sheltered communities and large industrial cities where economic opportunities and social assimilation amongst the migrant community were available for the migrants.

The high migration pattern of Caribbeans to the Midlands to join their kith and kin in the second phase of migration in the 1950s meant that cities such as Birmingham, Wolverhampton and Nottingham, and also Brixton in London, became the heartbeat of the West Indian expression of Pentecostalism. The practical features of the distinctive settlement pattern of Africans and Caribbeans is more apparent in the boroughs of inner London, as Africans and Caribbeans are more likely to live there, particularly in Lambeth, Hackney and Lewisham.

The "white flight" which is the urban migration of Whites from black conurbations in most urban cities has led to the emergence of almost exclusively black communities in some cities in Britain. This regional divide has contributed to the widening of the gulf of social non-integration amongst ethnic minority groups (inclusive of Africans and Caribbeans) and also between the indigenous and migrant communities. The demographic factors seem to have contributed to limiting the effectiveness of the Black Majority Churches in reverse mission, as most of the churches are revelling in "cultural captivity". Similar resonance has been observed with various other ethnic minority groups in Britain.

The 2001 Census reveals that London has the highest proportion of people from minority ethnic groups, apart from those who identified themselves as of Pakistani origin, of whom there is a higher proportion in Yorkshire and the Humber (2.9%) and the West Midlands (2.9%). Two per cent of the population of England and Wales are Indian, with Leicester having the highest proportion (25.7%). Bangladeshis formed 0.5% of the population of England and Wales, with the highest proportion in the London borough of Tower Hamlets (33.4%). It is often in the pursuit of social and economic aspirations that most migrants from the Caribbean and Africa express their faith and identity, which is interestingly reflective of their cultural identity. The statistics are quite compelling: London, for instance, has over 2,000 Black Majority Churches.[5] The massive church plant in London is not so much a missiological initiative but seems to be a deliberate repositioning of the denominational frontiers of some African and Caribbean churches or established Pentecostal churches that have their denominational headquarters in Nigeria, Ghana or the Caribbean. Schism and the pliability of Pentecostalism as a strand of the Christian faith have contributed significantly to the continued growth of Black Majority Churches in inner cities in Britain.

The Redeemed Christian Church of God is perhaps the fastest-growing church in the United Kingdom, with over 600 parishes and over 53% are situated in London. (Growth within this context is the number of churches planted, as this is a motivating factor for the conurbations of RCCG parishes globally: the vision is to plant churches like Starbucks cafés in developed countries within five minutes' driving distance and in developing countries within 10 minutes' driving distance.) Micklethwait and Wooldridge concur with my previous assertions, positing that "London's immigrant-packed East End is thought to have twice as many Pentecostal congregations as Church of England ones."[6] A similar trend can be seen on the Old Kent Road, in south-east London, which should be renamed "Church Street" in view of Black Majority Churches' "bombing" of the area in comparison to the historic denominations' presence in the neighbourhood.

I posit that the inner cities, especially in the third wave of the history of the Black Majority Church in Britain, are seen by the churches as denominational frontiers where they can reinvent and reposition their organizations with the claim of re-evangelizing Britain, but candidly, also, the churches are mission posts for the Diasporan community. Commenting on the growth of Black Majority Churches in Britain, Brierley said: "I asked one black church leader why they thought the black church was growing so much and the answer was: 'We put mission before justice.' They [Black Churches] are passionate, highly charismatic and focused on healing ... We need to learn from them."[7]

Brierley failed to ask why the charismatic disposition and passion has not translated into the conversion of the indigenous host communities in inner cities in Britain – or is healing the birthright of Africans and Caribbeans, or do the host indigenes present a typology of the dogs that are alien to the commonwealth of Israel? Black Majority Churches constitute a model for British historic denominations but Brierley failed to take cognizance of the effectiveness of the missional agenda within the British context of these churches which has not impacted the indigenous white community in consonance with Jesus' missional agenda as indicated in his valedictory admonition to the disciples in the closing verses of Matthew (Mt 28:18–20). Mission was not limited to ethnic or national boundaries: the world and its inhabitants constitute the church's *missio Dei* (Jn 3:16).

The purported claims of these churches as agents of re-evangelizing England might constitute a farce in the face of obvious irreconcilable facts, as a significant population of these churches are culturally captive while making little or no impact in attracting the indigenous community into their churches. Irukwu opined that, "We [Black Majority Churches] should carry on with the job at hand but the ascription of the term Black Church, Black-led or Black Majority Churches will be a misnomer when the host communities are attracted into our churches. I have expressed my views in private and public with respect to the usage of the word black."[8] Irukwu's assertion agrees with that of Hill: he opined that "it could be that the present all-black sects will one day begin to break through into the local white population".⁹ Irukwu's assertion is futuristic – it might have constituted a type of Noah's Ark in the midst of the moral and societal perverseness of his day, but his optimism only culminated in the salvation of its kith and kin.

This paradox seems to be experienced by most Black Majority Churches, as there exist minimal concerted proactive measures to move away from mono-cultural churches to multicultural congregations. Whether the Black Majority Churches will be able to bring the indigenous communities in Britain into their churches is a million-dollar question, but it seems quite achievable with a change in paradigm amongst Black Majority Churches' leadership. There is the need for proactive measures to engage the host culture, as there exist marked cultural differences in worship, theology and ecclesiology between Black Majority Churches and the historic denominations.

There is a subtle acknowledgement of inadequacies with respect to the growth of churches in inner cities in Britain and their missiological agenda. To missiologists, the alienation of the inherent British cultural paradigm, of which most Black Majority Churches are yet to take cognizance, has made most of these churches in inner cities consumerist and commuter-oriented. Mobility within the churches is akin to the consumer orientation of postmodern times. The level of commitment to a local church often cannot be guaranteed, as members of these churches continually shop around churches for their purported needs, demonstrating gregarious intra-migration and replicating the consumer mentality.

Black Majority Churches should come to terms with their inability to effect the changes in their *modus operandi*, that are required to effectively cope with the dynamic cultural shift which seems to have progressed at a geometric rate in the last sixty years in Britain. The inherent cross-cultural challenges and lack of understanding of the signs of the times as noted by Adedibu have contributed significantly to the continued cultural captivity of most Black Churches in inner cities in Britain.¹⁰ Black Majority Churches should adopt a countercultural stance which mirrors Jesus' values and simultaneously identify the various contemporary approaches of communicating the Gospel.

The religious exclusivity of most Black Majority Churches' congregations has contributed to social distance in terms of race relationships. Despite the uniqueness and the cross-cultural challenges of most Black Majority Churches in Britain, many such churches have been acknowledged as "contributing positively" to British society. In his speech delivered at Jesus House, Brent Cross, London, during his 59th birthday celebration, His Royal Highness Prince Charles said, "I want you to remember, that you are highly appreciated by me and more and more by other people. Too often, it seems that the media are interested in the negative and stereotypical but you [Jesus House] if I may say so, are a wonderful and shining example."[11]

A major distinctive feature of most inner-city churches in Britain is the attempt to continually be relevant to their immediate community. Black Majority Churches' contributions to inner cities' social life are represented in various social and community initiatives to combat some of the challenging social problems of inner cities in Britain. For instance, the New Testament Church of God's Evangelical Enterprise enjoyed state funding under the leadership of the former Secretary of State for Trade and Industry, Kenneth Clarke, initiated during a consultative meeting with Rev. Arnold, Clive Calver and the late Philip Mohabir of the Evangelical Alliance on 9 December 1986. The Deputy General Overseer of the New Covenant Church, Pastor Israel Kolade, recently launched Vision 2030 with a focus on providing leadership and mentoring initiatives to youths within the age bracket of 20–30 years of age as he observed that lifelong decisions and commitments are made within this age group.[12]

Glory House, led by Dr Albert Odulele, has contributed significantly to the educational and recreational life of youths in Newham Borough ranging from the Glory House Football Academy (which is now defunct) and a drop-in centre, to talent shows. House on the Rock, led by Pastor Omawunmi Efueye, is maximizing the use of its newly acquired property for neighbourhood regeneration through its "Touching the Community" programme, which focuses on youth, mentoring, education, community development and citizenship.

I concur with Brierley with respect to the future of Black Majority Churches in Britain.[13] He noted that these churches will make it in the future with strategic planning, a clear vision, and pneuma-centric theology. This also necessitates a review of the communication-cum-sociological paradox of the indigenous communities, to create a holistic commitment towards mission rather than a sense of utopianism and complacency in the wake of re-congregating the Diasporan population and perpetuating denominational frontiers. Black Majority Churches, especially in the inner cities of Britain, should consider contextualization of their doctrinal and religious observance in order to be relevant within the British social and religious landscape, and to escape the continued monolithic and cultural captivity as envisioned by the membership spectrum.

The religious ethos of Black Majority Churches is not just an evangelistic approach to conversion. Habermas, who described himself as "stone deaf in the religious sphere", provides a recipe for liberal states in the wake of the September 11 attacks in 2001. His proposition is a succinct model for Black Majority Churches in Britain. He states, concerning American religionists, including Christians: "It is they who must translate their religious convictions into a secular language before their arguments have any prospect of being accepted by the majority."[14] Contextualization is necessary because of the obvious antithetical worldviews alien to the Christian worldview.

## SOCIAL, ECONOMIC AND POLITICAL RELEVANCE

### Social Action and Pragmatism of Black Majority Churches in Britain

Historically, Christian Churches have had remarkable impact in shaping British society. This impact is reflected in community development, education and British heritage in the last five centuries. The perceived loss of sense of community in Britain has facilitated the process of engaging faith communities in social policy formulation for community and social development in recent decades in Britain. The second wave of the emergence of Black Majority Churches in Britain pioneered by the West Indian Churches initiated during the *Windrush* era culminated in various social, cultural and economic challenges for the *Windrush* migrants.

The immediate social ostracization of this generation precipitated social action towards their members which assuaged the social and racial challenges experienced by the members of the emerging churches. Emerging Black Majority Churches provided a social haven for the migrants, based on their faith, identity and cultural affiliations. The ingenuity of the founding fathers of the West Indian Churches brought about the implementation of the indigenous thrift and credit schemes to assist the members of their churches in the acquisition of properties to alleviate the housing constraints, a by-product of racism by British landlords in the 1950s.

This culminated in the emergence of the Pentecostal Credit Union started by Reverend Carmel Jones MBE (Member of the British Empire) through the former Credit Union League of Great Britain and incorporated in March 1980. The late Bishop Powell, the former presiding Bishop of the New Testament Assembly in England, observed that, "It is one of the best visions that we have come up with. When we first came to this country, banks refused to give us loans, so we had to go to private lenders and it was very stressful. PCU has alleviated that stress. It has built our stability and made the purchase of our properties much easier to achieve."[15] Black Majority Churches' social engagement initiatives have made significant contributions to urban and inner-city renewal, often in working with various governmental agencies, and this has been the case since the late 1980s.[16] This era marked the genesis of a "social theology and social gospel within their traditional evangelical and Pentecostal theology".[17] The New Testament Church of God (NTCG) is one of the foremost Black Majority Churches in Britain; it has made remarkable inroads in social actions and has fostered collaborative initiatives with governmental agencies.

One of the foremost publications on the social actions of Black Majority Churches was the publication of a former National Overseer of the NTCG, Selwyn Arnold, entitled *From Scepticism to Hope*. This publication gives a vivid historiographical narrative of the genesis of the social gospel of the NTCG and the circumstances that facilitated the social initiative. Arnold opined that the social action initiative of the New Testament Church of God was birthed as a result of its perception as "inept in its attitude to social issues and [its failure] to set Biblical and theological guideposts for its members".[18] It has been observed that apparent differences in worldview between the first generation and second generation West Indians on a wide range of social, financial and political issues in Britain culminated in reflective practice by the leadership of the New Testament Church of God. The fluidity of the host culture with regard to second-generation West Indians in the 1970s and 1980s led to dynamic tension in upholding the doctrinal tenets of the NTCG which was in conflict with the cultural perspective of some of the second-generation British Caribbeans. The second generation West Indians in the 1970s and 1980s were disillusioned by their experiences on account of the distinction between sacred and secular, and because many of the youth were unemployed or grossly underemployed. This was further compounded by the mistrust of the government's Youth Training Scheme, perceived as a farce because it offered very little meaning or hope for their future.[19]

The bedrock of the initiative was a dual model of social action: (a) the establishment of the NTCG Department of Social Responsibility and (b) the development of cooperation between African and Caribbean people to provide a defined organizational agenda that was not only diagnosing problems but also providing answers to social challenges within and outside the immediate context of the church. This provided the impetus for engagement with relevant state agencies on a wide range of social and economic issues, thereby repositioning the church as relevant to the needs of the British community: "We [the churches] are God's answer to the cry of the suffering."[20] A major shortcoming of Arnold's publication was that its focus was limited to the NTCG. It was not a broadly representative piece of work on the social action of Black-led Churches in Britain, but it demonstrated the potential within the Black-led Churches to respond to their social and community challenges.

In the last few years an observable trend is the upsurge in the social action initiatives of Black Majority Churches, especially African Diasporan churches. This presents a sharp contrast to the late 1980s and 1990s when West Indian churches were at the forefront of social action in Britain. The apparent differences between the Caribbean initiatives for social action and those of the new Neo-Pentecostal Churches like the RCCG might be a reflection of changes in statutory and regulatory functions of the Charity Commission. The recently introduced Public Benefit Test of the Charity Commission, introduced by the 2006 Charities Act, places responsibility on charities in England and Wales to provide evidence that they are benefiting the local community.[21] Asserting the statutory requirement as the basis for the upsurge in the community initiaves of Black Majority Churches in Britain might be very myopic. The influence and contribution of Christianity is reflected in the wide range of educational, social and community initiatives in which the Black Majority Churches have participated actively in Britain.

In October 2004, the Kingsway International Christian Centre (KICC) Walk of Champions was held at Hackney Marsh. It was organized by the KICC, London, who adopted the Sickle Cell Society as the Charity of the Year. The sponsored walk raised £40,808 for the Society, which represents 33.3% of all donations received in 2005. A cheque for this was presented by the KICC's Senior Pastor Matthew Ashimolowo, to Mr Linserd Miller, Chairman of the Society, at a congregation service in January 2005. Apart from staff of the Society, also in attendance at the cheque presentation were Mr Trevor Phillips OBE, Chair of the Commission for Racial Equality (CRE) and Patron of the Society, and Miss Simone Stuart, celebrity singer and supporter of the Society. The KICC has supported a charity annually since 2004 with the KICC Champions Walk. The recipient of the KICC Champions Walk donation in 2008 of over £21,000 was the charity Springboard for Children. The donation impacted 1,000 children and their families positively, giving them gifts that gave them hope for a better future, according to Dipo Oluyo, Chief Executive Officer of the KICC.[22]

The KICC recently demonstrated their commitment to reduce pollution by the acquisition of 30 Mercedes-Benz Sprinter Traveliners: the buses are fitted with the innovative ECO-Start system – this saves fuel and reduces emissions to the community. This is not only a business initiative in terms of saving cost and increasing comfort and safety, but also a commitment to improve the quality of life of the local community.

Within the RCCG network of churches in Britain, similar social action initiatives include those of the RCCG International Christian Centre, a church based in Romford, East London, noted for its initiative in alleviating the needs of the poor and disadvantaged. The "Five Loaves and Two Fishes" initiative of the RCCG International Christian Centre is well acknowledged within Romford Borough and has been embraced by the various state agencies through referrals. The credibility of the church within its community was noted by the University of East London, who voluntarily furnished the community centre of the church up to the tune of £50,000.[23]

A similar initiative making waves in Kingsborough is the Kingsborough Family Church, led by Pastor Tunde Balogun. Its food bank is the only one of its kind in the borough to assist members of the community in social crisis, the unemployed and the homeless. The food bank was launched by Deputy Mayor Councillor David Yarrow and Mrs Rita Kilroy, the Deputy Mayoress of Hillingdon, on 25 September 2009, but had received local media reviews since 20 May 2009, for example in the *Uxbridge Gazette* under the title: "A bank where the bonus is on saving lives". The social action of the church is further complimented by the Coat of Many Colours Nursery, which according to Balogun is "amongst the best nurseries in Kingsborough".[24] This assists in the gradual integration of nursing mothers back to work, as it is community focused.

The social action initiatives of Jesus House, Brent Cross, London, which is the flagship of the RCCG in the United Kingdom, are defined under the banner of Church Social Responsibility (CSR) as CSR International and Community Action. The basic idea of church social responsibility is that the leadership of Jesus House affirms that the church is a social entity and so they should play a role in the social issues of the day. They take seriously their "obligations to society" and actively try to fulfil them[25] but this concept has come under scrutiny within the financial and social sectors globally. The CSR of Jesus House is holistic, based on the Christian ethos, and has a global appeal. The vision of CSR International is to mobilize the human and material resources of Jesus House for all nations towards projects and initiatives that will impact the lives of the poor, the underprivileged and those marginalized in society. Burgess noted that the social initiative of Jesus House entails a huge capital outlay within and outside the United Kingdom.[26] Some of the social action initiatives include events such as the Mandate Men's Conference, the Soul 100 music concert, the annual free car wash week, the Barnet Week of Peace project, and the "Spreading Christmas Cheer" outreach.

The hub of the vision of CSR according to the website of the church[27] comes from Matthew 25:31–46, especially verse 40: "The King will reply, 'I tell you the truth, whatever you did for one of the least of these brothers of mine, you did for me.'" The five foundational objectives are:

1. To undertake projects all over the world that will improve the lives of the poor, downtrodden and underprivileged people in the societies where these projects are undertaken.
2. To create a "conscious awareness" of the social issues of poverty, injustice and related issues within Jesus House.
3. To create an understanding of our social responsibility as God's people to tackle the issues of poverty, injustice and related issues in the world.
4. To facilitate and encourage the active involvement of members of Jesus House in projects and initiatives that tackle these social issues.
5. To create the framework for partnership and strategic alliances with other groups and bodies to achieve the above aims.

The CSR International of Jesus House in 2009/2010 embarked on various projects in Asia, West, East and South Africa to alleviate poverty and enhance human dignity. Jesus House, Brent Cross, aims to use the interventionist approach: "Using diverse and innovative measures, the ministry works to bring a Christian response to the issues and challenges of the borough. Approaches include organizing various outreach projects and events designed to impact and transform the lives of the members of our community for the better." Jesus House aims to help "disadvantaged individuals and families facing challenges through practical projects like 'The Manna Project', and to influence change in the negative values and belief systems pervading society at large".[28]

The Manna Project is a multi-agency initiative focused on assisting various governmental agencies in Barnet Borough to minimize the effect of social challenges and poverty in one of the richest boroughs of London, as six of Barnet's areas are listed in the lowest 10% of the country's worst deprived areas. The Manna Project of Jesus House engages the members of the community in debt counselling, employment training, Youth Enterprise Schemes and asylum support groups.

Black Majority Churches have made remarkable inroads to foster community cohesion, equality, justice and peace within their sphere of influence. These churches are not only identifying social challenges but are also proffering solutions in active collaboration with state agencies. There has been an emergence of various social action initiatives not only from churches but also from non-governmental agencies, companies and charities led by various Christian leaders in Britain. The Nehemiah Housing Authority started by the Church of God of Prophecy is perhaps one of the most successful housing projects by a Black Majority Church tackling the challenges of housing in Britain. In order to extend the frontiers of the Nehemiah Housing Authority a merger was effected with the United Churches Housing Association with the newly formed company known as Nehemiah United Churches Housing Association (NUCHA) with 40 employees.

In the 2007 annual review of the organization, the chairman, Dick Owusu-Darkar, noted that "Nehemiah UCHA now has a turnover of nearly £4 million and works closely with over 6 local authorities across the West Midlands. We are determined to use our experience and influence to make sure that the voice of the BME [Black Minority Ethnic] community is heard by the UK government and in wider society and we are determined to keep our independence and grow as a successful organization with more homes and better lives for our tenants."[29]

Sturge noted the contributions of the Joint Council of Anglo-Caribbean Churches (JCACC) as far back as in the 1980s (led by Reverend Eseme Beswick who later became the President of Churches Together in England in 2000) in combating the menace of drug abuse in England.[30] The Ascension Trust, led by director Less Isaac, has been in existence for more than a decade and has made a remarkable impact with the Street Pastors initiative (co-founded with David Shosanya) in the last five years in Britain. The scheme assists night revellers in staying within defined boundaries of social life from 10pm to 4am on weekends in most major cities of Britain. The Street Pastors are serving the community, assisting the police in maintaining peace through non-threatening presence and enhancing a cohesive community.

The social impact of the Street Pastors has been applauded by public figures such as Prince Charles, the Prince of Wales. In a reception hosted for volunteers who worked with the Hope 08 project on 12 June 2008 at Clarence House, the Prince of Wales said, "I just wanted to say how full of admiration I am for all your extraordinary activities, your devotion and your ability to motivate other people." He further stated that "I do understand how difficult it can be in this day and age overcoming what I feel so often is rampant cynicism, which provides an enormous hurdle at the start. And I also have the feeling that there are an enormous amount of people out there who long to do more but feel terrified because they think they're going to be thought of as old-fashioned."

Peace Alliance is a local initiative in Haringey which started in 2001, an independent voluntary organization working to reduce crime and fear of crime, and to promote peace within the community. Peace Alliance is led by Nims Obunge as the chief Executive Director and the pastor of Freedom Ark based in London and recipient of the MBE for his contributions towards community services. The initiative is based around working with community voluntary/statutory/faith organizations, trying to ensure that there is a holistic response to the challenges of criminal justice in Britain. Peace Alliance makes use of educational, social-religious and institutional approaches towards the challenges of knife and gun crime in Britain.

Nims Obunge has always advocated for a collective community responsibility in the tackling of gun and drug problems in Britain. In the press release preceding the Ministers Together Conference held at the Kingsway International Christian Centre on 4 June 2007, he asserted that "drugs and guns are a menace to our society; we all need to work together with criminal justice agencies to help vulnerable young people and their families in order to keep guns off the street. To achieve this we must have vision and resources as well as political will, parental engagement and public support." This holistic approach resonated in Pastor Ashimolowo's press release preceding the conference as he identified that "Black-led churches have a key role to play in helping to tackle this issue at the grassroots by helping young people to find and fulfil their purpose in life and be the best they can be."[31]

Peace Alliance is noted for the annual Peace Week held in London since 2004 which has brought together various faith organizations in collaboration with the Metropolitan Police and various partners of Peace Alliance. The positive gains of London Peace Week include greater public awareness for community cohesion and inclusiveness through various social, educational and recreational initiatives.

Bishop Wayne Malcolm released an anti-drug CD resource for churches called "Overdose: what the drug dealers won't tell you", which gives an overview of the spiritual origin of drug taking, the obsession of being hooked on Class A drugs, the intrinsic relationship between mental health and drug taking and the impact of drug taking on the wider community.

One of the foremost African social engagement advocates is Rev. Ade Omoba, the co-pioneer of Christian Victory Group's "I Care" project and also Christian Concern for our Nation. In recent years he has been instrumental in engaging churches and their communities and policy-makers in Britain. Rev. Ade Omoba in the last seventeen years has contributed significantly to the establishment of over seventy social action projects with various churches in Britain. He recently opened up a nursery in Brixton at a cost of £1.2 million. Rev. Ade Omoba's proactive disposition is evident in the critique of Black Majority Churches to engage policy-makers on various social and governmental policies in addressing their concerns.

In the run-up to the May 2010 General Election in Britain, Rev. Ade Omoba initiated a hustings forum tagged "Christians and Candidates". Similar initiatives were held by New Wine, Woolwich led by Pastor Tayo Adeyemi and RCCG Holy Ghost Zone, Coventry. Jesus House, Royal Connections and a host of other churches embarked on educating the members of their congregations on the need to exercise their civic right as the politically inclined members of the churches highlighted the various economic, political and social agendas of the parties, while most Black Majority Churches held praying meetings for the success of the 2010 General Elections and the hope that a God-fearing leader would be elected as the prime minister.

One of the most engaging social action initiatives that has impacted Africans and Caribbeans outside the churches is Renewal, Advancement, Financial Freedom, Autonomy (RAFFA), an International Development Agency of the Church of God of Prophecy, which reflects holistic ministry for the twenty-first century. This is a social initiative that has a dynamic integrated approach in terms of the transfer of academic knowledge into the practicalities of the challenges of Blacks in Diaspora in Britain. RAFFA also facilitated a "Battlefield of the Mind" Faith & Spirituality Seminar, which demonstrated the need for the inclusion of spirituality in the provision of mental health services, held at Birmingham and Solihull Mental Health NHS Hospital in 2008. RAFFA is led in the United Kingdom by Rudi Page, co-founder and coordinator of London Joburg Initiative 2003, the first African Caribbean Trade Mission to South Africa representing the UK, supported by UK Trade & Investment and Business Link for London.

### Ecumenical Initiatives of Black Majority Churches

Black Majority Churches in Britain are involved in various social and community activities beyond their ecclesiological orientations; most of these activities provide immediate benefits to needy individuals and their families. Black Majority Churches are also actively involved in some ecumenical initiatives across Britain aimed at addressing various social challenges, such as the Bringing Hope Consortium, a partnership between the Council of Black-led Churches Birmingham, the Diocese of Birmingham and the Birmingham City Council's Community Safety Partnership.

The premise of Bringing Hope is based on the vision of "Christ Action" and "Social Action" that brings holistic, redemptive and transformative love from the heart of God out onto the streets and into the lives of people crying out in need of salvation. The uniqueness of this social action is that it defies denominational boundaries to tackle the problem of gun and knife crime in Birmingham. Similar community-based actions by black Christians include the Damilola Taylor Foundation that has fostered a dynamic working relationship with the Metropolitan Police and Criminal Justice Board, making use of educational, recreational and interventionist approaches in addressing the menace of gun and knife crime amongst youths in Britain.

The contributions of Churches Together in England (an ecumenical instrument which has taken cognizance of the growth of Black Majority Churches and appointed Joe Aldred as the Minority Ethnic Christian Affairs Officer) in the curtailing of gun and knife crime led to the publication of the report of a committee which included Aldred, a Bishop of the Church of God of Prophecy. The Rev. Dr David Cornick, General Secretary of Churches Together in England said: "This report reaffirms our belief that the Christian Church is a sign of God's love for our world. It emphasizes the unique value of each young person's life, and seeks to inspire the churches to reach out to young people in inner cities caught up in social disorder, as an act of good neighbourliness." The report is titled "Who is my neighbour?",[32] and highlighted various issues that can alleviate the current trend of gun and knife crime in Britain. These issues include the development of strategies to better support families, promote feedback events for young people and encourage members to move back into deprived communities. The report also suggests that the government should empower local people to tackle these issues themselves, and encourages inter-faith and inter-generational projects. The police are also advised to improve their involvement with Restorative Justice Projects and forge more dynamic partnerships with churches as key partners.

Some Black Majority Church buildings have been and are still being used to deliver a wide range of services to their community which cannot be underestimated, according to Finneron and Dinham.[33] The New Testament Church of God, Mile End, has initiated "Adopt a Cop" in which a local church adopts a police officer, prays for them and gets to know about the Police Force. This initiative has contributed significantly to Police Public Relations within the NTCG and encouraged some of the youths to consider the Police Force as a career. The stereotypical notion of black youths has significantly been blurred by the Adopt a Cop engagement as Police Officers' social, security and community responsibilities have consistently been reinforced.

The successes of Black Majority Churches might be incomparable to the contributions of historic denominations in the mould of the Church of England, or the Methodist and Catholic Churches in Britain, but ecumenical initiatives are significant. In one of the first major ecumenical acts after being enthroned as the Archbishop of Canterbury on 12 March 2003, Dr Rowan Williams added his name to a covenant signed by the Presidents of Churches Together in England. The other signatories to the covenant were Cardinal Cormac Murphy O'Connor, the Archbishop of Westminster, and the Reverend Esme Beswick, of the Joint Anglo-Caribbean Council of Churches. Reverend Beswick has distinguished ecumenical antecedents in Britain: she has served on several ecumenical bodies, including the Borough of the Dean of Lambeth, Brixton Council of Churches (as Chair), Churches Council of Britain and Former Inner Cities Religious Council. The original covenant was signed by the Presidents of Churches Together in England in the presence of Her Majesty Queen Elizabeth II immediately after the Jubilee Service at St George's Chapel, Windsor, while Dr George Carey was then the Archbishop of Canterbury.

The appointment of Joel Edwards, as the first black General Director of Evangelical Alliance UK, who succeeded Clive Calver in the summer of 1997, was a major contribution of Black Majority Churches to British evangelicalism. Joel Edwards was the Senior Pastor of the New Testament Church of God, Mile End for ten years and a probation officer for fourteen years. He has previously been involved in the Metropolitan Police Independent Advisory Group, the Government's "Working Together" interfaith consultation group and an advisory group to HM Prison Service.

Dr Joel Edwards was also appointed as a commissioner to the Equality and Human Rights Commission (EHRC) on 25 November 2007. After his tenure at the Evangelical Alliance, Joel Edwards, who received a medal of appreciation for services to Jamaica in 2003, and an honorary doctorate from St Andrews University in 2007, is now Micah Challenge's International Director. On 25 January 2011, Joel Edwards and a host of other members of the Micah Challenge team hosted an event entitled "What's Your Promise?" which was held in one of the House of Commons committee rooms with members of the British Parliament on eradicating poverty by 2015. In his speech at the Big Handover, Joel Edwards highlighted this remarkable response to Micah's call, saying: "The fact that 60 million Christians made promises shows that the global church is one of the most powerful and readied agents for change on poverty the world has ever seen." Joel Edwards is perhaps one of the few Black Church leaders who has crossed the boundaries of ethnic Christianity and is highly esteemed in British church circles.

The Black Christian Leaders' Forum (BCLF) was actively engaging with the Church of England prior to the bicentenary celebrations of the abolition of slavery in Britain in 2007. The climax was the active involvement of Black Majority Churches' leadership in the planning and celebration of the anniversary at Westminster Abbey in London, led by the Archbishop of Canterbury, Rowan Williams, with high profile state officials who included Queen Elizabeth II, the former Prime Minister Tony Blair, and Agu Irukwu, chairman of the Executive Council of the Redeemed Christian Church of God, who read the preamble to the prayer of confession and forgiveness.

The role and conduct of the Blacks in attendance at the ceremony has been criticized by pan-Africanist Toyin Agbetu: "I [Agbetu] don't believe it was right for us to have remained in a venue in which the British monarchy, government and church – all leading institutions of African enslavement during the Maafa – collectively refused to atone for their sins."[34] The confession and forgiveness prayer that was led by Agu Irukwu, RCCGUK Executive Council Chairman and Senior Pastor of Jesus House for All Nations, was ambiguous, as there was no clarity of the repentant race (Blacks or British). Beckford observed that "If the Black people were specifically being asked to recognize and forgive African complicity that is understandable. But if, as Mr. Agbetu and many others within the Abbey seem to think, they were being asked to forgive an event in which their ancestors were the victim, the lack of mass action and protest intrigues me."[35] Beckford's berating of the non-reaction of Africans at the Westminster Abbey event was due to the failure of the Africans to come to terms with the structural sin which "can be systemic, a domination system that is manifested in unjust social and political systems, within institutions as well as personal action. Awareness of structural sin facilitates a refocusing on how unjust historical processes have resulted in unjust enrichment and the pain and suffering of others."[36]

Inasmuch as the injustices and structural and economic inequalities created by the slave era are evident, with most of the former colonies still subservient to the British economy, it suffices to note that Africans and Caribbean leaders have contributed to the economic and social inequalities of their nations due to poor governance, corruption and leadership ineptitude which has aggravated the post-slavery syndrome.

In furtherance of its ecumenical relationship with Black Majority Churches in Britain, the head of the Church of England, the Archbishop of Canterbury, Rowan Williams, hosted the members of the Black Christian Leaders Forum at Lambeth Palace on 21 January 2010 to discuss modalities for continued engagement with the Black Majority Churches. This has led to the proposal for the development of a memorandum of understanding between the Church of England and Black Majority Churches. Black Majority Church leaders in attendance included Bishop Joe Aldred, Secretary of Minority Ethnic Affairs, Nims Obunge and David Muir, the former director of Public Policy of the Evangelical Alliance, UK. Others included Pastor Andrew Adeleke, Pastor of House of Praise, Charlton and member of the Executive Council of the RCCGUK.

### Social Capital of Black Majority Churches in Social Action

The concept of social capital has been noted to have multiplicities of usage and ambiguities. The concept of social capital was popularized by the work of American researcher Robert Putnam.[37] Social capital, according to the 1998 World Bank publication entitled *The Initiative of Defining, Monitoring and Measuring Social Capital*, is defined as "institutions, relationships and norms that shape the quality and quantity of a society's social interactions. Increasing evidence shows that social cohesion is critical for societies to prosper economically and for the development to be sustainable. Social capital is not just the sum of the institutions which underpin a society – it is the glue that holds them together."[38] This has been summed up by Gilchrist who noted that social capital has three components – Bonding, Bridging and Linking – as a result of the social–relational dynamics of people.[39]

Gilchrist opines that Bonding evolves from multifaceted relationships of similar orientations like family, friends, kith and kin, while Bridging is the convergence from extraneous relationships in which there exist diverse but overlapping interests amongst people such as neighbours, and Linking is the ability to reach out to more than the immediate sphere of influence of people. There exists the "dark side" of social capital, as observed by Taylor,[40] which includes the destructive capital associated with gangs and the criminal world. The repository of social capital in terms of infrastructural, social and state support over the years provide huge leverage for historic churches' social action initiatives. For instance, the "Church of England through its diocesan structure and its Church Urban Fund, and the Methodist Church through its Mission Alongside the Poor [a charitable organisation] initiative have developed capacity to support substantial involvement in Urban Regeneration informed by developed theologies", according to Farnell *et al.*[41]

This is a marked difference amongst the Black Majority Churches like the RCCG whose social theology is gradually evolving. The obvious social and relational capital created by Black Majority Churches contributes significantly to community cohesion and development. This view is corroborated by Putnam.[42] Moreover, a 2006 publication by the Joseph Rowntree Foundation, entitled *Faith as Social Capital: Connecting and Dividing?* noted that faith groups contribute to social capital through being socially rooted and having shared values. Social capital has been identified by policy-makers and politicians alike in Britain as a potential source of economic and social benefits. The effectiveness of most Black Majority Churches' social action is rooted in the *in situ* local knowledge of their neighbourhood, which can constitute vital information for statutory agencies' attempts to engage the community.

There exist various social action opportunities in Britain that Black Majority Churches are yet to explore, especially ecumenical initiatives. Sturge noted that the contribution of Black Majority Churches is a reflection of their identity, faith and economic class. He was of the opinion that most Black Majority Church members are middle class, "comprising by far the larger percentage of professionals and graduates than anywhere else in the community".[43] They provide a repertoire of skills for the social and religious life of black communities, but he also observed that "BMCs have not taken up opportunities available to them". Black Majority Churches are perhaps the most engaging in terms of youth and after-school clubs, and similar community actions are embarked on by members of these Churches to complement state agencies' provisions and creatively engage the youth in maximizing their potential.

The politicians and the law enforcement agencies seem unable to have a definite solution to the hydra-headed challenges of gun and knife crime in Britain, as politicians are calling on the church as a last beacon of hope for the community to assist through its people-centred approach and orientation. Councillor Alan Craig of the Christian People's Alliance, commenting after the fatal stabbing of 15-year-old Adam Regis in Plaistow in March 2007, said, "The police and local authorities can now be declared officially bankrupt of any meaningful solutions to youth violence in our capital." He further posits that "They [police and local authorities] have created a vacuum and – almost alone – the churches can fill it. It is time for the churches to ignore the authorities, to step into the breach and to take a lead in serving the community in their distinctive way in order to combat gang culture."[44]

He noted various church-based initiatives of Black Majority Churches that have made a remarkable impact on the community, such as STOP DA VIOLENCE, the Street Pastor scheme, the Eastside Young Leaders' Academy, the Peace Alliance and Glory House Football Academy. Senior Pastor of Glory House and initiator of Glory House Football Academy, Dr Albert Odulele, observed that "Youth crime is a serious issue in the borough [Newham], especially drug abuse and truancy." He further noted that "The Football Academy [which has 700 to 800 boys aged between 8 and 16 years] runs weekly, with the aim of providing mentoring for the young boys in the borough. We have children from various racial and religious backgrounds – black, white, Muslim, Hindu, Christians, and so on. We regularly have parent nights and award nights, where we tell the parents what the whole thing is about. They come along and participate."[45] It is rather unfortunate that the positive gain of the Glory House Football Academy was not sustained by the church due to the sudden demise of the academy.

In regard to addressing youth challenges in Britain, Councillor Alan Craig cited three main areas of influence where churches can contribute significantly:

(a) The traditional family values. He asserted that "There is no better long-term alternative to the burgeoning urban gang culture than the active promotion of stable and committed family life. Although the authorities refuse to recognize it, marriage is – literally – a Godsend to our fractured and alienated cities."

(b) The role of fathers in the development of children. He opined that "Christians alone see God as Father so the churches should be shouting from the rooftops that children – especially boys – need fathers. After years of marginalizing fathers, society now needs them more than ever. The churches should rapidly expand their successful fathering and mentoring schemes."

(c) Education for males. "Last week's Ofsted report on pre-school education highlighted that even from the earliest stages our over-feminized schooling system is failing the 50% of the population that God made distinctively male. Boys are unable to use their practical, focused, imaginative and often outdoor energies – and society is the loser."[46]

The involvement of faith communities with the state in various political or social initiatives has come under much scrutiny amongst academicians in various parts of the world. Dr Luke Bretherton, a lecturer at King's College London, presented a paper in 2005 at the conference *Faith's Public Role: Theology and Politics*. His paper was entitled "A New Establishment? Theological politics and the emerging shape of church–state relations". He was of the opinion that contemporary multicultural Britain has brought about the politics of relevance and requisition by various ethnic minorities for recognition and use of public resources in the furtherance of their faith communities as well as a vehicle for engagement of social services and provision of services rendered to their faith community.

The continued interaction of the state and the church is attributable to the organization and mobilization potential of faith communities, thus making the faith communities, of which Black Majority Churches are an integral part, indispensable to politicians in community consultation and engagement. The Black Majority Churches remain effective ways for reaching large segments of black ethnic minorities of the community, and for encouraging them to participate in initiatives such as New Deal for Communities and inner-city regeneration. It is apt to note that despite the thriving social action initiatives of these churches, the political theology of these churches is quite ineffective in challenging structural injustices prevalent within the British social landscape. A typical example is the criminal justice system that has almost stereotyped Blacks within the judicial system.

### *Transformational Church: Liverpool Lighthouse Fellowship*
One of the most influential and transformational churches in Britain within their community is the Lighthouse Fellowship, led by Dr Tami Omideyi, a Nigerian and an engineer. The social and community landscape of Anfield, Liverpool, has been significantly transformed by the social and community initiative of this local church.

[The journey to Anfield started with] a large house group that had been meeting in Wavertree. We [the Lighthouse Fellowship] relocated to Anfield in 1991 to a very racist area of Liverpool with a mixed congregation of 45 people. Anfield area was noted in appalling social statistics as 4th out of the 14 poorest wards as published: 74% claim benefits, 33% long term sick. Major entry point for Asylum seekers and Refugees with over 7,000 in 3 years and 20% unemployment level as at 2002. Over the next 7 years, we grew to about 120 people.[47]

The birthing of the transformational ethos of the Liverpool Lighthouse Fellowship was significantly influenced by Rick Warren's concept of reaching out to the community in his book, *The Purpose Driven Church*, and the influences of Dwight Smith. The inherent "Americanization" influences on Tami Omideyi gradually led to a paradigm shift in the organizational culture and the repositioning of the church as a missional church with focus on the un-churched and the community. The impact of the changes in the missional paradigm of the church was the catalyst that established the present home of the church at the former Gaumont cinema in Anfield, Liverpool, just 100 metres from the famous Anfield football ground. The building was in a very poor state of repair when purchased in 1998 but the owner gave the facility to the church until such time as the church could afford to pay for the property because he said, "I have noticed the good work that you have being doing in the community for a while."[48]

Liverpool Lighthouse is part of the Love and Joy Ministries Group and is Europe's first designated Urban Gospel Arts Centre. Liverpool Lighthouse uses urban gospel arts as a means for engaging groups at risk of exclusion, and for contributing to the transformation of its community. The uniqueness of Liverpool Lighthouse's social initiative is the holistic ethics which revolve around socio-educational, religious and economic initiatives. Love and Joy Ministries' community projects include: a Learn Direct centre; café; small business office space; recording studio; Harmonize – an alternative education programme which uses arts and music for children aged 14 to 16 who are excluded from school or in care, in partnership with Liverpool Local Education Authority (LEA); and Kaleidoscope – an over-55s community project. Other initiatives include card making, local history and a community choir in conjunction with the Capital of Culture Company; Skills for Work courses for the local community; and Integrate – helping asylum seekers and refugees learn English and other skills.

Liverpool Lighthouse had the remit to deliver for Liverpool Capital of Culture 2008 the "City Sings Gospel" international project. The

Lighthouse Fellowship demonstrates the implicit role of faith communities in urban regeneration, as people of faith assign importance to spiritual regeneration and the quality of human relationships in their localities. They also share the practical and material problems and concerns of their neighbours.[49] Love and Joy Gospel Choir, started in 1987, is a vibrant, multi-racial choir, based at the Temple of Praise, and has for many years been at the forefront of building relationships towards community cohesion and inclusion within and outside the United Kingdom. The choir has ministered at BBC's "Songs of Praise", Granada and Sky, and sung on local and national radio as well as on the BBC World Service.

The Love and Joy Ministries (LJM) have developed a dynamic working relationship with various state agencies and LJM Housing is a supported accommodation project for young people, developed in partnership with Social Services for more than a decade. The project operates from leased properties and can accommodate over 250 young people from 6 months to 18 months depending on their psychological and medical state "with noticeable success in re-engaging them with families and reducing the levels of hospital visits due to self-harm. The project also offered outreach support services to 105 young people in various locations, helping them to maintain their tenancies."[50]

## BLACK MAJORITY CHURCHES AND "LABELLING THEORY"

On account of palpable racial stereotyping and statistical evidence of the crime rate, especially gun and knife crime, amongst black youths in Britain, most Black Majority Church leaders have been motivated to rise to the challenge of refuting labelling theory and its associated criminalizing effects on black youths in Britain. Muncie gives the core argument of opponents of labelling theory: "behaviour may be labelled criminal but it is not this behaviour in itself that constitutes crime".[51] The dysfunctional behaviour of some youths is often associated with the societal and moral upheavals in relation with crime as youths are labelled as social deviants and a menace to the community. In order to address this perspective, Cullen and Agnew posit a reversal of orientation, as "labelling theory proposes that we focus our attention not on the behaviour of offenders, but on the behaviour of those who label, react to and otherwise seek to control offenders. Labelling theory argues that it is these efforts of social control that ultimately trigger the processes that trap individuals in a criminal career."[52]

The travesty of labelling theory within the British social landscape was further amplified by the former Prime Minister of Britain, Mr Tony Blair. Wintour noted that, "In 2007 the former Prime Minister claimed the spate of knife and gun murders in London was not being caused by poverty, but a distinctive black culture."[53] The assertion of Tony Blair was not only considered condescending but an uninformed opinion that was potentially divisive amongst black leaders in Britain, including church leaders. Wintour summed up Mr Blair's perspective as being "at odds with those of the Home Office minister Lady Scotland, who told the Home Office select committee last month [as at the time of the speech] that the disproportionate number of black youths in the criminal justice system was a function of their disproportionate poverty, not to do with a distinctive Black culture". It is imperative to note that delinquent behaviour is not only a black youth phenomenon but defies race. The media has been noted to be sensationalist in their reporting, which has contributed to the creation of a moral panic in the community.

The mechanism for such sensationalism is described by Jewkes, who observed that in news reporting "once a story has reached the required threshold it may have to meet further thresholds to stay on the agenda; the story is often kept alive due to the creation of news thresholds, some stories are used as 'fillers' during quiet news periods and tend to be reported in waves, suggesting widespread social problems rapidly reaching a crisis point".[54] Less Isaac agrees with this view on the influence of the British media in labelling British black youths: "I think there is overemphasis on young black men in jail. But the fact is – as I visit jails up and down the country – there is a very high disproportion of young black men in our institutions, hence it has, in one sense, demonized young black boys and men in the public's opinion. Every year I meet up with literally hundreds of black boys and girls who have accomplished their A-levels and are actively engaging in seeking further education at universities, yet they never get a glimpse in the public domain or media."[55]

The mass media might not have hyped the incidents of knife and gun crime in London since 2006, but "the image of Black boys and young men portrayed through the media is not a positive one".[56] The media do portray black youths in a negative and stereotypical manner, but it is indeed a matter of fact based on statistics that youth crime cannot be dismissed as moral panic exacerbated by the media. The general apathy with respect to the breakdown of traditional family values in Britain was echoed by Britain's Conservative Party leader, David Cameron, who said, "I believe that family breakdown is at the heart of so many of these problems and it is when families break down that gangs can sometimes take over."[57]

The breakdown of traditional family institutions in Britain today is a reflection of the changes in worldviews in the West in the last fifty years from modernity to postmodernity. The once typical British family headed by two parents (man and woman) has undergone substantial changes during the twentieth century as "marriage levels in Britain are at an all-time low. For every three weddings there are now two divorces – the highest rate in Europe. Cohabitation has risen 64% in a decade, with almost half of children now born outside wedlock. We [Britain] also have by far the highest proportion of lone parents in Europe – a quarter of children now live with a single mum."[58]

The African and Caribbean families which make up a significant proportion of the membership of most Black Majority Churches have similar dysfunctional family challenges as "the Commons Committee investigating young Black people and the criminal justice system was told that 57% of black Caribbean children grew up in lone parent households, compared with 25% of white children" according to Batmanghelidjh.[59] The intricacies of the dysfunctional social values of black British Caribbean youths can be a by-product of the racial experiences of the *Windrush* era characterized by social exclusion and material and social inequalities, as Burke observed that "the first group of Afro-Caribbeans to arrive in the UK came with high aspirations and ambitions but found themselves consigned to a force of cheap labour. Their children were subject to racial discrimination which resulted in endless pressure."[60]

The continued social deviation of some black youths in Britain might be induced by their survivalist mentality, changes in the cultural paradigm, an underclass culture and a general breakdown of traditional families. This might constitute a niche for further investigations with respect to the effects of "anomie syndromes" on the integration of second-generation African and Caribbean migrants in the UK.

Black Majority Churches' responses to labelling theory have been diverse and multifaceted. The Black Christian Leaders' Forum (BCLF) is one of the numerous frontiers that have being engaging the Department for Children, Schools and Families (DCSF). The BCLF has held regular consultations with government agencies since its inception in 2006. Joe Aldred, secretary for Ethnic Minority Affairs for Churches Together in England and a member of the Black Christian Leaders' Forum was of the opinion that black youths need black role models in order to navigate crucial challenges of life. He asserted that "it is crucial for people who have similar backgrounds to those boys to mentor and teach them at critical points in their lives when they are young and impressionable at school."[61]

The National Black Boys Can Association (NBBCA) led by Dr Cheron Byfield of Excell3, the charity under which NBBCA operates, is a direct response to counteract the inadequacies within the educational and community sectors for black British youths. The organization has a wide range of educational, social and community-based initiatives to empower black youths with strategies to cope with life challenges and acquire valuable life skills. The *modus operandi* of National Black Boys Can is the early intervention strategy which aims to maximize the potential of young black boys to adulthood, citizenship and career. The organization was selected in 2006 to be partners with the Home Office, Department of Communities and Local Government (DCLG) till 2009 which culminated in the production of parenting books commissioned by DCLG of which 100,000 copies were produced and distributed.

The Church of God of Prophecy has been actively involved in the National Black Boys Can project with the church coordinating the Croydon network of National Black Boys Can. The organization has launched the first educational web-based resource for black pupils – www.blackpupils.com – and developed a strategic partnership with Oxford University.

A media blitz was generated by the death of Victoria Climbié who died in the intensive care unit of St Mary's Hospital, Paddington on 25 February 2000, aged 8 years and 3 months. She was a victim of abuse and her death was caused by multiple injuries arising from months of ill-treatment and abuse by her great-aunt, Marie-Therese Kouao, and her great-aunt's partner, Carl John Manning. Victoria Climbié's case heralded a new phase in the labelling of Black Majority Churches as "rogues" and perversionists of the Christian doctrine. The appalling and shocking death of Victoria Climbié included an element of belief in possession and witchcraft by her guardians. Ethnic minority churches in Britain received further negative publicity in the media with the Metropolitan Police investigation into the identity of "Adam", the torso of a Nigerian boy found in 2001 in the River Thames. The media searchlight was focused again on the disappearance of 300 African boys missing from London school registers between July and September 2001. There are any number of purported unofficial explanations but it was noted that "there was no evidence at all to suggest anything sinister had happened to them" according to Commander Dave Johnston of the Child Abuse Investigation Command.[62] Dominic Casciani, BBC correspondent on Community Affairs in an interview on 22 May 2006, with Pastor Jean Boasco, a Congolese Pastor and community leader, expressed the ostracization and polarization of the Congolese community due to the sensationalism of the media reports about the abuse of a Congolese Christian. Bosco said, "We feel hurt by this – it's as if we have been demonized and put outside the mainstream Christian fellowship, as if we are not being recognized as proper Christians." This invariably had multiple social and religious resonances within the black community in Britain. Hackney North Member of Parliament Diane Abbott, the first black woman ever elected to the British Parliament in 1987 and later a contestant for the Leadership of the Labour Party, was quick to jump on the bandwagon in a column for London's *Evening Standard* of 7 June 2005 and laid the blame on the pastors who she said "make a good living off their congregations" in churches that "distort fundamental Christian teachings". She further called for the banning of "these witchcraft churches". Lord Stevens, a former commissioner of the Metropolitan Police, condemned African churches, which he said were "obsessed by witchcraft, exorcism and evil spirits". "We must," Lord Stevens railed in a Sunday newspaper column, "stop this madness costing children's lives."[63]

Paul Valley of the *Independent* newspaper of Monday 18 July 2005 noted utter disgust and refutation of the blanket labelling of the Black Majority Churches, and Nims Obunge, the pastor of Freedom's Ark Church in Haringey, North London, a police chaplain and a member of the national Crimestoppers board, described the level of reporting as "pathetic". Obunge noted the irreconcilable mass labelling of Black Majority Churches with the incidents of child abuse; he posited that "none of the three main incidents is really linked to responsibility by a church and yet we have been maligned unjustly by all these lies and innuendo, and the minds of the public have been prejudiced against us. Journalists can't seem to understand the difference between exuberant worship and child abuse. It's pitiful."[64]

The black community, especially the Black Majority Churches, were criminalized and discriminated against further by the BBC Newsnight broadcast "Exorcism or Witchcraft?" Reverend Katei Kirby, Director General of the African and Caribbean Evangelical Alliance until cessation of operations in April 2009, refuted the perceived campaign of calumny from the British media as she said, "Exorcism was totally misrepresented in it. The programme makers didn't understand. They made assumptions that people were being traumatised on the basis of observations." She further noted that "People in these services are not there against their will. And how they behave is not to do with trauma but is culturally determined. To sensationalise it because it's in an African context smacks of discrimination."[65] The rhetoric of the British press seems not only discriminatory but also smacks of Eurocentric ideals of centuries ago. As Beckford noted, "some of the coverage reminds me of the racist 19th-century anthropological literature".[66] Lee Jasper, a Christian and former adviser to London's former mayor, Ken Livingstone, accused the police of being responsible for "a very dangerous report" which was resulting in "a racist witch-hunt of African communities".[67]

The unfolding events generated a much-needed synergy and networking amongst Black Majority Church leaders to confront the labelling of Black Majority Churches. Irukwu opined that a poor consultative process by the government was a major contribution to the criminalization of Black Majority Churches as child abusers:

> We [Black Majority Church leaders] don't know the truth and real extent of what we are dealing with, and rumours are beginning to run rife. We are concerned that unless the government handles this wisely, it could in fact drive a wedge between black-majority churches and the wider society, particularly when the newer churches are beginning to make their contributions in addressing some of society's problems. We want to help to facilitate positive steps towards finding and applying meaningful solutions, but we cannot do so if the government does not consult with us adequately.[68]

The obvious labelling perceived to be orchestrated by the British media was effectively doused by the comments of Inspector Bob Pull, a Christian pastor and a former member of London Metropolitan Police's "Project Violet" unit investigating faith-related child abuse. During an interview with BBC News and Community Affairs correspondent Dominic Casciani on 22 May 2006, he said that "of the 42,000 child abuse allegations the Metropolitan Police has dealt with in the past five years, 52 of them were related to allegations against African spiritualists offering 'deliverance' from possession. Eight of these have ended up in court, although other investigations resulted in action by social services." This constitutes 0.1% of the total percentage of reported child abuse cases in Britain. This was further corroborated by the Eleanor Stobart Report which recommended sharing of information of children with various agencies involved in children's services, consultation with the faith communities and adoption of good practice codes as well as monitoring by immigration agencies on migrant children.

The irreconcilability of press reports with the empirical evidence from the Metropolitan Police smacks of discrimination and sensationalism of the press in the criminalizing of Black Majority Churches and obvious failings within the British social services. The House of Commons Report on the Victoria Climbié case observed that the case of child abuse was not entirely new to the British community; claims of abuse included cases such as Maria Colwell in 1973, Jasmine Beckford and Tyra Henry (both in 1984), Kimberley Carlile (1986), Leanne White (1992) and Chelsea Brown in 1999. The deaths of these children all share many points of similarity. The pattern does not even end with the death of Victoria Climbié; since that time there have been at least two more high-profile cases (Lauren Wright in 2000, and Ainlee Walker in 2002).

In fact the report noted that there had been over 70 public inquiries into major cases of child abuse since 1948 but most of the enquiries were left on the shelf with no implementation of the recommendations. This assertion is further corroborated by the Sub-Culture Alternatives Freedom Foundation (SAFF) website that has repositories of various abuses since 1988 entitled "The Black Museum of Priestly Abuse". The gross institutional inadequacies identified by the Laming report during the Victoria Climbié inquiry and the Eleanor Stobart Report have led to a change in paradigm within various governmental agencies in Britain. The "Baby P" incident of 2007 still shows that child abuse is not an issue of race but an act of perverseness by the perpetrators of this inhumane crime against human dignity as enshrined in the Human Rights Charter of the United Nations.

In terms of influencing governmental policies on youth and the criminal justice system, Black Majority Christian leaders are strategically influencing and articulating not only the Christian ethos but are adequately representing the ethnic minorities to ensure an egalitarian society. Nims Obunge, Pastor of Freedom's Ark, the Executive Director of Peace Alliance and Acting Chair for the London Criminal Justice Board advisory group and Less Isaac, the Director of the Ascension Trust were invited as witnesses by the House of Commons Committee on Young Black Boys and the Criminal Justice System on 7 November 2006 chaired by John Denham, Communities Secretary under the Gordon Brown Administration. Obunge and Isaac informed the committee of potential racial prejudice in its composition, as Obunge said, "I am a bit challenged by the present company, the Committee, because I do not see any black person on it. That, in itself, is a reflection of the challenge we have in the black community. If I am giving evidence, I had hoped to see somebody from my community sat with yourselves who would be able to tune things – and I am not talking about somebody sitting at the back of yourselves, but sitting in the centre." His opinion was graciously acknowledged by the committee but James Denham noted that the committee was a reflection of the composition of the House of Commons. Obunge and Isaac consistently reiterated the perceived lack of opportunities and institutional racism as experienced by black youths in the hands of the criminal justice system. Obunge, in an un-hypocritical stance, was quite empirical:

> When we look at stop and search rates, the facts speak for themselves. The black community is more likely to be stopped and searched. I have sat on the MPA [Metropolitan Police Authority] Stop and Search Scrutiny Panel and the Home Office Stop and Search Community Panel and the statistics are very high: up to six times more likely in some cases than their white counterparts. When that first encounter is going to take place with the police, black young people already feel persecuted.[69]

In his submissions to the House of Commons Committee on Young Black People and the Criminal Justice System, Obunge berated the lack of exit strategies to get young black boys out of crime. Some of them are willing to come clean of their vices, but the lack of protective custody from law enforcement personnel and the Home Office have kept many within the vicious circle of social deviance.

Black Majority Church leaders in the mould of Aldred, Byfield, Less Isaac, Nims Obunge and members of the Black Christians Forum are not only identifying but are prescribing and engaging with the challenges of labelling amongst black youths in Britain. This presents a holistic ministry that embodies the spiritual, social and communal wellbeing of Christians as well as the wider community. In order to articulate the black course in Britain there is a need to engage in empirical evidence, to address identified social and community constraints of African and Caribbean families. Professor Mullard in his speech at the launching of Faith in Britain, at the House of Commons on 5 October 2010, corroborated the need for evidence-based initiatives. Announcing the launch of a Commission of Enquiry into the challenges and opportunities of black families in Britain, he asserted that "the commission of inquiry will provide empirical data to inform public policy as well as facilitate conversation about the complex challenges facing families, especially among African and Caribbean families". A research-based initiative will eliminate doubts and misconceptions about whether labelling theory constitutes a challenge to Blacks in Britain or otherwise as the empirical data will not only identify but also be used in prescribing solutions to some of these challenges to the government.

## POLITICAL ACTIVISM OF BLACK MAJORITY CHURCHES IN BRITAIN

The political and economic activism of most Black Majority Churches is gradually evolving in comparison to the founding days of these churches in Britain. Most Black Majority Churches in their founding stages were insular and exclusive but a new paradigm has evolved as a by-product of the disaffection of the second generation of West Indian migrants in search of identity and expression of their cultural and religious ideals in the face of institutional racism. The holistic ministry of Christ in addressing the spiritual, economic, social and cultural challenges of his day provides a typology for the economic and political engagement for Black Majority Churches in Britain. Jesus in his Palestine days provided a unique leadership for his disciples that stood against the religious, political and social exploitation of his day.

The Black Majority Churches' political ideology is gradually evolving and taking shape. Aldred noted the misconception that Black Majority Churches were mainly preoccupied with ecclesiastical rites, insular, inclusive yet exclusive, identifying but not prescribing, utopian communities encumbered with futuristic parousia and politically inactive.[70] In retrospect, Black Church leaders in the mould of Olaudah Equiano, Ignatius Sancho and Ottobah Cugoano were active politically through their literary contributions to the demise of the slave trade in collaboration with the Clapham Sect [Clapham sect or saints were a group of influential likeminded Church of England reformers who shared common political views concerning the liberation of slaves, the abolition of slave trade and the reform of the Penal system] as observed by Sturge.[71] Aldred cited Beresford's assertion that Black Church leaders are politically active and engaging politicians.[72] One of the major strategic initiatives that has facilitated the relevance of Black Majority Churches in Britain is the Black Christian Leaders' Forum (BCLF).

This growing level of engagement in strategic high-level politics is emerging in numerous ways, significantly through the work of the Black Christian Leaders' Forum which is a consortium representing African and Caribbean Christians in the United Kingdom. The BCLF have met with the Prime Minister and departmental secretaries on a wide range of issues with respect to the black community. At a meeting held on 25 October 2007 with the former Prime Minister, Gordon Brown, who emphasized continued commitment towards cohesive community, Brown said, "We need to unlock the talent that exists in our communities, encouraging young people, even when they feel disengaged, that they have something to contribute. Let's get the message across and we can build a stronger society. It's appreciated throughout the whole country."[73]

The strategic and visionary appeal of the BCLF is that black Christian leaders are no longer perceived as faith leaders alone but vital in various community initiatives within their immediate ethnic strata that can be a vehicle to influence governmental policies and a sounding board for the ethnic or cultural ideals of their immediate constituencies. One of the remarkable fruits of the consultative process of the BCLF was the REACH Report which not only identified the challenges of black youths in Britain but adequately proffered solutions from a multifaceted perspective to empower and maximize the potential of black youths in Britain. The aftermath of the REACH Report was the initiation of REACH National Role Models in London on 3 December 2008, attended by the former Secretary of State for Communities and Local Government Hazel Blears, the Attorney General Baroness Scotland and broadcaster Kwame Kwei Armah.

Similar initiatives with an interventionist approach to education include From Boyhood to Manhood, led by Decima Francis, based in Peckham, Southwark, which works with young children who are about to be excluded or have been excluded from school and which has created the gun crime strategy for the Mayor of London.

The political engagement of Black Majority Churches in Britain might be misconstrued to be docile, but there exists a subtle and gradual entrenchment of members of these churches at various levels of governance as public servants, who have consciously maximized the opportunity to place Black Majority Churches on the governance radar. Lee Jasper, (former Policy Director for Equalities and Policing for the former Mayor of London, Ken Livingstone, Chair of the Trident Independent Advisory Group, a partnership trying to combat gun crime in the black community, and a member of the London Criminal Justice Board), resigned under frenzied media scrutiny when publicly funded organizations led by his friends and associates were accused of financial irregularities.

Lee Jasper unveiled the depth and influence his position provided for Black Majority Church leaders in Britain to covertly influence government policies. He has always been a member of Ruach Ministries led by Bishop John Francis, one of the most influential Black Majority Church preachers in Britain. Jasper leads over 5,000 congregants and has impacted Brixton through various social action initiatives in which many drug barons have been converted through his ministry. In an interview with *Keep the Faith* magazine in its 2009 maiden edition, he said, "many people *do not know, whilst in office* [emphasis mine] l brought the Black pastors together with the Mayor to discuss embedding the church into the Mayor's Office or that l moved heaven and earth to help KICC, another great church. Once people knew that we [Jasper and Black Majority Church leaders] were working together, praying together, marching for peace together, they launched their attack on me." However, though he inferred that his Christian antecedents and racial undertones were contributory factors to the media attention that led to his resignation, he was a type of Obadiah with his heart for Black Majority Churches, or an Esther "for such a time as this" in the subtle political clout of Black Majority Church leaders.

The process of engaging of the political class by Black Majority Church leaders to represent their view with respect to various governmental policies has entailed a series of mega-consultations and networking amongst these churches. For instance, Mr Tunji Adebayo of TA Properties Consultants, based at Willesden, submitted a 20,000-name petition to the former Mayor of London, Ken Livingstone, on the conversion of unused commercial properties to churches to serve as social outposts for communities and also provide ecclesiastical, pastoral and spiritual care for their adherents. Mr Adebayo, though a property consultant, also serves as the pastor of Central London Fellowship, a parish of the Redeemed Christian Church of God. He was not only engaging the government but was stra-tegically repositioning the needs of churches of which he is an active member whilst simultaneously challenging the government to change legislation on the issue.

Mr Adebayo, in a press release on his behalf by Paul Eddy of Paul Eddy Public Relations Limited, said: "Mr Livingstone says he's sympathetic, but it is up to central government and that he has no powers." Adebayo's ability to understand the signs of the times was to pique the conscience of the nation through the ongoing frenzied media reports on gun and knife crime. He posited that "the victims of crime in these areas, and the churches who want to help, do not want any more sympathy from politicians, they want joined-up action". He succinctly appealed to the public conscience: "In the middle of this political fudge is the fact that both central and local Governments have been calling on the Black communities to own the problems of violence, which has led to several people being stabbed to death in the last year alone in the capital. The Prime Minister himself has called on the Black community to become 'a part of the solution.'"[74]

The pragmatism of Black Majority Churches in terms of their political and social ideology is depicted by the consistency and emergence of diverse African/Caribbean initiatives to address their religious and social perceptions. The African and Caribbean Community Network (ACCN), one such initiative concerned with the welfare of the black community in Britain, organized a conference on Financing Church Buildings held at Jesus House, Brent Cross, with about 300 leaders of the Black Majority Churches in attendance. The preliminary phase for the conference was preceded by a luncheon hosted by Barclays Bank at their Headquarters in Canary Wharf, London.

One of the most pragmatic of the organizations that have been advocates of black engagement in politics is Operation Black Vote (OBV) led by Simon Woolley. The organization has created a broad-spectrum network within the black community and the wider society to sensitize and educate Blacks in Britain to be politically active in contributing positively to the governance and the political life of Britain. Simon Woolley's organization mounted a high-powered campaign on behalf of deselected Labour party candidates in June 2009 for the May 2010 election which included the mayor of Waltham Forest, Anna Mbachu. Simon Woolley, with a sense of pride and justice, stated that, "This is an excellent decision, and a just one too, which demonstrates what activism can do. OBV works to ensure that BME [Black Minority Ethnic] talent across all parties is recognised and not mistreated. We made it clear to the local Labour party early on that the deselections were unacceptable, and we demanded action while affording suggestions about ways forward."[75]

Bishop Wilton Powell, the presiding Bishop of the Church of God of Prophecy, visited the offices of Operation Black Vote in London on 11 February 2010. Bishop Powell reminded OBV's Director Simon Woolley that "if we want greater success in our communities we must invest time and effort in collaborative projects and strengthening relations". The meeting was judged to be thought-provoking as the two leaders looked forward to future collaborations. The political clout and influence of Operation Black Vote is a transatlantic phenomenon with active collaborations with American civil rights activists. In January 2010 OBV facilitated a meeting between Tottenham MP David Lammy and American civil rights activist Rev. Al Sharpton whilst on a visit to the United Kingdom, seeking a greater role for UK and US churches in Haiti.

This distinctive paradigm amongst Black Majority Church leaders has ushered in a new era in public theology in the history of these churches. The editorial of the first issue of the *International Journal of Public Theology* defined the term "public theology" as "a deliberate use of common language in a commitment to influence public decision-making, and also to learn from substantive public discourse ... an engagement of living religious traditions with their public environment – the economic, political and cultural spheres of common life".⁷⁶

This implies that, despite the fact that Christians are in the world but not of the world, Black Majority Church members are intimately connected to the social and civic structures that define their cultural, political, economic and civic life. This is akin to the intimate fellowship and the prescribed commandment to Adam in the account of the Book of Genesis (Gen 1:28; Gen 2:15–20). This provides a model for Black Majority Church leaders to speak prophetically to the economic and social policies of governance that promote a peaceful and egalitarian society based on Christian values.j198

As a prophetic witness, the Black Majority Churches need to abandon individualism for communalism, to stop living for denominational ideals, and be proactive and live out their Christian values. The prophetic witness is a responsibility of Black Majority Churches in Britain. As one of the most influential men of the twentieth century, Martin Luther King, asserted in his seminal Letter from Birmingham Jail, "[The] judgment of God is upon the church as never before. If today's church does not recapture the sacrificial spirit of the early church, it will lose its authenticity, forfeit the loyalty of millions, and be dismissed as an irrelevant social club with no meaning for the twentieth century."⁷⁷

De Gruchy's seven points present a typology for continued political relevance of Black Majority Churches in Britain; this could constitute a heptalogue for political activism of these churches:

1. BMCs should not seek to exalt Christianity above other faiths but to witness to values that Christian beliefs are essential for the good of all and sundry.
2. BMCs should ensure contextualization of Christian concepts, language and symbols to the public without losing the core feature of the Christian tradition that is accessible to people outside the Christian tradition.
3. BMCs' leadership requires adequate understanding of various governmental policies in relation to the Christian faith, consistently engaging in reflective practice and theological critique to determine the influence and effects of such policies on the BMCs.
4. The theology of BMCs should be multi-disciplinary in character by ensuring that the contents and processes are entwined.
5. BMCs should herald a new paradigm with respect to the point of view of oppressor and oppressed, and to the re-establishment of

impartiality; it sides with the helpless against the influential, and seeks to personify truth to power drawing its motivation from the visionary course in the Bible.
6. BMCs should consciously be nurtured and informed by biblical and theological reflection and a rich life of worship in relation to the British context in the light of their experiences and their missiological agenda.
7. BMCs require a spirituality which enables a lived experience of God, with people and with creation, fed by a longing for justice and wholeness and a resistance to all that prevent wellbeing.[78]

## FAITH COMMUNITIES: STATE AND SOCIAL PUBLIC POLICY IN BRITAIN

### Faith Communities: A Multifaceted Concept

The concept of "faith communities" within social public policy has been defined from a variety of perspectives, on account of the various functionalities of the phrase "faith communities" and its heterogeneous usage. Bretherton opined that the phrase "faith community" is problematic because "faith denotes 'Christianisation', or even 'Protestantisation' of other religious groups".[79] He noted the inadequacies of the concept in defining the diverse religious traditions of various faiths, and Farnell *et al.* identified this problem as a major constraint to policy formulators and statutory agencies' personnel due to religious illiteracy.[80]

This problem is further compounded by the homogenization of ethnic and faith communities. Farnell *et al.* noted that "Reformed Jews are not distinguished from ultra-Orthodox ones: evangelical and Pentecostal Christians are perceived as 'born again fundamentalists' who are inherently Right-wing and reactionary."[81] In view of the shortcomings identified by Bretherton, he proposed another synonym for faith communities – "Faith Designated Group" – which "indicates both the work of religious NGOs and the work undertaken by religious congregations, Mosques, Gudwaras, etc., in and of themselves".[82] The ingenuity of Bretherton's use of the phrase Faith Designated Group has not eliminated his abhorrence for the use of the word "faith" due to its religious interpretations and its central importance to the Christian faith.

The concept of faith communities is a political euphemism convenient to politicians and policy formulators in a bid to enlist the services of various non-religious and religious organizations. Their objective is mainly to engage the social and relational capital of the faith communities or Faith Designated Groups to enhance their political subscription to the "social mantra" of the "triad community manifesto", namely community development, community inclusion and community cohesion. The phrase "faith communities", in generic usage, is associated with ambiguities and misconceptions on account of the diversity of religious expressions. However, the term "faith" is more inclusive than divisive, as Bretherton asserted – if the phrase "church-based" had been used as a sub-set of the Faith Designated Group or faith communities, this would have excluded adherents of Judaism, Islam and others.[83] The obvious ambiguity of the concept of faith presents an ominous Pandora's Box for continued criticism of the interaction of state and religion in social policy with its inherent ambivalent position, as noted by researchers in America.[84]

The inherent ambiguities due to the heterogeneous composition of faith groups has never been a barrier to their contributions to community development, despite the misconception that most social action revolves round proselytization, especially in Black Majority Churches. The misconception of the *modus operandi* of Black Majority Churches has led to systematic bias in funding of some religious groups' social actions by the state. According to the *Report of the Policy Action Team on Community Self-help* by the Home Office in 1999, "in many cases faith groups ... will be the strongest around and yet their potential may be overlooked by funders and others engaged in programmes of community development". The faith communities have been noted to be inexplicably linked with continuous social and relational ties with their existing community, characterized by inherent leadership, infrastructural capabilities, human resources and relational and social capital.

Because of operational and network intricacies, faith communities often have more street credibility in reaching out to perceived "hard liners" which bureaucratic agencies might not be able to connect with. Farnell *et al.* observed that the continued interaction of the state and faith communities was a product of "the context of the modernization of local government" and "the need for local authorities to address social exclusion and reconnect local communities".[85] They further reiterated that no matter what the skill set is of most faith communities, there exists the need for the acquisition of a different skill set in engaging state agencies, and poor religious literacy constitutes a barrier to bureaucratic officers. The obvious resonance of "state political correctness" is found in the convergence of religious values and nuances in consonance with community ideals, which are common values of most ethnic or religious groups. Such ideals include integrity, good citizenship, egalitarian community, peace and good neighbourliness. It is apt to note that the recent religious intolerance and extremism in Britain has greatly underscored the common values of co-existence amongst various religious and ethnic groups.

### State and Social Public Policy

The "politics of relevance" in the words of Bretherton is due to the identification of the potential of "Black Minority Ethnic" which is an encompassing generic term used to designate various ethnic communities encompassing Asians, Africans and Caribbeans. A major component of this broad-spectrum classification is the Black Majority Churches in Britain. The importance of this sub-sector of the Black Minority Ethnic organizations was affirmed by McLeod *et al.* in their seminal work on Black and Minority Ethnic Voluntary and Community Organizations, but they posited that there are gross inadequacies within governmental policy framework, as often Black Majority Churches are "bypassed by grant regimes which tend to exclude support for the promotion of specific religion".[86] The positive discriminatory grounds are rooted in the ethos of grant-giving organizations' subscription that religion should be firmly compartmentalized to personal space.

It is rather ironic that the social capital of these churches in terms of infrastructure, relationship networks and values has been identified as vital to community development, as observed by Cote and Healy but yet it is a case of "identifying but not belonging".[87] Aldred opines that Black Majority Church leaders need to be pragmatic because of the "tension between the Caribbean-British led Churches and state agencies". Quoting an unidentified source he said, "we are a Black church when we apply for funding but just church when we worship".[88] This has gradually led to a reflective and proactive approach based on the experiential perspective of some Black Majority Churches that has led to the formation of charitable organizations that are devoid of any ecclesiastical or religious trappings to access government funds.

The political lexicon in Britain in the last two decades has significantly changed to include concepts such as social capital, faith communities, social inclusion and community cohesion. The new semantics have generated diverse interest within government research agencies in Britain such as the Inequalities Branch of the Office of National Statistics (ONS), which conducted research on social capital and public policy. The apparent integration of faith communities with the state in contemporary Britain is a sequel to the "new" multicultural Britain accentuated by post-war migration in the 1950s, but this presents a basis for the argument for religion to be limited to private space. McLeod *et al.* observed that prior to the new commonwealth migration of the 1950s the existence of Black Minority Ethnic Organizations in Britain before the First World War had a high presence at "maritime industries and port cities" with ethnic associations such as "Sons of Africa in Cardiff and African Progress Union in Liverpool".[89]

Post-war immigration led to the emergence of religious pluralism shaped by various religious groups, such as Islam, with 1.6 million adherents in Britain, according to a 2004 Home Office publication, *Working Together: Cooperation Between Government and Faith Communities*. This figure might be well over 2 million in the wake of attempts by Islamic fundamentalists to Islamize Britain.[90] The emergence of various religious groups undoubtedly has influenced public policy significantly to reflect the various multi-ethnic communities in Britain who are stakeholders in the country such as Jews, Shintoists, Jains, etc. The 2001 British Census heralded a new epoch in the history of the Census in the United Kingdom as religion became a factor in population enumeration. The 2001 Census revealed that 76.8% of the population have some religious subscription while 71.6% were identified as Christians, which constitutes the largest faith community in Britain. This high percentage of Christians is perhaps mostly made up of nominal Christians who are "believing but not belonging" in the words of Grace Davies. Historically, British social history has been progressively shaped by Christian churches in various perspectives ranging from education to community cohesion and welfarism.

This has contributed to the marked influence of Christian social thought in the social policy of Britain.[91] There exists a repertoire of divergent views with respect to the active engagement of faith communities into public policy. Toynbee[92] and Grayling[93] queried the rationale for the engagement of religious organizations in public social policy in Britain. It is asserted that the heterogeneous composition of the faith communities, rather than uniting, might constitute a divisive feature because of counter-religious beliefs, but sociological studies in America show that this assertion is ambivalent.[94] The inherent pyramidal structure of most religious organizations, in which power is vested at the apex of such organizations, similar to secular institutions, is antithetical to the kind of egalitarian ethos that should be created through community initiatives via a consultative process within the faith communities.

Grayling surmized that religion should be compartmentalized into the private sphere; this partition would eliminate any inhibition through prejudice, thereby creating a classless status for active participants in social public policy. The concept of community is a transatlantic phenomenon politically and philosophically, as the United States and Britain have been emphasizing the role of the community in development in relation to the engagement of faith communities. Annette opines that the resonance of communitarianism as depicted by the New Labour political polemics and the New Democrats has led to "compassionate conservatism".[95] He further posited that this has brought about community utopianism amongst members of the community as the beacon of engagement in urban regeneration and contributing to renewal of their communities.

This assertion by Annette is further corroborated by the Department of the Environment, Transport and the Regions' (DETR) publication of 1997 entitled *Involving Communities in Urban and Rural Regeneration,* which states that members of the faith community, too, are stakeholders in their communities, as are any other residents. The basis of this assertion is the notion that "faith communities are a good point of entry into involving the local community ... faith organisations may also be a signpost to regeneration partnerships to other contacts in the community; they may even help to organise local involvement".[96] These assertions are validated by Liverpool Lighthouse Fellowship, which is evident in its complementary social and community initiatives that have brought about the social transformation of the Anfield area of Liverpool.

In the run-up to the 2001 election, the former Prime Minister of Britain, Tony Blair, addressed a press conference of religious organizations from both Christian and other faith backgrounds under the auspices of the Christian Socialist Movement at Westminster Central Hall. He stated his own religious motivation in politics and emphasized the importance of religion in contemporary society. Blair spoke of "a new and vital energy about the practice of faith in the UK. A new and vital energy within the churches and other faith groups about engagement in the communities within which you work and have your being." He noted the contributions of church schools which were a pillar of the education system, "valued by very many parents for their faith character, their moral emphasis and the high quality of education they generally provide".[97]

Blair's assertions contributed to the discussions on the contributions of faith communities to social capital in consonance with the 2002 report of the Greater London Enterprise and London Churches Group. *Neighbourhood Renewal in London: The Role of Faith Communities* identified 7,000 projects and 2,200 faith buildings. This figure might no longer be relevant with the proliferation and success of Black Majority Churches that have "bombed" London and are continually striving to engage their community. The antecedent of the entwined relationship between religion and politicians was with the establishment of the Inner Cities Religious Council (ICRC) in 1992, which then metamorphosed into the Faith Communities Consultative Council (FCCC) and the Working Together Steering Group in April 2006. Before the change of nomenclature of the ICRC, it was a bridge that fostered collaboration between the government and faith community leaders to work on urban renewal and social exclusion. The overarching aim of the FCCC is "giving faith communities a strong role and clear voice in improving cohesion, regeneration and renewal in local communities".[98]

Bretherton further traced the interaction of the state and faith communities with the establishment of the Home Office Faith Communities Unit in 2003, the appointment of a faith envoy for the Prime Minister and the inclusion of religious leaders such as the monthly Black Leaders' Christian Forum (BLCF) in the formulation of public policy.[99] The government's continued patronage of faith communities was further articulated by the Department of Communities and Local Government publications *Improving Opportunity, Strengthening Society: The Government's Strategy to Increase Race Equality and Community Cohesion* (2005); *Our Shared Future, Commission on Integration and Cohesion* (2008) and *Face-to-Face and Side-by-Side: A Framework for Partnership in our Multi-faith Society* (2008). The continued reference to faith communities depicts state policies as being inclusive and creating community cohesion and emphasizes the various ethnic convergences in multi-ethnic, multicultural Britain.

A new era in the history of faith communities and the state in Britain's political history was heralded with the appointment of 13 faith advisers by John Denham, Labour Communities Secretary under Gordon Brown's administration on 6 January 2010. John Denham spoke of the role of faith in shaping the values and religious orientations of people. He opined that, "for millions of people the values instilled by their faith are central to shaping their behaviour. We should continually seek ways of supporting and enhancing the contribution faith makes to the decision-making process on the central issues of our time."[100] Amongst the appointees was Marcia Dixon, editor of *Keep the Faith* magazine, a publication distributed to Black Majority Churches.

British and American politicians in the early twenty-first century seem to have similar ideological orientations in the engagement of faith communities in social policy. The Bush (Jnr) and Blair regimes were noted to have brought about the renaissance of faith to the public space. Blair was noted to be quite pragmatic in his tenure at Downing Street as he avoided "playing religion". This was echoed by his press secretary Alistair Campbell who checkmated Tony Blair when he was asked by an American Journalist from *Vanity Fair* about his beliefs. Alistair Campbell, an atheist, interrupted and said, "We don't do God."[101] But Blair's religious persuasions contributed to his governmental policies on faith communities. Although he was reticent about his faith in public life, he admitted that faith was important to him as he was converted from Anglicanism to Catholicism in 2007. Bush, however, was quite vociferous with his love for evangelical Christianity, as there was the "God factor" not only in his personal life but in political decision-making. Micklethwait and Wooldridge[102] citing David Kuo, who worked in the White House promoting faith-based solutions to social problems, noted that Karl Rove and his political shop were nothing less than "obsessed" with evangelical voters.

The purported claim of community cohesion and inclusiveness has been queried by the Cantle Report. Bretherton opined that the state creates an antagonistic playing field, as the various bureaucratic frameworks designed to engage the faith communities are indirectly divisive, particularly in the area of competition for urban funds.[103] This presents a divergent view that religion in itself is divisive. He further referred to the change in the *modus operandi* of faith communities with stringent bureaucratic requirements which are often alien to the ecclesiastical orientation of most church bodies. Charles Glen argues that "professionalization, while it may raise the standards of service or teaching in significant respects, may also distance non-profit organisations or schools they serve from their communities".[104]

The compliance modalities required from faith communities before they can enjoy state funding might be a challenge for some faith communities, especially Black Majority Churches. From my experience as a member of the board of trustees of a faith community initiative, compliance with bureaucratic requirements for state funding, rather than being restrictive, often fosters a greater sense of accountability, prudence and transparency, as funds received are judiciously utilised, though elements of professionalism are required in some social initiatives. For instance, Jubilee House for All Nations, based in Romford and part of the network of the RCCG in Britain, is a church for people with special needs. This requires a greater level of professionalism and meeting statutory requirements for people with special needs such as provision of trained personnel, Criminal Record Bureau checks for personnel, provision of loop, handling and managing autistic members, etc. It is amazing that 98% of the professional skill requirements of the church is achieved through volunteers.

A major fault line in Bretherton's assertion was his inability to realize that some of the changes in the worldview and cultural dynamics in the Western world necessitate the bureaucratic structures. Though bureaucratic structure can be restrictive, it is not overtly a dominant feature. The perceived paradigm shift, from traditional pastoral and ecclesiastical responsibilities of a faith community to their adherents to engagement with the state's demands, is gradually being eliminated by some Black Majority Churches in Britain. The two observable approaches have been the utilization of skilled professional volunteers amongst the membership of the faith community or the incorporation of a separate charitable entity that is solely focused on some of the faith community initiatives. The purported shift in the missional objectives of the churches as noted by Bretherton is avoided by the leadership of some Black Majority Churches in Britain.

## SUMMARY

The proliferation of Black Majority Churches in Britain has brought about an urban resonance in the Christian faith which has impacted the urban religious landscape. The conurbation has gradually led to distinctive black communities in some of the cities with associated social challenges. The growth of these churches has alienated the purported claims of reverse mission but has led to continued extension of denominational frontiers.

The social action of Black Majority Churches has been dynamic, presenting an holistic perspective of the Gospel. The centrifugal force for the social action initiatives is social relevance and the incarnational model of the Gospels. The various approaches include religious, social and educational initiatives, often in collaboration with state agencies. These have received commendations from the state and public officers.

The political pragmatism of Black-led Churches is gradually evolving and is in sharp contrast to the political ideology of the Black Movement of America. The active involvement of various Black-led Church leaders, community groups and parachurch organizations is gradually shaping the political activities of Black Majority Churches.

The role of faith communities in the social public policy of Britain is based on the identified potential of these communities for community development and cohesion. The use of human, infrastructural facilities, and social and relational capital, is the hub of the contributions of the faith communities to the state, though the concept of faith communities is fraught with ambiguities because of its multiplicity of usage. The dearth of empirical research on the contributions of Black Majority Churches as members within the faith communities presents a research niche that is yet to be explored.

*Chapter Six*

# Applying the Lessons of History

∽

## INTRODUCTION

Black Majority Churches in Britain in the last one hundred years of existence have consistently shaped the diversity of British Christian history. The distinctive phases of the Diasporan experiences have brought about the emergence of a cultural and theological matrix in Black Majority Churches and in British black theology in comparison to American black theology. Indeed, the acorn seed planted in the wake of the Sunderland pneuma-centric experiences of 1907 has consistently modulated the Christian activism through the Black Majority Churches in Britain. This has tilted the pendulum of public opinion amongst historic denominations about Black Majority Churches away from scepticism, ignorance, cultural and racial dissonance to acceptance and celebration in the repositioning of the Christian faith in British public space.

This section provides a reflection on the annals of the history of Black Churches in Britain through a trifocal prism:

(a) Retrospect: an exploration of the black Christian faith's emergence from the fringes of obscurity to national status;
(b) Repositioning: an evaluative approach assessing the perceived or observable missional challenges of Black Majority Churches and the need for a paradigm shift to reflect the existential changes within the British cultural milieu;
(c) Resourcing: a proactive treatise to engage and maximize the potentials of Black Majority Churches in Britain, considering what the future might hold for these churches.

The appropriation of the trifocal prism of reflective practice outlined above provides a future construct of the likely theological, missiological and ecclesiastical agenda for Black Majority Churches in Britain. The shift in praxis in the light of the perceived inadequacies in the emerging phases of these churches and changes in the British socio-cultural milieu will inevitably necessitate a redefined missiological agenda for the continued relevance of Black Majority Churches in Britain.

### RETROSPECT: LOOKING BACK

*Transitional Overview of Black Majority Churches*

The Black Majority Churches over a century of existence provide a repertoire of historical, social, cultural, political and theological reflections of African and Caribbean Diasporans in Britain. These reflections have inevitably shaped the social, political and religious consciousness of Africans and Caribbeans in Britain. The uniqueness of the enthusiastic, persuasive, celebratory, oral liturgy-based, pneuma-centric theology and existential experiences have progressively shaped black British theology which is akin to Pentecostal theology globally. Black Majority Churches in Britain, despite their diversity in terms of ecclesiology, still have a convergence of uniformity, especially the Pentecostals with the ancient landmark of glossolalia. Britain, a Protestant nation by law, beholds Black Majority Churches with nostalgia and appreciation as the British Historic Churches' cultural commentators acknowledge that the growth and proliferation of Black Majority Churches has put spirituality and the Christian faith back on the public radar.

The road to today's accomplishments has been strewn with sacrifices of men and women despised, ridiculed, once nearly suppressed by racism and grossly misunderstood. Muir opined that "the growth and development of the Black Church Movement and the place of faith/religion in society should be seen in the context of wider philosophical and cultural discourse about God, spirituality and the forces of modernity".[1] The search for dignity, respect and relevant cultural and religious hegemony paid off significantly in the shaping of the theological and cultural matrix of Black Majority Churches in Britain; this has enabled the members of these churches in the last six decades through self-help and work ethics to "rise above their social deprivation and build on view points that inspire the realms of middle class respectability".[2]

The exploration of the black Christian faith in Britain is a watershed in the history of British Christianity: from under the dark alleys of the Railway Arch in Peckham in 1907, where Pastor Brem-Wilson's church was situated, to the social reconstruction of the Liverpool "brown babies" social action of Daniel Ekarte, to the *Windrush* era, accentuated further by the African Independent Churches in the late 1950s and 1960s in London.[3]

Alexander observed that the emergence and proliferation of African Independent Churches led to a "contextual and holistic response to the oppressive conditions with which its members and communities they represent are confronted", predicated on "'liberational spirituality' and a holistic understanding and response to the concerns of the oppressed", giving hope, affirmation, dignity and a sense of community not available in the wider British community because of racism, especially during the *Windrush* era. She further asserted that this spiritual explanation has its roots in "fundamental Christian beliefs and white southern state American values".[4] The diversity and growth dynamics were energized as a result of a multiplicity of internal push and pull factors.

The fissiparous nature of Black Majority Churches, akin to the global Pentecostals,[5] the effect of the declining fortunes of third world countries,[6] incorporation of religion as a factor in occupational mobility, and immigration have contributed to the success story of Black Majority Churches in Britain, though this was slightly curtailed by the 1962, 1965, 1968 and 1971 Immigration Acts.

Kalu, in the paper entitled "African Pentecostalism in Diaspora" read on his behalf posthumously by Allan Anderson during the Global Pentecostal Conference at Birmingham in 2009, noted the diversities of views and publications on African immigration, which is often precipitated by collapsed economies, natural causes and immigration policies of host communities to attract skilled migrants. He opined that there are "now three important moments in migration patterns: the departure, the migration route and the destination, each with a rich history and structure etched in human biographies".[7] Kalu's treatise on the migratory pattern of African Diaspora presents an interesting paradox which has a positive correlation with the immigration policies of the host countries, economic indices and cultural and technological trends, aptly termed globalization.

The social and racial experiences of the post-*Windrush* migrants from West Africa were much more civil in comparison with those of the *Windrush* migrants. Hill observed that the focal factor was more to do with educational aspirations in 1960. He asserted that,

> Those who came were mainly from West Africa from upper-class families who sent them to Britain as students for advanced education. Their objectives were to gain educational qualifications and return to Africa. Most of them had no desire to settle in Britain and returned to Africa where they

formed a new educated professional middle-class elite often locally known as the "Been Tos" – those who had been to Europe for their further education.[8]

This presents a similar paradigm to the *Windrush* migrants, who mostly migrated to work for a while and then go back to the Caribbean, though none migrated for academic purposes. The context of the similarities is a reflection of the challenges of assimilation and acculturation to the British socio-economic, religious and political structures. The intricate social and religious connotations of the migrant population gradually facilitated the "greater particularity as individuals search for ethnic, cultural or religious categories with which they can identify".[9]

Black Churches became safe havens for affirmation, social and religious reconstruction in Britain to cope with the racial, social and economic setbacks for the black communities. Despite the assimilation and acculturation challenges of most migrants, especially in the *Windrush* era, many believed that they were missionaries, and approximated the role of proclamation and affirmation of the limitless riches of Jesus Christ in Britain as far back as the 1960s.[10] The growth of these churches brought about various phases of development "characterised historically and sociologically from 'early mission' (1940s and 1950s); to a 'period of consolidation' (1960–1975); and from the 'diverse church' (1980–1993); to the 'maturing church' (2004 onwards)" according to Muir.[11]

### Rhetorics of Reverse Mission

Mohabir[12] and a few other *Windrush* migrants who might be classified as pioneers of reverse mission to Britain from the Caribbean during the third phase of the accentuation of Black-led Churches, present a view antithetical to that of Adogame, who claims that "the conscious missionary strategy by mother churches in Africa of evangelizing the Diaspora is a relatively recent one. Diaspora has been a key aspect to their response to European mission",[13] but this might constitute a myopic perspective, as the mission strategies of most African and Caribbean churches in Britain are either nascent or were non-existent originally.[14]

The prevalent trend within Black Majority Churches in Britain to redefine their migration using the language of spirituality "at a time like this" rather than viewing the motivating factor for migration as economic or political, gives a sense of "hyper-spiritual sensation" to the evangelization of Britain. Sunday Adelaja, the pastor of the single largest congregation in Europe (of over 20,000 membership with 99.9% Whites) subscribes to the theory of a "supernatural element" as he asserts that his success is astonishing because "He [God] plucked me from my small village in Africa. Then brought me by divine call to Ukraine and told me to start a church in Kyiv."[15] This spiritual perspective seems to be a transnational phenomenon, as Adogame rightly observed in his paper on the Embassy of the Blessed Kingdom of God for all Nations: it is "an interesting dynamic of how migration narratives are often sacralised and weaved as occurrences and mobility anchored on divine design rather than by any mundane accident. Testimony genres of several African migrants are rife with accounts of how they saw the mysterious 'hand of God' in shaping their life trajectories and migration histories."[16] The shift in Christianity from Global North to Global South has heralded a new epoch in European history and has been described by Jenkins as the "Southernization of European Christianity".[17]

This is reflected in the domination of various parts of Africa and the Caribbean by the Pentecostal movements, especially in the cities, for instance in Nigeria, where Pentecostal forms of Christianity have an overwhelming presence on the religious scene. Kalu refers to this as the "third response" to white cultural domination and power in the church, the previous responses being Ethiopianism and African Independent Churches or the Aladura movement.[18] This further reinforces the fact that the growth of Pentecostalism globally is a product of its "localization" ability within any cultural milieu. Pentecostalism is thus a "quintessential indigenous religion adapting readily to a variety of cultures" according to Klaus.[19]

There exists a strong American influence, as Bueno points out: "America's special place among nations" and a "conviction that other peoples ought to be guided and ruled by American principles, both civil and religious" is depicted by the current wave of prevalence of Pentecostalism in Sub-Saharan Africa that is "a rapidly growing sector of Christianity that is closely related to and heavily dependent on the United States".[20] Though the influence of American theology on African and Caribbean theologies is quite apparent, especially with the Health and Wealth ideologies, even in Britain, Black Majority Churches retain their indigenous character with a distinct worldview which is shaped by the cultural prism of Africans and Caribbeans akin to the Nigerian Pentecostal scene, as Kalu notes: "the originators continue to be Africans and Caribbeans, imitating foreigners, eclectically producing foreign theologies but transforming these for immediate contextual purposes".[21]

The broad generalization of the Health and Wealth gospel as a product of Americanization might not be true in its entirety, as there exist various reconstructions and distinctions that have a radically different context alien to the American Health and Wealth contexts.

The ingenuity of the Black Majority Church with distinctive cultural resonance is not only within the doctrinal position on Health and Wealth gospel, but permeates almost all facets of its ecclesiology, which strongly repudiates the purported claims of its reverse mission in Britain. There does exist, however, an undeniable "witness presence" within the British social space by the Black Majority Churches.

The missional flow from the normative states of Europe and America to Africa, Asia and other parts of the world until the late twentieth century was from the repository of the Catholic and Protestant brands of Christianity. There is now a paradigm shift, as what constituted mission fields hitherto are now sending missionaries to the Western world. Reverse mission has been defined as "the sending of missionaries to Europe and North America by churches and Christians from the non-Western world, particularly Africa, Asia and Latin America, which were at the receiving end of Catholic and Protestant missions as mission fields from the sixteenth to late twentieth century".[22]

In Black Majority Churches in Britain, especially African Churches, there exists a lot of self-representation and symbolic mapping. The image of Britain is projected as, in their words, a post-Christian nation with various connotative synonyms such as "dead continent", "prodigal nation" or "secularized Britain". These assertions tend to reinforce churches' legitimacy to engage in missions. This seems to be a transatlantic phenomenon amongst Diasporan congregations in the West and America.

The rapidity of exportation of missionaries to the Western world portrays Africa's role in the heart of contemporary Western Christian History. It is generally affirmed by most Black Majority Church leaders that the law of "sowing and reaping" is pivotal to reverse mission in Europe by African missionaries. Adeboye espouses the rhetoric of reverse mission:

> I believe the Almighty God is saying there is revival at the door, that a great revival is coming, that one day not too long from now the streets of London will be practically empty on Sunday morning because people have gone to church to worship the Almighty God. I believe that the glory that was lost *will be restored*. And I believe it to be very soon. I believe that all the prayers that these thousands are sending to the Almighty God saying, "Revive our soul, Lord! Revive our soul, Lord!" will receive an answer sooner than we expected.[23]

It is an observable feature, not only in Britain but also in Western Europe, due to the effects of ongoing secularization[24] and the decline of Christianity, that most immigrant churches, especially of the African and Caribbean Diaspora, are now involved in the re-evangelization of Europe, including the "dark" continent of Britain. Black Majority Churches, according to Anderson, "see the 'world' as a place to move into and 'possess' for Christ. Transnationalism and migration do not affect their essential character, even though their adherents may have to steer a precarious course between contradictory forms of identity resulting from the migratory experience."[25]

Thus Black Majority Churches seem to have an "invading army" agenda in terms of re-evangelizing Britain, but the success of these churches at best might be described as a repository of large ethnic churches, most of which are yet to reflect indigenous white memberships in these churches. However, Asamoah-Gyadu observed that there are practical lessons to be learnt from Black Majority Churches in Britain in the light of "the attention it draws to the fact that Christianity is about experience and that the power of God is able to transform circumstances that Western rationalist theologies will consider the preserve of psychology and scientific development".[26] Though this existential appeal has served as one of the attractions of Black Majority Churches to its followers, this has come under much scholarly scrutiny on account of perceived hermeneutical flaws.

Muir succinctly identified the basis of such "suspicion" in black theology: "[any] theology whose sources (and norms) derived from Scripture on the one hand and the black experience and culture on the other hand, is bound to raise tensions and cause a degree of hermeneutical suspicion".[27] Unveiling this aspect of black theology, Muir quoted Homer and Witvliet as having a unique perspective on this challenge; they assert that "indigenous sources of knowledge of God in black religion" is in danger of "assuming that knowledge can be anything but Black and private" but recognize the "danger of regarding the hermeneutical circle of black theology as a closed circle which does not have a single point of contact with that of so-called white theology". The array of criticisms against the existential hermeneutical practices within Black Majority Churches indeed is of a great concern, but "the politicisation of the hermeneutical circle in Black theological discourse is a real concern".[28] This further echoes Beckford's call for Liberation Experiential Theological Praxis to be considered as a valid hermeneutical tool in black theology in the West.

The continuous subscription by Black Majority Church leaders to missiological reasons for their proliferation presents an irony yet to be reconciled with observable trends in the membership of these churches. Irukwu's assertion that the continued generic classification of these churches as Black Majority Churches will be a misnomer when indigenous white communities are attracted to these churches[29] is in itself an admission that the Black Majority Churches' purported claim of reverse mission is yet to translate to substantial gain through proselytization and conversion of the indigenous white communities. In order for the Black Majority Churches in Britain to convert the gains of bringing God back on the agenda, the onus is on these churches to translate their "theology of presence" to missional gains through the development of appropriate contextualized theology that is indigenous to the Western world, and to refrain from the allurements of an attractional church model built around African cultural ideals which have been restrictive and which have led to the continued proliferation of mono-ethnic and mono-national churches.

The heterogeneous composition of Black Majority Churches is also replicated in diversities of church culture that are often counter-cultural to the indigenous British culture, and that might impede the missional outlook of these churches. A major proponent of the affirmation that Black Majority Churches are a repository of hope to re-evangelize Britain is Ian Bradley. Bradley opines that despite the missional inadequacies of these churches "Black Christianity may well prove to be a key agent in the re-evangelisation of Christian Britain".[30] Ukah, however, provides a sarcastic and metaphoric allusion to the rhetoric of reverse mission as explored through the history, growth and structure of the Redeemed Christian Church of God, United Kingdom. He titles his essay "Reverse Mission or Asylum Christianity?"[31] Ukah gives a critical appraisal of the church's purported claim to be one of the fastest-growing churches in England with a mandate to evangelize postmodern Britain or post-Christian Britain. Ukah opines, "part of the theology of re-missioning Europe is the (re)production of God and preservation of community identity (Yoruba/ Nigerian/ African/ Christian/ Pentecostal/ Global)".[32]

This is a similar paradigm to the *Windrush* churches of "believing but not belonging" to the larger British culture, which has resulted in the recreation of Yoruba/Nigeria/African dialectics, which in turn have militated against the impact of the RCCG in the British context. This repudiates the reverse mission mantra of the organization. In effect, the words and actions of RCCG churches, despite the varying efforts of rebranding and contextualization in terms of some of the network of churches such as Jesus House, Royal Connections and Trinity Chapel, have not translated to missional gains but have succeeded in reinterpreting the RCCG Pentecostal ideals in consumer- and market-orientated structures to attract the upwardly mobile Nigerians and Africans.[33]

The attractional attributes of the RCCG flagship churches in the United Kingdom, which include Jesus House, London, Royal Connections, Jesus House, Aberdeen, Fountain of Love, Aberdeen and Trinity Chapel, London, are reflected in the administrative and professional competence of the staff which can compete favourably with any corporate organization in Britain. Ukah noted that the basis of the "asylum branding" of the RCCGUK is potentially rooted in its carry-over syndrome of "Nigerianization" of its church-planting initiatives, as the transplanting is fraught with contextual and missional flaws such that these churches will continually attract Nigerian and African Diasporans.[34] I thus posit that the RCCG is a global brand, but its potential for global appeal is predicated on its dismantling of inherent authoritarianism and a high degree of contextualization of its ideals. Though Ukah's research was conducted in 2004, he noted that the success of the RCCG in re-evangelizing Europe might be predicated on engagement with other networks of Pentecostal churches, which was indeed a signpost for reflective engagement for the future of the church.

There have been significant changes in the strategic relationship and networking of RCCG leadership in the UK as suggested by Ukah. There exists a tripartite relationship among the leadership of the Redeemed Christian Church of God, New Testament Church of God and Church of God of Prophecy. Similar cross-fraternization is observable with Holy Trinity Church, Brompton and Jesus House, the flagship of the Redeemed Christian Church of God, UK. Because of multiple transnational and local transformations of Black Majority Churches in Britain on reverse mission, it is imperative to ask, after Ukah, whether these churches are missionally minded engaging in "reverse mission or diasporic mission".

## REPOSITIONING: LEARNING THE LESSONS

### Cultural Challenges

There has been a massive shift in the socio-cultural, political and religious landscape of Britain since the 1940s. Paradoxically, it is in the midst of these diversities and dynamic shifts that Black Majority Churches have re-emerged and proliferated. This therefore implies that the growth and proliferation of these churches was intricately dependent on the cultural and social revolution in Britain in this period. But the growth and proliferation of these churches in the midst of British social and cultural revolution is predicated more on migration, cultural and Diasporic nuances, pneumatic theology and the fissiparous nature of Pentecostals coupled with various internal branding of the various churches. Black Majority Churches must certainly come to terms with the fact that the British social, cultural and religious landscape that was shaped by the modern ethos has significantly metamorphosed. Black Majority Churches in Britain must be astutely aware of the monstrous challenges they confront and have the ability to be incarnational and do things in a new way.

Various black British theologians have challenged the status quo in the operational and ecclesiastical approaches of Black Majority Churches in Britain. These include the likes of Beckford[35] through Dread Theology, Anthony Reddie and Michael Jagessar,[36] and Joe Aldred,[37] with a clarion call for transformational approaches and a shift from conservative modalities in church practices. There is an undeniable need for the churches to be much more aware of these realities, as the inability of the church to interact with the culture can enhance or impair its missional objective. It is notable that most of the fastest-growing Black Majority Churches in Britain today, such as Kingsway International Christian Centre (KICC) led by Pastor Matthew Ashimolowo, Ruach Ministries led by Bishop John Francis, Christian Life City led by Malcolm Wayne, and Jesus House led by Agu Irukwu, to a large extent have demonstrated in-depth knowledge of the socio-cultural and political culture of Britain.

The rebranding and restructuring of the organizational ethos of the aforementioned churches is predicated on strategically repositioning the churches as relevant and contemporary by engaging in the creative use of technology seeker-friendly programmes and a consumer orientation akin to the prevailing postmodern ethos of consumerism and connectedness. It is pertinent to note that most of the theology of these churches is non-academic, but finds credibility amongst their adherents on account of their cultural and existential orientations. I concur with Burgess that theology has to be relevant, contextual, public and transformational.[38] However, Black Majority Churches' theology is characterized by a strong emphasis on humanism. Ukah pointedly avers that "because the churches are competing for the attention of young men and women who are ordinarily drawn to popular culture, there is a strong trend within these churches to creatively adapt church services and events to resemble forms of popular entertainment: including good music, trendy dressing, weekend picnics, sports events and a host of other activities".[39] Ironically this is a not a generic feature of the majority of the Black Majority

Churches. It is imperative, however, to note that even the leading churches amongst the Black Majority Churches are yet to attract the indigenous white communities.

The limited success of enculturation and contextualization has not translated to missional success for these churches. The forces shaping British culture are too many and too strong and there exists a diverse breakdown of historic values and norms characterized by social fragmentation. The lack of understanding of the British cultural milieu by most Black Majority Church leaders has contributed significantly to the continued cultural captivity of these churches. Mike Regele made a clarion call to churches in his seminal book *The Death of the Church*, querying the inaction of the church. He affirms that "if we [Black Majority Churches] do not understand the forces of change, we will be overwhelmed by them".[40] The changes from modernity to postmodernity have changed the status quo of our world and assumptions due to the complexities of the changes. Regele summed up the impact of the cultural revolution and its impact on the church as he observed that, "At the brink of the twenty-first century, the king who knew not Joseph is the collective culture of which we are part."[41]

The combined impact of the information age, postmodern thought, globalization and racial, ethnic and religious pluralism has displaced the historic role the church has traditionally played. As a result we are seeing the marginalization of the institutional church. The changes are quite stressful, great and encompassing, but most Black Majority Churches are still living in an illusionary world of the Enlightenment age, while the Western world thrives on the ethos of postmodernity. I am acutely aware of the diversity of views with respect to the concept of postmodernity, as some scholars argue that there is too much hype about the concept while scholars such as Giddens[42] and Habibis *et al.*[43] posit that the cultural shift be termed "second modernity". The undeniable fact is that there has been a shift from the cultural norm of modernity with variation in societal and cultural values. The future and potential of Black Majority Churches in Britain can only be maximized if the churches understand the dynamics of the cultural context of Britain.

Because of poor cross-cultural and missiological training most of the leaders of the Black Majority Churches are inundated with the postmodern ethos of pluralism which has paved the way for sacredness to exchange for perverseness, courtesy of "pick and mix" orientation. The intrigues of the cultural shift within the last seventy years in Britain are a challenge to all institutions within the British social and religious landscape, Black Majority Churches inclusive. This might be responsible for the continued cultural captivity of Black Majority Churches, as most of the churches are insular, dependent on an attractional model of church.

The obstacle that successfully repudiates the attempts of most Black Church leaders in Britain to engage the British community is lack of understanding of the prevailing British culture, and this has greatly impaired their missions agenda. The churches are locked into old ways of doing things; this means that they will not gain a hearing in a rapidly changing cultural environment. The "farce" of the growth of Black Majority Churches in Britain has meant that most of the churches do not acknowledge the swiftness of some of the historic denominations to address the challenges of the cultural changes.

The tripartite relationship of Church of England, Methodist Church and United Reformed Church is seen in "Fresh Expressions". Fresh Expressions is a response to the fragmented and postmodern culture; it aims to make the church relevant to the prevailing British context. Michael Moynagh said, "Emerging church is a mindset ('we'll come to you') rather than a model. It is a direction rather than a destination. It rests on principles rather than a plan. It arises out of a culture rather than being imposed on a culture. It is a mood, scarcely yet a movement."[44] The fluidity of the postmodern culture presents a continuous need for reflective practice by mission practitioners, especially Black Majority Churches, which are not conversant with the indigenous British culture and its dynamics. Moynagh observes:

> that is why many different expressions of church are emerging. Our society continues to fragment, and the church is tackling more varied forms to enter those segments. Single models of church will no longer do. Increasingly, as ministers return from the latest how-to-do-it conference, the model they bring back with them becomes car-sick and never makes the journey.[45]

It is expedient to note that neither am I an advocate of Eurocentric culture for Black Majority Churches, but if indeed Black Majority Churches are to be missional and re-evangelize the West, their missiological approaches must be creative and imaginative to engage the prevailing British culture and strongly repudiate any form of the culture that is antagonistic to the Christian faith.

### *Leadership Structure: Paradigm Shift*

A common feature of most Black Majority Churches in Britain, despite the complexities due to the heterogeneous nature of these churches, is the hierarchical or pyramidal model of leadership. The prevalence of this model of leadership is a reflection of the inherent predominance of this model in African and Caribbean countries, but it seems to be a major constraint to the empowerment of the laity and missions. The pyramidal model is the traditional model of leadership used by most Black Majority Churches, and it is prevalent in Africa. The crossover and transfer of successful processes created by some Black Majority Churches such as the RCCG into Britain has negatively impacted their reverse mission rhetoric as observed by Ukah.[46] Though the RCCGUK thrives on the network model in terms of their relational interface, as each network is a legal entity, many are steeped in the pyramidal model of leadership. There exist divergent views on the continued relevance of this leadership model within the Western context but some scholars like Leavitt (2004) still posit that it is the best organizational model.

Gibbs and Coffey, however, opined that this structure militates against effective missional initiatives. The inherent constraints of the pyramidal leadership structure which might become more prevalent include: (a) Building of dependency on hierarchies; (b) Core leadership becomes indispensable unknowingly; (c) Decision-making is from the top down, stifling initiatives and often control-modulated; (d) Strategy is imposed on the team; (e) Blame culture is prevalent within the structure; (f) Avoidance of dealing with problems.[47]

Most Black Majority Churches have inherited certain structures that may have served the organization well in times past but there is the need to adapt and develop them if they are to be serviceable in the new contexts of ministry in the West. Anderson noted that "many come to Europe unencumbered by out-of-date ecclesiastical structures and hierarchies. With a sense of divine call to do something important for God, they see the success of other expatriate Africans who have started significant churches and believe that they can do the same."[48] However, Anderson failed to acknowledge the fact that the purported growth is not evaluated in the light of missional effectiveness of these churches, as the bulk of the large churches consists mostly of African and Caribbean migrants. It is becoming increasingly clear that if Black Majority Churches are to respond to cultural changes in a thoroughly missional manner, they will have to adapt their structures to ones that empower their members for effective action.

The changes in cultural dynamics within the Western context provide great opportunities for reflective practice. The cultural chaos in the West has affected every facet of British society, the church inclusive. The shifts from modernity to postmodernity or late modernity, as described by various scholars, have far-reaching implications on the operational modalities of churches within the Western context and missions.

As a consequence, many of the old certainties in British society have long been abandoned and moral, intellectual and political environments are undergoing constant change. Church structures, too, must change in order to keep pace with the cataclysmic upheavals brought about by new paradigms in science and theories of knowledge. That is not to say that the essential message of the Gospel has been lost but, rather, that its relevance has to be established afresh in each new cultural context.

Britain of today is a post-Christian secularized society characterized by (a) relativity, (b) pluralism, and (c) fragmentation. In the light of these cultural changes, the leadership concept within British fragmented society is moving from the traditional pyramidal model to a model in which decentralized decision-making empowers the practitioners. Amazingly, most Black Majority Churches make use of the pyramidal leadership model, which is very restrictive on account of its inherent disadvantages. As Robert Greenleaf observes, "To be a lone chief atop a pyramid is abnormal and corrupting."[49] Commenting on the inability of current Western organizations to fulfil their functions effectively, Greenleaf goes on to say, "Part of the failure of our institutions [churches inclusive] to serve with distinction may be the interaction between two reinforcing elements: low levels of trusteeship and the concept of the single executive."[50] Robinson and Smith pick up on this when they observe:

> What Greenleaf has to say about institutions in general is particularly true of the church. Not only is the principle of the lone leader "abnormal and corrupting", but its impact on those who are led can be astonishingly painful. Moreover, the failure to lead well results in the impoverishment of Christ's people. In such structures, the gifts of the many are not recognised and developed. The goal is not empowerment but submission.[51]

Pyramidal structures are concerned with control rather than performance because it is considered that control systems will maximize performance. However, this assumption is, at best, doubtful, in terms of reaching out to people locked into contemporary thought forms. McLaren observes, "Control is less important than catalyzing positive action", and he goes on to quote William Easum who distinguishes between control structures and permission-giving structures. Easum says: "the top-down oppressive approach of the bureaucracy is on its way out. In its place are emerging permission-giving networks. These networks are freeing and empowering people to explore their spiritual gifts individually and in teams on behalf of the body of Christ."[52] Hierarchical structure is concerned with delivering uniform procedures so that everybody in the system knows where they are and what is required of them, according to Gibbs and Coffey.[53] In the words of Bob Dylan, "times are changin'". The most rapidly growing churches across the Atlantic with a similar cultural context to Britain are apostolic networks where leadership is strong but lithe enough to let other leaders into their ministry against the background of supportive relationship. This is often almost an exception amongst the Black Majority Churches.

A notable exception to this is the leadership of Jesus House that provides not only relational support for all church plants but also provides continuous financing and mentoring opportunities for the new church leaders. This seems to be a recent initiative because in 1996 Fola-Alade was given only £250 by Jesus House to start Trinity Chapel. The changes in the operational strategies of Jesus House since then have contributed to a low turnover of personnel within the organization. The focus and leadership ethos is to recreate daughter churches that will replicate the DNA of the Agu Irukwu-led organization but also function responsibly to compete with corporate organizations and impact their society by taking the "church away from the church" while retaining their organizational uniqueness, which I describe as "Rapu and Agu Mitosis Syndrome" (RAMS) within the RCCGUK network of churches. Tony Rapu's Christian ideology right from the inception of the third model parish of the RCCG at Apapa, Nigeria on 5 May 1991 also translated to the core values of Jesus House, London, which he pioneered, and resonates in almost all RCCG pastors that were under his tutelage even at Jesus House. Agu's relational and organizational skills, however, have greatly enhanced the organization.

However, most Black Majority Churches that are still using the pyramidal leadership model are in a very precarious situation which often leads to schism as a result of not harnessing the pool of resources available to the leadership of these churches. Common amongst some "dysfunctional" Black Majority Churches are sycophancy, blind loyalty and absolute negation of stipulated internal regulatory responsibilities of the Board of Trustees, so that church leaders' appointees are lame ducks or cronies that often times will not constructively challenge procedural and operational modalities of the church leaders. A typical example was the infamous Douglas Goodman saga. This was possible because there was no clear separation in the management of Victory Christian Centre (VCC) and the ecclesiastical functions of the pastor. The outcome of this was that the Charity Commission announced "they were going to pursue Pastor Douglas Goodman and his wife for misappropriating £3million from

VCC" according to Sturge.⁵⁴ While Black Majority Churches move forward and embrace necessary changes to cope with the cultural challenges, it is expedient that they should not move too far from the NT models as so many UK denominations have done to their loss of real spiritual impact. It is quite obvious within the British social landscape that the modern generation yearn for spiritual renewal, not cultural cosmetics.

In retrospect, Black Majority Churches will be more effective if there is a shift in emphasis from positional to relational authority, in order to enhance the missional agenda of these churches. Most Black Churches' authority is vested in the hands of very few people because of their hierarchical position in the organization. Clearly, a certain amount of authority will always be inherent in a person's position in any given structure because that position allows them access to resources that other people need. However, the way in which such resources are used tends to depend on the relational influence of the authority figure. Intra-church transfer, which is one of the growth factors of Black Majority Churches in Britain, profits from the resentment of many Pentecostal adherents, as people vote with their feet and re-congregate elsewhere because of personal dissatisfaction. Most of these churches thrive on volunteers who give their skill in return for purported claims of divine blessing for their services and contribute through effective financial principles of tithing and faith offerings that enable them to transfer their skills to another church should they become dissatisfied with their current position. In such a climate, authority is more a matter of moral and pragmatic influence based on relationship rather than the exercise of naked power. The strong emphasis on Charismatic leadership of African and Caribbean churches at times is fraught with a concept of leadership that is "autocratic and total utilitarian"⁵⁵ and that negates even statutory regulatory checks and balances, as such personalities are held in so much awe and reverence.

There has to be a paradigm shift from *demanding* to *equipping* – it will no longer suffice for most Black Majority Church leaders to *demand results* from organizational members: they will have to *facilitate action*. Apart from setting vision and direction for these churches, the main function of leaders in more open networks will be that of equipping team members for the tasks to which they are called. Most leaders are highly opinionated and at times abuse the sacredness of their office by not empowering their members. This facilitative process can be achieved by mentoring, coaching and counselling those under their pastoral care. Visionary leaders may not have all the skills required to prepare and encourage team members in every facet of needed training but they should acquire the skill of identifying and facilitating those who can.

Eddie Gibbs points out the limitations of the "in house" apprenticeship training approach. He comments:

> This can result in a narrow vision and in producing leaders who know how to do only what is already being done. What's more, ministry competencies do not consist simply in technical expertise. If a church is to operate as a transformational missional presence in any society, be it traditional, modern or postmodern, its leaders require theological training and missiological preparation as well as the development of ministry skills. [56]

The best missiological and theological training within Black Majority Churches comes from Bible Colleges that are designed for denominational ideals without secular accreditation. In the 1960s and 1970s most of the churches established denominational colleges without any academic validation. The situation is gradually changing, however, within institutions like Christ Redeemers College, the theological training arm of the RCCG, now accredited by Middlesex University. The role and enthusiasm of Hollenweger, the first Professor of Mission of the University of Birmingham, for intercultural study cannot be overemphasized. The partnership that evolved in 1977 through a meeting at Selly Oak Colleges, Birmingham, with Black-led church leaders in the mould of Martin Simmonds (First United Church of Jesus Christ Apostolic), Samuel Owusu-Akuffo (Divine Prayer Society), Olu Abiola and the Department of Theology lecturers (particularly the innovative and broadminded Hollenweger) was quite pivotal to the genesis of intercultural studies. This eventually culminated in the emergence of a pilot theological training attended by forty-five leaders from different churches including Pentecostals and African Independent Churches.[57] The Selly Oak Colleges have become part of The Queen's Foundation, Birmingham, whose degrees are awarded by the University of Birmingham, and which for quite a while has been the only British theological college that provided contextual theological training in black and Asian theology until it was recently joined by Oxford Brookes University.

### The Nature of Church Leadership

A major distinguishing feature of Pentecostals globally is pneumacentrism. This is a complete departure from the historic denominations. It is apt to note that until recently most Black Majority Churches exhibited apathy towards theological or missional training. Theological training apathy is a by-product of anti-intellectualism due to the strong emphasis on the role of the Holy Spirit by Pentecostals; the basis of ministerial functionalities is based on "Divine call", and the ability to effectively function is given by the anointing of the Holy Spirit. As Klaus and Triplett point out, the "general minimizing of the clergy/laity barrier" is because "the emphasis has been on the whole body as ministers supernaturally recruited and deployed. Since the Holy Spirit speaks to all believers equally, regardless of education, training or worldly rank, each member is capable of carrying out the task".[58] Most ministers and church leaders amongst the Black Majority Churches are indeed engaged in the ministry because of the Holy Spirit leading "often through some spiritual revelation like prophecy, a dream or a vision and even through audible voice perceived to be that of God in comparison to Missio Dei of Older Catholic and Protestant missions".[59]

Anderson observes the missionary agenda of Pentecostals as being dependent on the Holy Spirit, as he quotes Roswell, a Pentecostal, who wrote in 1908 that "When the Holy Spirit comes into our hearts, the missionary spirit comes in with it; they are inseparable ... Carrying the gospel to hungry souls in this and other lands is but a natural result."[60] An observation of most Black Majority Churches' leadership reinforces this school of thought. It is thus a common trend amongst these churches to see young men of diverse professional backgrounds leading congregations but having no theological training or pastoral training. Hollenweger, who is not necessarily cynical about Pentecostals, as he was formerly one, gave a concise comparison between Pentecostals and the Presbyterian Church in the dedication of his book: "To my friends and teachers in the Pentecostal Movement who taught me to love the Bible and to my teachers and friends in the Presbyterian Church who taught me to understand it."[61]

The strong emphasis on the universal priesthood of believers has greatly contributed to the over-reliance on identifying members or workers within these churches that have charismatic gifting to lead these congregations through in-house training and denominational ideals over time, or at best as graduates of their denominational colleges, but these churches worked through the appointing of national pastors and evangelists to build congregations and reach out to the community. What most leaders of Black Majority Churches lack in theological and pastoral training is made up for by implicit faith in God and missionary zeal. This however, does not compensate for inadequacies of theological and pastoral training but might be one of the reasons that has made the Black Majority Church attractive to its adherents and culturally modulated experiential nuances.

The Black Majority Churches' emphasis on church growth, humanism and eschatological triumphalism contributed to the insular nature of these churches, as until recently theological training was not on the radar of most Black Majority Churches. For instance the first black British woman to complete her PhD in religious studies and theology was Valentina Alexander in 1996 at the University of Warwick with a groundbreaking thesis on "Breaking Every Fetter? To What Extent has the Black-Led Church in Britain Developed a Theology of Liberation?" This was ninety years after the emergence of the first Pentecostal church in Britain! It is worth noting that the trend is gradually changing amongst these churches. The obvious inference is that the "missionary spirit" of the Pentecostals as it were amongst Black Majority Churches in Britain has only succeeded in recreating ethnic churches or Diasporic churches in Britain, but is this just a comma in the journey of faith of these churches, or the end of the storyline? This raises continued interest in relation to the reverse mission agenda of these churches.

### Metaphors of Black British Theologians

Theological metaphors over the years have contributed significantly to enhance and enrich people in appreciating and understanding models of God. The use of theological metaphors is a deconstructionist approach revealing God and its functionalities based on making God accessible to people. McFague opines that "we construct the worlds we inhabit, but also that we forget we have done so".[62] The purpose of the use of metaphors is to cause people to see things differently. The impact of the shift in perception leads to "contemporary experiences of relatedness to God"[63] which resonate in the worldview of Christians to give a coherent explanation of their experiences and understanding of God.

The last three decades have seen progressive positive changes in the emergence of black British theologians who have contributed significantly with various theological metaphors to the richness and diversity of black British theology. Such metaphors have evolved in recent years in Britain and serve as the screen through which black British theology has been advocated. The theological metaphors are quite cognitive and often poetic, offering a unique prism through which to view the new theological praxis while not embellishing the old; they accomplish this through seeing similarity in the dissimilar. Amongst notable metaphors that have evolved amongst black British theological scholars is that of Valentina Alexander, whose seminal thesis employs a liberation, passive and active radicalisation metaphor in ascertaining the social-political engagement of African-

Caribbean Christianity. The influence of black American theology or liberation theology has been quite pronounced and has influenced the theological leanings of emerging black British scholars, though in the last couple of years there is agitation amongst black British scholars like Aldred and Muir for a shift in praxis from the liberation theology of North America. Kee, in his critique of British black theology, observed the influence of black American theology on black British scholars and the dependence on metaphors that has evolved in black American theology/political activism.[64]

Anthony Reddie's book, entitled *Nobodies to Somebodies: A Practical Theology for Education and Liberation,* lends credence to the covert influence of American Liberation theology which is markedly different from the British context, as Kee observed that the objective of the book was to "contribute to ... the discipline of Black and Womenist theology and transformative education" while it completely negated the British context.[65] Kee's critique of various black British theologians' publications reveals that black theology within the British context has gradually evolved in the last twenty years. Africans and Caribbeans have just begun to articulate their theology and ecclesiology within their cultural framework that is essentially free from white theology, but also to foster and enhance intercultural theology and missions.

David's Muir assertion, as quoted by Kee, that black theology is underdeveloped in Britain, is succinct and true. Black British theologians, except for Robert Beckford, Joe Aldred and David Muir, are Pentecostals, while the likes of Anthony Reddie, Emmanuel Lamptey, Michael Jagessar, Kate Coleman and Valentina Alexander are members of the historic churches. The rich historical and theological traditions of the historic churches are leverages that Reddie, Jagessar, Coleman and Alexander have maximized in articulating their scholarly contributions. In view of the focus of this work which is black British Pentecostalism, it is important to critique the works of black British Pentecostal theologians. The two black British Pentecostal theologians who have contributed significantly to black British theology through the use of metaphors are Robert Beckford, with his Dread Canon, which has challenged white theology and has produced indigenous metaphors identifiable by Africans and Caribbeans, and Joe Aldred, with the Theology of Respect.

*Dread Theology: Beckford's Political and Social Mobilization*
Robert Beckford's work might have been the answer to Hollenweger's concerns about the future of black theology in Britain, as there were few

black students in theological training and higher institutions while he was lecturing in England.

Robert Beckford is an enigma and one of the pioneers of black British theology: an author, researcher, academician, broadcaster and public speaker. Beckford's theological persuasion is defined by the "Dread" analysis which is a fusion of Caribbean Rastafarianism and theological persuasions calculated to upstage social and political injustice within the British public space for the Black-led Churches. Beckford's seminal publication in 1998 heralded this distinctive theo-cultural focus with *Jesus is Dread: Black Theology and Black Culture in Britain*. His second publication was in 2000: *Dread and Pentecostal: A Political Theology for the Black Church in Britain*. Subsequent publications included *God of the Rahtid: Redeeming Rage* (2001), *God and the Gangs* (2004) and *Jesus Dub: Theology, Music and Social Change* (2006).

Beckford utilizes Paul Tillich's "revised critical correlation" principle in the use of "dread" as metaphor. Prior to his work "dread" was synonymous with negativity, fear and misconceptions, even in the Caribbean. As observed by Muir, "back in Jamaica, Rastas were outcast, the dregs, the insane of society. To see their children embrace this apparently bizarre cult drove many older West Indians to distraction."[66] But Kee gives insight into the genesis of Rasta language, observing that Beckford's enthusiasm in the use of Rastafarianism stems from the Caribbean subversion towards continued imperialism, leading to the deconstruction of the English language which was a feature of Rastafarian revolt. Kee, quoting Ernest Cashmore, explains, "language was one of the blades used by the Rastaman to cut his links with the encompassing Babylon. It aided maximal detachment from the everyday experience of white society and encouraged insularity and the development of in-group solidarity."[67] This counter-cultural dissociation from imperialism presents a political and social metaphor as espoused by Beckford for Black Majority Churches in Britain.

Beckford's counter-cultural reversal of Dread was a Utopian approach of creating and enlightening the Black Majority Churches on political activism, on challenges of social and political integration in Britain.[68] His thesis is hinged on the tripartite hub of liberation, oppression and exclusion with the sole objective of defining black British political ideology. Beckford's ideal in the adoption of Rastafarian ideology and iconography in asserting black identity and as a theological resource also smacks of lack of broad cultural acceptance considering the diversity of the Black Majority Churches and multicultural metaphors prevalent in the diversity. It is rather ironic that with the much-vaunted claims of theologizing within the socio-political praxis of Black Majority Churches, his work is almost bereft of examples of his political subscription. The prophetic role and socio-political constructions of Beckford's Dread canon was indeed a reflective practice that identified a niche not yet explored by Black Majority Churches then. His effort has been assessed as informing, radical and academic but "problematic",[69] and "politically incorrect and emotionally disturbing for most Black preachers ... Dread stands up as a coherent intellectual tool for a Black Paradigm but will ring hollow for most Pentecostals".[70]

The irreconcilable positivism of Beckford is perceived as alien to the Black Majority Churches he seeks to serve as prophet, as Edwards further asserts: "the danger is that the spokesperson would not be recognised by his constituency that he seeks to represent".[71] This is rather a paradox to Beckford's immediate constituency that has not been able to reconcile the pioneering effort to articulate black British theology from their cultural nuances. Beckford's Dread theology is riddled with various cultural ambiguities and clarification of usage of terms like politics, which has a broad spectrum of meanings, but he ruffled the feathers of the Black-led Churches by calling for a prophetic voice and a paradigm shift from "selfish faith" to "selfless faith".[72] This essentially is a wake-up call for re-engineering of the political theology of Black Majority Churches in Britain.

The starting point for Beckford's Dread hermeneutics is Rastafarianism; this is antithetical to Cone's recipe, as cited by Muir:

> In God's revelation in Scripture we come to the recognition that the divine liberation of the oppressed is not determined by our perceptions but by the God of the Exodus, the prophets and Jesus Christ who calls the oppressed into a liberated existence ... And if it can be shown that God as witnessed in the Scriptures is not liberator of the oppressed, then Black Theology would have either to drop the "Christian" designation or choose another starting point.[73]

Though Dread theology presents a pioneering praxis as the "cultural focus", as Muir further asserts, there are not "sufficient grounds for turning to Rastafari to find a theo-cultural focus for politicising African Caribbean Christianity".[74] The fundamental flaw of Beckford's Dread paradigm is its minimal engagement with the Bible. Any theological discourse or metaphor that is biblically shy is perceived by African Christians as alien because African Christians are "Biblified".

Beckford's Dread paradigm also asserted that Jamaican music icon Bob Marley was a "black liberation theologian"; Beckford affirms that

Marley was committed towards "radical social transformation and non-cooperation with the system" and a "psychological liberation with the poor and oppressed". Social and political semantics is the centrepiece of Beckford's theology and his total abhorrence for the inaction of Britain's Black-led Churches to this assertion gives a very myopic and limited perspective with respect to the moral school of thought regarding Marley's use of "*ganja*" (marijuana). A major challenge of this approach of Beckford is also noted in the use of Bob Marley's song "Get Up, Stand Up". Marley's lyrics explored the ethos of black liberation as he sang "if you know what life was worth, you would fight for yours on earth". This is a familiar victim/oppressor paradigm that many Pentecostals can identify with. Beckford also recognized the frailties or "negative ideologies" in Marley's canon, but he failed to reconcile the Pentecostals' flight from negative ideologies, as the divine status attributed to Haile Selassie in Rastafarianism is totally irreconcilable to the Christian ethos.[75] I concur with Reddie and Jagessar who noted that such an interpretation is problematic for two reasons: first "it reveals an uncritical approach to the text. Second, it relies heavily on an idealized and romanticized view of African history."[76]

Beckford's paradigm resonates within the liberation/oppression prism. Aldred noted that, "by presenting wrath as yet another aspect of Caribbean British Christian life that needs liberation or redemption, Beckford [in *God of the Rahtid: Redeeming Rage*] demonstrates the intractable nature of the oppression/liberation dialectic. In effect, this is a self-perpetuating philosophy that has the potential to have Blacks perpetually beholden to White benevolence, or dependent upon their eventual overthrow."[77]

Despite the myriad criticisms of Beckford's Dread, a major contribution was that he made an attempt to construct a political theology for Black Majority Churches, albeit fraught with counter-cultural ambiguities, impracticalities and minimal biblical engagement. Beckford's Dread further heightens cultural discontinuities in contextualization, rather than helping to bring about a culturally modulated theology which informs and maintains its distinctiveness while meeting the existential needs of Black British Churches. Without an iota of doubt, Dread is authentic and intellectually engaging, but is missionally flawed because of the limited scope of its cultural paradigm in relation to the *missio Dei* of the Gospel.

*Theology of Respect*
Joe Aldred is a Bishop of the Church of God of Prophecy, but has been actively involved in ecumenical initiatives at local and national levels in

Britain. Joe Aldred studied Theology at Sheffield University where he completed his PhD. He is an ecumenist, published author and editor of several books which include *Sisters with Power* (2000) *Praying with Power* (2002), *Respect: British Caribbean Christianity* (2006) and is also co-editor of *Black Church in the 21st Century* (2010). He also hosts a radio broadcast on BBC West Midlands.

Joe Aldred is involved in various educational and health care initiatives with several local and national organizations, including: Birmingham and Solihull Mental Health Foundation Trust, Partnership for Achievement, Sickle Cell and Thalassaemia User Support Group, Rookery House Restoration, Faith Communities Consultative Council, REACH Programme and the National Society for the Prevention of Cruelty to Children (NSPCC).

*Respect: British Caribbean Christianity* is the adaptation of Joe Aldred's PhD thesis which is one of the major contributions to scholarship on black British theology through his theology of Respect. Aldred's contribution to emerging black British theological discourse was predicated on his call for a shift in praxis from the North American oppressor/victim paradigm to a theology of respect. Though he had had reservations about the continued exploration of the oppressor/victim paradigm by black British scholars, he made use of Aretha Franklin lyrics; this indicates that American black theology is an ensemble of diversity and creativity that black British theologians can still utilize, while not necessarily adopting the oppressor/victim paradigm. It is not so much of an indigenization approach but more of the context of application in Aldred's use of the lyrics. The criticism of Jagessar (2007) reveals not weakness but the crossover nature of Aldred while yet maintaining the distinctiveness of his theology.

The focus of Aldred's treatise *Respect* was to articulate Caribbean British Christianity. The hybrid nature of his Respect theology was noted by Jagessar in the review of the publication as he noted, "I wonder about theology in the Caribbean, which is, for the most part, still very British (and of a certain era) in its articulation." Much of Jagessar's critique of *Respect* stems from his assertion that Aldred's theology "reflects an undeconstructed Caribbean British Christian expounding much of white inherited theology . . . There is much that is British and European and little that is Caribbean." This repudiates Aldred's objective to "unmask the true Caribbean Identity".[78] This presents quite an interesting dynamic: could Aldred's Caribbean identity have been shaped by the British context so much that he is more British than Caribbean in his theological leanings? Aldred's Incarnational theory is the starting point for the understanding of the Theology of Respect and his rejection of the Exodus story as a paradigm which is inherent in Beckford's black theology.

However, Reddie observed the discontinuities of Aldred's Respect theology:

> [the] work is weakened by the failure to build into his conceptualization for a contextualized Caribbean British black theology and any acute sense of constructive social analysis or politicized conscientization. Simply asserting that one is a human being and then claiming equality on that basis, without additional systematic analysis or structural models of conscientization simply leads to debilitating forms of false consciousness and theological escapism.[79]

The incarnational model of Aldred's Respect is the consciousness of being the express image of God, as exemplified in Genesis 1:26. This model is a conscious postulation to replace the victim/oppressed disposition with an acceptance of the tripartite nature of God. Inasmuch as I agree with Beresford and Reddie that asserting one's humanity, dignity and spirituality should not be misconstrued as "an attempt to liquidate centuries of economic and social justice", I wish to posit further that neither the process of politicization nor that of conscientization can retrospectively change the human and economic wastage of centuries. It is imperative that the black British theological position should see beyond the "post-slavery syndrome" to a theology that revolves around a political and social agenda for the future of the Black Majority Churches in the quest to be a transformational agent while simultaneously engaging the British communities as a prophetic witness.

Aldred's view of black British theology is not what black Christians used to be but what today and the future holds for Caribbean British Christianity, and how to effectively live within such a cultural prism and biblical worldview that creates a unique tapestry within the Christian world that is progressive.

Aldred recognizes the injustices of the *Windrush* era but strongly affirms the need for the appropriation of a new identity for black Caribbean Christians and the construction of a theology that is in conformity with God's view about equality of humans, and is not defined by a liberation and oppression worldview. This marks the distinction between Aldred's and Beckford's theological positions, though both scholars can be said to be creative, expressive and imaginative knights of black British theology in the last one hundred years of the existence of Black Majority Churches.

Kee describes *Respect* as "bold, perceptive and even courageous".[80] It is inherently a volte-face from the North American black theological rhetoric. It is indeed a post-Exodus view which gives impetus to view the experience of liberation as an interlude in the journey of self-discovery and celebration of black Caribbean Christians in Britain. It has wider applicability to Black Majority Churches because of its strong biblical focus, although a major constraint to wider acceptance is the defined focus of the publication which is Caribbean British Christianity.

## RESOURCING: MAXIMIZING THE FUTURE

Since Britain's Black Majority Churches have moved from the fringes of social irrelevance in their founding days to public recognition in over a century of existence, one is indeed right to predict that Black Majority Churches are here to stay. Sturge opined that the future of Black Majority Churches in Britain will be modulated by extraneous factors over which Black Majority Churches have no control, and by internal factors which are dependent on the willingness of the churches to engage in critical retrospection of their *modus operandi* in order to be able to clearly articulate the continued relevance and growth of these churches or remain as "asylum churches".[81]

The immigration policy of Britain was greatly overhauled recently with the introduction of a Points-Based System (PBS), but the intended changes to Britain's immigration policy in the light of the political evolution of the LibDem/Conservative coalition (i.e. to cap migration of non-European migrants) might be a major constraint to the continued growth of Black Majority Churches in Britain. Sturge observed that there exist historical antecedents in the Western world as they are "happy to underwrite flawed economic, immigration and social policies in order to achieve political and commercial objectives".[82] He further says that in spite of the proliferation of these (Black) churches, empirically the strength and character of the growth phenomenon seems inconsequential in relation to the British population, as black people make up only 2% of British society, made up of 1% black Caribbean, 0.8% black African, 0.2% black others.

The purported growth and reverse mission rhetoric from these churches whose members are predominantly Africans and Caribbeans suggests a flawed missional agenda. Britain is still very much a mission field because of various existential changes in the socio-religious life of the nation. The growth of these churches might plateau unless there is a paradigm shift to attract the other ethnic groups, including the indigenous white community, but interestingly Sturge noted that the continued relevance of Black Majority Churches should not be predicated on proliferation or growth; he posited that the Jewish faith, despite its small size, "continued to have incredible leverage in every area of society".[83] Although Beresford articulates in his thesis that Black Majority Churches are politically and socially active in Britain, the political activism might not be a reflection of their congregational aspirations but of the leadership fraternization and relevance within the socio-political climate of Britain.[84] This in itself is quite important in the light of legislation that is often aimed at social inclusion and community cohesion, which at times violate Christian convictions. A major shift that is required in the orientation of Black Majority Churches is their continued relevance in British social political life.

There has to be a wider understanding of holistic ministry amongst Black Majority Churches, because social, cultural and political engagement in the wider society is an integral part of God's agenda for the church. The Administrative Bishop of the New Testament Church of God, Bishop Eric Brown, is a strong adherent of this affirmation with the BIG MOVE initiative. Political and social responsiveness constitute core values in the BIG MOVE initiative as indicated in the governing document of New Testament Church of God (NTCG):

> ... as Christians we are members of the kingdom of God as well as a social order of the world. Obedience to God requires us to act in a responsible manner as citizens of our country ... Therefore we should support civil law and order; hold our leaders in respect and pray for them; participate in school, community and governmental activities; exercise our voting rights; and speak out on clear-cut moral issues.[85]

There has to be an increase in the number of Black Majority Churches which have public policy statements on social-cultural and political engagements. This is quite pivotal if the Black Majority Churches are to adequately inform, educate and be agents of transformation.

### Missional Framework for Black Majority Churches

Black Majority Churches of the twenty-first century must develop a definite missiological agenda that is Christo-centric, relevant, missional and engaging with the cultural realities of Britain. The missiological framework should shift from the earlier liberation/oppression paradigm which was the prevailing basis of articulation of the Black Churches with peculiar cultural and sociological nuances. What I am advocating is a framework based on reflective practices that made these churches the hub of Christian activism.

Black Majority Churches are faced with the challenges of connecting with the realities of postmodern Britain and constructing an engaging paradigm that challenges social injustice and is mission-oriented. This will invariably entail a move towards establishment of missional churches. The missional concept is associated with so much fluidity due to the multi-faceted usage and misconceptions associated with the concept, but Frost and Hirsch described a missional church as

> Incarnational, not attractional, in its ecclesiology. By Incarnational we mean it does not create sanctified spaces into which unbelievers must come to encounter the gospel. Rather, the missional church disassembles itself and seeps into the cracks and crevices of a society in order to be Christ to those who don't yet know Him.[86]

This entails the deconstruction of the Black Majority Churches' attitude to church and missions, as Frost and Hirsch further argue that "as people of a missionary God, we ought to engage the world the same way he does by going out rather than just reaching out".[87] This is counter-cultural to Black Majority Churches' ethos, which is often averse to risk-taking, and satisfied to perpetuate the "maintenance mode" of their denominations. This stance is in sharp contrast to Gibbs and Coffey's ideals of missional churches: "Churches living out the apostolic paradigm define themselves in missional terms and are prepared to embark on risk-taking initiatives. This bold willingness to take new missionary risks is their distinctive feature and gifting that challenges the great majority of churches stuck in a survival mode."[88]

The Lausanne Conference on World Evangelisation in 2004 averred that missional churches are "those communities of Christ-followers who see the church as the people of God who are sent on a mission". The concept of the priesthood of believers indeed might seem to support this within Black Majority Churches' theology, but there exists a deviation from this assertion, as missions often are constructed as an integral part of the church, but the church is supposed to be missional, thus limiting the general engagement of the members of these churches in the public space outside the secular–religious divide where there is a veritable pool of mission opportunities that are not understood and not appropriated.

The prevailing scenario amongst most Black Majority Churches in Britain is that little or no resources are committed to missions. A church that is missionally committed will see huge capital and human resources invested in missions. The concept of mission often has an overlapping inference to church planting amongst these churches. Akhazemea, citing Cindi John, suggested that the increase in church attendance on Sunday in London was due to the mission efforts of these churches based on the assertion that people of African and Caribbean origin make up 2% of the UK's population but account for more than two-thirds of Sunday church-goers in London and 7% of worshippers nationwide,[89] but it is imperative to note that the black ethnic minorities within the historic churches have increased significantly.

There needs to be a major shift in mission initiatives of Black Majority Churches in order for these churches to be transformational. According to the Church of England report on Mission Shaped Churches, "a missionary church seeks to shape itself in relation to the culture in which it is located or to which it is called. Whenever it is called to be cross-cultural then its long-term members or initial team lay aside their cultural preferences about church to allow the emergence of a form of church to be shaped by those it is seeking to reach."[90] These churches need to be incarnational and responsive to the cultural nuances of the host communities in order to consciously engage in cross-cultural missions, as acculturation is pivotal to the future of these churches. Jesus presents a unique model for this subscription, as he adjusted to the cultural realities of his days but was quite emphatic on kingdom principles and denounced any culture that was antagonistic to the kingdom worldview.

Paul also presented a similar paradigm in his sermon at Athens in Acts 17. His knowledge of the socio-cultural and political dynamics of the Jewish people contributed to his missional effectiveness as he engaged with the Athenian worldview in order to unravel the kingdom worldview to his audience. His approach was quite constructive and engaged with the Athenians' beliefs and worldviews. He found common ground in Stoic teachings that the Athenians were conversant with, but it has been noted by Wright that it is "travelling on the slippery slope towards syncretism".[91] Contextualization is expedient, but skilful delineation of boundaries is essential, as over-contextualization leads to syncretism. Over-contextualization to a great extent has caused some of these churches to lose their distinctiveness as Christian churches and become more or less "social clubs".

The New Testament model of church and missions was not built around mono-ethnic remits. The New Testament illustrates the concept of building congregations based on the empowerment of the Holy Spirit to bring about reconciliation to God irrespective of racial divide. The current trend within most Black Majority Churches is in itself not deliberate, but building congregations around a homogenous grouping is a sociological principle based on what is cosy and marketable. This seems ironical in view of the pneuma-centric theology of empowerment of the Black Majority Churches. In as much as l agree with Akhazemea in his thesis that some Black Majority Churches in the mould of the Redeemed Christian Church of God have a genuine missional drive,[92] it is apparent that the drive is yet to translate to well-articulated missional churches that are willing to step out of the homogenous trappings and engage the dynamic British culture; it is more about Diasporic congregations, at best described as "church away from home".

Brandon in an unequivocal manner stated that if the *modus operandi* of African Churches in Britain does not change and if they "persist in perpetuating Africa on British soil, their missionary potential will never be realised".[93] Brandon is not a prophet of doom for African churches, but this paints a very gloomy picture for the future of Black Majority Churches in Britain: indeed the growth might stagnate if there is no shift in the missional orientation of these churches. He further admonished that "the success mentality could ultimately militate against the evangelistic engagement with the nation". Changes in the ecclesiology of Black Majority Churches will invariably reflect in the missiological approaches within the British context as the field is ripe but the labourers are culturally conditioned.

### *Regulatory and Statutory Challenges*

The phenomenal proliferation of Black Majority Churches in Britain, especially the Neo-Pentecostal African churches, in the last twenty years is unprecedented in British Church history. The Kingsway International Christian Centre's administrative takeover in 2003 by the Charity Commission of England and Wales raised a lot of concerns with respect to compliance requirements of the Commission and of the Inland Revenue. The continuous changes in legislation over time will contribute to compliance challenges as these churches strive to meet the increasing requirements of Health and Safety, governance, Criminal Records Bureau checks, Child Protection legislation and Trusteeship. The stipulated policies and procedures required by the law are pivotal in creating checks and balances especially amongst the Black Majority Churches, most of which have charitable status. One of the positive effects of the KICC 2003 saga was that for the first time in the history of the Charity Commission of England and Wales, there was a conscious effort by the Commission to understand the peculiarities and cultural nuances of Black Majority Churches, though Osgood noted the hyper-sensationalism of the British media in the reporting of the KICC investigation.[94] The investigations culminated in better understanding of the cultural and biblical worldview of Black Majority Churches by the Charity Commission and an increased ability to accommodate Black Church culture in Britain.

Even the former Prime Minister, Tony Blair, said that the charity law was outdated. In a foreword to a report entitled "Private Action, Public Benefit. A Review of Charities and the Wider Not-For-Profit Sector" he said: "The current law is unclear, has not evolved in a way which best meets the needs of contemporary communities, and does not reflect the diversity of organisations which operate for the public benefit."[95] On account of the continuous changes in the regulatory dictates of the Charity Commission and the legislation, it is incumbent upon Black Majority Churches that still want to enjoy charitable status to comply continually with all regulatory requirements and changes to UK legislation. A major shift has already taken place in the social and political landscape of Britain with the proposed "Big Society" by the Liberal Democratic Party/Conservative Party coalition led by Mr David Cameron. The third sector, which is the voluntary sector including the faith and charitable organizations, will be expected to meet stipulated government requirements to be able to benefit from the process of localization of some services that might be better delivered by the faith communities. This might inevitably imply that huge capital outlay will be available to the third sector, but there exist two major constraints that might work actively against Black Majority Churches. These are (a) bureaucratic illiteracy on faith concepts and (b) the inability of the Black Majority Churches to meet the policy requirements to access funding to implement their social initiatives. It has been ascertained that currently only 75% of existing charities are funded by government, which implies huge opportunities for inclusive funding for Christian charities to be paid for their services to the community.

As a church leader amongst Black Majority Churches I have observed a reluctance by some of these churches to engage in ecumenical initiatives in Britain. Various ecumenical organizations are willing to assist and make available various instruments to some of the Black Majority Churches in Britain. The pioneering Caribbean Churches have formed formidable partnerships with various ecumenical organizations and this has greatly broadened the understanding of the cultural tapestry of Black Majority Churches by the ecumenical organization. For the future of Black Majority Churches and the Christian faith in Britain greater partnership with ecumenical bodies is pivotal and there is a rich historical antecedent that Black Majority Churches need to learn from. Brandon noted that African Churches (Black Majority Churches) can learn from British Church history: "in no more than one or two generations, the church can go into sharp spiritual decline. At present BMCs in the United Kingdom are riding on the momentum of a wave of African revivalism."[96] There are already diverse challenges with second-generation members of Black Majority Churches in Britain as they have been significantly culturally conditioned as British rather than Africans or Caribbeans.

Indeed, perhaps the future of Black Majority Churches depends on whether the second and third generations can actualize their desire to re-evangelize Britain. Brandon further argues that the second and third generations will be "culturally far better equipped to take the nation [Britain] for Christ"[97] but the challenge is whether these generations are willing to walk in the lines of the first-generation commitment to the Gospel. The reality of the future is defined by the actions and commitment of the present leadership of Black Majority Churches. For instance, I previously noted that the second-generation Nigerians in churches are already shaped by the prevailing British culture and posited re-assessment of the leadership model, missiological agenda, communication model and ecclesiological approaches of Nigerian Churches in the South-East of London.[98]

## SUMMARY

The last one hundred years of Black Majority Churches have brought about so much resilience, determination and optimism that is due to the growth and proliferation of these churches in Britain. The future of Black Majority Churches is predicated on their ability to engage in reflective practice, and to carry out concise appraisals of the developments of these churches from the fringes of irrelevance to a celebratory status in British Church history. This practice entails a deliberate effort that is critical but yet objective and that will celebrate the strengths of the Black Majority Church while simultaneously addressing perceivable flaws prevalent in these churches.

The reverse mission rhetoric of Black Majority Churches so far has not led to any significant progress in the re-evangelization of Britain but has contributed to putting God on the agenda in British public space. Most of the Black Majority Churches are homogenous mono-ethnic or mono-national churches characterized by various cultural nuances of the prevailing diverse nationalities.

In order to actualize the reverse mission agenda of Black Majority Churches, there has to be a review of their organizational ethos, which often is antithetical to the British cultural norms. The inability of these churches to understand British social and cultural norms has affected their acculturation and contextualization. In the last twenty years there have emerged distinguished black theologians who have consistently contributed to black British theology. Two such outstanding contributors with a Pentecostal background are Robert Beckford and Joe Aldred. Their contributions are creative, engaging and with a distinctive cultural flavour that has challenged white theology in Britain.

The future of Black Majority Churches in Britain is hinged on both external and internal factors. The extraneous factors are modulated by prevailing immigration policy which can be politically motivated. Changes to immigration and social political policies in Britain will have a reverberating effect on the growth and proliferation of Black Majority Churches. There has to be a shift in paradigm from attractional churches to missional churches in order for Black Majority Churches to engage the host culture. The current composition of Black Majority Churches, almost 99% Africans and Caribbeans, does not reflect the reverse mission rhetoric of the churches.

There is a need for various organizational structures, especially the pyramidal leadership model, which is quite restrictive and controlling, to be replaced by the open network model which is empowering and missionally inclined. The process is vital to overcome constraints within the leadership of some of these organizations. Black Majority Churches are pneuma-centric, akin to global Pentecostals, and as such there is little or minimal emphasis on training.

National government statutory regulations will continue to be a challenge to Black Majority Churches in the future because of changes within the regulatory and monitoring instruments of the Charity Commission of England and Wales. In order to prepare for the future there must a conscious and deliberate effort by Black Majority Church leaders to learn from British Church history and to chart a new course of action that will prepare the second- and third-generation Diasporans to take up leadership responsibilities. Their commitment will be pivotal to the future of Black Majority Churches.

*Chapter Seven*

# Conclusion

British church history has been transformed remarkably in the last sixty years with the growth and proliferation of Black Majority Churches. This further signifies and authenticates previous assertions and claims of scholars regarding the shift in the hub of Christianity to the Global South, for previously classified mission fields are now sending missionaries to the Western world.[1] The focus of this book is the origin, growth, distinctiveness and contributions of Black Majority Churches to British Christianity.

The origin of Black Majority Churches in Britain was ascertained to have been 1906. It is inexplicably linked with the genesis of British Pentecostalism which occurred in Sunderland in October 1907 at the invitation of Norwegian Pentecostal Preacher Thomas Ball Barrat by Alexander A. Boddy (1854–1930), vicar of All Saints, Monkwearmouth, Sunderland. The Azusa Street revival outpouring of 1906 had a cataclysmic effect of global proportions with respect to the spread of Pentecostalism: adherents fanned the flame of missions as ordinary people travelled to different parts of the world in a short while. The message of the "missionaries", hinged on premillennialism which created a sense of urgency in the proclamation of the Gospel to all hearts, culminated in diverse resonance in Europe, as Norway emerged as the Azusa of Europe. It was noted by Anderson that the Azusa Street revival was not the only hub of the outpouring of the Holy Spirit in America: there were other towns not on the radar of most scholars:

> [There were] other important early centres of Pentecostalism independent of Azusa Street, in particular Marie and Robert Brown's Glad Tidings Tabernacle in New York City (commenced in 1907), William H. Piper's Stone Church in Chicago (which became a Pentecostal in 1907), and Ellen and James Hebden's Queen Street Mission in Toronto (the Hebdens were baptised in the Spirit in 1906).[3]

Anderson further alludes to the emergence of "Jerusalems" globally which were independent of the Azusa Street revival. Anderson's story shows how

Creech has perverted the history of Pentecostalism.[4] Anderson's assertions included the emergence of Korean Pentecostalism in 1907–8 which "commenced at a convention in Pyongyang" which was preceded by a revival amongst Methodist Missionaries in Wosnan in 1903. Anderson[5] noted that the revival had similar resonance with the Welsh revival of 1903–4 characterized by mass conversion, emotionalism, revelatory visions and experiential and boisterous prayers, but Desmond Cartwright, the official historian of Elim Pentecostal Church, Great Britain, repudiated the notion that glossolalia was part of the Welsh revival.[6]

The uniqueness of the origin of Pentecostalism as asserted by Anderson was that Pentecostalism, like revivalism, had been known in South India as far back as 1860 when glossolalia and other manifestations of the Spirit were reported prior to the 1905 revival in Khasi Hills, India, "where Welsh Presbyterian missionaries were working".[7] These assertions further corroborate the conclusive statement of McGee on the origin of Pentecostalism that before the North American account, Pentecostalism in India was fully established "before the word of Azusa reached the subcontinent".[8] The overt misconception or simplification of the history of Pentecostalism with respect to the Western countries is to see them as the hub, sending missionaries to Africa, Asia and Latin America, but Anderson noted that the various Pentecostal revivals were not primarily movements from the Western world to foreign lands but more significantly movements "within these continents themselves".[9]

The relevance of Anderson's account from the global perspective to this book is that I posit that there might exist elements of imperialism where the development of movements recorded in non-Western sources has been discounted.

The inference with respect to Britain's Black Majority Churches is that most of the records and publications on the origin of Black Majority Churches were newspaper articles and newsletters like *Pentecost* (edited by Donald Gee), *Redemption Tidings*, etc, which were produced by Western organizations where essentially the focus was more on Eurocentric missions. It seems the origin of the first Black Church in Britain was not so much on the radar of most religious commentators in its infancy probably because a Black Church was adjured as a misnomer in Britain as far back as 1906. This was the genesis of reverse mission as Brem-Wilson became the forerunner of the African and Caribbean Pentecostal churches in Britain. Though I subscribe that the genesis of Black Churches in Britain was missiological, also it is providential, as Sunderland became the turning point for Brem-Wilson's ministry through the exploration of his contact with various historic denominational leaders who acknowledged his ministry credentials and benevolence to their cause.

Augustus Cerillo, a Pentecostal historian, noted that there exist four basic approaches to understanding the origin of American Pentecostalism. These are: "(1) Providential. The belief that the movement came 'from heaven' through a sudden, simultaneous and spontaneous outpouring of the Spirit" – Pentecostals subscribe to this view wholly and it is strongly rooted in the biblical antecedents of the Lukan account in Acts 2; "(2) Historical, where Christianity the movement is seen as continuous with the nineteenth century revivalist Christianity, (3) multicultural (4) functional or sociological, which looks at the social context to provide an explanation for its emergence."[10] Although Anderson subscribes to the multicultural interpretative approach for the origin of global Pentecostalism which is appropriate for the global historiography of the movement, it is imperative to note that the emergence of the movement in each context varies significantly.

I wish to posit, using Cerrillo's interpretative model, a fifth approach, which is alien to the emergence of the American context but unique to the emergence of the first Black Pentecostal Church in Britain. The fifth interpretative model is the missiological and providential approach. Biblical antecedents to this assertion are observed in Luke 10:19 but subsequently had the providential experience of the Holy Spirit (Acts 2 and Luke 24:49). Brem-Wilson was baptized in the Holy Spirit at Sunderland at the beginning of British Pentecostalism. It was reminiscent of the biblical Pentecost, when people came to celebrate the feast of Pentecost in Jerusalem on the fateful day with pronounced linguistic diversity: 120 people spoke in heavenly "languages" that brought forth the first glossolalic community. In the case of black British Pentecostalism, Bro. Brem-Wilson became an Apostle for black British Pentecostalism to London, which providentially is the hub of black British Pentecostalism in the twenty-first century.

To the Pentecostals mission without providential experience is deemed to be ineffective, as the providential experience is synonymous with empowerment. This approach to the emergence of the first Black Pentecostal Church in Britain presents a unique approach, as the mission work was "not a clearly well thought out theological decision and so policy and methods were formed mostly in the crucible of missionary praxis".[11]

The second and third phases of the re-emergence of Black Majority Churches through Daniel Ekarte and the *Windrush* era have similar missiological resonance. Though slavery was effectively abolished before the emergence of Black Majority Churches in Britain, these churches experienced hostile and unreceptive beginnings in Britain. The aftermath was a gradual sense of withdrawal from the larger British communities, but there was a rapid evolution of experiential, theological and doctrinal orientations in order to cope with the challenges of assimilation; this process was enhanced by the Pentecostal ideals of fluidity in various cultural contexts. All this has led to a clarion call for a better understanding of what African, Caribbean and Asian churches thrive on. Gerloff asks for the "understanding of what the Asian, African and the worldviews of Indians have to offer about the 'spirit world', human empowerment, healing and a wholesome concept of the cosmos over and against progressing misery of people".[12]

Brem-Wilson was the first Black Pentecostal pastor in modern Britain; his missiological initiative dates back to 1906, when he and Bro. Newlands established the first Black Church in Britain. Evangelist Brem-Wilson's accomplishments have not been on the radar of British Pentecostalism and black British Pentecostal historiographies, but evidently his ministry impacted his generation. A contributory factor to his non-recognition by black British scholars might be the typical tradition in which historical antecedents are passed on orally. It is rather amazing that as a missionary school master from Ghana, and as a businessman and investor, he failed to engage in any literary work with the exception of his article in *Riches of Grace* in 1924. Killingray opined that the entries in his diaries do not capture the entire length of his ministry.[13] This thus constitutes a unique niche for further research into Brem-Wilson's antecedents. In retrospect, the ministry of Brem-Wilson as an evangelist was quite celebrated amongst the white community, as his congregation was affiliated to the Apostolic Church, Great Britain, and at his "mission" meetings crowd control was a major problem for the organizers. The Baptism of Holy Spirit and the simplicity of his preaching were quite astonishing.

Most scholars have hitherto associated the origin of Black Majority Churches in Britain with the *Windrush* era. It is apt to submit that this account is inaccurate. Similar inadequacies were observed by Anderson in his historical account of global Pentecostalism.[14] Based on the observable trend from Anderson's assertions, it seems that the global history of Pentecostalism, including Britain's Black Majority Churches, has not been adequately articulated on account of poor intellectual contributions by Pentecostals. Many historical accounts have been lost because most of them have been written from an outsider's perspective. The ability of Pentecostal teachings and practices to infiltrate various cultural contexts is quite evident, as these churches have proliferated globally and this has resulted in Pentecostalism being referred to as a missionary religion.

Pentecostalism constitutes a "missionary institution" but its missionary drive has not been based on a well-thought-out missiological agenda or missionary praxis. Ironically this was so in the emerging days of Black Majority Churches in Britain. Mohabir, perhaps one of the most well-respected pioneers of reverse mission from the West Indies, copiously affirmed that he came to England to give hope to the English people on account of their social and moral decadence and the relegation of the Christian faith to the fringes of public life as far back as the 1950s.[15] In the midst of racial and social ostracization, Mohabir never retreated from proclamation evangelism in London. In their infancy Black Majority Churches in Britain were without any missiological agenda, but a few in the mould of Mohabir placed emphasis on missions and evangelism similar to North American Pentecostalism.

## MIGRATION, DIASPORA AND RELIGIOUS IDENTITY

The contemporary migratory pattern to the Western world might be attributed to the multifaceted effect of globalization, as the world is now a global village made possible by technological advancement and migration. This has invariably led to the emergence of multicultural communities, especially in Western Europe and America, and has grossly changed the social and economic landscape of these continents, but it has also brought about the emergence of religious diversities in these contexts. The dynamics and direction of global mobility and the various immigration restrictions have checked the flow of legal migration but also served as catalysts for illegal migrants, which include Christians.

The shift is replicated with the growth and proliferation of Black Majority Churches in Britain, which has heralded a distinctive phase in the chequered British church history. This has progressively led to various researches on the interconnectedness of religion, Diaspora and migration in relation to religious creativity; all of these have contributed to the shaping of the spiritual landscape of these contexts.[16] The migratory pattern has been towards Western Europe and America. The role of religious communities in Diasporic communities constitutes a major feature of the Africans and Caribbeans because of the intrinsically religious nature of Africans. Gerrie Ter Haar examined the dynamics which are at play:

> The reversal of roles implied by the notion of an African mission to Europe stands many conventional ideas on their head. Europeans traditionally see

Africans as being on the receiving end, and themselves on the giving end, of a relationship which is often equated with black–white relations. Moreover Europeans are inclined to believe that the proper place for Africans is in Africa. The idea of an African mission to Europe thus appears inappropriate to the marginal status of black immigrants in their society. To many native Europeans the recent foundation of African Christian congregations is an anomaly. In fact, the rise of African and other non-Western Christian congregations is nothing less than a new phase in the religious history of Europe.[17]

The concluding statements of Ter Haar further support the age-long misconception that the emergence of Black-led Churches in Europe is a new phenomenon in its entirety, but in Britain, Black-led Churches have been in existence for over a century. She also failed to highlight the pull and push factors that have contributed to the emergence of Black Churches in Europe.

A major feature of the migratory pattern of Africans and Caribbeans is the positive correlation of migration and religious affirmation. Often, however, living in a different cultural context has facilitated great diversity, leading to the modification of religious practices in order to reflect spiritual thirst and to gain more converts, which often are viewed as a messianic seal on the faith of the migrants. Britain's Black Majority Churches represent a mosaic of religious diversity in Europe which is currently under the consideration of religious historians, anthropologists, sociologists and theologians seeking to define the emerging transnational phenomenon and sociological mechanism of Diasporic religiosity.[18] The emerging religious landscape in Europe has a definitive imprint of Africa, as Jenkins opined: "for the next few decades, the face of religious practice across Europe should be painted in Brown and Black".[19]

These churches, whose emergence spans over a century, and which fulfil definite missiological, social and cultural needs of Africans and Caribbeans, have metamorphosed into a formidable constituency that has heralded a new chapter in British church history. However, there has been a noticeable decline in the growth and proliferation of the *Windrush* Caribbean Churches in comparison with the African Neo-Pentecostal Churches in the last twenty years. The migratory pattern is not mainly a transatlantic phenomenon, as Zeleza noted that migration is often intra-African migration.[20] The migratory pattern to Europe from Africa and the Caribbean is reminiscent of colonial historical antecedents, and is reflected in the educational, linguistic and economic indices adopted by the colonies. This also shapes the migration trends of economic, social and forced migration which have led to the emergence of African and Caribbean communities in Britain.

The explosion of African and Caribbean immigrants to Europe, Britain included, has led to the emergence of African communities with their religious subscriptions. This culminated in the emergence of the Caribbean brand of Christianity during the *Windrush* era which was a by-product of the prevailing post-war challenges of rebuilding Britain and skill shortages in some sectors of the British economy, as discussed in Chapter Two. The migratory pattern to Britain from the West Indies during this dispensation was also greatly influenced by the Caribbean agrarian economy and post-war reconstruction challenges. As noted, a British Labour MP described Jamaica as a "tropical slum".[21]

The exploration of opportunities in the Western world for economic and social benefits of the migrants has been due to a moral economy of corruption by the leadership of African nations, but this also contributes to the continued impoverishment of the African continent while Europe has a compensatory brain gain. The West Indian and African migrants may have migrated for economic and social reasons or for family reunions, but they also migrated with their religious idiosyncrasies, as noted in Chapter Two. Juxtaposing this within global migration, Adogame and Weissköppel posit that religion, hitherto not a "motor or driving force" is vital in the formation of African Diaspora.[22] This has further been corroborated by transnational researchers on the RCCG in Germany, the Netherlands and Britain that "religion is to some extent a driving factor in the migration process, albeit a small one",[23] as 7% of RCCG pastors surveyed in the United Kingdom are primarily in the country for Christian ministry, while 55% of the sampled pastors indicated that Christian ministry in Britain was one of the motivating factors for choosing to stay in the United Kingdom.

The sending of missionaries to the West constitutes a shift in the concept of mission from the European perspective. The territorial "*from* the West *to* the rest of the world" model was prevalent during the halcyon days of the Western missionary movement (1850–1950). The change in prevailing mission praxis is unique and might continue for quite a while despite immigration constraints imposed on migrants from Africa and Asia to Europe and America. Andrew Walls has observed that "the great new fact of our time – and it has momentous consequences for mission – is that the great migration has gone into reverse. There has been a massive movement, which all indications suggest will continue, from the non-Western to the Western world."[24] It is an undeniable fact that most Black Majority Churches are engaged in cross-cultural missions, but are often faced with a lack of impact on the indigenous natives whose lack of interest in the Good News is unparalleled. The resultant effect of minimal impact on the host indigenes leads to self-affirmation of their obedience to the global mandate for evangelization (Mk 16:16–18) as the word of God is proclaimed within the geographical and spiritual boundaries of the nation.

It is rather ironic that the repository of migrants from Africa and Asia to Britain with their Christian or religious orientations not only contribute significantly to the British economy but also bring about vitality to the Christian faith whose voice is almost lost in the effects of pluralism, relativism and secularism that have prided themselves in "the death of God" in Britain. The welfare disposition of Britain presents a safe haven for the economically disadvantaged, the oppressed and refugees fleeing from natural disasters in the third world.

The Church of Scotland Church and Nation Committee, "Refugees and Migration", reported to the Church of Scotland General Assembly 2005 in Edinburgh:

> the West and North are not neutral observers of their plight but bear part of the responsibility for their plight ... We cannot answer the question of why people become refugees simply in terms of internal politics and discrimination within a country, while ignoring international responsibility for the environment, and the effects of a globalised economy and politics on the poorest of the world.[25]

It is upon the crest of the massive migration to the West from Africa and the Caribbean that Black Majority Churches proliferated during the *Windrush* era and African Neo-Pentecostal churches, with their distinct identity and socio-cultural values, grew in the 1980s and 1990s in Britain. The third phase of growth of Black Majority Churches in Britain as chronicled in this study further supports the views of various transatlantic researchers that have identified the role of religion in ethnic and identity formation in a new context.[26]

The proliferation of the West Indian churches from the 1950s and the African Neo-Pentecostal Churches in the 1980s and 1990s has highlighted the interrelatedness of religious practices in the homelands of migrants and in Britain. The mitigating circumstances in the 1950s in Britain were twofold, primarily the effects of racism and the culture shock associated with the English church culture and the wider British culture. The prevailing British culture in the post-war era brought a gradual social and cultural revolution in Britain which led to the renunciation of the accepted norms of British life: family values and the sacredness of marriage were tossed to the wind. The effects of secularization and the attendant challenges of the new industrial revolution contributed significantly to the missionizing of Britain by African and Caribbean Christians.

Andrew Walls highlighted the need for migrants to re-evangelize Britain as he remarked that "the developed world is faced with a paradox: it needs immigrants, but does not want them. In a public forum where the presence of Christian voices can be less and less taken for granted, Western Christians may find themselves increasingly called to take stances that are unpopular."[27] The religious identity created by the proliferation of Black Majority Churches in Britain in the light of reverse mission has enabled the migrants in Diaspora to have social support networks to cope with the challenges of assimilation into the host communities. The churches function as a hub of restructuring and transforming the self-worth and economic worth of their members through dissemination of information about job opportunities.[28]

Miller and Yamamori's observation that Pentecostalism "often attracts people who are suffering from what sociologists refer to as anomie"[29] is apt if the migration pattern of the Pentecostal Churches is a local migratory pattern, but the uniqueness of the Black Majority Churches was that adherents suffered from "transnational anomie". This is the impact of the social, economic and political challenges as a result of migration from undeveloped economies to developing economies. This often constitutes major restraint in the acculturation of members of Black Majority Churches to the host communities and other ethnic communities in Britain. It is thus a common trend amongst the members of the Black Majority Churches to be selective in their assimilation into British society.

Selective assimilation is borne out of elements of social and religious discontinuities, observed or imagined by migrants, which is fostered by social interaction and religious repository within ethnic churches where the indigenous migrant cultural worldviews are upheld. The process of selective assimilation entails linguistic, educational and some social ideals, but also a deep preference for an African or Caribbean religious flavour, as noted by Ebaugh and Chafetz.[30] It is expedient to note that the challenges of assimilation of the third phase of the emergence of Black Majority Churches in Britain are incomparable to the first and second phases because of changes within the social and legislative worldview of Britain, in which certain legislative measures have been put in place to check racism. However, it is still pertinent to note that racism is an ideology that manifests at various levels of engagement.

Burgess *et al.*, after asserting that religious commitment is a major factor in transnational migration of Nigerian-initiated churches in the mould of the RCCG, cited a number of church leaders within the RCCG in the United Kingdom, Germany and the Netherlands to whom this applies. The names included Agu Irukwu, RCCGUK Executive Council Chairman and Senior Pastor of Jesus House, Sola Fola-Alade (Trinity Chapel) and Ibrahim Abarshi, the pastor of Jesus House Holland, a church plant of Jesus House London.[31] Agu Irukwu, before his redeployment to the United Kingdom from Freedom Hall, Apapa, Nigeria, was a merchant banker. He is a graduate of law from Warwick University, UK, and the son of Professor Joe Irukwu, the "controversial former president of the Pan-Igbo cultural organization, Ohaneze Ndi Igbo".[32] Sola Fola-Alade is a Nigerian-trained medical doctor whose father is Chief (Dr) Isaac Fola-Alade, who had an illustrious career in the federal civil service of Nigeria and served as Federal Permanent Secretary (Special Duties) for Nigerian Armed Forces, Supreme Headquarters between November 1976 and October 1979.

The assemblage of the young upwardly mobile Africans that migrated in the 1990s to Britain were well educated, middle class and had privileged backgrounds, but came with their religious "backpacks" to Britain. Other economic migrants that have since left their economic pursuits include David Sola-Oludoyi and Grace Sola-Oludoyi (of Royal Connections, an RCCG parish in London) who are Russian-trained medical doctors. It is unimaginable to most Western observers that a first-class graduate psychiatrist doctor like Grace Sola-Oludoyi would abandon the stethoscope to proclaim the limitless riches of Jesus Christ. The list seems endless, as names like Sola Fola-Alade, Jonathan Oloyede, Albert Odulele, Dipo Oluyomi, Tayo Adeyemi and Sola Adeaga have also bid farewell to their medical vocation to be agents of "soul renewal and transformation".

Black Majority Churches in Britain have succeeded in creating a major religious identity that is not just a cultural ghetto, but they have created sacred spaces where transitional experiences are articulated in familiar symbolic constructs which are often disconnected from the worldview of the outside community. These articulations are based on a common worldview and religious praxis, which creates a community of people with high self esteem, belief and pride in overcoming perceived social injustices or alienation.

## UNIQUENESS OF THE BLACK MAJORITY CHURCH PRAXIS

The theological and doctrinal persuasions of Black Majority Churches were considered in Chapter Four in relation to the liturgical and preaching models of these churches in Britain. It suffices to note that spirituality is greatly influenced by the context of expression of such a faith. The British context has significantly contributed to the unique theological and hermeneutical praxis of Black Majority Churches. The experiential nature of Black Majority Churches in Britain further reiterates the existential nature of black Christian spirituality which is relevant, holistic and promises to give answers to all challenges of life. Britain's Black Majority Churches' spirituality is not different from the Global Pentecostal spirituality which is exemplified by oral liturgy, narrative theology and witness, participatory, experiential and metaphorical interpretations of visions and dreams, and pneuma-centrism. Similar resonance is found amongst Pentecostals globally, despite the diversities of cultural context in the expressions of Pentecostalism. This view is adequately corroborated by Droogers.[33] The organized spontaneity of black British Pentecostals has tremendous appeal that is due to its experiential nature devoid of formalism, and many of the attendees cannot but appreciate an encounter with God which is holistic, characterized by being the solution to myriads of challenges.

Asamoah-Gyadu asserts that this experiential element has contributed significantly to Western Christianity: "One of the major contributions of African Christians, particularly Pentecostals and Charismatics, to Western Christianity is the attention it draws to the fact that Christianity is about experience and that the power of God is able to transform circumstances that Western rationalist theologies will consider the preserve of psychology and scientific development."[34] The major hallmark that constitutes the uniqueness is the cultural context of the expression of the Pentecostals: its inherent ability to acculturate itself to any culture has been a contributory factor to the proliferation of Pentecostalism globally.

Brem-Wilson's church in its infancy at Walworth Road, London, was given the pejorative name the "black man's church" with complaints that their meetings were too noisy: this must have been as a result of the emotionalism associated with Pentecostal meetings, like those experienced at Azusa Street. The racially insulated British community prevalent in 1907 was similar to the American context in the days of William Seymour, but the unity of faith of Seymour's leadership and Brem-Wilson's church was unique: "at the time, people within ethnic minorities discovered the sense of dignity and community denied them in the larger urban culture".[35]

Black Majority Churches have similar praxis with William Seymour's Azusa Street revival. The indigenous nature of Afrocentrism was reflected in Seymour's religious expressions, as Nelson noted that these "expressions were a reflection of African religious culture from which slaves had been abducted and Seymour himself was deeply affected by black slave spirituality".[36] This was characterized by the jerking, rolling and shouting prevalent during the Azusa Street revival, which is currently a feature of African-American church culture, and might have been influences from African slave religion, but Harris avers that "these are patterns that are translated as expressions of Christian spirituality among African Americans rather than simply an extension of African religion".[37]

The Pentecost of Azusa did not eliminate racism in its totality, as Cox notes how Seymour's disenchantment with white Pentecostals affected his perception of the gift of tongues: "finding that some people could speak in tongues and continue to abhor their black fellow Christians convinced him that it was not tongue speaking but the dissolution of racial barriers that was the surest sign of the Spirit's Pentecostal presence and the approaching New Jerusalem".[38] Pentecostalism generally is a missionary religion and this is hinged on the twin portals of evangelism and missions. The first twenty years of Pentecostalism were described as "chaotic operations" due to a strong over-emphasis on being moved by the Spirit devoid of a rational, systemic approach towards mission and evangelism. This has created, for most Black Majority Churches' preachers, a unique preaching tapestry that uses strong metaphors that resonate with the prevailing social and economic challenges of their members.

The Old Testament is invariably a ready source of encouragement on account of its multiplicity of meta-migratory narratives which entail leaving, separation and Diasporic experiences. Preachers will use the Exodus story or the Abrahamic call to articulate the Diasporic worldview and associated challenges of the migrant communities with distinct religious identity against the backdrop of coping with the socio-economic diversities of living in a foreign land. The Exodus story is a well-known illustration, which is pleasing for migrants because it talks also about the opportunity of safeguarding communal distinctiveness without the preservation of the original territorial or national context. Though Black-led Churches' hermeneutics have been noted to derive their theology from the Bible, they often have a "bumper sticker" or "literalist experientialism" approach[39] in their exegesis, as many scriptures are utilised out of historical context. This uncritical hermeneutic is generally synonymous with Pentecostalism, as Gifford noted that African Pentecostals make their theology relevant within their context.[40]

The re-orientation of their members through such exegesis has come under much scrutiny of scholars[41] for its hermeneutical inadequacies hinged on literalism which is consistent with the North American holiness, healing and Pentecostal movements. For most Black Majority Churches, their biblical exegesis is based on revelatory experience, the affirmation of the Word, and their own consequent faith, not on experiential investigation or argument. Beckford calls for the recognition of the Liberation Theological Praxis (LTP) as an authentic means of interpretation of scriptures because it meets the existential realities of African and Caribbean Diasporans.[42]

Closely connected to the depiction of evil in the construction of migrant religious identity is the inclination to emphasize "power" in their religious discourse. This channel of communication can range from everyday life exchanges and interventions ("Jesus power is super power!") to inter-textual biblical exegesis and ritual praxis. The concept of evil is central to the religious subscriptions of African Christians, with Satan as the source of suffering, the greatest enemy of mankind and originator of evil.[43] The reasons are complex because of the traditional African cosmic worldview: "the result is that many people no longer accommodate angered spirits by propitiating them, but must drive them out since they have come to be seen as evil" according to Gerrie Ter Haar.[44]

This has contributed to the popularity of many Black Majority Churches in Britain with the strong emphasis on the fight against evil "in new religious movements as well as among Africans in Diaspora".[45] The resonance of African and Caribbean cosmology within the Pentecostal ideals brings about a replacement functionality of African Traditional Religion in coping with the exigencies of life.

## RAISING THE STAKES: BLACK MAJORITY CHURCHES' SOCIAL CAPITAL

The growth and proliferation of Black Majority Churches in Britain in over a century of existence has ushered in a distinctive shift in praxis in social capital contributions to Britain as articulated in Chapter Five of this work. This is further complimented by the charitable status of these organizations with the stringent requirements of the Charity Commission position on the public benefit test. This invariably creates a measure of fiscal and community accountability to the wider society while simultaneously creating avenues for additional funding through the British government's "Gift Aid" scheme. These churches present a holistic view of mission which includes active political and civic engagement. This has gradually led to the development of huge infrastructural facilities that are complementary to government initiatives.

The Nehemiah Housing Authority started by the Church of God of Prophecy is perhaps one of the most successful housing projects by a Black Majority Church tackling the challenges of housing in Britain. In order to extend the frontiers of the Nehemiah Housing Authority a merger was effected with the United Churches Housing Association, and the newly formed company was known as Nehemiah United Churches Housing Association (NUCHA) with 40 employees and an annual turnover of over £4 million. The various social initiatives invariably connect with the social and political ideals of the wider public. This has certainly bridged the gap to foster a better understanding of the nascent social and political theology of Black Majority Churches in Britain. Though there exist divergent views with respect to the political ideology of Black Majority Churches in Britain, Beresford has demonstrated that Black Majority Churches are quite political in their social engagement, although the social theology and political ideology of Black Majority Churches is still very incoherent in comparison with that of historic British denominations.[46] It is apt to note that there are yet unconquered territories as Black Majority Churches need to move from provision of social services to fighting structural inequalities within British society, such as the criminal justice system, addressing racial and economic inequalities and the criminalizing of black youths.

It is thus not out of place to classify Britain's Black Majority Churches as "progressive Pentecostals" in relation to overly "Health and Wealth" Pentecostals. The contributions of these churches as highlighted in this study gives further credence to the social entrepreneurship of Black Majority Churches in Britain as espoused by Miller and Yamamori.[47] Black Majority Churches are gradually becoming a social force in Britain on account of the multiplicity of their engagements with the larger communities and their assistance of the migrant communities in social, economic and linguistic integration to the host communities masked with cultural nuances, although Black Majority Churches are faced with multiple challenges in the West, especially the Health and Wealth ideology, which British evangelicalism strongly repudiates.[48]

The post-*Windrush* era heralded a shift in praxis of Black Majority Churches' engagement with British mainstream Christianity with the Zebra Project in north-west London to explore a better working relationship between Black-led Churches and the historic churches.[49] Much of this initiative, as observed by Parsons, stems from the joint working party representatives of Black-led Churches and the British Council of Churches.[50] He noted that the report for the initiative was published as "Coming Together in Christ, Building Together in Christ and Learning in Partnership". He further asserted that this basically culminated in a national agenda to stimulate a dynamic working relationship between Black-led Churches and White Churches through the British Council of Churches in 1978 and 1979. This was the basis of the emergence of the Centre for Black and White Christian Partnership at Selly Oak in Birmingham, with strong emphasis on partnering in leadership between black and white churches through education and intercultural theology.

Philip Mohabir was one of the most forward-thinking adherents and enthusiasts of ecumenical engagement as he identified that if Black-led Churches were to make significant inroads in Britain there must be wider collaboration with British Evangelical Churches, but he opined that there were very few Black-led Churches in the British Council of Churches and disproportionate representation in the management of the organization. In 1984 the West Indian Evangelical Alliance was founded by Mohabir, including among its aims "working with the existing (White-led) Evangelical Alliance and fostering relationships between the West Indian churches and other British churches". The ecumenical tapestry has changed significantly since Mohabir's initial effort, as Aldred states:

> of the twenty-eight churches and agencies in membership of Churches Together in England, ten can be described as Black-led, of which nine are Pentecostal, with pending membership applications ... But it could also be argued that the Black churches are coming of age, growing in confidence and are now ready to engage and share fellowship with others with whom they do not necessarily agree doctrinally and theologically.[51]

Osgood's thesis gives a very commendable account of the relationship of British Evangelicalism with African Neo-Pentecostal Churches in Britain, which is considered as the third phase of the emergence of Black Majority Churches in this work.[52] He demonstrated deep residual knowledge and personal engagement between the two streams of the Christian faith, as each is unwilling to shift ground on their historic subscriptions. I also concur with Osgood's concluding remark:

interactions between British evangelicalism and African Neo-Pentecostalism that took place from 1985 to 2005 illustrate three strong commitments: first, evangelicalism's commitment to inclusiveness; second, African Neo-Pentecostalism's commitment to distinctiveness; third, evangelicalism's own commitment to distinctiveness. It is these three commitments that have led to the constant interplay between adherence to principles and adoption of practicalities throughout the twenty year period.[53]

The street credibility and broad understanding of the socio-cultural dynamics of most migrants by the Black Majority Churches is a profound leverage to meet the needs of their communities. The level of engagement of these churches is dependent on the available resources, the identified social challenges and level of engagement with other social or community initiatives. The changes within the political landscape of Britain in the light of the LibDem/Conservative party alliance and the "Big Society" initiative which is hinged on the localization of various community services into the hands of the private and third sectors might further reinforce more engagement of the Black Majority Churches.

The social capital at the disposal of Black Majority Churches will be a huge asset in their engagement with the Big Society agenda with the ideal of pushing decentralization: from central government to local government, and driving the initiative to community and boroughs. It is apt to note that the general articulations of the Big Society agenda in terms of community and neighbourhood engagement are the mainstay of most Black Majority Churches. In view of the community focus of most of these churches, the Big Society might provide the leverage for recognition and access to public funds for Black Majority Churches. Although the Big Society agenda has been criticized by various organizations and people in relation to the public policy of a reduction in the budget deficit by the Cameron/Clegg coalition, it might be the turning point to address perceived disproportionate funding between most Black Majority Churches and historic denominations if Black Majority Churches are able to meet the statutory requirements for project funding. The perceived discrimination in terms of release of grants and winning bids by many projects of the historic churches are a by-product of well-organized, structured, resource-based initiatives with a track record of consistency in delivery of community-based projects.

However, the objective of making use of the Big Society Bank to increase financial and encourage social investment by linking up private investors with community organizations to promote long-term sustainability of the voluntary and community sector will only be enjoyed by Black Majority

Churches if they are able to develop empirical and systemic processes and use of professional bid writers to articulate their community initiatives.

## MISSIONARY CHALLENGES

In order to consider the future of Britain's Black Majority Churches, it is expedient to reflect on the various missionary challenges that are enumerated in this study. The proliferation of these churches in Britain is "laity driven" with strong emphasis on pneuma-centrism. The first, second and third phases of the emergence of Black Majority Churches highlighted in this study have demonstrated that the proliferation and growth of these churches were hinged on migration while religion constituted a major factor in the migration trend to the West. The migratory pattern has also been accentuated by the ability of Pentecostalism to transcend various cultural strands. Church growth statistics of Black Majority Churches are difficult to measure but a general overview of these churches shows that London is the hub of the growth of these churches. The majority of the churches have experienced growth in urban cities but London perhaps has the highest population of Black Majority Churches. The urban concentration of Black Majority Churches might be due to the migratory pattern of migrants from Africa and Asia.

The Redeemed Christian Church of God has covered 68% of Britain's urban cities in their church planting initiative. A major reason for the proliferation of these churches has been their fissiparous nature which is generally a global trait of the Pentecostal movement. Schism is a common occurrence amongst Black Majority Churches. Various churches have emerged as a result of schism, often as a result of high-handed authoritarian leadership, insecurity of leadership, poor management skills, moral ineptitude and other extraneous factors.

One of the major ethical challenges within the Black Majority Churches in Britain is the direct ecclesiastical transplant to Britain. This is a major cog in the wheel of progress for these organizations. This is compounded by not taking cognizance of the prevailing worldview of the British context, although in the first and second phases of the emergence of Black Majority Churches in Britain such ecclesiastical transplanting was effective because the recreation of familiar structures in the host country provided a safe haven for the ostracized migrants during the process of acculturation.

Black Majority Churches at the turn of the twenty-first century have begun to attract affluent and educated people, a departure from the global and British historical antecedents of the emergence of Pentecostalism. The elimination of clericalism in most Black Majority Churches places a strong emphasis on a universal priesthood of believers, leading to mentoring and discipleship, as the laity is effectively mobilized into the church's life. The subscription of Pentecostals globally to the doctrine of a priesthood of believers, which eliminates the distinction between the clergy and laity, has contributed significantly to the growth of Black Churches in the United Kingdom. However, it has had a negative impact on their missional agenda, and has contributed significantly to their anti-intellectualism until recently, as most of these churches shun formal pastoral and missiological training. The clarion call to end this apathy is reflected in Beckford's articulation as a major flaw that has allowed the continued bewitchment of Blacks in their mission agenda through colonial influences.[54] This seems to be a recurring feature of Pentecostals globally, as Saayman noted that the "Spirit speaks equally to all believers regardless of gender, education, or social status, and so each Pentecostal believer is potentially a minister and missionary."[55]

Britain's Black Majority Churches have not risen to the missionary challenge of the British community. It is apparent that the *modus operandi* through the purported claims of power evangelism, in the words of Wimber, has not translated to attracting the host communities into these churches. The prevailing scenario is a sharp contrast to claims of reverse mission in the West. Though the proliferation of these churches has succeeded to some extent in putting God back on the public radar, these churches have continued to be cultural ghettos in the light of *missio Dei*. This situation stems from a lack of pragmatic missionary initiative or missional engagement with the host culture: the "dark and prodigal continent of Britain" is yet to be revived despite the huge transnational networks that these churches have spawned in the last fifty years in Britain.

Brandon in an interview noted the missiological deficiencies of most leaders of these churches as he asserted that "research denotes that pastors of BMCs generally derive their sense of self-worth and status from the size of their churches. The pastor of a large and growing church often becomes a 'religious celebrity' with power and influence in Britain's shrinking religious sub-culture."[56] There is no doubt about the endless celebrity culture around so-called successful black pastors: this has so much African cultural resonance that failure to acknowledge it is totally unacceptable within the African culture – but doing so to excess constitutes idolatry. This presents a cult-like symbolism and often leads to gross abuse and neglect of the important hub of the Christian faith, which is mission. The commitment of most churches to mission is seen in the annual budget for missions which is a far cry from other allocations of their budget.

Brandon further clarifies his earlier views on some of the leaders of Black Majority Churches:

> the senior executives of these churches are not prepared to implement the radical changes that will facilitate the evangelism of Britain's diverse ethnic population. Admittedly, they want the kudos associated with a multi-ethnic congregation but on their own cultural terms. I can empathise with their predicament. Why risk the security and status of being a pastor of a large African [and Caribbean] congregation for the more dangerous and uncertain vocation of pioneering a multicultural church? Why sacrifice success and a very generous wage agreement, for the precarious life of a missionary to post-Christian Britain? Christ renounced "success", "power", "glory" and "status" in order to redeem a world.[57]

These remarks will be greatly contested by many church leaders within Black Majority Churches but a careful self-assessment might reveal the need for renewal amongst the leadership of Black Majority Churches in Britain.

Clark opined that the failure of West Indian Churches in the 1960s and 1970s in Britain eventually culminated in the gradual decline of these churches.[58] He further posited that the church planting strategies of African churches have greatly contributed to the ongoing vitality of the African-led Churches in Britain. Though African Neo-Pentecostal Churches seem to be the new wine in the old bottle in the history of Black Majority Churches since the 1980s, through their entrepreneurial skills, passionate prayer and leverage with historic denominations, they have failed to emerge with a distinct missionary strategy that is contextually relevant and engaging to the indigenous British communities.

Black Majority Churches in Britain are replicating the mistakes of the missionary enterprise to Africa, according to Mudimbe, who asserted that "the missionary does not enter into dialogue with pagans and 'savages' but imposes the law of God that he incarnates".[59] The failure to engage the British worldview is a militating factor for the continued missional inadequacies of Black Majority Churches. There is the need for re-imagination of missions and evangelism by Black Majority Churches as a missionary community rather than a nomad sanctuary. This will involve dramatic changes in ecclesiology and totally new patterns of evangelism, but "If

African churches persist in perpetuating Africa on British soil, their missionary potential will [might] never be realised" according to Brandon.[60] Moreover, the proliferation and growth of Black Majority Churches has created a "triumph mentality" amongst some segments of these churches which could ultimately militate against evangelistic engagement with the nation.

There seems to be a sense of general accomplishment amongst these churches but it is imperative that the missiological, linguistic and cultural inadequacies of the first and second generations of Africans be overcome by the third and fourth generations of Africans and Caribbeans so that they might impact the host community. This proposition should be embraced with much caution, and a hope that the subsequent generations of Africans and Caribbeans will be as passionate and committed to the Christian faith as the preceding generations of African and Caribbean leaders.

Black Majority Churches should endeavour to be more committed to theological and missiological education amongst their leadership. The dearth of theological and cross-cultural training is replicated in avoidable challenges in the operational modalities of these churches. This endeavour will further assist in intercultural studies that will help to establish black theological underpinnings in Britain.

There must be a conscious and systemic development of black intelligentsia who are committed to the process of articulating the historical dynamics of Black Majority Churches in Britain. This approach will preserve the various stages of evolution of the Black Majority Churches in the light of objective and critical appraisal with respect to the future relevance of these churches. The effect of such initiatives will be the development of a repository of scholars and writers to espouse and articulate the theological underpinnings of Black Majority Churches while avoiding potential drift from the Pentecostal ideals.

There is a need for consistent re-appraisal of the theological ideals of these churches in the light of Diasporic socio-political nuances in Britain. The development of political and social synergy by Black Majority Churches will not only be a vehicle for social equality but also will inevitably be an avenue to engage the wider British communities through their social theology. Black Majority Churches' ecumenical engagement should be encouraged by their respective denominations. This will create leverage to constructively engage in various public issues and will enable democratic representation for Black Majority Churches and the wider constituency. There have to be proactive initiatives by the leadership of

Black Majority Churches to explore diverse forms of social and economic enterprise that will contribute significantly to the holistic ministry of these churches. The divisive denominational intrigues of Black Majority Churches that have truncated black British parachurch organizations should be addressed by focusing on more unifying factors of the Christian faith.

# Notes

## CHAPTER ONE: INTRODUCTION

[1] Peter Brierley, former Director of Christian Research UK, in the last two decades has qualitatively sensitized British Church leaders about the decline in attendance in historic denominations in comparison to the Black Majority Churches which have proliferated in urban cities in Britain. For further reading see P. Brierley, 1984. *Christians in England.* London: MARC Europe; P.Brierley (ed.), 2005. *UK Christian Handbook: Religious Trends Vol. 5.* Worcester: Christian Research; P. Brierley (ed.), 2006. *Religious Trends in the UK.* Worcester: Christian Research.

The growth and proliferation of Black-led Churches in Britain was first analysed by sociologists and social anthropologists in the wake of the 1948 *Windrush* era due to the social, religious and racial challenges in the process of acculturation and assimilation to British life. For further reading about the study of West Indians in Britain in the post-*Windrush* era see the following publications: C. Hill, 1963. *West Indian Migrants and the London Churches.* London: Oxford University Press; S. Patterson, 1965. *Dark Strangers: A Sociological Study of the Absorption of a Recent West Indian Migrant Group in Brixton, South London.* London: Tavistock Publications; G. Parsons (ed.), 1993. *The Growth of Religious Diversity: Britain from 1945.* London: Routledge.

[2] An observable feature of this study is the interchangeable use of Black Church, Black-led Church and Black Majority Churches. I am quite aware of the potential controversy for adopting such a position but l wish to posit that the use of these labels is reflective of the historical antecedents and the challenges that these churches have overcome; the true identity of these churches is based on their prophetic and Christian commitments to the diverse expressions of the Christian faith in Britain. An observable trend amongst most of the African and Caribbean Diasporic churches is that most of these churches prefer their denominational names as many are indifferent to Sturge's rebranding. (See M. Sturge, 2005. *Look What the Lord has Done! An Exploration of Black Christian Faith in Britain.* Bletchley: Scripture Union.)

Rev. Arlington Trotman, whose background was in the Wesleyan Holiness Church, now a Methodist who currently serves as Moderator (Chairman) of the Churches' Commission for Migrants in Europe (CCME) refuted the label Black-led Church as he noted that "there is no logical or ethical reason for black people to justify our heritage by using defensive or polemic language given to us to define our religious experiences". Trotman's disputation is due to the imperialistic and Eurocentric ideals of Whites in creating a secondary status for Blacks, although he noted the challenges of a new terminology that will reflect a broad-spectrum appeal due to the diversities of these churches in terms of their theology, ecclesiology, cultural and experiential perspectives. (For Trotman's contribution on this discourse see Arlington Trotman, "Black, Black-led or What?" *In* Joel Edwards (ed.), *Let's Praise Him: An African Caribbean Perspective on Worship*. London: Kingsway.)

Sturge further heightened this discourse and faulted Trotman's recipe for a new terminology to identify ethnic minority churches that have broad spectrum resonance as he posited that using the labels "Holiness" or "Pentecostals" or "Pentecostalism" is fraught with contextual ambiguities due to their multifaceted use and use by African Methodist Episcopal (AME) churches and Lutheran Churches (see Sturge, *Look What the Lord has Done!*, p26). He further posited that the inter-relatedness of the Holiness revival and Pentecostal revival of the nineteenth and twentieth centuries constitutes a major barrier to Arlington's proposed terminologies. In pursuit of an acceptable nomenclature for African and Caribbean Diasporic churches, Sturge argued that due to the growth and internal dynamics of these churches, and as many their members are stakeholders in the community, it was imperative to strategically manage the change of name through the African Caribbean Evangelical Alliance (ACEA) in his days as the General Secretary of the organization. It is apt to appreciate the contributions of Sturge and the ACEA leadership in the "strategic" rebranding of African and Caribbean Diasporic Churches to Black Majority Churches as "a worshipping Christian Community whose composition is made up of more than 50% of people from African or Caribbean heritage". Though this might seem more acceptable due to his arguments, he acknowledged the inadequacies of the new nomenclature (Ibid.).

Joe Aldred, Director of the Minority Ethnic Christian Affairs group at Churches Together in England, asked what is more excellent about "Black Majority Churches" in relation to Sturge's rebranding of African and Caribbean Diasporic churches in his book *Respect* (see J. Aldred, 2006. *Respect: Understanding Caribbean British Christianity*. Peterborough: Epworth). Aldred's earlier assertion is further espoused in his latest anthology, with Keno Ogbo, on Black Churches in the twenty-first century. Aldred and Ogbo both posited that "dispensing with suffixes like 'led' and 'majority' after Black permits certain clarity of identity. Church is always a compound term and in this case the Black Church refers to that multi-dimensional Christian tradition that has been established in Britain". (See J. Aldred and K. Ogbo (eds), 2010. *The Black Church in the 21st Century*. London: Darton Longman and Todd, p1.)

Peter Brierley, the former Director of Christian Research also added his voice to the ongoing discourse as he referred to Britain's African and Caribbean churches as Black Majority Independent Churches (BMICs). Brierley's position is reflective of the changes within the historic denominations as some churches' memberships are made up of more than 50% African and Caribbeans, and thus there is the need for further distinction of the context of the evaluation. It is important to note that despite all the semantics, the word "black", which is a signifier of sociological classification, is prevalent in all the terminologies used in describing these churches. It adds credence to the fact that Trotman's and Sturge's polemics were invariably hinged on the denigrating status associated with the word "black" since the plutocratic dispensation, but the context of Trotman's earlier position was greatly influenced by the *Windrush* era's racial and social ostracization of the West Indian immigrants of 1948. (For further reading see R. Hood, 1994. *Begrimed and Black: Christian Traditions on Blacks and Blackness*. Minneapolis: Augsburg Fortress.)

Obunge, during the Christian Resource Exhibition (CRE), in the seminar entitled "Black in White Space", has always been an advocate of the Christological approach as he articulated that salvation is not only for the Jews but also Gentiles and as such he detests the use of Black Church, or Black Majority Church, but he failed to take cognisance of the fact that the term "black" is neither nuanced as denigrating nor is it exclusive to the communion of the saints. (N. Obunge, 2009. "Black Church in White Space." A lecture given at Christian Resource Exhibition, Esher, Surrey, United Kingdom. 15 May 2009.)

3 V. Francis, 1998. *With Hope in Their Eyes: Compelling Stories of the Windrush Generation*. London: The X Press.

4 cf. M. Calley, 1965. *God's People: West Indian Pentecostal Sects in England*. London: Oxford University Press, p38.

5 C. Hill, 1971. *Black Churches, West Indian and African Sects in Britain*. London: Community and Race Relations Unit of the British Council of Churches, p4.

6 V. Howard, 1987. *A Report on Afro-Caribbean Christianity in Britain*. Leeds: University of Leeds Department of Theology and Religious Studies, Community Religions Project Research Papers, New Series, 4, pp10, 13.

7 Quoted in J. Petre, 2006. "Migrants Fill Empty Pews as Britons Lose Faith." [Web]

8 J. Aldred, 2007. *Black Churches Contributing to Cohesion or Polarising Christians and Other Faith Groups*. [Web]

9 Sturge, *Look What the Lord has Done!*

10 D. Killingray and J. Edwards, 2007. *Black Voices: The Shaping of Christian Experience*. Nottingham: InterVarsity Press.

11 cf. S. Hunt and N. Lightly, 2001. "The British Black Pentecostal 'Revival': Identity and Belief in the 'New' Nigerian Churches." *Ethnic and Racial Studies*, 24.1; S. Hunt, 2002. "Neither Here Nor There: The Construction of Identities and Boundary Maintenance of West African Pentecostals." *Sociology*, 36 (1).

12 G. Elton, 1987. *The Practice of History*. London: Fontana Press, p67.

13 Elton, *The Practice of History*; A. Marwick, 1979. *The Nature of History: Knowledge, Evidence, Language*. London: Macmillan.

14 Marwick, *The Nature of History*.

15 C. Oshun, 1981. *Christ Apostolic Church of Nigeria: A Suggested Pentecostal Consideration of its Historical, Organizational and Theological Developments, 1918–1975*. PhD dissertation. Exeter: University of Exeter; I. MacRobert, 1989. *Black Pentecostalism: Its Origin, Functions and Theology: With Special Reference to a Midland Borough*. PhD dissertation. Birmingham: University of Birmingham; C. Oshun, 1990. *Aladura Diaspora in Britain as a Model for Mission: A Study of Selected Churches*. PhD dissertation. Birmingham: University of Birmingham; A.

Ukah, 2007. *The Redeemed Christian Church of God (RCCG), Nigeria: Local Identities and Global Processes in African Pentecostalism.* PhD dissertation. Bayreuth: University of Bayreuth; L. Beresford, 2008. *African-Caribbean Pentecostal Church Leaders and Socio-political Engagement in Contemporary Britain.* PhD dissertation. Birmingham: University of Birmingham.

[16] J. Aldred, 1995. *A Black Majority Church's Future.* M.Min dissertation. Sheffield: University of Sheffield; B. Adedibu, 2007. *Impact of Postmodernity on Second Generation Nigerians in Churches in South East of London.* MA dissertation. Cardiff: University of Wales.

[17] Hunt and Lightly, "The British Black Pentecostal 'Revival'"; Hunt, "Neither Here Nor There; A. Adogame, 2007. *The Rhetoric of Reverse Mission: African Christianity and the Changing Dynamics of Religious Expansion in Europe.* Outline of lecture presented at the conference "South Moving North: Revised Mission and its Implications", Protestant Landelijk Dienstencentrum, Utrecht; A. Adogame, 2008. "Up, Up Jesus! Down, Down Satan! African Religiosity in the Former Soviet Bloc – the Embassy of the Blessed Kingdom of God for all Nations." *Exchange Journal of Missiological and Ecumenical Research*, Vol. 37; R. Burgess, 2008. "Nigerian Pentecostal Theology in Global Perspective." *PentecoStudies*, Vol. 7, No. 2; Ukah, *The Redeemed Christian Church of God.*

[18] I. MacRobert, 1989. "The New Black-led Churches in Britain." *In* Badham, P. (ed.), *Religion, State and Society in Modern Britain.* Lampeter: Edwin Mellen. See also D. Gee (ed.), 1950. *Pentecost Magazine. In* T. Cauchi, 2008. Pentecost. A complete run of 77 Pentecost magazines 1947–1966 (CD ROM); C. Ireson, 1970. *My Life and Thought.* Bradford: Puritan Press.

[19] T. Barratt, 1927. *When the Fire Fell: An Outline of My Life.* Oslo: Alfons Hansen & Sonner; Gee, *Pentecost Magazine.*

[20] R. Beckford, 1998. *Jesus is Dread: Black Theology and Black Culture in Britain.* London: Darton, Longman and Todd; R. Beckford, 2000. *Dread and Pentecostal: Political Theology for Black Churches in Britain.* London: SPCK; R. Beckford, 2001. "Theology in the Age of Crack: Crack Age, Prosperity Doctrine and Being There." *Black Theology in Britain*, 4 (1); R. Beckford, 2006. *Jesus Dub: Theology, Music and Social Change.* London: Routledge; R. Beckford, 2009. *Challenges of Black Pentecostal Leadership in the 21st Century From Mission to Maintenance: Resisting the Bewitchment of Colonial Christianity.* A paper presented at the Oliver Lyseight Annual Lecture organized by the Education Department of the New Testament Church of God, Northampton. March 2009. [Web]

[21] Sturge, *Look What the Lord has Done*; Aldred, *Respect.*

[22] P. Jenkins, 2002. *The Next Christendom: The Coming of Global Christianity.* New York: Oxford University Press; P. Jenkins, 2006. *The New Faces of Christianity: Believing the Bible in the Global South.* New York: Oxford University Press; A. Anderson, 2004. *An Introduction to Pentecostalism: Global Charismatic Christianity.* Cambridge: Cambridge University Press.

[23] Aldred, *Black Churches Contributing to Cohesion.*

## CHAPTER TWO: THE ORIGIN OF BLACK CHURCHES IN GREAT BRITAIN

1. MacRobert, "The New Black-led Churches in Britain", p120.
2. Sureway International Christian Ministries. 2006. *100 Years of Centenary Celebrations: Our Journey So Far*. London: Sureway International Christian Ministries, p4.
3. P. Fryer, 1984. *Staying Power: History of Black People in Britain since 1504*. London: Pluto Press, p1.
4. Quoted in S. Arnold, 1992. *From Scepticism to Hope: One Black-led Church's Response to Social Responsibility*. Nottingham: Grove Books, p13.
5. P. Edward, and J. Walvin, 1983. *Black Personalities in the Era of Slave Trade*. London: Macmillan, pp1, 2.
6. Fryer, *Staying Power*, p2.
7. Ibid., p4; Edward and Walvin, *Black Personalities*, p6.
8. Edward and Walvin, *Black Personalities*, p11.
9. Fryer, *Staying Power*, p5.
10. F. Shyllon, 1977. *Black People in Britain*. Oxford: Oxford University Press, p6.
11. Fryer, *Staying Power*, p10.
12. Ibid., p12.
13. C. Bailey, 1991. "Beyond Identification: The Use of Africans in Old Testament Poetry and Narratives." In C.H. Felder (ed.), *Stony the Road We Trod: African American Biblical Interpretation*. Minneapolis: Fortress Press.
14. R. Hood, 1994. *Begrimed and Black: Christian Traditions on Blacks and Blackness*. Minneapolis: Augsburg Fortress, p47.
15. Shyllon, *Black People*, p6.
16. Postlethwayth, quoted in Fryer, *Staying Power*, p17.
17. Fryer, *Staying Power*, p3.
18. Ibid., p17.
19. Quoted in Edward and Walvin, *Black Personalities*, p23.
20. G. Wilmore, 1976. *Black and Presbyterian: The Heritage and the Hope*. Philadelphia: Geneva Press, p5.
21. Fryer, *Staying Power*, pp429–430.
22. Long, quoted in J. Walvin, 1971. *Black Presence: A Documentary History of the Negro in England*. London: Macmillan, p68.
23. Edward and Walvin, *Black Personalities*, p145.
24. Fryer, *Staying Power*, p425.
25. Walvin, *Black Presence*.
26. Fryer, *Staying Power*, pp157–161.
27. Shyllon, *Black People*, p225.
28. Fryer, *Staying Power*, p66.
29. Shyllon, *Black People*, pp22–28.
30. Fryer, *Staying Power*, p114.
31. J. Wilkinson, 1993. *Church in Black and White*. Edinburgh: Saint Andrew Press, p23.
32. Ibid., p24.
33. A. Raboteau, 2004. *Slave Religion: The "Invisible Institution" in the Antebellum South*. New York: Oxford University Press.

34. Fryer, *Staying Power*, p147.
35. MacRobert, *Black Pentecostalism*, p12.
36. D. Kortright, 1990. *Emancipation Still Comin': Explorations in Caribbean Emancipatory Theology.* New York: Orbis, p35.
37. O. Equiano, 1969. *The Life Of Olaudah Equiano, Or Gustavus Vassa, The African.* New York: Negro Universities Press, p150.
38. Shyllon, *Black People*, pp22–24.
39. Fryer, *Staying Power*, pp113–132.
40. Admiral Lord Nelson, cited by E. Metaxas, 2007. *Amazing Grace: William Wilberforce and the Heroic Campaign to End Slavery.* San Francisco: Harper One, p107.
41. K. Belmonte, 2007. *William Wilberforce: A Hero for Humanity.* Grand Rapids: Zondervan, p97.
42. Fryer, *Staying Power*, pp212–215.
43. T. Baehr et al., 2007. *The Amazing Grace of Freedom: The Inspiring Faith of William Wilberforce, the Slaves' Champion.* Green Forest, AR: New Leaf Press, pp62–63.
44. Beckford, *Challenges of Black Pentecostal Leadership.*
45. Raboteau, *Slave Religion*, pp4, 5.
46. Washington, quoted by MacRobert, "The New Black-led Churches in Britain", p8.
47. Ibid.
48. V. Synan, 1975. *Aspects of Pentecostal-Charismatic Origins.* New York: Logos, p117.
49. D. Shakarian, 1975. *The Happiest People on Earth.* New Jersey: Fleming Revell, pp12–13.
50. Anderson, *An Introduction to Pentecostalism*, p1.
51. D. Barrett and T. Johnson, 2003. "Annual Statistical Table on Global Missions: 2003." *International Bulletin of Missionary Research*, 27 (1).
52. Anderson, *An Introduction to Pentecostalism*, p32.
53. R. Anderson, 1979. *Vision of the Disinherited: The Making of American Pentecostalism.* Peabody: Hendrickson, p69.
54. D. Faupel, 1996. *The Everlasting Gospel: The Significance of Eschatology in the Development of Pentecostal Thought.* Sheffield: Sheffield Academic Press, pp202–205.
55. Anderson, *An Introduction to Pentecostalism*, p84.
56. W. Kay, 1986. "Alexander Boddy and the Outpouring of the Holy Spirit in Sunderland." *Journal of the European Pentecostal Theological Association*, Vol. 5, No. 2.
57. M. Robinson, 1976. *The Charismatic Anglican – Historical and Contemporary: A Comparison of the Life and Work of Alexander Boddy (1854–1930).* M.Litt dissertation. Birmingham: University of Birmingham. This position is acutely corroborated by Rev. Thomas Barrat in his biography as he noted on 13 October 1907 in the *London Chronicle* an article entitled "Revival wonders – Old and young speak in tongues – Alleged healing – North Country stirred by strange signs". Barrat observed that the article "gives a good idea of the perfect absence of spiritual insight". The article was quite denigrating in the last paragraph and this

could have necessitated the inclusion of the whole article in Barrat's memoirs. The writer said of Barrat that "there is another figure in the strange landscape: the Evan Roberts of the present movement, Pastor Barrat, Cornishman, naturalised, Norwegian, a dreamer if you will: a madman if you like; but the heart and soul of religious movement before which others pale". Other newspapers that publicized the Sunderland revival included Thomsen's *Weekly News* with the headline "Extraordinary revival scenes – Gift of Tongues at Sunderland: persons speak in unknown languages" and the *North Mail:* "Utility of the Gift of Tongues, Pentecostal services at Wearmouth: young man's testimony". For detailed study read: T. Barratt, 1927. *When the Fire Fell: An Outline of My Life.* Oslo: Alfons Hansen & Sonner.

58 Anderson, *Vision of the Disinherited,* p4; cf. Robinson, *The Charismatic Anglican.*
59 V. Synan, 1971. *The Holiness/Pentecostal Tradition: Charismatic Movements in the Twentieth Century.* Grand Rapids: Eerdmans, p99; cf. *Yorkshire Post* report dated 27 December 1904.
60 C.G. Williams, 1981. *Tongues of the Spirit: A Study of Pentecostal Glossalalia and Related Phenomena.* Cardiff: University of Wales Press, p55.
61 D. Cartwright, 2008. Email correspondence with Desmond Cartwright on Welsh Revival.
62 T. Turnbull, 1963. *Brothers in Arms.* Bradford: Puritan Press, pp25–28.
63 Gee, *Pentecost Magazine,* p12.
64 Barratt, *When the Fire Fell,* p150.
65 MacRobert, "The New Black-led Churches in Britain", p138.
66 D. Killingray, 2009. Telephone interview, 23 November 2009. David Killingray is retired Emeritus Professor of History at Goldsmiths College, London; he was introduced to the author by David Cartwright, the official historian of Elim Pentecostal, UK in 2009 during the course of this research. Killingray delivered a lecture on 2 February 2010 at the School of Arts and Science (SOAS), London, entitled *An African Pentecostal Pioneer in Peckham; The Hidden life of Thomas Brem-Wilson (1855–1929).* He is duly credited for his contributions to my research on Thomas Brem-Wilson. Killingray's first contact with Brem-Wilson's historical antecedents coincided with mine at the preliminary stages of my literature review for my PhD thesis through MacRobert, "The New Black-led Churches in Britain" and Aldred, *Respect,* as the author noted that there was evidence of an organized Black Pentecostal Church in London as far back as 1907. Killingray, in his article on "African Research and Documentation" dated 10 January 2010, said, "two years ago [2008] I came across [Brem-Wilson's] name in a footnote to an article in a journal which stated that he had helped found an early Pentecostal church in south London. Through the wonders of the web I contacted his grandson, who sent me photographs and mentioned that his sister had diaries. Another member of the family contacted me and produced more than one hundred letters and documents. I have now transcribed the diaries which run intermittently from 1899–1925. Although many entries are one-liners, they include names and places that, with a good knowledge of the contemporary Gold Coast as well as the black Diaspora in Britain, enabled me to reconstruct the religious, commercial, social, and political networks that Brem-Wilson inhabited during the first decade of the twentieth century. The

67   diary transcripts, with my edited notes, in due course will be deposited in a number of libraries and archives." Killingray also noted that Thomas Brem-Wilson's widow died in 1962 in Keston, Kent. For further reading see D. Killingray, 2010, *African Research and Documentation*. [Web]
67   Killingray, Telephone interview.
68   Gee, *Pentecost Magazine*, p12.
69   Sureway, *100 Years*, p4; S.A. Smith, 2009. *British Black Gospel: The Foundations of this Vibrant UK Sound*. London: Monarch Books, p46.
70   MacRobert in R. Gerloff, 1992. *A Plea for British Black Theologies: The Black Church Movement in Britain in its Transatlantic Cultural and Theological Interaction with Special References to the Pentecostal Oneness (Apostolic) and Sabbatarian Movements*. Frankfurt: Peter Lang, p44.
71   D. Cartwright, 2007. "Black Pentecostal Churches in Britain." *Journal of the European Pentecostal Theological Association*. Vol. 23, No. 2.
72   MacRobert in Badham, *Religion, State and Society*, p138.
73   Sureway, *100 Years*, p4.
74   Cartwright, "Black Pentecostal Churches".
75   Sureway, *100 Years*, p4.
76   Cartwright, "Black Pentecostal Churches", p127.
77   G. Weeks, 2003. *Chapter Thirty-two: A History of the Apostolic Church*. Barnsley: Prontaprint, p84.
78   D. William (ed.), 1923. *Riches of Grace. 1923, July edition*. Bradford: Apostolic International Missionary Council, p24.
79   Ibid., p31.
80   Ibid., p13.
81   *Redemption Tidings*, 1939, Vol. 15:6. *In* T. Cauchi, *Redemption Tidings 1924–1939*. Revival Library (CD ROM).
82   Gee, *Pentecost Magazine*, p12.
83   Viden, as recorded in *Redemption Tidings*.
84   Anderson, *Vision of the Disinherited*, p69.
85   Ibid., p222.
86   Gerloff, *A Plea for British Black Theologies*, p44.
87   Cartwright, "Black Pentecostal Churches", pp126–138.
88   William, *Riches of Grace*, pp27–29.
89   Cartwright, "Black Pentecostal Churches", p3.
90   Ibid.
91   Ibid.
92   Killingray, Telephone interview.
93   C. Van der Laan, 1992. "Discerning the Body: Analysis of Pentecostalism in the Netherlands." *In* J. Jongeneel (ed.), *Pentecost, Mission and Ecumenism: Essays on Intercultural Theology*. Studies in the Intercultural History of Christianity, 75. Frankfurt: Peter Lang, p126.
94   D. Cartwright, 1981. *From The Backstreets to the Royal Albert Hall: British Pentecostalism 1907–1928*. Unpublished paper delivered at the First European Pentecostal Theological Association Conference, Leuven. 28–29 December, p6. [Web]
95   Ibid.

[96] Sturge, *Look What the Lord has Done!*, p73.
[97] D. Killingray and J. Edwards, 2009. *Black Voices: The Shaping of our Christian Experience*. Leicester: InterVarsity Press, p31. [Web]
[98] Ibid., p36.
[99] C. Wilson, 1992. "Racism and Private Assistance: The Support of West Indian and African Missions in Liverpool, England, During the Interwar Years." *African Studies Review*, Vol. 35, No. 2 (Sep. 1992), p57.
[100] Ibid., p67.
[101] Ibid., p68.
[102] Fryer, *Staying Power*, p3.
[103] B. Carey, 2003. *"The Extraordinary Negro": Ignatius Sancho, Joseph Jekyll, and the Problem of Biography*. [Web]
[104] Killingray and Edwards, *Black Voices*, p43.
[105] N. File and C. Power, 1991. *Black Settlers in Britain 1555–1958*. Oxford: Heinemann, p1.
[106] Fryer, *Staying Power*, pp425–426.
[107] Killingray and Edwards, *Black Voices*, p58.
[108] File and Power, *Black Settlers*, p4.
[109] Carey, *"The Extraordinary Negro"*.
[110] V. Carretta (ed.), 1996. *Unchained Voices: An Anthology of Black Authors in the English-Speaking World of the Eighteenth Century*. Lexington: The University Press of Kentucky, pp107, 108.
[111] Sturge, *Look What the Lord has Done!*, p76.
[112] Killingray and Edwards, *Black Voices*, p95.
[113] Fryer, *Staying Power*, p324.
[114] Sturge, *Look What the Lord has Done!*, p82.
[115] Ibid.
[116] T. Sewell, 1999. *Keep on Moving: The Windrush Legacy*. London: Voice Enterprises Ltd., p35.
[117] E. Williams, 1970. *From Columbus to Castro: The History of the Caribbean, 1492–1969*. London: Andre Deutsch, p498.
[118] Sewell, *Keep on Moving*.
[119] Jonathan Clarke quoted in Sewell, *Keep on Moving*, p10.
[120] J. Rex and R. Moore, 1967. *Race, Community and Conflict*. London: Oxford University Press, p157.
[121] N. Deakin, 1970. *Colour and Citizenship in British Society*. London: Panther Books, p238.
[122] Cited in P. Edmead, 1999. *The Divisive Decade: A History of Caribbean Immigration to Birmingham in the 1950s*. Birmingham: Birmingham City Council Department of Leisure and Community Services, p9.
[123] Ibid., p15.
[124] M. Eden (ed.), 1993. *Britain on the Brink*. Nottingham: Crossway Books, p102.
[125] C. Hill, 2009. "Black Churches in White Space." A seminar held at the Christian Resource Exhibition, Esher, Surrey, United Kingdom. 13 May 2009.
[126] Hill, *West Indian Migrants*.
[127] Patterson, *Dark Strangers*, p226.
[128] M. Banton, 1959. *White and Coloured: The Behaviour of British People Towards*

*Coloured People.* London: Jonathan Cape, p122; cf. K. Little, 1972. *Negroes in Britain: A Study of Racial Relations in English Society.* London: Routledge & Kegan Paul, p252.

[129] Banton, *White and Coloured,* pp222, 224, 227.
[130] Little, *Negroes in Britain,* p252.
[131] Banton, *White and Coloured,* p121.
[132] I. MacRobert, 1988. *The Black Roots and White Racism of Early Pentecostalism in the USA.* London: Macmillan.
[133] I. Brooks, 1983. *Where Do We Go From Here?* London: Brooks, p13.
[134] Eden, *Britain on the Brink,* pp100–116.
[135] Gee, *Pentecost Magazine,* p2.
[136] Hill, *Black Churches,* p12.
[137] Howard, *A Report on Afro-Caribbean Christianity,* p9.
[138] O. Lyseight, 2009. *Extract from "Sceptism and Hope".* [Web]
[139] M. Dempster, B. Klaus and D. Petersen (eds), 1999. *The Globalisation of Pentecostalism.* Irvine: Regnum Press, pxviii.
[140] P. Mohabir, 1988. *Building Bridges: Dramatic Personal Story of Evangelism and Reconciliation.* London: Hodder and Stoughton, p111.
[141] See note 2, p253 this volume.
[142] Gerloff, *A Plea for British Black Theologies,* p2.
[143] M. Calley, 1965. *God's People: West Indian Pentecostal Sects in England.* London: Oxford University Press, p38; Hill, *Black Churches,* p4; P. Charman, 1979. *Reflections: Black and White Christians in the City.* London: Zebra Project, p44; Howard, *A Report on Afro-Caribbean Christianity,* pp10, 13.
[144] Gerloff, *A Plea for British Black Theologies*; Sturge, *Look What the Lord has Done!*.
[145] J. Ashworth and I. Farthing, 2007. *Churchgoing: A Research Report on Church Attendance in UK.* [Web]
[146] Aldred, *Black Churches Contributing to Cohesion.*
[147] J. Rex and S. Tomlinson, 1979. *Colonial Immigrants in a British City: A Class Analysis.* London: Routledge & Kegan Paul, p248.

## CHAPTER THREE: THE NUMERICAL GROWTH OF BLACK MAJORITY CHURCHES IN GREAT BRITAIN SINCE THE 1950S

[1] This section primarily focuses on the historical and the sociological factors that have contributed to the numerical growth of Black Churches in Britain since the 1950s. The numerical growth is predicated on the interplay of local factors and the global processes. This approach is akin to various research perspectives on Pentecostalism globally (H. Cox, 1995. *Fire From Heaven: The Rise of Pentecostal Spirituality and the Reshaping of Religion in the Twenty-first Century.* Mowbray: Continuum International Publishing Group; S. Coleman, 2000. *The Globalisation of Charismatic Christianity: Spreading the Gospel of Prosperity.* Cambridge: Cambridge University Press; Anderson, *An Introduction to Pentecostalism*), but there are very few specific case studies of specific denominations of Black Majority Churches with the exception of N. Toulis, 1997. *Believing Identity, Pentecostalism and the Mediation of Jamaican Ethnicity and Gender in England.* Oxford: Berg Publishers and S. Arnold, 1992. *From Scepticism*

to Hope: One Black-led Church's Response to Social Responsibility. Nottingham: Grove Books. The inherent broad spectrum scope of the research of over five decades of sociological and historical analysis commensurately was a major constraint in comparison to a case study of a denomination.
2. Black Majority Churches Directory, 2008 [Web]; Ashworth and Farthing, Churchgoing.
3. R. Burgess, 2009. Transnational Religious Networks and Social Transformation in Britain. GloPent Conference, University of Birmingham. 6–7 February 2009; H. Harris, 2006. Yoruba in Diaspora: An African Church in London. New York: Macmillan; S. Hunt, 2000. The "New" Black Pentecostal Churches in Britain. [Web]; S. Hunt, 2002. Deprivation and Western Pentecostalism Revisited: Neo-Pentecostalism. [Web]; Hill, Black Churches; Hill, "Immigrant Sect Development in Britain"; M. Calley, 1965. God's People: West Indian Pentecostal Sects in England. London: Oxford University Press.
4. A. Walls, 1993. The Significance of African Christianity. Friends of St. Colm's Public Lecture, Church of Scotland St. Colm Education Centre and College, 21 May 1989. Printed by the Overseas Ministry Study Centre, New Haven, CT, p2.
5. Together in Mission, 2004. MA lecture notes on Missions in Contemporary Society. Martin Robinson, Lecturer. Birmingham: Together in Mission.
6. Aldred, Respect; I. Smith and W. Green, 1989. An Ebony Cross: Being a Black Christian in Britain Today. London: Harper Collins, pp2–40.
7. J. Mbiti, 1980. "The Encounter of Christian Faith and African Religion." Christian Century 97.
8. Fryer, Staying Power, p69.
9. D. Miller and T. Yamamori, 2007. Global Pentecostalism: The New Face of Christian Social Engagement. California: University of California Press, p23.
10. Gerloff, A Plea for British Black Theologies, p108.
11. Paul C. Boyd, 1991. The African Origin of Christianity, A Biblical and Historic Account. Vol. 1. London: Karia Press, p160.
12. C. Griggs, 1991. Early Egyptian Christianity: From its Origins to 451 CE. Leiden: Brill, p16.
13. MacRobert, "The New Black-led Churches in Britain", p127.
14. Booth, We True Christians.
15. Hill, "Immigrant Sect Development"; Wilkinson, Church in Black and White, pp13, 15.
16. Patterson, Dark Strangers, p205.
17. Calley, God's People, pp140, 142, 144.
18. Patterson, Dark Strangers, p51.
19. Hill, West Indian Migrants, p22.
20. Parsons, The Growth of Religious Diversity, p247.
21. Ibid.
22. E. Pemberton and F. Pemberton (eds), 1983. Pilgrims in Progress. J.R. Maxwell.
23. Mohabir, Building Bridges, p38.
24. Ibid., p81.
25. Ibid., pp111, 112.
26. Gerloff, A Plea for British Black Theologies, p56.
27. Arnold, From Scepticism to Hope, p19.

28 Ibid., p21.
29 Gerloff, *A Plea for British Black Theologies*, p57.
30 Ibid., p56.
31 Cox, *Fire From Heaven*, pp81–88.
32 Ibid., p86; Anderson, *An Introduction to Pentecostalism*, p200.
33 Cox, *Fire From Heaven*, p92.
34 Ibid., p95.
35 W. Hollenweger, 1986. "Intercultural Theology." *Theology Today*, 43.1, p29
36 O. Kalu, 1998. "The Third Response: Pentecostalism and the Reconstruction of Christian Experience in Africa, 1970–1995." *Journal of African Christian Thought*, 1:2, p2.
37 A. Adogame, 2000. "'Aiye loja, orun nile': The Appropriation of Ritual Space-time in the Cosmology of the Celestial Church of Christ." *Journal of Religion in Africa*, 30.1.
38 L. Harvey, 1987. "From Rejection to Liberation: The Development of the Black Christians in Britain and United States." *In* "Claiming the Inheritance", *Racial Justice*, No. 6, Spring 1987, Birmingham: Evangelical Christians for Racial Justice, p29.
39 F. Ludwig, 2005. "The Proliferation of Cherubim and Seraphim Congregation in Britain." *In* A. Adogame and C. Weissköppel (eds), *Religion in the Context of African Migration*. Bayreuth African Studies Series, No. 75. Bayreuth: Breitinger, p346.
40 Mbiti, "The Encounter of Christian Faith".
41 Oshun, *Aladura Diaspora in Britain*.
42 Jenkins, *The New Faces of Christianity*, p152.
43 Oshun, *Christ Apostolic Church of Nigeria*.
44 Kalu, "The Third Response".
45 B. Ray, 1993. "Aladura Christianity." *Journal of Religion in Africa*, 23.3.
46 K. Enang, 2000. *Nigerian Catholics and the Independent Churches: A Call to Authentic Faith*. Immensee, Switzerland: Neue Zeitschrift fur Missionswissenschaft, Supp 45, p31.
47 H. Turner, 1979. *Religious Innovations in Africa: Collected Essays on New Religious Movements*. Boston, MA: G.K. Hall & Co., pp159–172.
48 R. Mitchell, 1979. "Strains and Facilities in the Interpretation of an African Prophet Movement." *In* L. Kriesberg (ed.), *Research in Social Movements, Conflicts and Change*, Vol. 2. Greenwich, CT: JAI Press, p188; see also R. Mitchell, 1964. "Africa's Prophetic Movement." *Christian Century*, 18, pp1427–1429.
49 B. Meyer, 1992. "If You are a Devil You are a Witch and if You are a Witch You are a Devil. The Integration of 'Pagan' Ideals into the Conceptual Universe of Ewe Christians in South Eastern Ghana." *Journal of Religion in Africa*, 22.2; B. Meyer, 1999. *Translating the Devil, Religion and Modernity Among Ewe in Ghana*. Edinburgh: Edinburgh University Press.
50 L. Sanneh, 1991. *Translating the Message: The Missionary Impact on Culture*. Maryknoll, NY: Orbis.
51 B. Meyer, 2004. "Christianity in Africa: From African Independent to Pentecostal-Charismatic Churches." *Annual Review of Anthropology*, 33.
52 Harris, *Yoruba in Diaspora*.

53 Ibid., pp233–234.
54 Meyer, *Translating the Devil*; D. Maxwell, 2001. "Sacred History, Social History: Traditions and Texts in the Making of a Southern African Transnational Religious Movement." *Comparative Studies in Society and History*, 43.3; A. Ukah, 2003. *The Redeemed Christian Church of God, Nigeria. Local Identities and Legitimacy and the State in Twentieth-Century Africa: Essays in Honour of A.H.M. Greene*. London: Macmillan Press.
55 Sturge, *Look What the Lord has Done!*, p135.
56 Oshun, *Aladura Diaspora in Britain*; see also Patterson, *Dark Strangers*; B. Gates (ed.), 1980. *Afro Caribbean Religion*. London: Wardlock Publishing, p67.
57 T. Booth, 1984. *We True Christians*. PhD dissertation. Birmingham: University of Birmingham.
58 Ludwig in Adogame and Weissköppel, *Religion in the Context of African Migration*, pp349–355.
59 Hunt, *Deprivation and Western Pentecostalism Revisited*.
60 S. Burgess, G. McGee, and P. Alexander (eds), 1998. *Dictionary of Pentecostal and Charismatic Movements*. Grand Rapids: Zondervan.
61 P. Gifford, 1998. *African Christianity: Its Public Role*. London: Hurst & Company.
62 Hunt, *Deprivation and Western Pentecostalism Revisited*.
63 S. Hunt, 2000. *The "New" Black Pentecostal Churches in Britain*. [Web]
64 R. Marshall, 1991. "Power in the Name of Jesus: Social Transformation and Pentecostalism in Western Nigeria 'Revisited'." *Review of African Political Economy*, 52.
65 C. Wagner and J. Thompson (eds), 2004. *Out of Africa*. California: Regal Books, pp9–10.
66 Ibid., p10.
67 Ibid.
68 J.K. Asamoah-Gyadu, 2009. *Spirit, Mission and Transnational Influence: Nigerian-led Pentecostalism in Eastern Europe*. A paper presented at the 2009 GloPent Conference, University of Birmingham, UK. 6–7 February 2009.
69 Cited in Wagner and Thompson, *Out of Africa*, p118.
70 E. Adeboye, 2009. Speech at the Opening Ceremony of the Administrative Office of the Redeemed Christian Church of God, Central Office, Knebworth, Hertfordshire, UK, 16 November 2009.
71 Sturge, *Look What the Lord has Done!*.
72 Hunt, *The "New" Black Pentecostal Churches in Britain*.
73 A. Irukwu, 2009. "Pastor Agu Irukwu." *Keep the Faith* magazine. Issue 47. Bury: Black Publications UK.
74 Miller and Yamamori, *Global Pentecostalism*, p12.
75 Beckford, *Challenges of Black Pentecostal Leadership*.
76 Cited in A. Anderson, 2005. "New African Initiated Pentecostalism and Charismatics in South Africa." *Journal of Religion in Africa*, 35.1.
77 O. Adebayo, 2007. *Mayor of London Has No Power to Help Black Churches Convert Redundant Buildings*. [Web]; A. Irukwu, 2006. Speech during annual Ministers' Conference of the Redeemed Christian Church of God, United Kingdom, held at Pontins Conference Centre, Blackpool.
78 Anderson, "New African Initiated Pentecostalism".

79. L. Etan-Adollo, 2006. *Growth in Afro-Caribbean Pentecostal Churches.* London: Athena Press, p23.
80. B. Birch, 1991. *Let Justice Roll Down: Old Testament, Ethics and Christian Life.* Louisville: Westminster/John Knox, p89.
81. Quoted in Anderson, *An Introduction to Pentecostalism*, p237.
82. Etan-Adollo, *Growth in Afro-Caribbean Pentecostal Churches.*
83. M. Hill (ed.), 1971. *A Sociology Yearbook of Religion in Britain.* London: SCM Press Ltd, pp1–20.
84. Wilson, cited in ibid., pp7, 9.
85. S. Adedeji, 2004. *Church Cash Charity Mismanaged.* [Web]
86. L. Newbigin, 1957. *The Household of God: Lectures on the Nature of the Church.* London: SCM, p39.
87. S. Bruce, 2002. *God is Dead: Secularisation in the West.* Oxford: Blackwell, pp22, 24.
88. L. Gerlach and V.H. Hine, 1970. *People, Power, Change: Movements of Social Transformation.* New York: Bobbs-Merrill, pp53, 54.
89. Gerlach and Hine, *People, Power, Change.*
90. Stammer, cited in Jenkins, *The New Faces of Christianity*, p237; cf. Anderson, *An Introduction to Pentecostalism*, pp45, 52.
91. R. Wallis, 1984. *The Elementary Forms of the New Religious Life.* London: Routledge & Kegan Paul.
92. Ukah, *The Redeemed Christian Church of God.*
93. Ibid., p68.
94. A. Omoyajowo, 1982. *Cherubim and Seraphim: The History of an African Independent Church.* New York: NOK Publishers, p193.
95. E. Lawless, 1983. "Shouting for the Lord: The Power of Women's Speech in the Pentecostal Religious Service." *Journal of American Folklore*, 96 (382); E. Lawless, 1987. "Piety and Motherhood: Reproductive Images and Maternal Strategies of Women Preachers." *Journal of American Folklore*, 100 (398); E. Lawless, 1988. *Handmaidens of the Lord: Pentecostal Women Preachers and Traditional Religion.* Philadelphia: University of Pennsylvania Press; E. Lawless, 1991. "Rescripting their Lives and Narratives: Spiritual Life Stories of Pentecostal Women Preachers." *Journal of Feminist Studies in Religion*, 7.1.
96. E. Brusco, 1995. *The Reformation of Machismo: Evangelical Conversion in Columbia.* Austin: University of Texas Press.
97. Cucchiari, S. 1990. "Between Shame and Sanctification: Patriarchy and its Transformation in Sicilian Pentecostalism." *American Ethnologist*, 17.4.
98. Toulis, *Believing Identity*, p221.
99. Ibid., p225.
100. J. Parratt, 1995. *Reinventing Christianity: African Theology Today.* Grand Rapids: Eerdmans, p207.
101. J. Hanciles, 2008. *Beyond Christendom: Globalization, African Migration, and the Transformation of the West.* Maryknoll: Orbis Books, pp357, 358.
102. R. Burgess, 2009. "African Pentecostal Spirituality and Civic Engagement: The Case of the Redeemed Christian Church of God in Britain." *Journal of Beliefs & Values*, 3, p258.
103. J. Comaroff and John L. Comaroff, 1999. "Occult Economies and the Violence of

Abstraction: Notes from the South African Postcolony." *American Ethnologist*, 26.3.
[104] Meyer, "Christianity in Africa".
[105] D. Maxwell, 2007. *African Gifts of the Spirit: Pentecostalism and the Rise of a Zimbabwean Transnational Religious Movement*. Athens: Ohio University Press.
[106] Ukah, *The Redeemed Christian Church of God*, pp642–643.
[107] Burgess, "African Pentecostal Spirituality", p258.
[108] Jesus House, 2007. "Going the Extra Mile." In Review. London: Jesus House; cf. Arnold, *From Scepticism to Hope*, p72.
[109] Arnold, *From Scepticism to Hope*; E. Foster, 1990. "Out of this World: A Consideration of the Development and Nature of Black-led Churches in Britain." In P. Grant and R. Patel (eds), *A Time to Speak: Perspectives of Black Christians in Britain*. A joint publication of Racial Justice and the Black Theology Working Group, Birmingham, p68; Howard, *A Report on Afro-Caribbean Christianity*, pp22–23.
[110] Parsons, *The Growth of Religious Diversity*, p257.
[111] Adeboye, Speech at the Opening Ceremony.
[112] Arnold, *From Scepticism to Hope*.
[113] Charity Commission of England and Wales, 2008. *Public Benefit Guidance Information*, p29. [Web]
[114] Arnold, *From Scepticism to Hope*, p72.
[115] A. Quass, 2009. "Representations of Transnationality in Nigeria and Germany." A paper presented at GloPent Transnational Conference on Transnational Pentecostalism in Europe at Birmingham University. 6–7 February 2009.
[116] A. Adogame, 2004. "Contesting the Ambivalences of Modernity in a Global Context: The Redeemed Christian Church of God, North America." *Studies in World Christianity*, 10/1.
[117] Quass, "Representations of Transnationality".
[118] A. Adogame, 2009. *Transnational Migration and Pentecostalism in Europe*. Paper delivered at European Research Network on Global Pentecostalism Conference at the University of Birmingham.
[119] O. Kalu, 2009. "African Pentecostalism." A paper presented at the 2009 GloPent Transnational Conference, Birmingham, UK.
[120] Jenkins, *The New Faces of Christianity*, p52.
[121] O. Kalu, 2008. *African Pentecostalism: An Introduction*. Oxford: Oxford University Press, pp266–267.
[122] Gifford, *African Christianity*, p333.
[123] J.K. Asamoah-Gyadu, 2004. *African Charismatics: Current Developments Within Indigenous Pentecostalism in Ghana*. Studies of Religion in Africa: 27. Leiden: Brill, p215.
[124] A. Adogame, 2005. *Dealing with Local Satanic Technology: Deliverance Rhetoric in the Mountain of Fire and Miracles Ministry*. Paper presented at the CESNUR international conference on "Religious Movements, Globalization and Conflict: Transnational Perspectives", Palermo, Sicily, pp6–7.
[125] Edwards in Eden, *Britain on the Brink*, p106; Sturge, *Look What the Lord has Done!*, pp81–111; J. Aldred, 2002. "The Development of BMCs. Presentation given as part of the CTBI consultation with BMCs." In Sturge, *Look What the Lord has Done!*.

[126] Gerloff, *A Plea for British Black Theologies*, pp55–61.
[127] Ibid., p44.
[128] Gee, *Pentecost Magazine*, p12; cf. Smith, *British Black Gospel*, p40.
[129] Gerloff, *A Plea for British Black Theologies*.
[130] Edwards in Eden, *Britain on the Brink*, pp100–118.
[131] Aldred, *Respect*.
[132] Sturge, *Look What the Lord has Done!*.
[133] Ireson, *My Life and Thought*, p8.
[134] Ibid., pp50, 58.
[135] Ibid., p50.
[136] Ibid., pp11–15.
[137] *Ashburton Guardian*. 19 November 1920, p4.
[138] Fryer, *Staying Power*.
[139] M. Sherwood, 1994. *Pastor Daniel Ekarte and the African Churches Mission*. London: Savannah Press, p24.
[140] Ibid., p24.
[141] Wilson, "Racism and Private Assistance", pp55–76.
[142] Ibid., p59.
[143] Ibid.
[144] Quoted in Sherwood, *Pastor Daniel Ekarte*, pp28–31.
[145] Arnold, *From Scepticism to Hope*, pp63–80; Sturge, *Look What the Lord has Done!*, p110.
[146] A. Anderson, 1992. *Bazalwane: African Pentecostals in South Africa*. Pretoria: Unisa Press, pp2–6, 64–72.
[147] Arnold, *From Scepticism to Hope*, p18.
[148] Gerloff, *A Plea for British Black Theologies*, p42.
[149] Ibid., p56.
[150] O. Lyseight, 1995. *Forward March: An Autobiography*. London: G.S. Garwood, pp46, 47.
[151] Edwards in Eden, *Britain on the Brink*, p105.
[152] Oshun, *Aladura Diaspora in Britain*.
[153] Gerloff, *A Plea for British Black Theologies*, p57.
[154] Ibid.
[155] Ibid.
[156] Sturge, *Look What the Lord has Done!*, p94.
[157] Weeks, *Chapter Thirty-two*, p263.
[158] J. Aldred, 2008. Personal interview held at Birmingham in October 2008.
[159] Gerloff, *A Plea for British Black Theologies*; Sturge, *Look What the Lord has Done!*.
[160] Beckford, *Jesus is Dread*, pp115–127.
[161] Gerloff, *A Plea for British Black Theologies*, p59.
[162] Aldred, *Respect*, p102.
[163] Ibid.
[164] Virgina Beecher, cited in Sturge, *Look What the Lord has Done!*, p101.
[165] Sturge, *Look What the Lord has Done!*, p95.
[166] Aldred, *Respect*, p106.
[167] Ibid., p107.
[168] A. Adeleke, 2009. Interview held in May 2009 at RCCG House of Praise,

Charlton, London. (Interviewer Babatunde Adedibu: audio recording.)
169 Sturge, *Look What the Lord has Done!*, pp96–97.
170 J. Aldred, 1999, *A Black Majority Church*. MA dissertation. Sheffield: University of Sheffield, p16.
171 Sturge, *Look What the Lord has Done!*, p102.
172 H. Osgood, 2006. *African Neo-Pentecostal Churches and British Evangelicalism 1985–2005: Balancing Principles and Practicalities*. PhD dissertation. London: University of London, p92.
173 Smith, *British Black Gospel*, p148.
174 Ibid., p147.
175 Sturge, *Look What the Lord has Done!*, p99.
176 Ibid., p103.
177 M. Sturge, *Christianity Today* (9 August 2005).
178 Aldred, *Respect*, p106; cf. Sturge, *Look What the Lord has Done!*, p97.
179 Adeleke, Interview.
180 Obunge, "Black Church in White Space".
181 Irukwu, "Pastor Agu Irukwu".
182 R. Stedman, 1972. *Body Life: The Church Comes Alive!*. Ventura: Regal Books, p106.
183 R. Warren, 1995. *The Purpose Driven Church: Growth Without Compromising Your Message and Mission*. Grand Rapids: Zondervan; C. Schwarz, 1996. *Natural Church Development: A Guide to Eight Essential Qualities of Healthy Churches*. Carol Stream, IL: ChurchSmart Resources; E. Dever, 1998. *Nine Marks of a Healthy Church*. Washington DC: Center for Church Reform; S. Macchia, 2001. *Becoming a Healthy Church Workbook: A Dialogue, Assessment, and Planning Tool*. Grand Rapids: Baker Books.
184 C. Chaney, and R. Lewis, 1997. *Design for Church Growth*. Nashville: Broadman Press, p87.
185 G. Barna, 1990. *Marketing the Church*. Colorado Springs: Navpress, p15.
186 Hunt, *The "New" Black Pentecostal Churches in Britain*.
187 Burgess, "Nigerian Pentecostal Theology".
188 J. Aldred, 2009. Personal correspondence with author; Aldred, *A Black Majority Church*.
189 Hunt, *The "New" Black Pentecostal Churches in Britain*.
190 Burgess, "Nigerian Pentecostal Theology".
191 W. Chadwick, 2001. *Stealing the Sheep: The Church's Hidden Problems with Transfer Growth*. Downers Grove: InterVarsity Press, p10.
192 Warren, *The Purpose Driven Church*, p102.
193 Chadwick, *Stealing the Sheep*, p159.
194 Ibid., p157.
195 Macchia, *Becoming a Healthy Church*.
196 Burgess, "Nigerian Pentecostal Theology".
197 J. Sepulveda, 1997. "To Overcome the Fear of Syncretism: A Latin American Perspective." *In* P. Lynne, J. Sepulveda and G. Smith (eds), *Mission Matters*. Frankfurt am Main: Peter Lang, p167.
198 W. Hollenweger, 1997. *Pentecostalism: Origins and Developments Worldwide*. Peabody: Hendrickson Publishers, p25.

199 Ibid.
200 Sturge, *Look What the Lord has Done!*, p126.
201 Wilkinson, *Church in Black and White*, p106.
202 A. Essien, 2000. "New Religious Movements and the Gospel of Prosperity: The Nigerian Experience." *The Oracle*, 1, p40.
203 A. Anderson, 1987. "Prosperity Message in the Eschatology of Some New Charismatic Churches." *Missionalia*, 15.2.
204 Irukwu, Speech during annual Ministers' Conference.
205 Ukah, *The Redeemed Christian Church of God*, p642.
206 Sturge, *Look What the Lord has Done!*.
207 www.eauk.org/media/black-church-leaders.cfm. [Accessed 12 October 2011].
208 Ibid., CCPAS is the Churches Child Protection Advisory Services.
209 Burgess, "Nigerian Pentecostal Theology".

## CHAPTER FOUR: THE DISTINCTIVE THEOLOGICAL AND PRACTICAL FEATURES OF BLACK-LED CHURCHES IN GREAT BRITAIN

1 Hollenweger, "Intercultural Theology", pp28–35.
2 E. Graham, H. Walton and F. Ward, 2005. *Theological Reflection: Methods*. London: SCM Press, p10.
3 Gerloff, *A Plea for British Black Theologies*, p49.
4 Ibid.
5 Aldred, *Respect*.
6 D. Reid-Salmon, 2008. *Home Away from Home: The Caribbean Diasporan Church in the Black Atlantic Tradition*. London: Equinox, pp83, 84.
7 Kalu, "The Third Response"; O. Kalu, 2000. *Power, Poverty and Prayer: The Challenges of Poverty and Pluralism in African Christianity, 1960–1996*. Frankfurt am Main: Peter Lang.
8 P. Gifford, 1998. *African Christianity: Its Public Role*. London: Hurst & Company.
9 Beckford, *Challenges of Black Pentecostal Leadership*.
10 Beckford, *Jesus is Dread*; Aldred, *Respect*.
11 Hollenweger, "Intercultural Theology", pp28–29.
12 Beckford, *Challenges of Black Pentecostal Leadership*, p10.
13 J. Aldred, 2007. *The Experience of Black Churches in the United Kingdom. Change and Diversity – Impact of Migration in Church and Society*. EEA3. Conference Forum-Migration. Sibiu, Romania. 4–9 September 2007, p5.
14 Gerloff, *A Plea for British Black Theologies*, p52.
15 W. Hollenweger, 1972. *The Pentecostals*. London: SCM Press, pp405, 406.
16 MacRobert, *The Black Roots*, p29.
17 MacRobert, "The New Black-led Churches in Britain", p120.
18 *Black Majority Churches Directory*.
19 Aldred, Personal interview.
20 Gerloff, *A Plea for British Black Theologies*, p50.
21 MacRobert, *Black Pentecostalism*.
22 Parsons, *The Growth of Religious Diversity*, p248.

23 Aldred, Personal correspondence; MacRobert, *Black Pentecostalism*.
24 David K. Bernard, 1991. *Oneness and Trinity A.D. 100–300: The Doctrine of God in Ancient Christian Writings*. Hazelwood, MO: Word Aflame Press, pp160, 161.
25 C. Brumback, 1977. *Like a River*, USA: Gospel Publishing House, p99.
26 Cited in Gerloff, *A Plea for British Black Theologies*, p87.
27 Gerloff, *A Plea for British Black Theologies*.
28 J. Ankerberg and J. Weldon, 1991. *Cult Watch*. Eugene, OR: Harvest House, pp367–368; cf. Hollenweger, *The Pentecostals*, p31.
29 Anderson, *An Introduction to Pentecostalism*, p48.
30 Anderson cited in MacRobert, *Black Pentecostalism*; Hollenweger, *The Pentecostals*, p24.
31 D.E. Harrell, 1971. *White Sects and Black Men in the Recent South*. Nashville: Vanderbilt University Press, pp130–131.
32 Anderson, *Vision of the Disinherited: The Making of American Pentecostalism*. Peabody: Hendrickson, p113.
33 Miller and Yamamori, *Global Pentecostalism*, p21, cf. Anderson, *An Introduction to Pentecostalism*, pp40, 44.
34 M. Crews, 1990. *The Church of God: A Social History*. Tennessee: University of Tennessee Press, pp1–18.
35 Burgess *et al.*, *Dictionary of Pentecostal and Charismatic Movements*, pp938–939.
36 Mitchell quoted in Gerloff, *A Plea for British Black Theologies*, p53.
37 Peter Brierley, UK Church Statistics 2005–2010, section 9.5.
38 Ibid.
39 Gerloff, Roswith, *A Plea for Black British Theologies*, p53.
40 Ibid.
41 MacRobert, "The New Black-led Churches in Britain", p130.
42 Ibid., p132.
43 MacRobert, *Black Pentecostalism*, p288.
44 Ibid.
45 Ibid.
46 MacRobert, "The New Black-led Churches in Britain", p133.
47 Boyd, *The African Origin of Christianity*, p10.
48 Bernard, *Oneness and* Trinity, pp293–294; cf. MacRobert, *Black Pentecostalism*, p133.
49 Bernard, *Oneness and Trinity*, p288.
50 R. Bowman, 1985. "Oneness Pentecostalism and the Trinity: A Biblical Critique." *Forward* 8 (Fall 1985), p23.
51 Milne, B. 1982. *Know the Truth*. Leicester: InterVarsity Press, pp62–63.
52 G. Prestige, 1988. *God in Patristic Thought*. London: SPCK, p157.
53 Ibid., p248.
54 Ibid., p237.
55 K. Barth, 1936. *Church Dogmatics* 1/1, Edinburgh: T&T Clark, p368.
56 Ibid., pp355–359.
57 T. Torrance, 1995 *The Christian Doctrine of God: One Being, Three Persons*. Edinburgh: T&T Clark, pp203–234.
58 C. Gunton, 1995. "Relation and Relativity: The Trinity and the Created World."

In C. Schwobel (ed.), *Trinitarian Theology Today: Essays on Divine Being and Act*. Edinburgh: T&T Clark, pp92–112.
59 A. Grudem, 1994. *Systematic Theology. An Introduction to Biblical Doctrine*. Grand Rapids: Zondervan, pp253–254.
60 Boyd, *The African Origin of Christianity*, pp62–63; cf. J. Fortman, 1999. *The Triune God. A Historical Study of the Doctrine of the Trinity*. Eugene, OR: Wipf and Stock, pp162–163.
61 J. McNeill, (ed.) 1960. *John Calvin: Institutes of the Christian Religion*. Philadelphia: Westminster Press, pp113–114.
62 Boyd, *The African Origin of Christianity*, pp59–62.
63 MacRobert, *Black Pentecostalism*, p292.
64 Cited in MacRobert, *Black Pentecostalism*, p293.
65 Boyd, *The African Origin of Christianity*, pp144–145.
66 MacRobert, *Black Pentecostalism*, p294.
67 Bernard *Oneness and* Trinity, pp170–180.
68 Boyd, *The African Origin of Christianity*, pp140–141.
69 MacRobert, *Black Pentecostalism*, p295.
70 G.R. Beasley-Murray, 1994. *Baptism in the New Testament*. Grand Rapids: Eerdmans Publishing Company, pp90–92.
71 Ibid.
72 Reid-Salmon, *Home Away from Home*, p79.
73 Aldred, *Respect*.
74 Curtin cited in Reid-Salmon, *Home Away from Home*, p84.
75 Sturge, *Look What the Lord has Done!*, p113.
76 Aldred, Personal interview.
77 Warrington, K. 2008. *Pentecostal Theology: A Theology of Encounter*. London: T&T Clark, pvii.
78 Kalu, *African Pentecostalism*, p291.
79 Ibid., p250.
80 MacRobert, *Black Pentecostalism*, pp247, 252.
81 A. Reddie and N. Jagessar (eds), 2007. *Black Theology in Britain*. London: Equinox, p82.
82 Beckford, *Dread and Pentecostal*, p171.
83 Hollenweger, "Intercultural Theology", pp28–29.
84 Schreiter, R. 2004. *The New Catholicity: Theology Between the Global and the Local*. New York: Orbis Books, pp127–128.
85 Jenkins, *The New Faces of Christianity*; C. Chike, 2007. *African Christianity in Britain: Diaspora, Doctrine and Dialogue*. Milton Keynes: Author House; Jenkins, *The Next Christendom*.
86 J. Mbiti,1986. *Bible and Theology in African Christianity*. Tanzania: Oxford University Press Tanzania Ltd, p44.
87 A. Anderson, 2009. *African Europeans in Global Pentecostalism*. A paper presented at the annual academic lecture of Christ Redeemer Christian College and Redeemed Christian Church of God held at Jesus House, London. 6 October 2009, p6.
88 I. Phiri and J. Maxwell, 2007. *Gospel Riches: Africa's Rapid Embrace of Prosperity Pentecostalism Provokes Concern – and Hope*. [Web]
89 R. Burgess, 2009.*The Challenges of Second Generation Africans in Churches in*

*Britain*. A paper presented at the Annual Academic Lecture of Redeemed Christian Church of God United Kingdom, Christ Redeemer College, London. 6 October 2009.

90   Chike, *African Christianity in Britain*.
91   Phiri and Maxwell, *Gospel Riches*.
92   A. Walsh, 2007. "First Church of Prosperidad." *Christianity Today*. [Web]
93   Chike, *African Christianity in Britain*.
94   Burgess, *The Challenges of Second Generation Africans*.
95   Jenkins, *The New Faces of Christianity*, p83.
96   L. Sanusi, 2007. *Take it by Force: How to Possess your Possessions*. Crayford: Oraword Publications Ltd, p37.
97   Chike, *African Christianity in Britain*.
98   Achebe cited in Jenkins, *The New Faces of Christianity*, p59.
99   Nasimiyu-Waske, cited in Jenkins, ibid.
100  Majioga cited in Jenkins, ibid.
101  P. Akinola, 2004. *Why I Object to Homosexuality and Same-sex Unions*. [Web]
102  N. Wright, 1996. *The Radical Evangelical: Seeking a Place to Stand*. London: SPCK, p9.
103  R. Stronstad, 1993. The *Charismatic Theology of St Luke*. Peabody: Hendrickson Publishers, p1.
104  Vinson, cited in Burgess *et al.*, *Dictionary of Pentecostal and Charismatic Movements*, pp326–327.
105  Fackre in Wright, *The Radical Evangelical*, p6.
106  Cited in Jenkins, *The New Faces of Christianity*, p4.
107  S. Pak, U. Lee, J. Kim and M. Cho, 2005. *Singing the Lord's Song in a New Land*. Louisville: John Knox Press; T. Carnes and F. Yang (eds), 2004. *Asian American Religions: The Making and Remaking of Borders and Boundaries*. New York: New York University Press; F. Matsuoka and E.S. Fernandez (eds), 2003. *Realizing the America of Our Hearts*. St Louis: Chalice Press.
108  Brierley, *Religious Trends*.
109  J. Penny, 1997. *The Missionary Emphasis of Lukan Pneumatology*. Journal of Pentecostal Theology Supplement Series 12. Sheffield: Continuum International Publishing Group; S. Ellington, 1996. "Pentecostalism and the Authority of Scripture." *Journal of Pentecostal Theology*, 9; L. McQueen, 1995. *Joel and the Spirit: The Cry of a Prophetic Hermeneutic*. Sheffield: Continuum International Publishing Group.
110  J. Moltmann, 1992. *The Spirit of Life: A Universal Affirmation*. Minneapolis: Augsburg Fortress Publishers, p6.
111  Ibid., p17.
112  C. Pinnock, 2004. "The Recovery of the Holy Spirit in Evangelical Theology." *Journal of Pentecostal Theology*, 10.
113  Reddie and Jagessar, *Black Theology in Britain*, p153.
114  J. Cone, 2003. "Black Spirituals: A Theological Interpretation." *In* W. Cornel and S. Eddie (eds), *African American Religious Thought: An Anthology*. Louisville, Kentucky: Westminster John Knox Publisher, p783.
115  Beckford in Reddie and Jagessar, *Black Theology in Britain*, p89.
116  Ibid.

117 Ibid., p90.
118 Ibid.
119 G. Fee, 2000. *Listening to the Spirit in the Text*. Cambridge: William B. Eerdmans Publishing, p8; cf. G. Fee, 1991. *Gospel and Spirit: Issues in New Testament Hermeneutics*. Peabody: Hendrickson Publishers, pp85–86.
120 Ferguson, cited in Chike, *African Christianity in Britain*, p25.
121 Ukah, *The Redeemed Christian Church of God*; Chike, *African Christianity in Britain*; Fee, *Listening to the Spirit*.
122 K. Coleman, 2006. *Exploring Métissage: A Theological Anthropology of Black Christian Women's Subjectivities in Postcolonial Britain*. PhD dissertation. Birmingham: University of Birmingham; Aldred, *Respect*; Beckford, *Dread and Pentecostal*; R. Beckford, 2001. "Theology in the Age of Crack: Crack Age, Prosperity Doctrine and Being There." *Black Theology in Britain*, 4 (1); Hyacinth Sweeney in J. Aldred (ed.), 2000. *Sisters with Power*. London: Continuum.
123 B. Klaus and L. Triplett, 1991. "National Leadership in Pentecostal Missions." *In* M. Dempster, B. Klaus and D. Petersen (eds), *Called and Empowered: Global Mission in Pentecostal Perspective*. Peabody: Hendrickson, p226.
124 Sheppard, cited in Burgess *et al.*, *Dictionary of Pentecostal and Charismatic Movements*; Aldred, *Respect*; Beckford, *Dread and Pentecostal*; Beckford "Theology in the Age of Crack".
125 Asamoah-Gyadu, *African Charismatics*, p215.
126 Ukah, *The Redeemed Christian Church of God*.
127 Jenkins, *The New Faces of Christianity*, p35.
128 Kalu, *African Pentecostalism*, pp266–267.
129 Zinkuratire cited in Jenkins, *The New Faces of Christianity*, p36.
130 W. Ariarajah, 2000. "Changing Frontiers of Ecumenical Theology: A Challenge to Ecumenical Formation." *Ministerial Formation*, 89 (April 2000).
131 Reddie and Jagessar, *Black Theology in Britain*, p11.
132 Chike, *African Christianity in Britain*, p193.
133 Sweeney in Reddie and Jagessar, *Black Theology in Britain*, pp154–160.
134 M. Clark, H. Larderle *et al.*, 1989. *What is Distinctive About Pentecostal Theology?* Pretoria: University of South Africa, p69.
135 Ibid., p102.
136 J. MacArthur, 1992. *Charismatic Chaos*. Grand Rapids: Zondervan, p116.
137 H. Ervin, 1985. "Hermeneutics: A Pentecostal Option." *In* P. Ebert (ed.), *Essays on Apostolic Themes*. Peabody: Hendrickson, p28.
138 T. Cargal, 1993. "Beyond the Fundamentalist-Modernist Controversy: Pentecostals and Hermeneutics in a Postmodern Age." *Pnuema*, 15, No. 2.
139 M. Cartledge, 1996. "Empirical Theology: Towards an Evangelical-Charismatic Hermeneutic." *Journal of Pentecostal Theology*, 9, pp121–125.
140 Pinnock, "The Recovery of the Holy Spirit", pp16–17.
141 Tomlin, cited in Reddie and Jagessar, *Black Theology in Britain*, p229.
142 Sturge, *Look What the Lord has Done!*, p124.
143 D. Dayton, 1987. *Theological Roots of Pentecostalism*. Massachusetts: Hendrickson Publishers, p23.
144 Penny, *The Missionary Emphasis*, p12.
145 A. Yong and T. Richie, 2010. "The Spirit Encounter: Theology of Religions –

Pentecostal and Pneumatological Perspectives." *In* A. Anderson, M. Begrunder, A. Droogers and C. Van der Laan, *Studying Global Pentecostalism. Theories and Methods*. California: California University Press, p258; cf. M. Welker, 2004. *God the Spirit*. Minneapolis: Fortress Press.
146  Suurmond in A. Yong, 2005. *The Spirit Poured Upon All Flesh: Pentecostalism and the Possibility of Global Theology*. Grand Rapids, Michigan: Baker Academic, p195.
147  D. Martin, 2002. *Pentecostalism: The World in Their Parish*. London: Blackwell, p114.
148  Kalu, *African Pentecostalism*, p251.
149  Anderson, *African Europeans*, p10.
150  Miller and Yamamori, *Global Pentecostalism*, p139.
151  Ukah, *The Redeemed Christian Church of God*.
152  J. Peel, 2000. *Religious Encounter and the Making of the Yoruba*. Indianapolis: Indiana University Press, p91.
153  Lindon cited in Burgess, "Nigerian Pentecostal Theology", p13.
154  Burgess, "Nigerian Pentecostal Theology".
155  Ukah, *The Redeemed Christian Church of God*, p179.
156  One of the most outstanding texts that is not only a scholarly but an irenic text on Health and Wealth prosperity teaching is the report on "Word of Faith and Positive Confession" Theologies initiated by the Evangelical Alliance (UK) Commission on Unity and Truth among Evangelicals. The uniqueness of the text is due to the effort of the authors to give a balance and critical assessment of the Health and Wealth ideology not only in terms of textual criticism of Health and Wealth proof-texting of scriptures and literalism but also a comprehensive historical analysis of the emergence of the ideology in America and a seminal treatise within the United Kingdom context. For further reading see A. Perriman (ed.), 2003. *Faith: Health and Prosperity. A Report on "Word of Faith and Positive Confession"*. Carlisle: Paternoster Press.
157  Reddie and Jagessar, *Black Theology in Britain*, p12.
158  S. Hunt, 1998. "Magical Moments: An Intellectualist Approach to the Neo-Pentecostal 'Faith' Ministries." *Religion*, 28 (3), p272.
159  Burgess, "Nigerian Pentecostal Theology".
160  F. Price, 2005. *Name it and Claim it! The Power of Positive Confession*. Benin City: Marvellous Christiana Publication.
161  D. Ayegboyin, 2006. "A Rethinking on Prosperity Teaching in the New Pentecostal Churches in Nigeria." *Black Theology*, Vol. 4, No. 1.
162  Asamoah-Gyadu, *African Charismatics*, pp215–222.
163  Hunt, *The "New" Black Pentecostal Churches in Britain*.
164  Cox, *Fire From Heaven*, p272; cf. S. Coleman, 1993. "Conservative Protestantism and the World Order: The Faith Movement in the United States and Sweden." *Sociology of Religion*, 54 (4), p335.
165  J. Robinson, 2003. *Another View of the Prosperity Gospel*. [Web]
166  B. Meyer, 1998. "The Power of Money: Politics, Occult Forces and Pentecostalism." *African Studies Review*, 41.3.
167  Burgess, "Nigerian Pentecostal Theology".
168  Ukah, *The Redeemed Christian Church of God*.

[169] M. Ojo, 1996. "Cha̤  .tic Movements in Africa." In C. Fyfe and A. Walls (eds), *Christianity in Africa ι the 1990s*. Edinburgh: University of Edinburgh Centre of African Studies, p106.
[170] Beckford, "Theology in the Age of Crack", pp15–16.
[171] Sturge, *Look What the Lord has Done!*, p139.
[172] Miller and Yamamori, *Global Pentecostalism*, p215.
[173] Ukah, *The Redeemed Christian Church of God*; cf. Ayegboyin, "A Rethinking on Prosperity Teaching", pp70–86; cf. D. Oyedepo, 1997. *Understanding Financial Prosperity*. Lagos: Dominion Publishing, pp156–157.
[174] Hacketh in R. Roberts, 1995. *Religion and Transformation of Capitalism: Comparative Approaches*. London: Routledge, pp199–214.
[175] Hunt, *The "New" Black Pentecostal Churches in Britain*.
[176] O. Adeboye, 2005. "Transnational Pentecostalism in Africa: The Redeemed Christian Church of God, Nigeria." In L. Fourchard, A. Mary and R. Otayek (eds), *Enterprises religieuses transnationales en Afrique de l'Ouest*. Paris: Karthala, pp438–465; Anderson, "New African Initiated Pentecostalism", pp66–92; Hunt, *The "New" Black Pentecostal Churches in Britain*.
[177] G. Folarin, 2007. "Contemporary State of the Prosperity Gospel in Nigeria." *Asia Journal of Theology*, 21 (1), p80.
[178] Jenkins, *The New Faces of Christianity*, p93.
[179] M. Ashimolowo, 2003. *The 10Ms of Money*. London: Mattyson Media, p68.
[180] K. Copeland, 1987. *Our Covenant with God*. Fort Worth: Kenneth Copeland Publications, p89; cf. K. Hagin, 1995. *Financial Prosperity*. Tulsa: Faith Publication Library, pp10–13.
[181] K. Copeland, 1974. *The Laws of Prosperity*. Fort Worth: Manna Christian Outreach, p51.
[182] Cox, *Fire From Heaven*, p271.
[183] Hagin, *Financial Prosperity*; M. Ashimolowo, 2000. *101 Answers to Money Problems*. Vols 1–4. London: Matthew Ashimolowo Media Ministries; Ashimolowo, *The 10Ms of Money*.
[184] K. Sarles, 1986. "A Theological Evaluation of the Prosperity Gospel." *Bibliotheca Sacra*, 143, p337.
[185] Ashimolowo, *The 10Ms of Money*, p68; Hagin, *Financial Prosperity*, p56; R. Tilton, 1983. *God's Word About Prosperity*. Dallas, TX: Word of Faith Publications, p6.
[186] Sturge, *Look What the Lord has Done!*, p141.
[187] Perriman, *Faith: Health and Prosperity*, pp9–11.
[188] Osgood, *African Neo-Pentecostal Churches*.

## CHAPTER FIVE: THE CONTRIBUTIONS OF BLACK MAJORITY CHURCHES AND THEIR MEMBERS TO BRITISH CHRISTIANITY

[1] R. Williams in J. Petre, 2006. "Migrants Fill Empty Pews as Britons Lose Faith." *The Telegraph*. [Web]
[2] P. Brierley, 2009. Report of interview in M. Mackay, 2009. *Strategic Planning Essential to Church's Future*. [Web]
[3] Aldred, *Respect*, p107.

4. Beckford, *Challenges of Black Pentecostal Leadership.*
5. *Black Majority Churches Directory.*
6. J. Micklethwait and A. Wooldridge, 2009. *God is Back: How the Global Rise of Faith is Changing the World.* USA: Allen Lane, p137.
7. Brierley, Report of interview.
8. A. Irukwu, 2009. "Pastoral Perspective of Second Generation Africans in Churches in Britain." A paper presented at the annual academic lecture of Christ Redeemers College/Redeemed Christian Church of God, held at Jesus House, 6 February 2009.
9. Hill, *Black Churches.*
10. B. Adedibu, 2009. *Storytelling: An Effective Communication Appeal in Preaching.* London: Wisdom Summit, pp25, 26.
11. Prince Charles, 2007. *Prince Charles Marks 59th Birthday with Tribute to Black Churches in the UK.* [Web]
12. Pastor Kolade is the Deputy Overseer of New Covenant Church, a Nigerian and Missionary to Britain. The 2030 national leadership seminar was held on 19 September 2009. The aim of the seminar was to teach delegates to communicate confidently and persuasively, to introduce useful techniques for leading or representing a group, and to show delegates how to motivate and inspire others by example, enhance presentation skills and build trust. See www.ncc2030vision.org/speakers.html. [Accessed 25 October 2010]
13. Brierley, Report of interview.
14. Habermas cited in Micklethwait and Wooldridge, *God is Back,* p139.
15. *Keep the Faith* magazine, Issue 50.
16. Arnold, *From Scepticism to Hope*; Foster, "Out of this World", p68; Howard, *A Report on Afro-Caribbean Christianity,* pp22–23.
17. Parsons, *The Growth of Religious Diversity,* p257.
18. Arnold, *From Scepticism to Hope,* p37.
19. Ibid., pp36–38.
20. Grey cited in Arnold, *From Scepticism to Hope,* p71.
21. Charity Commission, *Public Benefit Guidance Information,* p29.
22. D. Oluyomi, 2009. *Appeal by Kingsway International Christian Centre and the London Development Agency,* p22. [Web]
23. A. Adedoyin, 2009. "RCCG Churches Leading Role in Fighting Poverty in London." *In Festival News.* Official Publication of the London Festival of Life. London: Festival of Life, p11.
24. T. Balogun, 2009. Private discussion at Jesus House, London. 6 October 2009.
25. R. Freeman and D. Gilbert, 1988. *Corporate Strategy and the Search for Ethics.* Englewood Cliffs: Prentice Hall, p89.
26. Burgess, "Nigerian Pentecostal Theology".
27. www.jesushouse.org.uk. [Accessed 25 October 2010]
28. Ibid.
29. www.nehemiah-ucha.co.uk. [Accessed 25 October 2010]
30. Sturge, *Look What the Lord has Done!,* p109.
31. M. Ashimolowo, 2007. *Gun and Knife Crime to be Tackled by Church Leaders.* Press Release by Kingsway International Christian Centre. 4 June 2007. [Web]
32. J. Aldred, S. Hebden and K. Hebden, 2008. *Who is my Neighbour? A Church*

*Response to Social Disorder Linked to Gangs, Drugs, Guns and Knives.* London: Churches Together in England.

33 D. Finneron and A. Dinham, 2002. *Building on Faith: Faith Buildings in Neighbourhood Renewal.* London: Church Urban Fund.
34 Agbetu cited in Beckford, *Challenges of Black Pentecostal Leadership*, p7.
35 Beckford, *Challenges of Black Pentecostal Leadership*, p7.
36 Ibid., p8.
37 R. Putnam, 1995. "Bowling Alone: America's Declining Social Capital." *Journal of Democracy* 6 (1); R. Putnam, 2001. *Bowling Alone – The Collapse and Revival of American Community.* New York: Simon & Schuster; R. Putnam and L. Feldstein with D. Cohen, 2003. *Better Together: Restoring the American Community.* New York: Simon & Schuster.
38 World Bank. 1998. *The Initiative of Defining, Monitoring and Measuring Social Capital*, p8. [Web]
39 A. Gilchrist, 2004. *The Well-connected Community: A Networking Approach to Community Development.* Bristol: The Policy Press, p6.
40 M. Taylor, 2000. "Communities in the Lead: Power, Organisational Capacity and Social Capital." *Urban Studies*, 37, No. 5–7, p1027; cf. J. Lynch, P. Due, C. Muntaner and G. Davey Smith, 2000. "Social Capital – Is It a Good Investment Strategy for Public Health?" *Journal of Epidemiology and Community Health*, 54, pp404–408; cf. D. Halpern, 1999, *Social Capital: The New Golden Goose.* Faculty of Social and Political Sciences, Cambridge University, unpublished review; cf. A. Portes, 1998. "Social Capital: Its Origins and Applications in Modern Sociology." *Annual Review of Sociology*, 24.
41 R. Farnell, *et al.*, 2003. *Faith in Urban Regeneration? Engaging Faith Communities in Urban Regeneration.* Bristol: The Policy Press, p10.
42 Putnam, *Bowling Alone.*
43 Sturge, *Look What the Lord has Done!*, p110.
44 A. Craig, 2007. *Time for Churches.* [Web]
45 I. Madonko, 2007. *What Role do Churches Have in Newham?* [Web]
46 Craig, *Time for Churches.*
47 T. Omideyi, 2009. "Building and Sustaining a Multicultural Church." A paper presented at the African Consultative Leaders Forum held at the Redeemed Christian Church of God, Victory Parish, London. October 2009.
48 Ibid.
49 Farnell *et al., Faith in Urban Regeneration?.*
50 www.ljmgroup.org.uk. [Accessed 18 October 2010]
51 J. Muncie and B. Goldson (eds), 2004. *Youth Crime and Justice.* London: Sage Publications Ltd, p117.
52 F. Cullen and T. Agnew, 2004. *Criminological Theory: Past to Present: Essential Readings.* Los Angeles: Roxbury Park, p295.
53 P. Wintour and V. Dodd, 2007. "Tony Blair Blames Spate of Murders on Black Culture." The *Guardian.* 19 April 2007. [Web]
54 Y. Jewkes, 2004. *Media and Crime.* London: Sage, p41.
55 L. Isaac, 2007. Interview with Home Office Affairs Committee Report on Young Black People and the Criminal Justice Board, second session 2006–2007, chaired by John Denham. [Web]
56 REACH Report, 2007. [Web]

57 D. Cameron, 2007. Cited in V. Bone, *Questions Asked Over Teens Murders.* [Web]
58 M. Easton, 2007. *How Much is Family Life Changing?* [Web]
59 C. Batmanghelidjh, 2006. *Black Women Also Cause Splits.* [Web]
60 R. Burke, 2005. *An Introduction to Criminological Theory.* 2nd edn. Devon: Willan Publishing, p116.
61 *Keep the Faith* magazine, Issue 36, p22.
62 P. Valley, 2005. "Are Britain's Fringe Churches Preaching a Deadly Message?" The *Independent.* 18 July 2005.
63 Cited in I. Cobain and V. Dodd, 2005. "How Media Whipped up a Racist Witch-hunt." The *Guardian.* 25 June 2005. [Web]
64 Valley, "Are Britain's Fringe Churches Preaching a Deadly Message?".
65 Kirby cited in Valley, ibid.
66 Beckford cited in Valley, ibid.
67 Livingstone cited in Cobain and Dodd, "How Media Whipped up a Racist Witch-hunt."
68 Irukwu cited in Valley, "Are Britain's Fringe Churches Preaching a Deadly Message?".
69 N. Obunge, 2007. *In* Home Office Affairs Committee Report on Young Black People and the Criminal Justice Board, second session 2006–2007 chaired by John Denham, p26. [Web]
70 J. Aldred, 2008. *Challenges of Black Pentecostal Leadership in the 21st Century.* A paper presented at the first Oliver Lyseight Annual Lecture held at New Testament Church of God, Leadership Training Centre, Northampton.
71 Sturge, *Look What the Lord has Done!,* p67.
72 Aldred, *Challenges of Black Pentecostal Leadership.*
73 G. Brown, 2007. *Prime Minister to Work with Christian Leaders to Address Community Issues.* [Web]
74 Adebayo, *Mayor of London Has No Power.*
75 www.obv.org.uk. [Accessed 24 October 2010]
76 S. Kim, 2007. "Editorial." *International Journal of Public Theology* 1 (1).
77 M. King, 2008. "Letter from Birmingham Jail." *In* G. Fairchild and J. Robinson, "Unlearned Lessons from *Letter from Birmingham Jail*: The Work Begun, the Progress Made, and the Task Ahead." *Business and Society,* 47.
78 J. De Gruchy, 2007. "Public Theology as Christian Witness: Exploring the Genre." *International Journal of Public Theology* 1 (1), pp26–41.
79 L. Bretherton, 2005. "A New Establishment? Theological Politics and the Emerging Shape of Church-State Relations." *Political Theology,* 7.3.
80 Farnell *et al., Faith in Urban Regeneration?.*
81 Ibid.
82 Bretherton, "A New Establishment?".
83 Ibid.
84 R. Wuthnow, 2004. *Saving America? Faith Based Services and the Future of Civil Society.* Princeton: Princeton University Press.
85 Farnell *et al., Faith in Urban Regeneration?,* p6.
86 M. McLeod, D. Owen and C. Khamis, 2001. *Black and Minority Ethnic Voluntary and Community Organisations.* London: Polity Press, p80.
87 S. Côté and T. Healy, 2001. *The Well-being of Nations: The Role of Human and Social Capital.* Organisation for Economic Co-operation and Development.

Paris: OECD Publishing, p41; cf. S. Baron, J. Field and T. Schuller (eds), 2000. *Social Capital, Critical Perspectives.* Oxford: Oxford University Press.

[88] Aldred, *Respect*, p111.

[89] McLeod *et al., Black and Minority Ethnic Voluntary and Community Organisations*, p11.

[90] E. Husain, 2007. *The Islamist: Why I Joined Radical Islam in Britain: What I Saw Inside and Why I Left.* London: Penguin Books.

[91] R. Farnell, S. Lund, R. Furbey *et al.*, 1994. *Hope in the City? The Local Impact of the Church Urban Fund.* Sheffield: Centre for Regional Economic and Social Research, Sheffield Hallam University, pp34–37.

[92] P. Toynbee, 2001. "We Don't Need the Church to Educate our Children." The *Guardian.* 15 June 2001.

[93] A. Grayling, 2001. "The Third Way: The Last Word on Religious Schools." The *Guardian.* 24 February 2001; A. Grayling, 2001. "Keep God Out of Public Affairs." The *Observer.* 12 August 2001.

[94] Wunthnow, *Saving America?*.

[95] J. Annette, 2009. *Globalising Citizenship Education, Ambitions and Realities.* A paper presented at the fifth CITIZED International Conference held at Hong Kong Institute of Education. 24–26 June 2009; see also J. Roger, 2000. *From a Welfare State to a Welfare Society: The Changing Context of Social Policy in a Postmodern Era.* Basingstoke: Macmillan, pp117–118; N. Johnson, 1999, "The Personal Social Services and Community Care". *In* M. Powell (ed.), *New Labour, New Welfare State? The Third Way in British Social Policy.* Bristol: The Policy Press, p92; R. Levitas, 1998. *The Inclusive Society? Social Exclusion and New Labour.* Basingstoke: Palgrave Macmillan.

[96] Department of Environment, Transport and the Regions. 1997. *Involving Communities in Urban and Rural Regeneration: A Guide for Practitioners.* London: Department of Environment, Transport and the Regions, pp149–150; Department of Environment, Transport and the Regions. 2000. *Indices of Deprivation.* Regeneration Summary Research, Number 31. London: Department of Environment, Transport and the Regions, p1.

[97] T. Blair, 2001. *Faith in Politics.* Speech to the Christian Socialist Movement at Westminister Central Hall, London. [Web]

[98] www.communities.gov.uk. [Accessed 25 October 2010]

[99] Bretherton, "A New Establishment?".

[100] www.christiantoday.co.uk/article/government.appoints.faith.advisors/25040.htm

[101] Blair's religious values were reflective of the rebranding of the socialist values of the Labour Party in the 1990s. This is vividly illustrated by the Foreword to a collection of sermons and speeches by some senior Labour politicians and published by the Christian Socialist Movement. Blair proposed the reconsideration of the Labour Party's values, saying: "By rethinking and re-examining our values, and placing them alongside those of the Christian faith, we are able, politically, to rediscover the essence of our beliefs which lies not in policies or prescriptions made for one period of time, but in principles of living that are timeless. By doing so, we can better distinguish between values themselves and their application, the one constant and unchanged, the other changing constantly. To a Labour Party now undertaking a thorough and necessary

analysis of our future, this is helpful." For further reading see T. Blair, 1993, Foreword. *In* C. Bryant (ed.), *Reclaiming the Ground: Christianity and Socialism*, London: Spire, pp9–12.

102 Micklethwaite and Wooldridge, *God is Back*, p111.
103 Bretherton, "A New Establishment?".
104 Glen cited in Bretherton, ibid., p6.

## CHAPTER SIX: APPLYING THE LESSONS OF HISTORY

1 D. Muir, 2010. "Theology and the Black Church." *In* J. Aldred and K. Ogbo, *The Black Church in the 21st Century*. London: Darton Longman and Todd, p10.
2 Y. Channer, 1999. *I am a Promise: The School Achievement of British African Caribbeans*. Stoke-on-Trent: Trentham Books, pp34–35.
3 Harris, *Yoruba in Diaspora*.
4 V. Alexander, 1996. *Breaking Every Fetter? To What Extent Has the Black-led Church in Britain Developed a Theology of Liberation?* PhD dissertation. Warwick: University of Warwick, p219.
5 Cox, *Fire From Heaven*.
6 A. Ukah, 2008. *A New Paradigm of Pentecostal Power: A Study of the Redeemed Christian Church of God*. New Jersey: Africa World Press.
7 Kalu, "African Pentecostalism", p1.
8 C. Hill, 2009. "The Third Generation Hypothesis." A lecture delivered at the annual Academic Lecture of Christ Redeemers College/Redeemed Christian Church of God. London. 6 October 2009.
9 Harris, *Yoruba in Diaspora*, p224.
10 Mohabir, *Building Bridges*.
11 D. Muir, 2008. "An Obituary for the Wrong Subject: A Response to Alistair Kee's *The Rise and Demise of Black Theology*." *Pneuma*, 30; cf. Sturge, *Look What the Lord has Done!*.
12 Mohabir, *Building Bridges*, p67.
13 A. Adogame, 2010. *Reverse Missions: Europe – A Prodigal Continent?*, p1. [Web]
14 A. Ukah, 2005. "Mobilities, Migration and Multiplication: The Expansion of the Religious Field of the Redeemed Christian Church of God (RCCG), Nigeria." *In* Adogame and Weisskӧppel, *Religion in the Context of African Migration*, p338.
15 S. Adelaja, 2008. *Church Shift – Revolutionizing Your Faith, Church, and Life for the 21st Century*. Florida: Charisma House, pxxv.
16 Adogame, "Up, Up Jesus!", p317; cf. A. Dobrovolsky (ed.), 2007. *Olorunwa: There is God – Portrait of Sunday Adelaja*. Kyiv: Fares Publishing, pp180,181.
17 P. Jenkins, 2008. *God's Continent: Christianity, Islam, and Europe's Religious Crisis*. Oxford: Oxford University Press, p91.
18 Kalu, "The Third Response", p8.
19 M. Dempster, B. Klaus and D. Petersen (eds), 1999. *The Globalisation of Pentecostalism*. Irvine: Regnum Press, p127.
20 Ibid., p269.
21 Kalu, "The Third Response", p3.
22 Hanciles, *Beyond Christendom*; M. Ojo, 2007. "Reverse Mission". *In* Jonathan Bonk (ed.), *Encyclopaedia of Missions and Missionaries*. New York/London:

Routledge, p30; G. Ter Haar, 1998. *Halfway to Paradise: African Christians in Europe.* Cardiff: Cardiff Academic Press.
23. E. Adeboye, 2007. *We Can't Find a Place Large Enough.* [Web]
24. Asamoah-Gyadu, *African Charismatics.*
25. Anderson, *African Europeans*, p2.
26. Asamoah-Gyadu in Ter Haar, *Halfway to Paradise*, p4.
27. Muir, "An Obituary for the Wrong Subject", pp299–307.
28. Ibid.
29. A. Irukwu, 2009. "Pastoral Perspective of Second Generation Africans in Churches in Britain." A paper presented at the annual academic lecture of Christ Redeemers College/Redeemed Christian Church of God, held at Jesus House, 6 February 2009.
30. Bradley cited in D. Muir, 2009. *Changing Church – Changing Society.* [Web]
31. A. Ukah, 2009. "Reverse Mission or Asylum Christianity. A Nigerian Church in Europe." *In* T. Falola and A. Agwuele (eds), *Africans and Politics of Popular Cultures.* Rochester, NY: University of Rochester Press, pp104–132.
32. Ibid.
33. R. Burgess, 2010. *Reverse Mission, Symbolic Mapping and the Re-Occupation of Public Space: Nigerian Pentecostals in Britain.* A paper presented at GloPent Conference, Amsterdam. 19 February 2010.
34. Ukah, "Reverse Mission", pp104–132.
35. Beckford, *Jesus is Dread.*
36. Reddie and Jagessar, *Black Theology in Britain.*
37. Aldred, *Respect.*
38. Burgess, "Nigerian Pentecostal Theology", pp29–63; see also D. Forrester, 2000. *Truthful Action: Exploration in Practical Theology.* Edinburgh: T&T Clark, pp127–128; D. Tracy, 1981. *The Analogical Imagination: Christian Theology and the Culture of Pluralism.* London: SCM Press, p5.
39. Ukah, "Reverse Mission", p114.
40. M. Regele and M. Schulz, 1995. *The Death of the Church.* Grand Rapids: Zondervan, p23.
41. Ibid., p11.
42. A. Giddens, 2006. *Sociology.* 5th edn. Cambridge: Polity Press.
43. R. Habibis, *et al.*, 2005. *Sociology: Themes and Perspectives.* 5th edn. Glasgow: Collins Educational.
44. M. Moynagh, 2004. *Emergingchurch.intro.* Grand Rapids: Monarch Books, p214.
45. Ibid., p45.
46. Ukah, "Reverse Mission".
47. E. Gibbs and I. Coffey, 2001. *Church Next: Quantum Changes in Christian Ministry.* Downers Grove: InterVarsity Press.
48. Anderson, *African Europeans*, p11.
49. R. Greenleaf, 1977. *Servant Leadership: A Journey into the Nature of Legitimate Power and Greatness.* New York: Paulist Press, p63.
50. Ibid., p83.
51. M. Robinson and D. Smith, 2003. *Invading Secular Space: Strategies for Tomorrow's Church.* London: Monarch Books, p126.
52. B. McLaren, 2000. *The Church on the Other Side: Doing Ministry in the Postmodern Matrix.* Grand Rapids: Zondervan, p105.

## Notes

53 Gibbs and Coffey, *Church Next*, p74.
54 Sturge, *Look What the Lord has Done!*, p213.
55 Burgess, *Reverse Mission*.
56 Gibbs and Coffey, *Church Next*, p86.
57 R. Gerloff, 1992. "Theological Education in Black and White: The Centre for Black and White Christian Partnership." *In* J. Jongeneel and W. Hollenweger (eds), *Pentecost, Mission and Ecumenism: Essays on Intercultural Theology*. Frankfurt: Peter Lang, p47.
58 Klaus and Triplett, "National Leadership in Pentecostal Missions", pp225–241.
59 Anderson, "New African Initiated Pentecostalism", p206.
60 Ibid.
61 Hollenweger in Fee, *Gospel and Spirit*, p83.
62 S. McFague, 1987. *Models of God: Theology for an Ecological, Nuclear Age*. Philadelphia: Fortress, p6.
63 T. Hart, 1989. *Regarding Karl Barth: Essays Toward a Reading of his Theology*. Carlisle: Paternoster, p181.
64 A. Kee, 2008. *Reclaiming Liberation Theology: The Rise and Demise of Black Theology*. England: SCM Publishers, p168.
65 Ibid.
66 Muir, "Theology and the Black Church", p15.
67 Kee, *Reclaiming Liberation Theology*, p162.
68 Beckford, *Jesus is Dread*, pp145–146.
69 L. Campbell, 2002. "An Evaluation of Theological Methodology at Work Through a Critical Appraisal of *Jesus Dread: The Black Theology and Black Culture in Britain* by Robert Beckford." *In* unedited manuscript: D. Muir, 2009. *Theology and the Black Church*.
70 Edwards cited in Aldred and Ogbo, *The Black Church*.
71 Ibid.
72 Beckford, *Jesus is Dread*, p55.
73 Muir, "Theology and the Black Church", p10.
74 Ibid.
75 Beckford, *Jesus is Dread*, p125.
76 Reddie and Jagessar, *Black Theology in Britain*, p87.
77 Aldred, *Respect*, pp160–161.
78 M. Jagessar, 2007. "Review of *Understanding Caribbean British Christianity* by J. Aldred." *Black Theology: An International Journal*, 5.1, p128.
79 Reddie cited in Beresford, *African-Caribbean Pentecostal Church Leaders*, pp104,105.
80 Kee, *Reclaiming Liberation Theology*, p174.
81 Sturge, *Look What the Lord has Done!*, p205.
82 Ibid., p207.
83 Ibid.
84 Beresford, *African-Caribbean Pentecostal Church Leaders*.
85 D. Muir, 2009. *Black Majority Churches: Political and Civic Engagements*, p3. [Web]
86 M. Frost and A. Hirsch, 2003. *The Shaping of Things to Come*. Peabody: Hendrickson Publishers, p12.
87 Ibid.
88 Gibbs and Coffey, *Church Next*, p226.

89 D. Akhazemea, 2010. *Missional Implications of Growth of Black Majority Led Churches in London: A Critical Assessment.* MA dissertation. Cardiff: University of Wales.
90 Church of England, 2004. *Mission Shaped Church*, p81. [Web]
91 Wright, *The Radical Evangelical*, p81.
92 Akhazemea, *Missional Implications of Growth.*
93 Brandon in ibid., p114.
94 Osgood, *African Neo-Pentecostal Churches.*
95 T. Blair, 2002. *Private Action, Public Benefit.* Strategy Unit Report, September 2000, p6. [Web]
96 Brandon in Akhazemea, *Missional Implications of Growth*, p69.
97 Ibid.
98 Adedibu, *Storytelling.*

## CHAPTER SEVEN: CONCLUSION

1 Jenkins, *God's Continent*, p91.
2 Beckford, *Challenges of Black Pentecostal Leadership.*
3 Anderson, *An Introduction to Pentecostalism*, p44.
4 J. Creech, 1996. "Visions of Glory: The Place of the Azusa Street Revival in Pentecostal History." *Church History*, 65, pp405–424.
5 Anderson, *An Introduction to Pentecostalism.*
6 D. Cartwright, 2009. Email correspondence with Desmond Cartwright on origin of Black Pentecostal Churches in Britain.
7 Nongsiej, cited in Anderson, *An Introduction to Pentecostalism.*
8 Burgess *et al., Dictionary of Pentecostal and Charismatic Movements*, pp645–648.
9 Anderson, *An Introduction to Pentecostalism.*
10 Cerrillo cited in Anderson, *An Introduction to Pentecostalism*, pp43–44.
11 W. Saayman, 1993. "Some Reflections on the Development of the Pentecostal Mission Model in South Africa." *Missionalia*, 21.1, p22.
12 A. Adogame, R. Gerloff and K. Hock, 2009. *Christianity in Africa and the African Diaspora.* London: Continuum, p209.
13 D. Killingray, 2010. "Brem-Wilson: The Hidden Life of the First Pentecostal Pastor in Modern Britain." A lecture delivered in February 2010 at School of Oriental and African Studies (SOAS), London.
14 Anderson, *An Introduction to Pentecostalism*, p44.
15 Mohabir, *Building Bridges.*
16 H. Ebaugh and J. Chafetz, 2000. *Religion and the New Immigrants: Continuities and Adaptations in Immigrant Congregations.* Walnut Creek: Altamira Press; Y. Haddad, J. Smith and J. Esposito (eds), 2003. *Religion and Immigration: Christian, Jewish, and Muslim Experiences in the United States.* Walnut Creek, CA: Altamira Press; M Vasquez and M. Marquardt, 2003. *Globalizing the Sacred: Religion Across the Americas.* New Brunswick: Rutgers University Press; Harris, *Yoruba in Diaspora*; Ukah, "Mobilities, Migration and Multiplication"; P. Kalilombe, 1997. "Black Christianity in Britain." *Ethnic and Racial Studies*, 20/2, pp305–308.
17 Ter Haar, *Halfway to Paradise*, p3.

18 R. Burgess, K. Knibbe and A. Quaas, 2010. "Nigerian-initiated Pentecostal Churches as a Social Force in Europe: The Case of the Redeemed Christian Church of God." *PentecoStudies* 9:1. [Web]; Adogame, Gerloff and Hock, *Christianity in Africa*; Ukah, "Reverse Mission"; R. Marshall, 2009. *Political Spiritualities: The Pentecostal Revolution in Nigeria*. Chicago: The University of Chicago Press; Burgess, "Nigerian Pentecostal Theology"; Ukah, A *New Paradigm*.
19 Jenkins, *The Next Christendom*, p99; see also C. Währisch-Oblau, 2000. "From Reverse Mission to Common Mission ... We Hope: Immigrant Protestant Churches and the 'Programme for Cooperation between German and Immigrant Congregations' of the United Evangelical Mission." *International Review of Mission*, 89 (354); C. Währisch-Oblau, 2009. *The Missionary Self-Perception of Pentecostal/Charismatic Church Leaders from the Global South in Europe: Bringing Back the Gospel*. Global Pentecostal and Charismatic Studies 2. Leiden: Brill.
20 P. Zeleza, 2002. "Contemporary African Migrations in a Global Context." *African Issues*, 30/1, p9.
21 MacRobert, "The New Black-led Churches in Britain", p127.
22 Adogame and Weissköppel, *Religion in the Context of African Migration*, p5.
23 Burgess, Knibbe and Quaas, "Nigerian-initiated Pentecostal Churches", pp107–108.
24 A. Walls, 2002. "Mission and Migration: The Diaspora Factor in Christian History." *Journal of African Christian Thought*, Vol. 5/2 (December), p10.
25 Church of Scotland Church and Nations Committee, 2005. *Refugees and Migration. Reports to the Church of Scotland General Assembly 2005*. Edinburgh: Church of Scotland Board of Practice and Procedure.
26 A. Adogame, 2003. "Betwixt Identity and Security: African New Religious Movements and the Politics of Religious Networking in Europe." *Nova Religio: The Journal of Alternative and Emergent Religions*, 7.2; A. Adogame, 2004. "Engaging the Rhetoric of Spiritual Warfare: The Public Face of Aladura in Diaspora." *Journal of Religion in Africa*, 34/4; Haddad, Smith and Esposito, *Religion and Immigration*.
27 Walls, "Mission and Migration", p10.
28 Ukah, "Reverse Mission", p121.
29 Miller and Yamamori, *Global Pentecostalism*, p23.
30 Ebaugh and Chafetz, *Religion and the New Immigrants*, p456.
31 Burgess, Knibbe and Quaas, "Nigerian-initiated Pentecostal Churches".
32 Ukah, "Reverse Mission", p121.
33 A. Droogers, 2001. "Globalisation and Pentecostal Success." *In* A. Corten and R. Marshall-Fratani (eds), *Between Babel and Pentecost: Transnational Pentecostalism in Africa and Latin America*. Indianapolis: Indiana University Press, pp41–46.
34 Asamoah-Gyadu cited in Ter Haar, *Halfway to Paradise*, p1.
35 Anderson, *Vision of the Disinherited*, p69; cf. Anderson, *An Introduction to Pentecostalism*.
36 Nelson cited in Anderson, *An Introduction to Pentecostalism*, p43; cf. Hollenweger, *Pentecostalism*, p23.
37 Harris in Adogame, Gerloff and Hock, *Christianity in Africa*, p224.

38. Cox, *Fire From Heaven*, p63.
39. Kalu, *African Pentecostalism*, pp266–267.
40. P. Gifford, 1998. "Some Recent Developments in African Christianity." *African Affairs*, 21, p333.
41. Kalu, *African Pentecostalism*, pp266–267.
42. Beckford, *Jesus is Dread*.
43. E. Adeboye, 2010. "Head Under Siege?" *Open Heavens: A Daily Guide to Close Fellowship with God*. Vol. 10. London: First Call, p147.
44. G. Ter Haar, 2009. *How God Became African: African Spirituality and Western Secular Thought*. Philadelphia: University of Pennsylvania, p36.
45. Ibid.
46. Beresford, *African-Caribbean Pentecostal Church Leaders*.
47. Miller and Yamamori, *Global Pentecostalism*.
48. Osgood, *African Neo-Pentecostal Churches*.
49. I. Smith and T. Holden, 1983. *Dialogue Between Black and White Christians: Two Papers*. London: Zebra Project.
50. Parsons, *The Growth of Religious Diversity*, p258.
51. Aldred, *Respect*, p4.
52. Osgood, *African Neo-Pentecostal Churches*.
53. Ibid., p237.
54. Beckford, *Challenges of Black Pentecostal Leadership*.
55. Saayman cited in Anderson, *An Introduction to Pentecostalism*, p208.
56. Brandon in Akhazemea, *Missional Implications of Growth*, p117.
57. Ibid.
58. C. Clark, 2010. "Old Wine and New Wine Skins: West Indian and the New West African Pentecostal Churches in Britain and the Challenge of Renewal." *Journal of Pentecostal Theology*, Vol. 19, No. 1.
59. Mudimbe cited in Marshall, *Political Spiritualities*, p54.
60. Brandon in Akhazemea, *Missional Implications of Growth*, p114.

# Bibliography

Adebayo, O. 2007. *Mayor of London Has No Power to Help Black Churches Convert Redundant Buildings.* [Web] http://www.inspiremagazine.org.uk/news.aspx?action=view&id=1263 [Date of access: 27 May 2009]

Adeboye, E. 2007. *We Can't Find a Place Large Enough.* [Web] http://www.e-n.org.uk/p-3713–'We-can't-find-a-place-large-enough'.htm [Date of access: 23 February 2010]

────── 2009. Speech at the Opening Ceremony of the Administrative Office of the Redeemed Christian Church of God, Central Office, Knebworth, Hertfordshire, UK, 16 November 2009.

────── 2010. "Head Under Siege?" *Open Heavens: A Daily Guide to Close Fellowship with God.* Vol. 10. London: First Call.

Adeboye, O. 2005. "Transnational Pentecostalism in Africa: The Redeemed Christian Church of God, Nigeria." *In* Fourchard, L., Mary, A. and Otayek, R. (eds), *Enterprises religieuses transnationales en Afrique de l'Ouest.* Paris: Karthala. pp438–465.

Adedeji, S. 2004. *Church Cash Charity Mismanaged.* [Web] http://news.bbc.co.uk/1/hi/england/northamptonshire/3635230.stmhttp://news.bbc.co.uk/1/hi/england/northamptonshire/3635230.stm [Date of access: 25 February 2009]

Adedeji, Y. 2004. *Preacher Declines to Give Evidence.* [Web] http://news.bbc.co.uk/1/hi/england/northamptonshire/2994496.stm [Date of access: 23 February 2009]

Adedibu, B. 2007. *Impact of Postmodernity on Second Generation Nigerians in Churches in South East of London.* MA dissertation. Cardiff: University of Wales.

────── 2009. *Storytelling: An Effective Communication Appeal in Preaching.* London: Wisdom Summit.

Adedoyin, A. 2009. "RCCG Churches Leading Role in Fighting Poverty in London." *In Festival News.* Official Publication of the London Festival of Life. London: Festival of Life.

Adelaja, S. 2008. *Church Shift – Revolutionizing Your Faith, Church, and Life for the 21st Century.* Florida: Charisma House.

Adeleke, A. 2009. Interview held in May 2009 at RCCG House of Praise, Charlton, London. (Interviewer Babatunde Adedibu: audio recording.)

Adogame, A. 2000. "'*Aiye loja, orun nile*': The Appropriation of Ritual Space-time in the Cosmology of the Celestial Church of Christ." *Journal of Religion in Africa*, 30.1: 3–29.

────── 2003. "Betwixt Identity and Security: African New Religious Movements and the Politics of Religious Networking in Europe." *Nova Religio: The Journal of Alternative and Emergent Religions*, 7.2: 24–41.

────── 2004a. "Contesting the Ambivalences of Modernity in a Global Context: The Redeemed Christian Church of God, North America." *Studies in World Christianity*, 10/1: 25–48.

—— 2004b. "Engaging the Rhetoric of Spiritual Warfare: The Public Face of Aladura in Diaspora." *Journal of Religion in Africa*, 34/4: 493–522.

—— 2005. *Dealing with Local Satanic Technology: Deliverance Rhetoric in the Mountain of Fire and Miracles Ministry*. Paper presented at the CESNUR international conference on "Religious Movements, Globalization and Conflict: Transnational Perspectives", Palermo, Sicily.

—— 2007. *The Rhetoric of Reverse Mission: African Christianity and the Changing Dynamics of Religious Expansion in Europe*. Outline of lecture presented at the conference "South Moving North: Revised Mission and its Implications", Protestant Landelijk Dienstencentrum, Utrecht.

—— 2008. "Up, Up Jesus! Down, Down Satan! African Religiosity in the Former Soviet Bloc – the Embassy of the Blessed Kingdom of God for all Nations." *Exchange Journal of Missiological and Ecumenical Research*, Vol. 37.

—— 2009. *Transnational Migration and Pentecostalism in Europe*. Paper delivered at European Research Network on Global Pentecostalism Conference at the University of Birmingham.

—— 2010. *Reverse Missions: Europe – A Prodigal Continent?*. [Web] http://www.edinburgh2010.org/fileadmin/files/edinburgh2010/files/News/Afe_Reverse%20mission_edited.pdf [Date of access: 24 April 2010]

Adogame, A. and Weissköppel, C. 2005a. "Introduction." *In* Adogame, A. and Weissköppel, C. (eds), *Religion in the Context of African Migration*. Bayreuth African Studies Series, No. 75. Bayreuth: Breitinger.

—— (eds) 2005b. *Religion in the Context of African Migration*. Bayreuth African Studies Series, No. 75. Bayreuth: Breitinger.

Adogame, A. Gerloff, R. and Hock, K. 2009. *Christianity in Africa and the African Diaspora*. London: Continuum.

Afolabi, M. 2009. *Redeemed Christian Church of God, Church Planting: A Case Study of Growth of Black Majority Church in United Kingdom* (Unpublished). Archives of RCCG, Central Office, Knebworth.

Akhazemea, D. 2010. *Missional Implications of Growth of Black Majority Led Churches in London: A Critical Assessment*. MA dissertation. Cardiff: University of Wales.

Akinola, P. 2004. *Why I Object to Homosexuality and Same-sex Unions*. [Web] http://www.anglican-nig.org/Pri_obj_Homo.htm [Date of access: 20 October 2009]

Akoko, M. 2002. "New Pentecostalism in the Wake of the Economic Crisis in Cameroon." *Nordic Journal of African Studies*, 11 (3): 359–376.

Aldred, J. 1995. *A Black Majority Church's Future*. M.Min dissertation. Sheffield: University of Sheffield.

—— 1999, *A Black Majority Church*. MA dissertation. Sheffield: University of Sheffield.

—— (ed.) 2000. *Sisters with Power*. London: Continuum.

—— 2002. "The Development of BMCs. Presentation given as part of the CTBI consultation with BMCs." *In* Sturge, M. 2005. *Look What the Lord has Done! An Exploration of Black Christian Faith in Britain*. Bletchley: Scripture Union.

—— 2006. *Respect: Understanding Caribbean British Christianity*. Peterborough: Epworth.

—— 2007a. *The Experience of Black Churches in the United Kingdom. Change and Diversity – Impact of Migration in Church and Society*. EEA3. Conference Forum-Migration. Sibiu, Romania. 4–9 September 2007.

—— 2007b. *Black Churches Contributing to Cohesion or Polarising Christians and Other Faith Groups*. [Web] www.joealdred.com/?q=node/30 [Date of access: 23 April 2008]

—— 2008a. *Challenges of Black Pentecostal Leadership in the 21st Century.* A paper presented at the first Oliver Lyseight Annual Lecture held at New Testament Church of God, Leadership Training Centre, Northampton.
—— 2008b. Personal interview held at Birmingham in October 2008.
—— 2009. Personal correspondence with author.
—— 2010. Personal correspondence on Black Majority Churches' representation at Ecumenical Initiatives.
Aldred, J., Hebden, S. and Hebden, K. 2008. *Who is my Neighbour? A Church Response to Social Disorder Linked to Gangs, Drugs, Guns and Knives.* London: Churches Together in England.
Aldred, J. and Ogbo, K. (eds) 2010. *The Black Church in the 21st Century.* London: Darton Longman and Todd.
Alexander, V. 1996. *Breaking Every Fetter? To What Extent Has the Black-led Church in Britain Developed a Theology of Liberation?* PhD dissertation. Warwick: University of Warwick.
Anderson, A. 1987. "Prosperity Message in the Eschatology of Some New Charismatic Churches." *Missionalia,* 15.2: 72–83.
—— 1992. *Bazalwane: African Pentecostals in South Africa.* Pretoria: Unisa Press.
—— 2004a. "Pentecostal-Charismatic Spirituality and Theological Education." *PentecoStudies,* Vol, 3. No. 1. [Web] www.globpent.net/pentecostudies .ISSN1871769 [Date of access: 24 June 2009]
—— 2004b. *An Introduction to Pentecostalism: Global Charismatic Christianity.* Cambridge: Cambridge University Press.
—— 2005. "New African Initiated Pentecostalism and Charismatics in South Africa." *Journal of Religion in Africa,* 35.1: 66–92.
—— 2009. *African Europeans in Global Pentecostalism.* A paper presented at the annual academic lecture of Christ Redeemer Christian College and Redeemed Christian Church of God held at Jesus House, London. 6 October 2009.
Anderson, R. 1979. *Vision of the Disinherited: The Making of American Pentecostalism.* Peabody: Hendrickson.
Ankerberg, J. and Weldon, J. 1991. *Cult Watch.* Eugene, OR: Harvest House.
Annette, J. 2009. *Globalising Citizenship Education, Ambitions and Realities.* A paper presented at the fifth CITIZED International Conference held at Hong Kong Institute of Education. 24–26 June 2009.
Ariarajah, W. 2000. "Changing Frontiers of Ecumenical Theology: A Challenge to Ecumenical Formation." *Ministerial Formation,* 89 (April 2000): 10.
Arnold, S. 1992. *From Scepticism to Hope: One Black-led Church's Response to Social Responsibility.* Nottingham: Grove Books.
Asamoah-Gyadu, J.K. 2004. *African Charismatics: Current Developments Within Indigenous Pentecostalism in Ghana.* Studies of Religion in Africa: 27. Leiden: Brill.
—— 2009. *Spirit, Mission and Transnational Influence: Nigerian-led Pentecostalism in Eastern Europe.* A paper presented at the 2009 GloPent Conference, University of Birmingham, UK. 6–7 February 2009. [Available online: doi:10.1558/ptcs.v9i1.74 *Penteco Studies* (online) ISSN 1871-7691]
*Ashburton Guardian,* 1920, Volume XLI, Issue 9371, 19 November 1920: 4 [Web] http://www.paperspast.natlib.govt.nz/cgi-bin/paperspast?a=d&d =AG19201119.2.13 [Date of access: 21 January 2010]
Ashimolowo, M. 2000. *101 Answers to Money Problems.* Vols 1–4. London: Matthew Ashimolowo Media Ministries.

—— 2003. *The 10Ms of Money*. London: Mattyson Media.
—— 2006. *The Coming Wealth Transfer*. London: Matthew Ashimolowo Media Ministries.
—— 2007. *Gun and Knife Crime to be Tackled by Church Leaders*. Press Release by Kingsway International Christian Centre. 4 June 2007. [Web] www.kicc.org.uk /.../070523-sk-ministers%20together%20-%204th%20June%20press%20release%20FINAL.pdf [Date of access: 16 May 2009]
Ashworth, J. and Farthing, I. 2007. *Churchgoing: A Research Report on Church Attendance in UK*. [Web] http://www.tearfund.org/webdocs/Website/News/TAM%20Final%20Version%208.5.07.pdf [Date of access: 16 October 2008]
Ayegboyin, D. 2006. "A Rethinking on Prosperity Teaching in the New Pentecostal Churches in Nigeria." *Black Theology*, Vol. 4, No. 1: 70–86.
Badham, P. (ed.) 1989. *Religion, State and Society in Modern Britain*. Lampeter: The Edwin Mellen Press.
Baehr, T., Wales, S. and Wales, K. 2007. *The Amazing Grace of Freedom: The Inspiring Faith of William Wilberforce, the Slaves' Champion*. Green Forest, AR: New Leaf Press.
Bailey, C. 1991. "Beyond Identification: The Use of Africans in Old Testament Poetry and Narratives." *In* Felder, Cain Hope (ed.), *Stony the Road We Trod: African American Biblical Interpretation*. Minneapolis: Fortress Press. pp165–166.
Balogun, Tunde, 2009. Private discussion at Jesus House, London. 6 October 2009.
Banton, M. 1955. *The Coloured Quarter: Negro Immigrants in an English City*. London: Jonathan Cape.
Banton, M. 1959. *White and Coloured: The Behaviour of British People Towards Coloured People*. London: Jonathan Cape.
Barna, G. 1990. *Marketing the Church*. Colorado Springs: Navpress.
Baron, S., Field, J. and Schuller, T. (eds) 2000. *Social Capital, Critical Perspectives*. Oxford: Oxford University Press.
Barratt, T. 1927. *When the Fire Fell: An Outline of My Life*. Oslo: Alfons Hansen & Sonner.
Barrett, D. and Johnson, T. 2003. "Annual Statistical Table on Global Missions: 2003." *International Bulletin of Missionary Research*, 27 (1): 25.
Barth, K. 1936. *Church Dogmatics* 1/1, Edinburgh: T&T Clark.
Batmanghelidjh, C. 2006. *Black Women Also Cause Splits*. [Web] http://news.bbc.co.uk/1/hi/6080096.stm [Date of access: 26 August 2009]
Beasley-Murray, G.R. 1994. *Baptism in the New Testament*. Grand Rapids: Eerdmans Publishing Company.
Beckford, R. 1998. *Jesus is Dread: Black Theology and Black Culture in Britain*. London: Darton, Longman and Todd.
—— 2000. *Dread and Pentecostal: Political Theology for Black Churches in Britain*. London: SPCK.
—— 2001. "Theology in the Age of Crack: Crack Age, Prosperity Doctrine and Being There." *Black Theology in Britain*, 4 (1): 9–24.
—— 2006. *Jesus Dub: Theology, Music and Social Change*. London: Routledge.
—— 2007. "Liberation Theological Praxis (LTP)." *In* Jagessar, M and Reddie, A. (eds), *Black Theology in Britain*. London. Equinox. pp89–90.
—— 2009. *Challenges of Black Pentecostal Leadership in the 21st Century From Mission to Maintenance: Resisting the Bewitchment of Colonial Christianity*. A paper presented at the Oliver Lyseight Annual Lecture organized by the Education Department of the New Testament Church of God, Northampton. March 2009. [Web] www.ntcg.org.uk/education/2009annuallecture-beckford.stm [Date of access: 6 May 2009]

Beecher, V. 1995. *Black Church Traditions in Britain.* Centre for Black and White Christian Partnership and West Hill RE Centre. *In* Sturge, M. 2005. *Look What The Lord Has Done! An Exploration of Black Christian Faith in Britain.* UK: Scripture Union.

Belmonte, K. 2007. *William Wilberforce: A Hero for Humanity.* Grand Rapids: Zondervan.

Beresford, L. 2008. *African-Caribbean Pentecostal Church Leaders and Socio-political Engagement in Contemporary Britain.* PhD dissertation. Birmingham: University of Birmingham.

Bernard, David K. 1991. *Oneness and Trinity A.D. 100–300: The Doctrine of God in Ancient Christian Writings.* Hazelwood, MO: Word Aflame Press.

*Black Majority Churches Directory,* 2008 [Web] http://www.bmcdirectory.co.uk/ [Date of access: 4 April 2009]

Blair, T. 1993. Foreword. *In* Bryan, C. (ed.), *Reclaiming the Ground: Christianity and Socialism,* London: Spire.

—— *Faith in Politics.* Speech to the Christian Socialist Movement at Westminster Central Hall, London. [Web] www.britishblogs.co.uk/categories/christian-socialist-movement/ [Date of access: 6 October 2009]

—— 2002. *Private Action, Public Benefit.* Strategy Unit Report, September 2000 [Web] www.cabinetoffice.gov.uk/media/cabinetoffice/.../strat%20data.pdf [Date of access: 28 January 2010]

Birch, B. 1991. *Let Justice Roll Down: Old Testament, Ethics and Christian Life.* Louisville: Westminster/John Knox.

Bonk, J. 2007. *Routledge Encyclopaedia of Missions and Missionaries.* London: Routledge.

Booth, T. 1984. *We True Christians.* PhD dissertation. Birmingham: University of Birmingham.

Bowman, R. 1985. "Oneness Pentecostalism and the Trinity: A Biblical Critique." *Forward* 8 (Fall 1985): 22–27.

Boyd, Paul C. 1991. *The African Origin of Christianity, A Biblical and Historic Account.* Vol. 1. London: Karia Press.

Brandon, A. 2009. "Comments on BMC." *In* Akhazemea, D. 2010. *Missional Implications of Growth of Black Majority-Led Churches in London: A Critical Assessment.* MA dissertation. Cardiff: University of Wales. pp110–115.

Brem-Wilson, T. "The Palm." *In* Williams, D. (ed.), *Riches of Grace.* Penygroes: Apostolic Church Great Britain. pp27–29.

Bretherton, L. 2005. "A New Establishment? Theological Politics and the Emerging Shape of Church-State Relations." *Political Theology,* 7.3: 371–392.

Brierley, P. 1984. *Christians in England.* London: MARC Europe.

—— (ed.) 2005. *UK Christian Handbook: Religious Trends Vol. 5.* Worcester: Christian Research.

—— (ed.) 2006. *Religious Trends in the UK.* Worcester: Christian Research.

—— 2009. Report of interview in Mackay, M. 2009. *Strategic Planning Essential to Church's Future.* [Web] www.christiantoday.com/article/strategic.planning.essential.to.churchs.future/23490.htm [Date of access: 4 January 2010]

Brooks, I. 1983. *Where Do We Go From Here?* London: Brooks.

Brown, G. 2007. *Prime Minister to Work with Christian Leaders to Address Community Issues.* [Web] http://www.eauk.org/media/bclf.cfm [Date of access: 18 May 2009]

Bruce, S. 1993. "Religion and Rational Choice: A Critique of Economic Explanations of Religious Behaviour." *Sociology of Religion,* 54 (2): 193–205.

—— 2002. *God is Dead: Secularisation in the West.* Oxford: Blackwell.

Brumback, C. 1977. *Like a River,* USA: Gospel Publishing House.

Brusco, E. 1995. *The Reformation of Machismo: Evangelical Conversion in Columbia.*

Austin: University of Texas Press.
Bueno, R. 1999. "Listening to the Margins: Re-Historicizing Pentecostal Experiences and Identities." *In* Dempster, M., Klaus, B. and Petersen, D. (eds), *The Globalisation of Pentecostalism*. Irvine: Regnum Press.
Burgess, R. 2008. "Nigerian Pentecostal Theology in Global Perspective." *PentecoStudies*, Vol. 7, No. 2: 29–63.
—— 2009a. *The Challenges of Second Generation Africans in Churches in Britain*. A paper presented at the Annual Academic Lecture of Redeemed Christian Church of God United Kingdom, Christ Redeemer College, London. 6 October 2009.
—— 2009b. "African Pentecostal Spirituality and Civic Engagement: The Case of the Redeemed Christian Church of God in Britain." *Journal of Beliefs & Values*, 3 (December): 255–273.
—— 2009c. *Transnational Religious Networks and Social Transformation in Britain*. GloPent Conference, University of Birmingham. 6–7 February 2009.
—— 2010a. *Reverse Mission, Symbolic Mapping and the Re-Occupation of Public Space: Nigerian Pentecostals in Britain*. A paper presented at GloPent Conference, Amsterdam. 19 February 2010.
—— 2010b. Personal correspondence on the future of BMCs in Britain. March 2010.
Burgess, R., Knibbe, K. and Quaas, A. 2010. "Nigerian-initiated Pentecostal Churches as a Social Force in Europe: The Case of the Redeemed Christian Church of God." *PentecoStudies* 9:1. [Web] http://www.equinoxjournals.com/PENT/article/view/7221/pdf [Date of access: 15 April 2010]
Burgess, S., McGee, G. and Alexander, P. (eds) 1998. *Dictionary of Pentecostal and Charismatic Movements*. Grand Rapids: Zondervan.
Burke, R. 2005. *An Introduction to Criminological Theory*. 2nd edn. Devon: Willan Publishing.
Calley, M. 1965. *God's People: West Indian Pentecostal Sects in England*. London: Oxford University Press.
Cameron, D. 2007. Cited in Bone, V. *Questions Asked Over Teens Murders*. [Web] http://news.bbc.co.uk/1/hi/uk/6464853.stm [Date of access: 17 August 2008]
Campbell, L. 2002. "An Evaluation of Theological Methodology at Work Through a Critical Appraisal of *Jesus Dread: The Black Theology and Black Culture in Britain* by Robert Beckford." *In* unedited manuscript: Muir, D. 2009. *Theology and the Black Church*.
Cantle, T. 2001. *Community Cohesion: A Report of the Independent Review Team*. London: HMSO. [Web] http://image.guardian.co.uk/sysfiles/Guardian/documents/2001/12/11/communitycohesionreport.pdf [Date of access: 25 January 2010]
Carey, B. 2003. "*The Extraordinary Negro*": *Ignatius Sancho, Joseph Jekyll, and the Problem of Biography*. [Web] http://www.brycchancarey.com/Carey_BJECS_2003.pdf [Date of access: 16 October 2008]
Cargal, T. 1993. "Beyond the Fundamentalist-Modernist Controversy: Pentecostals and Hermeneutics in a Postmodern Age." *Pnuema*, 15, No. 2: 203–215.
Carnes, T. and Yang, F. (eds) 2004. *Asian American Religions: The Making and Remaking of Borders and Boundaries*. New York: New York University Press.
Carretta, V. (ed.) 1996. *Unchained Voices: An Anthology of Black Authors in the English-Speaking World of the Eighteenth Century*. Lexington: The University Press of Kentucky.
Cartledge, M. 1996. "Empirical Theology: Towards an Evangelical-Charismatic Hermeneutic." *Journal of Pentecostal Theology*, 9: 115–126.
Cartwright, D. 1981. *From The Backstreets to the Royal Albert Hall: British Pentecostalism*

*1907–1928*. Unpublished paper delivered at the First European Pentecostal Theological Association Conference, Leuven. 28–29 December. [Web] www.smithwigglesworth.com/pensketches/brixton.htm [Date of access: 10 February 2009]
—— 2007. "Black Pentecostal Churches in Britain." *Journal of the European Pentecostal Theological Association.* Vol. 23, No. 2: 128–137.
—— 2008. Email correspondence with Desmond Cartwright on Welsh Revival.
—— 2009. Email correspondence with Desmond Cartwright on origin of Black Pentecostal Churches in Britain.
—— 2010. Personal correspondence with Desmond Cartwright on origin of Black Pentecostal Churches in Britain.
Casciani, D. 2006. *Witchcraft and the "Missing" Report.* BBC News report. 22 May 2006. [Web] http://news.bbc.co.uk/1/hi/magazine/5002054.stm [Date of access: 3 January 2010]
Chadwick, W. 2001. *Stealing the Sheep: The Church's Hidden Problems with Transfer Growth.* Downers Grove: InterVarsity Press.
Chaney, C. and Lewis, R. 1997. *Design for Church Growth.* Nashville: Broadman Press.
Channer, Y. 1999. *I am a Promise: The School Achievement of British African Caribbeans.* Stoke-on-Trent: Trentham Books.
Chanter, H. (ed.) 1924a. "From the Midland." *In The Apostolic Church Missionary Herald.* April 1924. Vol. 1, No. 5. Bradford: Apostolic Church International Missionary Council.
—— (ed.) 1924b. "A Word from the Midland Headquarters." *The Apostolic Church Missionary Herald.* November 1924. Vol. 1, No. 6. Bradford: Apostolic Church International Missionary Council. pp183–185.
Charity Commission of England and Wales. 2008. *Public Benefit Guidance Information* [Web] www.charity-commission.gov.uk [Date of access: 17 March 2009]
Charlton, L. 1923. "Letters from the Great City." *In* William, D. (ed.), *Riches of Grace.* Vol. 11. No. 5. December 1923. Penygroes: Apostolic Church International Missionary Council. pp13–14.
Charman, P. 1979. *Reflections: Black and White Christians in the City.* London: Zebra Project.
Chike, C. 2007. *African Christianity in Britain: Diaspora, Doctrine and Dialogue.* Milton Keynes: Author House.
Church of England. 2004. *Mission Shaped Church.* [Web] www.cofe.anglican.org/info/papers/mission_shaped_church.pdf [Date of access: 27 January 2010]
Church of Scotland Church and Nation Committee. 2005. *Refugees and Migration. Reports to the Church of Scotland General Assembly 2005.* Edinburgh: Church of Scotland Board of Practice and Procedure.
Clark, C. 2010. "Old Wine and New Wine Skins: West Indian and the New West African Pentecostal Churches in Britain and the Challenge of Renewal." *Journal of Pentecostal Theology,* Vol. 19, No. 1: 143–154.
Clark, M., Larderle, H. *et al.* 1989. *What is Distinctive About Pentecostal Theology?* Pretoria: University of South Africa.
Cobain, I. and Dodd, V. 2005. "How Media Whipped up a Racist Witch-hunt." *The Guardian.* 25 June 2005 [Web] http://www.guardian.co.uk/uk/2005/jun/25/children.pressandpublishing [Date of access: 3 January 2009]
Coleman, K. 2006. *Exploring Métissage: A Theological Anthropology of Black Christian Women's Subjectivities in Postcolonial Britain.* PhD dissertation. Birmingham: University of Birmingham.

Coleman, S. 1993. "Conservative Protestantism and the World Order: The Faith Movement in the United States and Sweden." *Sociology of Religion*, 54 (4): 353–373.
—— 2000. *The Globalisation of Charismatic Christianity: Spreading the Gospel of Prosperity.* Cambridge: Cambridge University Press.
Comaroff, J. and Comaroff, John L. 1999. "Occult Economies and the Violence of Abstraction: Notes from the South African Postcolony." *American Ethnologist*, 26.3: 279–301.
—— 2000. "Millennial Capitalism: First Thoughts on a Second Coming." *Public Culture*, 12.2: 291–343.
Cone, J. 2003. "Black Spirituals: A Theological Interpretation." *In* Cornel, W. and Eddie, S. (eds), *African American Religious Thought: An Anthology.* Louisville, Kentucky: Westminster John Knox Publisher.
Cone, J.H. and Wilmore, G. (eds) 1979. *Black Theology: A Documentary History. 1966–1979.* Maryknoll: Orbis Books.
Conn, C.W. 1959. *Where the Saints Have Trod: A History of Church of God Missions.* Cleveland: Pathway Press.
Copeland, K. 1974. *The Laws of Prosperity.* Fort Worth: Manna Christian Outreach.
—— 1987. *Our Covenant with God.* Fort Worth: Kenneth Copeland Publications.
Corten, A. and Marshall-Fratani, R. (eds) 2001. *Between Babel and Pentecost: Transnational Pentecostalism in Africa and Latin America.* Indianapolis: Indiana University Press.
Côté, S. and Healy, T. 2001. *The Well-being of Nations: The Role of Human and Social Capital.* Organisation for Economic Co-operation and Development. Paris: OECD Publishing.
Cox, H. 1995. *Fire From Heaven: The Rise of Pentecostal Spirituality and the Reshaping of Religion in the Twenty-first Century.* Mowbray: Continuum International Publishing Group.
Craig, A. 2007. *Time for Churches.* [Web] http://www.transformnewham.com/Articles/74104/Homepage/Newham_Life/Newham_News/Time_for_churches.aspx [Date of access: 20 July 2009]
Creech, J. 1996. "Visions of Glory: The Place of the Azusa Street Revival in Pentecostal History." *Church History*, 65: 405–424.
Crews, M. 1990. *The Church of God: A Social History.* Tennessee: University of Tennessee Press.
Cucchiari, S. 1990. "Between Shame and Sanctification: Patriarchy and its Transformation in Sicilian Pentecostalism." *American Ethnologist*, 17.4: 687–707.
Cullen, F. and Agnew, T. 2004. *Criminological Theory: Past to Present: Essential Readings.* Los Angeles: Roxbury Park.
Dayton, D. 1987. *Theological Roots of Pentecostalism.* Massachusetts: Hendrickson Publishers.
De Gruchy, J. 2007. "Public Theology as Christian Witness: Exploring the Genre." *International Journal of Public Theology* 1 (1): 26–41.
Deakin, N. 1970. *Colour and Citizenship in British Society.* London: Panther Books.
Dempster, M., Klaus, B. and Petersen, D. (eds) 1991. *Called and Empowered: Global Mission in Pentecostal Perspective.* Peabody: Hendrickson.
—— 1999. *The Globalisation of Pentecostalism.* Irvine: Regnum Press.
Department of Environment, Transport and the Regions. 1997. *Involving Communities in Urban and Rural Regeneration: A Guide for Practitioners.* London: Department of Environment, Transport and the Regions.
—— 1998. *Modernising Local Government: In Touch with People.* Cmnd 4014. London: The Stationery Office.

—— 2000. *Indices of Deprivation*. Regeneration Summary Research, Number 31. London: Department of Environment, Transport and the Regions.
Dever, E. 1998. *Nine Marks of a Healthy Church*. Washington DC: Center for Church Reform.
Dobrovolsky, A. (ed.) 2007. *Olorunwa: There is God – Portrait of Sunday Adelaja*. Kyiv: Fares Publishing.
Droogers, A. 2001. "Globalisation and Pentecostal Success." *In* Corten. A. and Marshall-Fratani, R. (eds), *Between Babel and Pentecost: Transnational Pentecostalism in Africa and Latin America*. Indianapolis: Indiana University Press. pp44–46.
Easton, M. 2007. *How Much is Family Life Changing?* [Web] http://news.bbc.co.uk/1/hi/uk/7078004.stm [Date of access: 5 January 2010]
Ebaugh, H. and Chafetz, J. 2000. *Religion and the New Immigrants: Continuities and Adaptations in Immigrant Congregations*. Walnut Creek: Altamira Press.
Eden, M. (ed.) 1993. *Britain on the Brink*. Nottingham: Crossway Books.
Edmead, P. 1999. *The Divisive Decade: A History of Caribbean Immigration to Birmingham in the 1950s*. Birmingham: Birmingham City Council Department of Leisure and Community Services.
Edward, P. and Walvin, J. 1983. *Black Personalities in the Era of Slave Trade*. London: Macmillan.
Edwards, J. 1993. "The British Afro-Caribbean Community." *In* Eden, M. (ed.), *Britain on the Brink*. Nottingham: Crossway Books. pp100–116.
Ellington, S. 1996. "Pentecostalism and the Authority of Scripture." *Journal of Pentecostal Theology*, 9: 16–38.
Elton, G. 1987. *The Practice of History*. London: Fontana Press.
Enang, K. 2000. *Nigerian Catholics and the Independent Churches: A Call to Authentic Faith*. Immensee, Switzerland: Neue Zeitschrift fur Missionswissenschaft, Supp 45.
Equiano, O. 1969. *The Life Of Olaudah Equiano, Or Gustavus Vassa, The African*. New York: Negro Universities Press.
Ervin, H. 1985. "Hermeneutics: A Pentecostal Option." *In* Ebert, P. (ed.), *Essays on Apostolic Themes*. Peabody: Hendrickson. pp23–35.
Essien, A. 2000. "New Religious Movements and the Gospel of Prosperity: The Nigerian Experience." *The Oracle*, 1: 40–46.
Etan-Adollo, L. 2006. *Growth in Afro-Caribbean Pentecostal Churches*. London: Athena Press.
Falola, T. and Agwuele, A. 2009. *Africans and the Politics of Popular Culture*. New York: University of Rochester.
Farnell, R., Lund, S., Furbey, R. et al. 1994. *Hope in the City? The Local Impact of the Church Urban Fund*. Sheffield: Centre for Regional Economic and Social Research, Sheffield Hallam University.
Farnell, R. et al. 2003. *Faith in Urban Regeneration? Engaging Faith Communities in Urban Regeneration*. Bristol: The Policy Press.
Faupel, D. 1996. *The Everlasting Gospel: The Significance of Eschatology in the Development of Pentecostal Thought*. Sheffield: Sheffield Academic Press.
Fee, G. 1991. *Gospel and Spirit: Issues in New Testament Hermeneutics*. Peabody: Hendrickson Publishers.
—— 2000. *Listening to the Spirit in the Text*. Cambridge: William B. Eerdmans Publishing.
File, N. and Power, C. 1991. *Black Settlers in Britain 1555–1958*. Oxford: Heinemann.
Finneron, D. and Dinham, A. 2002. *Building on Faith: Faith Buildings in Neighbourhood*

*Renewal.* London: Church Urban Fund.

Folarin, G. 2007. "Contemporary State of the Prosperity Gospel in Nigeria." *Asia Journal of Theology*, 21 (1): 69–95.

Forrester, D. 2000. *Truthful Action: Exploration in Practical Theology.* Edinburgh: T&T Clark.

Fortman, J. 1999. *The Triune God. A Historical Study of the Doctrine of the Trinity.* Eugene, OR: Wipf and Stock.

Foster, E. 1990. "Out of this World: A Consideration of the Development and Nature of Black-led Churches in Britain." *In* Grant, P. and Patel, R. (eds), *A Time to Speak: Perspectives of Black Christians in Britain.* A joint publication of Racial Justice and the Black Theology Working Group, Birmingham.

Francis, V. 1998. *With Hope in Their Eyes: Compelling Stories of the Windrush Generation.* London: The X Press.

Freeman, R. and Gilbert, D. 1988. *Corporate Strategy and the Search for Ethics.* Englewood Cliffs: Prentice Hall.

Frost, M. and Hirsch, A. 2003. *The Shaping of Things to Come.* Peabody: Hendrickson Publishers.

Fryer, P. 1984. *Staying Power: History of Black People in Britain since 1504.* London: Pluto Press.

Fyfe, C. and Walls, A. (eds) 1996. *Christianity in Africa in the 1990s.* Edinburgh: Centre of African Studies, University of Edinburgh.

Gates, B. (ed.) 1980. *Afro Caribbean Religion.* London: Wardlock Publishing.

Gee, D. (ed.) 1950. *Pentecost Magazine. In* Cauchi, T. 2008. Pentecost. A complete run of 77 Pentecost magazines 1947–1966 (CD ROM).

Gerlach, L. and Hine, Virginia H. 1970. *People, Power, Change: Movements of Social Transformation.* New York: Bobbs-Merrill.

Gerloff, R. 1992a. *A Plea for British Black Theologies: The Black Church Movement in Britain in its Transatlantic Cultural and Theological Interaction with Special References to the Pentecostal Oneness (Apostolic) and Sabbatarian Movements.* Frankfurt: Peter Lang.

—— 1992b. "Theological Education in Black and White: The Centre for Black and White Christian Partnership." *In* Jongeneel, J. and Hollenweger, W. (eds), *Pentecost, Mission and Ecumenism: Essays on Intercultural Theology.* Frankfurt: Peter Lang. pp41–59.

Gibbs, E. and Coffey, I. 2001. *Church Next: Quantum Changes in Christian Ministry.* Downers Grove: InterVarsity Press.

Giddens, A. 2006. *Sociology.* 5th edn. Cambridge: Polity Press.

Gifford, P. 1998a. "Some Recent Developments in African Christianity." *African Affairs*, 21: 334–336.

—— 1998b. *African Christianity: Its Public Role.* London: Hurst & Company.

—— 2004. *Ghana's New Christianity: Pentecostalism in a Globalising African Economy.* Bloomington: Indiana University Press.

Gilchrist, A. 2004. *The Well-connected Community: A Networking Approach to Community Development:* Bristol: The Policy Press.

Goff, J. 1988. *Fields White Unto Harvest: Charles F. Parham and the Missionary Origins of Pentecostalism.* Fayetteville: University of Arkansas Press.

Graham, E., Walton, H. and Ward, F. 2005. *Theological Reflection: Methods.* London: SCM Press.

Grayling, A. 2001a. "The Third Way: The Last Word on Religious Schools." The *Guardian*. 24 February 2001.

—— 2001b. "Keep God Out of Public Affairs." The *Observer*. 12 August 2001.
Greenleaf, R. 1977. *Servant Leadership: A Journey into the Nature of Legitimate Power and Greatness*. New York: Paulist Press.
Griggs, C. 1991. *Early Egyptian Christianity: From its Origins to 451 CE*. Leiden: Brill.
Grudem, A. 1994. *Systematic Theology. An Introduction to Biblical Doctrine*. Grand Rapids: Zondervan.
Gunton, C. 1995. "Relation and Relativity: The Trinity and the Created World." *In* Schwobel, Christoph (ed.), *Trinitarian Theology Today: Essays on Divine Being and Act*. Edinburgh: T&T Clark. pp92–112.
Habibis, R. *et al.* 2005. *Sociology: Themes and Perspectives*. 5th edn. Glasgow: Collins Educational.
Haddad, Y., Smith, J. and Esposito, J. (eds) 2003. *Religion and Immigration: Christian, Jewish, and Muslim Experiences in the United States*. Walnut Creek, CA: Altamira Press.
Hagin, K. 1995. *Financial Prosperity*: Tulsa: Faith Publication Library.
Halpern, D., 1999, *Social Capital: The New Golden Goose*. Faculty of Social and Political Sciences, Cambridge University, unpublished review.
Hanciles, J. 2008. *Beyond Christendom: Globalization, African Migration, and the Transformation of the West*. Maryknoll: Orbis Books.
Harrell, D.E. 1971. *White Sects and Black Men in the Recent South*. Nashville: Vanderbilt University Press.
Harris, H. 2006. *Yoruba in Diaspora: An African Church in London*. New York: Macmillan.
Hart, T. 1989. *Regarding Karl Barth: Essays Toward a Reading of his Theology*. Carlisle: Paternoster.
Harvey, L.1987. "From Rejection to Liberation: The Development of the Black Christians in Britain and United States." *In* "Claiming the Inheritance", *Racial Justice*, No. 6, Spring 1987, Birmingham: Evangelical Christians for Racial Justice.
Hill, C. 1963. *West Indian Migrants and the London Churches*. London: Oxford University Press.
—— 1970. *Immigration and Integration: A Study of the Settlement of Coloured Minorities in Britain*. Oxford: Pergamon.
—— 1971a. *Black Churches, West Indian and African Sects in Britain*. London: Community and Race Relations Unit of the British Council of Churches.
—— 1971b. "Immigrant Sect Development in Britain: A Case of Status Deprivation." *Social Compass*, 18: 231–236.
—— 2009a. Interview held at Centre for Contemporary Ministries, Moggerhanger, Bedford. 21 May 2009.
—— 2009b. "Black Churches in White Space." A seminar held at the Christian Resource Exhibition, Esher, Surrey, United Kingdom. 13 May 2009.
—— 2009c. "The Third Generation Hypothesis." A lecture delivered at the annual Academic Lecture of Christ Redeemers College/Redeemed Christian Church of God. London. 6 October 2009.
Hill, M. (ed.) 1971. *A Sociology Yearbook of Religion in Britain*. London: SCM Press Ltd.
Hine, V. and Gerlach, L. 1970. *People, Power, Change: Movements of Social Transformation*. New York: Bobbs Merrill.
Hollenweger, W. 1972. *The Pentecostals*. London: SCM Press.
—— 1986. "Intercultural Theology." *Theology Today*, 43.1: 28–35.
—— 1997. *Pentecostalism: Origins and Developments Worldwide*. Peabody: Hendrickson Publishers.
Hood, R. 1994. *Begrimed and Black: Christian Traditions on Blacks and Blackness*.

Minneapolis: Augsburg Fortress.
Horton, W. and Conn, C. 1964. *The Glossolalia Phenomenon*. Cleveland: Pathway Press.
Howard, V. 1987. *A Report on Afro-Caribbean Christianity in Britain*. Leeds: University of Leeds Department of Theology and Religious Studies, Community Religions Project Research Papers, New Series, 4.
Hunt, S. 1998. "Magical Moments: An Intellectualist Approach to the Neo-Pentecostal 'Faith' Ministries." *Religion*, 28 (3): 271–280.
—— 2000. *The "New" Black Pentecostal Churches in Britain*. [Web] www.cesnur.org/conferences/riga2000/hunt.htm [Date of access: 12 October 2008]
—— 2002a. "Neither Here Nor There: The Construction of Identities and Boundary Maintenance of West African Pentecostals." *Sociology*, 36 (1): 147–169.
—— 2002b. *Deprivation and Western Pentecostalism Revisited: Neo-Pentecostalism*. [Web] www.glopent.net/pentecostudies/2002/hunt2002-2.pdf/view [Date of access: 12 October 2009]
Hunt, S. and Lightly, N. 2001. "The British Black Pentecostal 'Revival': Identity and Belief in the 'New' Nigerian Churches." *Ethnic and Racial Studies*. 24.1: 104–124.
Husain, E. 2007. *The Islamist: Why I Joined Radical Islam in Britain: What I Saw Inside and Why I Left*. London: Penguin Books.
International Organization for Migration. 2003. *World Migration 2003. Managing Migration: Challenges and Responses for People on the Move*. Geneva: International Organization for Migration.
Ireson, C. 1970. *My Life and Thought*. Bradford: Puritan Press.
Irukwu, A. 2006. Speech during annual Ministers' Conference of the Redeemed Christian Church of God, United Kingdom, held at Pontins Conference Centre, Blackpool.
—— 2009a. "Pastoral Perspective of Second Generation Africans in Churches in Britain." A paper presented at the annual academic lecture of Christ Redeemers College/Redeemed Christian Church of God, held at Jesus House, 6 February 2009.
—— 2009b. "Pastor Agu Irukwu." *Keep the Faith* magazine. Issue 47. Bury: Black Publications UK.
Isaac, L. 2007. Interview with Home Office Affairs Committee Report on Young Black People and the Criminal Justice Board, second session 2006–2007, chaired by John Denham. [Web] www.parliament.the-stationery-office.co.uk/pa/cm200607/.../181ii.pdf [Date of access: 15 March 2010]
Jagessar, M. 2007. "Review of *Understanding Caribbean British Christianity* by J. Aldred." *Black Theology: An International Journal*, 5.1: 128–130.
Jenkins, P. 2002. *The Next Christendom: The Coming of Global Christianity*. New York: Oxford University Press.
—— *The New Faces of Christianity: Believing the Bible in the Global South*. New York: Oxford University Press.
—— 2008. *God's Continent: Christianity, Islam, and Europe's Religious Crisis*. Oxford: Oxford University Press.
Jesus House, 2007. "Going the Extra Mile." *In Review*. London: Jesus House.
Jewkes, Y. 2004. *Media and Crime*. London: Sage.
Johnson, N., 1999, "The Personal Social Services and Community Care". *In* M. Powell (ed.), *New Labour, New Welfare State? The Third Way in British Social Policy*. Bristol: The Policy Press.
Kalilombe, P. 1997. "Black Christianity in Britain." *Ethnic and Racial Studies*, 20/2: 308–315.
Kalu, O. 1998. "The Third Response: Pentecostalism and the Reconstruction of Christian

Experience in Africa, 1970–1995." *Journal of African Christian Thought*, 1:2: 3–16.
────── 2000. *Power, Poverty and Prayer: The Challenges of Poverty and Pluralism in African Christianity, 1960–1996.* Frankfurt am Main: Peter Lang.
────── 2008. *African Pentecostalism: An Introduction.* Oxford: Oxford University Press.
────── 2009. "African Pentecostalism." A paper presented at the 2009 GloPent Transnational Conference, Birmingham, UK.
Kay, W. 1986. "Alexander Boddy and the Outpouring of the Holy Spirit in Sunderland." *Journal of the European Pentecostal Theological Association*, Vol. 5, No. 2: 44–56.
Kee, A. 2008. *Reclaiming Liberation Theology: The Rise and Demise of Black Theology.* England: SCM Publishers.
Kelsey, M. 1968. *Tongues Speaking.* New York: Doubleday.
Killingray, D. 2009. Telephone interview, 23 November 2009.
────── 2010a. "Brem-Wilson: The Hidden Life of the First Pentecostal Pastor in Modern Britain." A lecture delivered in February 2010 at School of Oriental and African Studies (SOAS), London.
────── 2010b. *African Research and Documentation.* [Web] http://www.faqs.org/periodicals/201001/2166008011.html [Date of access: 2 December 2010]
Killingray, D. and Edwards, J. 2007. *Black Voices: The Shaping of our Christian Experience.* Leicester: InterVarsity Press.
────── 2009. *Black Voices: The Shaping of our Christian Experience.* Leicester: InterVarsity Press. [Web] http://www.setallfree.co.uk/downloads/black_voices.pdf [Date of access: 25 June 2009]
Kim, S. 2007. "Editorial." *International Journal of Public Theology* 1 (1): 1–4.
Kimball, D. 1977. *The Emerging Church: Vintage Christianity for New Generations.* Grand Rapids: Zondervan.
King, M. 2008. "Letter from Birmingham Jail." In Fairchild, G. and Robinson, J. "Unlearned Lessons from *Letter from Birmingham Jail*: The Work Begun, the Progress Made, and the Task Ahead." *Business and Society*, 47: 484–522.
Klaus, B. and Triplett, L. 1991. "National Leadership in Pentecostal Missions." In Dempster, M., Klaus, B. and Petersen, D. (eds), *Called and Empowered: Global Mission in Pentecostal Perspective*. Peabody: Hendrickson. pp225–241.
Kortright, D. 1990. *Emancipation Still Comin': Explorations in Caribbean Emancipatory Theology.* New York: Orbis.
Lawless, E. 1983. "Shouting for the Lord: The Power of Women's Speech in the Pentecostal Religious Service." *Journal of American Folklore*, 96 (382): 434–459.
────── 1987. "Piety and Motherhood: Reproductive Images and Maternal Strategies of Women Preachers." *Journal of American Folklore*, 100 (398): 471–478.
────── 1988. *Handmaidens of the Lord: Pentecostal Women Preachers and Traditional Religion.* Philadelphia: University of Pennsylvania Press.
Lawless, E.J. 1991. "Rescripting their Lives and Narratives: Spiritual Life Stories of Pentecostal Women Preachers." *Journal of Feminist Studies in Religion*, 7.1: 53–71.
Leveatt, H. 2004. *Top Down, Why Hierarchies Are Here to Stay and How to Manage Them More Effectively*, Harvard Bussines School Press, Waterton.
Levitas, R. 1998. *The Inclusive Society? Social Exclusion and New Labour.* Basingstoke: Palgrave Macmillan.
Little, K. 1972. *Negroes in Britain: A Study of Racial Relations in English Society.* London: Routledge & Kegan Paul.
Ludwig, F. 2005. "The Proliferation of Cherubim and Seraphim Congregation in Britain." In Adogame, A . and Weissköppel, C. (eds), *Religion in the Context of African*

*Migration*. Bayreuth African Studies Series, No. 75. Bayreuth: Breitinger. pp343–357.

Lynch, J., Due, P., Muntaner, C. and Davey Smith, G. 2000. "Social Capital – Is It a Good Investment Strategy for Public Health?" *Journal of Epidemiology and Community Health*, 54: 404–408.

Lyseight, O. 2009. *Extract from "Sceptism and Hope"*. [Web] www.ntcg.org.uk/corporate/OLyseight_bookextract.stm [Date of access: 5 March 2009]

—— 1995. *Forward March: An Autobiography*. London: G.S. Garwood.

MacArthur, J. 1992. *Charismatic Chaos*. Grand Rapids: Zondervan.

Macchia, S. 2001. *Becoming a Healthy Church Workbook: A Dialogue, Assessment, and Planning Tool*. Grand Rapids: Baker Books.

MacRobert, I. 1988. *The Black Roots and White Racism of Early Pentecostalism in the USA*. London: Macmillan.

—— 1989a. *Black Pentecostalism: Its Origin, Functions and Theology: With Special Reference to a Midland Borough*. PhD dissertation. Birmingham: University of Birmingham.

—— 1989b. "The New Black-led Churches in Britain." *In* Badham, P. (ed.), *Religion, State and Society in Modern Britain*. Lampeter: Edwin Mellen. pp119–133.

Madonko, I. 2007. *What Role do Churches Have in Newham?* [Web] www.bbc.co.uk/london/content/articles/2007/07/03/church_newham.shtml [Date of access: 4 January 2010]

Marshall, R. 1991. "Power in the Name of Jesus: Social Transformation and Pentecostalism in Western Nigeria 'Revisited'." *Review of African Political Economy*, 52: 21–38.

—— 2009. *Political Spiritualities: The Pentecostal Revolution in Nigeria*. Chicago: The University of Chicago Press.

Martin, B. 1995. "New Mutations of the Protestant Ethic among Latin American Pentecostals." *Religion*, 25: 101–117.

Martin, D. 2002. *Pentecostalism: The World in Their Parish*. London: Blackwell.

Marwick A. 1979. *The Nature of History: Knowledge, Evidence, Language*. London: Macmillan.

Matsuoka, F. and Fernandez, E.S. (eds) 2003. *Realizing the America of Our Hearts*. St Louis: Chalice Press.

Maxwell, D. 2001. "Sacred History, Social History: Traditions and Texts in the Making of a Southern African Transnational Religious Movement." *Comparative Studies in Society and History*, 43.3: 502–524.

—— 2007. *African Gifts of the Spirit: Pentecostalism and the Rise of a Zimbabwean Transnational Religious Movement*. Athens: Ohio University Press.

Mbiti, J. 1980. "The Encounter of Christian Faith and African Religion." *Christian Century* 97: 817–820.

—— 1986. *Bible and Theology in African Christianity*. Tanzania: Oxford University Press Tanzania Ltd.

McFague, S. 1982. *Metaphorical Theology: Models of God in Religious Language*. Philadelphia: Fortress Press.

—— 1987. *Models of God: Theology for an Ecological, Nuclear Age*. Philadelphia: Fortress.

McGavran, D. and Arn, W. 1973. *How to Grow a Church: Conversations about Church Growth*. Glendale: Regal Books.

McLaren, B. 2000. *The Church on the Other Side: Doing Ministry in the Postmodern Matrix*. Grand Rapids: Zondervan.

McLeod, M., Owen, D. and Khamis, C. 2001. *Black and Minority Ethnic Voluntary and*

*Community Organisations.* London: Polity Press.
McNeill, J. (ed.) 1960. *John Calvin: Institutes of the Christian Religion.* Philadelphia: Westminster Press.
McQueen, L. 1995. *Joel and the Spirit: The Cry of a Prophetic Hermeneutic.* Sheffield: Continuum International Publishing Group.
Metaxas, E. 2007. *Amazing Grace: William Wilberforce and the Heroic Campaign to End Slavery.* San Francisco: Harper One.
Meyer, B. 1992. "If You are a Devil You are a Witch and if You are a Witch You are a Devil. The Integration of 'Pagan' Ideals into the Conceptual Universe of Ewe Christians in South Eastern Ghana." *Journal of Religion in Africa,* 22.2: 98–132.
—— 1998. "The Power of Money: Politics, Occult Forces and Pentecostalism." *African Studies Review,* 41.3: 15–37.
—— 1999. *Translating the Devil, Religion and Modernity Among Ewe in Ghana.* Edinburgh: Edinburgh University Press.
—— 2004. "Christianity in Africa: From African Independent to Pentecostal-Charismatic Churches." *Annual Review of Anthropology,* 33: 447–474.
Micklethwait, J. and Wooldridge, A. 2009. *God is Back: How the Global Rise of Faith is Changing the World.* USA: Allen Lane.
Miller, D. and Yamamori, T. 2007. *Global Pentecostalism: The New Face of Christian Social Engagement.* California: University of California Press.
Milne, B. 1980. *Know the Truth.* Leicester: InterVarsity Press.
Mitchell, R. 1964. "Africa's Prophetic Movement." *Christian Century,* 18: 1427–1429.
—— 1979. "Strains and Facilities in the Interpretation of an African Prophet Movement." In Kriesberg, L. (ed.), *Research in Social Movements, Conflicts and Change,* Vol. 2. Greenwich, CT: JAI Press. pp187–218.
Mohabir, P. 1988. *Building Bridges: Dramatic Personal Story of Evangelism and Reconciliation.* London: Hodder and Stoughton.
Moltmann, J. 1992. *The Spirit of Life: A Universal Affirmation.* Minneapolis: Augsburg Fortress Publishers.
Moynagh, M. 2004. *Emergingchurch.intro.* Grand Rapids: Monarch Books.
Muir, D. 2008. "An Obituary for the Wrong Subject: A Response to Alistair Kee's *The Rise and Demise of Black Theology.*" *Pneuma,* 30: 299–307.
—— 2009a. *Black Majority Churches: Political and Civic Engagements.* [Web] http://docs.google.com/viewer?a=v&q=cache:7ruWnTpW_C8J:www.susa.info/data/susa/downloads/pdf/Black%2520majority%2520churches%2520political%2520and%2520civic%2520engagement.pdf+Black+Majority+Churches:+Political+and+Civic+Engagements.&hl=en&pid=bl&srcid=ADGEESjUoOMxalSvSq-Hf2DrLxwgnxhiArWFNXGfnTYIcVtlg4Bm6UGYD8Lgaqr9f1VNBrhCm_-DygkECpkTxYMvwrQZbcD8pQe8LEInkXvlRQjqFIZkQShKk3V9LY2TqVH5BbadE531&sig=AHIEtbTZsaB_2VyZQRQt94jaELtLl36J7Q [Date of access (requires Google account): 29 March 2010]
—— 2009b. *Changing Church – Changing Society.* [Web] www.eauk.org/idea/changing-church-changing-society.cfm [Date of access: 24 February 2010]
—— 2010. "Theology and the Black Church." In Aldred, J. and Ogbo, K. *The Black Church in the 21st Century.* London: Darton Longman and Todd. pp8–27.
Muncie, J. and Goldson, B. (eds) 2004. *Youth Crime and Justice.* London: Sage Publications Ltd.
Naipaul, V. 2002. *The Middle Passage.* London: Andre Deutsch.
Newbigin, Lesslie. 1957. *The Household of God: Lectures on the Nature of the Church.*

London: SCM.

Nieswand, B. 2005. "Charismatic Christianity in the Context of Migration: Social Status, the Experience of Migration and the Construction of Selves Among Ghanaian Migrants in Berlin." *In* Adogame, A. and Weisskőppel, C. (eds), *Religion in the Context of African Migration.* Bayreuth African Studies Series, No. 75. Bayreuth: Breitinger. pp243–266.

Obunge, N. 2007. *In* Home Office Affairs Committee Report on Young Black People and the Criminal Justice Board, second session 2006–2007 chaired by John Denham. [Web] http://www.blackboyscansmallheath.co.uk/other_resources.html [Date of access: 24 March 2009]

—— 2009. "Black Church in White Space." A lecture given at Christian Resource Exhibition, Esher, Surrey, United Kingdom. 15 May 2009.

Ojo, M. 1988. "The Contextual Significance of the Charismatic Movements in Western Nigeria." *Africa* 57 (2): 175–192.

—— 1996. "Charismatic Movements in Africa." *In* Fyfe, C. and Walls, A. (eds), *Christianity in Africa in the 1990s.* Edinburgh: University of Edinburgh Centre of African Studies.

—— 2007. "Reverse Mission." *In* Jonathan Bonk (ed.), *Encyclopaedia of Missions and Missionaries.* New York/London: Routledge.

Olaiya, J. 2004. "God Promises." *In* Wagner, C. and Thompson, J. (eds), *Out of Africa.* California: Regal Books.

Oluyomi, D. 2009. *Appeal by Kingsway International Christian Centre and the London Development Agency.* [Web] http://www.havering.gov.uk/index.aspx?articleid=15288 [Date of access: 29 October 2009]

Omideyi, T. 2009. "Building and Sustaining a Multicultural Church." A paper presented at the African Consultative Leaders Forum held at the Redeemed Christian Church of God, Victory Parish, London. October 2009.

Omoyajowo, A. 1982. *Cherubim and Seraphim: The History of an African Independent Church.* New York: NOK Publishers.

Osgood, H. 2006. *African Neo-Pentecostal Churches and British Evangelicalism 1985–2005: Balancing Principles and Practicalities.* PhD dissertation. London: University of London.

Oshun, C. 1981. *Christ Apostolic Church of Nigeria: A Suggested Pentecostal Consideration of its Historical, Organizational and Theological Developments, 1918–1975.* PhD dissertation. Exeter: University of Exeter.

—— 1990. *Aladura Diaspora in Britain as a Model for Mission: A Study of Selected Churches.* PhD dissertation. Birmingham: University of Birmingham.

Oyedepo, D. 1997. *Understanding Financial Prosperity.* Lagos: Dominion Publishing.

Pak, S., Lee, U., Kim, J. and Cho, M. 2005. *Singing the Lord's Song in a New Land.* Louisville: John Knox Press.

Parratt, J. 1995. *Reinventing Christianity: African Theology Today.* Grand Rapids: Eerdmans.

Parsons, G. (ed.) 1993. *The Growth of Religious Diversity: Britain from 1945.* London: Routledge.

Patterson, S. 1965. *Dark Strangers: A Sociological Study of the Absorption of a Recent West Indian Migrant Group in Brixton, South London.* London: Tavistock Publications. (2nd edn. Middlesex: Penguin.)

Peel, J. 2000. *Religious Encounter and the Making of the Yoruba.* Indianapolis: Indiana University Press.

Pemberton, E. and Pemberton, F. (eds) 1983. *Pilgrims in Progress.* J.R. Maxwell.

Penny, J. 1997. *The Missionary Emphasis of Lukan Pneumatology.* Journal of Pentecostal Theology Supplement Series 12. Sheffield: Continuum International Publishing Group.

Perriman, A, (ed.) 2003. *Faith: Health and Prosperity. A Report on "Word of Faith and Positive Confession".* Carlisle: Paternoster Press.

Petre, J. 2006. "Migrants Fill Empty Pews as Britons Lose Faith." The *Telegraph.* [Web] www.telegraph.co.uk/news/uknews/1529106/Migrants-fill-empty-pews-as-Britons-lose-faith.html [Date of access: 23 April 2008]

Phiri, I. and Maxwell, J. 2007. *Gospel Riches: Africa's Rapid Embrace of Prosperity Pentecostalism Provokes Concern – and Hope.* [Web] www.ctlibrary.com/ct/2007/july/12.22.html [Date of access: 23 October 2009]

Pinnock, C. 2004. "The Recovery of the Holy Spirit in Evangelical Theology." *Journal of Pentecostal Theology,* 10: 35–84.

Portes, A. 1998. "Social Capital: Its Origins and Applications in Modern Sociology." *Annual Review of Sociology,* 24: 1–24.

Prestige, G. 1986. *God in Patristic Thought.* London: SPCK.

Price, F. 2005. *Name it and Claim it! The Power of Positive Confession.* Benin City: Marvellous Christiana Publication.

Prince Charles, 2007. *Prince Charles Marks 59th Birthday with Tribute to Black Churches in the UK.* [Web] http://www.assistnews.net/Stories/2007/s07110095.htm [Date of access: 28 October 2008]

Putnam, R. 1993. "The Prosperous Community: Social Capital and Public Life." *The American Prospect,* no. 13.

—— 1995. "Bowling Alone: America's Declining Social Capital." *Journal of Democracy* 6 (1): 65–78.

—— 2001. *Bowling Alone – The Collapse and Revival of American Community.* New York: Simon & Schuster.

Putnam, R. and Feldstein, L. with Cohen, D. 2003. *Better Together: Restoring the American Community.* New York: Simon & Schuster.

Quass, A. 2009. "Representations of Transnationality in Nigeria and Germany." A paper presented at GloPent Transnational Conference on Transnational Pentecostalism in Europe at Birmingham University. 6–7 February 2009.

Raboteau, A. 2004. *Slave Religion: The "Invisible Institution" in the Antebellum South.* New York: Oxford University Press.

Ray, B. 1993. "Aladura Christianity." *Journal of Religion in Africa,* 23.3: 266–291.

—— 2000. *African Religions: Symbols, Ritual and Community.* 2nd edn. New Jersey: Pearson Education.

REACH Report. 2007. [Web] http://www.communities.gov.uk/publications/communities/reachreport [Date of access: 29 September 2009]

Reddie, A. 2006. *Black Theology in Transatlantic Dialogue.* Hampshire: Palgrave Macmillan.

Reddie, A. and Jagessar, N. (eds) 2007. *Black Theology in Britain.* London: Equinox.

*Redemption Tidings.* 1939. Britain: Assemblies of God. *In* Cauchi, T. *Redemption Tidings 1924–1939.* Revival Library (CD ROM).

Regele, M. and Schulz, M. 1995. *The Death of the Church.* Grand Rapids: Zondervan.

Reid-Salmon, D. 2008. *Home Away from Home: The Caribbean Diasporan Church in the Black Atlantic Tradition.* London: Equinox.

Rex, J. and Moore R. 1967. *Race, Community and Conflict.* London: Oxford University Press.

Rex, J. and Tomlinson, S. 1979. *Colonial Immigrants in a British City: A Class Analysis.*

London: Routledge & Kegan Paul.

Roberts, R. 1995. *Religion and Transformation of Capitalism: Comparative Approaches.* London: Routledge.

Robinson, M. 1976. *The Charismatic Anglican – Historical and Contemporary: A Comparison of the Life and Work of Alexander Boddy (1854–1930).* M.Litt dissertation. Birmingham: University of Birmingham.

Robinson, J. 2003. *Another View of the Prosperity Gospel.* [Web] http://www.charismamag.com/index.php/features2/286-spiritual-maturity/7460-another-view-of-the-prosperity-gospel [Date of access: 29 October 2009]

Robinson, M. and Smith, D. 2003. *Invading Secular Space: Strategies for Tomorrow's Church.* London: Monarch Books.

Roger, J. 2000. *From a Welfare State to a Welfare Society: The Changing Context of Social Policy in a Postmodern Era.* Basingstoke: Macmillan.

Saayman, W. 1993. "Some Reflections on the Development of the Pentecostal Mission Model in South Africa." *Missionalia,* 21.1: 40–56.

Sanneh, L. 1991. *Translating the Message: The Missionary Impact on Culture.* Maryknoll, NY: Orbis. Cited in Meyer, B. 1992. "If You are a Devil You are a Witch and if You are a Witch You are a Devil. The Integration of 'Pagan' Ideals into the Conceptual Universe of Ewe Christians in South Eastern Ghana." *Journal of Religion in Africa,* 22.2: 98–132.

Sanusi, L. 2007. *Take it by Force: How to Possess your Possessions.* Crayford: Oraword Publications Ltd.

Sarles, K. 1986. "A Theological Evaluation of the Prosperity Gospel." *Bibliotheca Sacra,* 143: 329–350.

Schreiter, R. 2004. *The New Catholicity: Theology Between the Global and the Local.* New York: Orbis Books.

Schwarz, C. 1996. *Natural Church Development: A Guide to Eight Essential Qualities of Healthy Churches.* Carol Stream, IL: ChurchSmart Resources.

Sepulveda, J. 1997. "To Overcome the Fear of Syncretism: A Latin American Perspective." *In* Lynne, P., Sepulveda, J. and Smith, G. (eds), *Mission Matters.* Frankfurt am Main: Peter Lang. pp142–160.

Sewell, T. 1999. *Keep on Moving: The Windrush Legacy.* London: Voice Enterprises Ltd.

Shakarian, D. 1975. *The Happiest People on Earth.* New Jersey: Fleming Revell.

Sherwood, M. 1994. *Pastor Daniel Ekarte and the African Churches Mission.* London: Savannah Press.

Shyllon, F. 1977. *Black People in Britain.* Oxford: Oxford University Press.

Smelser, N. 1962. *Theory of Collective Behaviour.* London: Routledge & Kegan Paul.

Smith, S.A. 2009. *British Black Gospel: The Foundations of this Vibrant UK Sound.* London: Monarch Books.

Smith, I. and Green, W. 1989. *An Ebony Cross: Being a Black Christian in Britain Today.* London: Harper Collins.

Smith, I. and Holden, T. 1983. *Dialogue Between Black and White Christians: Two Papers.* London: Zebra Project.

Stedman, R. 1972. *Body Life: The Church Comes Alive!* Ventura: Regal Books.

Stronstad, R. 1993. The *Charismatic Theology of St Luke.* Peabody: Hendrickson Publishers.

Sturge, M. 2005. *Look What the Lord has Done! An Exploration of Black Christian Faith in Britain.* Bletchley: Scripture Union.

Sureway International Christian Ministries. 2006. *100 Years of Centenary Celebrations: Our Journey So Far.* London: Sureway International Christian Ministries.

Synan, V. 1971. *The Holiness/Pentecostal Tradition: Charismatic Movements in the*

*Twentieth Century*. Grand Rapids: Eerdmans.
—— 1975. *Aspects of Pentecostal-Charismatic Origins*. New York: Logos.
Taylor, M. 2000. "Communities in the Lead: Power, Organisational Capacity and Social Capital." *Urban Studies*, 37, No. 5–7: 1019–1035.
—— 2003. *Public Policy in the Community*. Basingstoke: Palgrave Macmillan.
Ter Haar, G. 1998. *Halfway to Paradise: African Christians in Europe*. Cardiff: Cardiff Academic Press.
—— 2009. *How God Became African: African Spirituality and Western Secular Thought*. Philadelphia: University of Pennsylvania.
Tilton, R. 1983. *God's Word About Prosperity*. Dallas, TX: Word of Faith Publications.
Together in Mission, 2004. MA lecture notes on Missions in Contemporary Society. Martin Robinson, Lecturer. Birmingham: Together in Mission.
Toulis, N. 1997. *Believing Identity, Pentecostalism and the Mediation of Jamaican Ethnicity and Gender in England*. Oxford: Berg Publishers.
Torrance, T. 1995. *The Christian Doctrine of God: One Being, Three Persons*, Edinburgh: T&T Clark.
Toynbee, P. 2001. "We Don't Need the Church to Educate our Children." The *Guardian*. 15 June 2001.
Tracy, D. 1981. *The Analogical Imagination: Christian Theology and the Culture of Pluralism*. London: SCM Press.
Trotman, A. 1992. "Black, Black-led or What?" In Joel Edwards (ed.), *Let's Praise Him: An African Caribbean Perspective on Worship*. London: Kingsway.
Turnbull, T. 1963. *Brothers in Arms*. Bradford: Puritan Press.
Turner, H. 1979. *Religious Innovations in Africa: Collected Essays on New Religious Movements*. Boston, MA: G.K. Hall & Co.
Ukah, A., 2003. *The Redeemed Christian Church of God, Nigeria. Local Identities and Legitimacy and the State in Twentieth-Century Africa: Essays in Honour of A.H.M. Greene*. London: Macmillan Press.
—— 2005. "Mobilities, Migration and Multiplication: The Expansion of the Religious Field of the Redeemed Christian Church of God (RCCG), Nigeria." *In* Adogame, A. and Weisskӧppel, C. (eds), *Religion in the Context of African Migration*. Bayreuth African Studies Series, No. 75. Bayreuth: Breitinger. pp317–341.
—— 2007. *The Redeemed Christian Church of God (RCCG), Nigeria: Local Identities and Global Processes in African Pentecostalism*. PhD dissertation. Bayreuth: University of Bayreuth.
—— 2008. *A New Paradigm of Pentecostal Power: A Study of the Redeemed Christian Church of God*. New Jersey: Africa World Press.
—— 2009. "Reverse Mission or Asylum Christianity. A Nigerian Church in Europe." *In* Falola, T. and Agwuele, A. (eds), *Africans and Politics of Popular Cultures*. Rochester, NY: University of Rochester Press. pp104–132.
Valley, P. 2005. "Are Britain's Fringe Churches Preaching a Deadly Message?" The *Independent*. 18 July 2005.
Van der Laan, C. 1992. "Discerning the Body: Analysis of Pentecostalism in the Netherlands." *In* Jongeneel, J. (ed.), *Pentecost, Mission and Ecumenism: Essays on Intercultural Theology*. Studies in the Intercultural History of Christianity, 75. Frankfurt: Peter Lang. pp123–142.
Vasquez, M. and Marquardt, M. 2003. *Globalizing the Sacred: Religion Across the Americas*. New Brunswick: Rutgers University Press.
Wagner, C. and Thompson, J. (eds) 2004. *Out of Africa*. California: Regal Books.

Wagner, P. 1976. *Your Church Can Grow: Seven Vital Signs of a Healthy Church.* Glendale: Regal Books.
—— 1979. *Your Church Can Be Healthy.* Nashville: Abingdon Press.
Währisch-Oblau, C. 2000. "From Reverse Mission to Common Mission ... We Hope: Immigrant Protestant Churches and the 'Programme for Cooperation between German and Immigrant Congregations' of the United Evangelical Mission." *International Review of Mission,* 89 (354): 467–483.
—— 2009. *The Missionary Self-Perception of Pentecostal/Charismatic Church Leaders from the Global South in Europe: Bringing Back the Gospel.* Global Pentecostal and Charismatic Studies 2. Leiden: Brill.
Wallis, R. 1984. *The Elementary Forms of the New Religious Life.* London: Routledge & Kegan Paul.
Walls, A. 1993. *The Significance of African Christianity.* Friends of St. Colm's Public Lecture, Church of Scotland St. Colm Education Centre and College, 21 May 1989. Printed by the Overseas Ministry Study Centre, New Haven, CT.
—— 2002. "Mission and Migration: The Diaspora Factor in Christian History." *Journal of African Christian Thought,* Vol. 5/2 (December): 10.
Walsh, A. 2007. "First Church of Prosperidad." *Christianity Today.* [Web] www.christianitytoday.com/ct/2007/july/13.26.html [Date of access: 23 October 2009]
Walvin, J. 1971. *Black Presence: A Documentary History of the Negro in England.* London: Macmillan.
Walvin, J. and Edwards, P. 1983. *Black Personalities in the Era of the Slave Trade.* Hong Kong: Macmillan.
Warren, R. 1995. *The Purpose Driven Church: Growth Without Compromising Your Message and Mission.* Grand Rapids: Zondervan.
Warrington, K. 2008. *Pentecostal Theology: A Theology of Encounter.* London: T&T Clark.
Weeks, G. 2003. *Chapter Thirty-two: A History of the Apostolic Church.* Barnsley: Prontaprint.
Welker, M. 2004. *God the Spirit.* Minneapolis: Fortress Press.
Wilkinson, J. 1993. *Church in Black and White.* Edinburgh: Saint Andrew Press.
William, D. (ed.) 1923. *Riches of Grace. 1923, July edition.* Bradford: Apostolic International Missionary Council.
Williams, C.G. 1981. *Tongues of the Spirit: A Study of Pentecostal Glossolalia and Related Phenomena.* Cardiff: University of Wales Press.
Williams, E. 1970. *From Columbus to Castro: The History of the Caribbean, 1492–1969.* London: Andre Deutsch.
Williams, R. 2006. Cited in Petre, J. 2006. "Migrants Fill Empty Pews as Britons Lose Faith." The *Telegraph.* [Web] www.telegraph.co.uk/news/uknews/1529106/Migrants-fill-empty-pews-as-Britons-lose-faith.html [Date of access: 23 April 2008]
Wilmore, G. 1976. *Black and Presbyterian: The Heritage and the Hope.* Philadelphia: Geneva Press.
Wilson, C. 1992. "Racism and Private Assistance: The Support of West Indian and African Missions in Liverpool, England, During the Interwar Years." *African Studies Review,* Vol. 35, No. 2 (Sep. 1992): 55–76.
Wilson, J. 1971. "The Sociology of Schism." *In* Hill, M. (ed.), *A Sociology Yearbook of Religion in Britain.* London: SCM Press Ltd. pp7–9.
Wintour, P. and Dodd, V. 2007. "Tony Blair Blames Spate of Murders on Black Culture." The *Guardian.* 19 April 2007. [Web] http://www.guardian.co.uk/politics/2007/apr/12/ukcrime.race [Date of access: 5 January 2010]
Witvliet, T. 1987. *The Way of the Black Messiah: The Hermeneutical Challenge of Black*

*Theology as a Theology of Liberation*. London: Meyer-Stone Books.
Woolcock, N. 2004. "TV Preacher Sexually Abused his Worshippers." *The Times*. 7 May 2004. [Web] www.timesonline.co.uk/tol/news/uk/article417711.ece [Date of access: 27 February 2009]
World Bank. 1998. *The Initiative of Defining, Monitoring and Measuring Social Capital*. [Web] http://www.google.co.uk/#hl=en&expIds=17259,27744,27753,27824,27868&xhr=t&q =THE+INITIATIVE+ON+DEFINING%2C&cp=0&pf=p&sclient=psy&site=&source =hp&aq=f&aqi=&aql=&oq=&gs_rfai=&pbx=1&fp=daa8df45e47eaf70 [Date of access: 25 February 2009]
Wright, N. 1996. *The Radical Evangelical: Seeking a Place to Stand*. London: SPCK.
Wuthnow, R. 2004. *Saving America? Faith Based Services and the Future of Civil Society*. Princeton: Princeton University Press.
Yong, A. 2005. *The Spirit Poured Upon All Flesh: Pentecostalism and the Possibility of Global Theology*. Grand Rapids, Michigan: Baker Academic.
Yong, A. and Richie, T. 2010. "The Spirit Encounter: Theology of Religions – Pentecostal and Pneumatological Perspectives." *In* Anderson, A., Begrunder, M., Droogers, A. and Van der Laan, C. *Studying Global Pentecostalism. Theories and Methods*. California: California University Press.
Zeleza, P. 2002. "Contemporary African Migrations in a Global Context." *African Issues*, 30/1: 9–14.

# Index

ACEA *see* Evangelical Alliance, African Caribbean
Adeboye, Enoch 70, 77–8, 148, 202
Adeboye, Folu 78, 106
Adedibu 158
Adogame 82–3, 200–1, 236
Africans 4, 7–10, 12, 17–19, 32, 35, 43–5, 52, 62–4, 66–8, 70, 84, 90, 94–6, 102, 105, 115–6, 118, 127–9, 131–5, 140, 144, 147, 150–1, 154, 156–7, 167, 170–1, 191, 198, 201, 205, 209, 216, 222, 228–9, 234–5, 239, 242, 249
African American 24, 28, 128, 241
African Traditional Religion 17, 65, 242
Akindayomi, Esther 78
Akindayomi, Josiah 78
Aladura 64–7, 78, 90–1, 201
Aladura movement 66, 201
Aldred 2, 5, 83–4, 93–5, 98, 110, 114–16, 128–9, 136, 154, 168, 171, 178, 183–4, 191, 206, 216, 219–21, 229, 244
America 10–13, 19–23, 29, 34–5, 46, 52, 54, 59–61, 69, 79, 82, 89–91, 100–3, 111–12, 114, 118–19, 121, 122, 129–30, 135–6, 149–53, 192, 197, 199, 201–2, 216, 220, 222, 230, 234, 236, 240–2
Americans 33, 37–8, 46, 53, 100, 128, 137, 160, 171, 187, 194–5
Americanization 89–91, 149–53, 175, 201–2, 216
American philosophy 149
Anderson, Allan 20, 24, 29, 73, 88, 120–1, 131, 144–5, 199, 203, 209, 214, 230–3
Ashimolowo 83, 94, 96, 101, 108, 151, 162, 166, 206

Baptism 7, 13–16, 21–6, 28, 33, 42, 48, 52–3, 118, 120, 123, 125–7, 232–3
Barratt 23–6, 48, 230
Beckford, Robert 5, 17, 73, 93, 96, 115–7, 131, 137–8, 150, 155, 170, 181, 203, 206, 216–19, 221, 229, 242, 247
Bible 15–16, 37, 79, 82, 96, 104, 123, 130–8, 140–1, 144, 153, 189, 213–14, 218, 241
Blacks, 7–19, 23, 32–4, 36–8, 43–6, 52, 54–5, 60, 64, 73, 79, 85–9, 113, 115–17, 120–1, 128, 137, 140, 167, 170, 174, 183, 187, 219, 247
BMCs *see* Churches, Black Majority
Brem-Wilson 7, 26–31, 48, 53–4, 59, 84–6, 111, 198, 231–3, 240
Brierley 121, 157, 159
Britain 1–6, 7–48, 49–111, 113–53, 154–96, 197–213, 215–24, 226–40, 242–50
British 1–2, 5–6, 8–12, 14, 17–20, 23–6, 28–30, 36–46, 48–52, 54–57, 61, 63, 68, 71–2, 74–6, 80, 83–4, 86, 88, 90–3, 95–7, 101, 106, 108, 112, 114–16, 121–2, 128, 130, 132–3, 136–7, 146, 148–9, 153–5, 157–62, 169–71, 174, 176–82, 189, 191–2, 194, 197–200, 202, 204–10, 212–13, 215–23, 226–9, 230, 232–8, 240–50

Caribbean 1–2, 4–5, 7–8, 10, 16, 18–19, 39–47, 49, 51–2, 54–60, 62, 64, 68–70, 74–6, 81–4, 88–90, 93–5, 97–8, 101–2, 104–5, 108, 113–17, 119, 121, 127–30, 132–4, 136, 144, 146–7, 150, 153–7, 161–2, 165, 167, 169, 171, 178, 180, 183–4, 186–7, 191, 198, 200–1, 203, 209, 212, 216–22, 225, 227–9, 231, 233–8, 242, 248–9
Catholic 20–1, 38, 65, 85, 110, 131, 134, 169, 195, 202, 214
Charity Commission 81, 87, 94, 107–9, 119, 162, 211, 226–7, 229, 242
Charismatics 21, 24, 63, 69, 74, 79, 88, 94–5, 119, 135, 141, 144, 149–51, 212, 214, 240
Christianity 1–7, 10, 14–17, 19–22, 25–39,

## Index

41–5, 47–58, 60–72, 74, 76–9, 83–90, 92–8, 100–8, 110, 112–17, 119, 123–5, 128, 131–7, 139–40, 142, 144, 146, 148–9, 152–4, 156, 160, 162–8, 170–1, 173, 178–86, 188–9, 192–9, 201–6, 208, 210–1, 215–16, 218–27, 230, 232, 234–8, 240–4, 247–50
Christianity, African 62–3, 114–15, 128–9, 131–4, 218, 235, 240, 242
Christianity, British 1–2, 4–6, 20, 51, 136, 154–96, 197–8, 230
Christianity, British Caribbean, 5, 114, 219–22
Church, African Independent 65, 90–1, 94, 111, 152, 198–9, 201, 213
Church, Catholic 20, 65, 110, 134, 169, 202, 214
Church growth 76, 99–103, 111–12, 155–60, 215, 246
Church of God, New Testament 31, 45–6, 59–60, 78–9, 81, 88–90, 92, 119, 122, 159, 161, 169, 205, 223
Church of God of Prophecy 54, 59, 81, 89–90, 92, 95, 101, 118–20, 122, 129, 136, 165, 167–8, 179, 187, 205, 219, 243
Church history, British 8, 20, 39, 48, 49–112, 153, 226, 228–9, 230, 234–5
Church leaders, Jamaican 88
Churches, African 31–2, 47, 65, 67, 70, 86–7, 95, 103, 109–10, 114, 129, 149, 151, 180, 202, 226, 228, 248–9
Churches, Black 1–6, 7–48, 49–53, 55–62, 68–9, 72–5, 77, 79–80, 83–4, 87–8, 90–1, 93, 97–101, 103–4, 106–8, 110, 112–13, 117–18, 128–9, 136, 149, 153–4, 157–8, 184, 191, 197–8, 200, 208, 212, 217, 219–20, 223, 227, 231, 233, 235, 244, 247
Churches, Black-led 7, 19–20, 25, 29–32, 39, 41–7, 53, 56–64, 66, 69, 72–3, 75–7, 79–80, 82, 83–98, 99–100, 104–5, 113–53, 162, 166, 168, 196, 200, 213, 215, 217–9, 235, 241, 243–4
Churches, Black Majority 1–7, 20, 30, 46–8, 49–112, 113–14, 117–9, 122, 127–33, 135–53, 154–96, 197–215, 217–19, 221–240, 240–6, 247–50
Churches, British 5, 36, 51–2, 56–7, 80–1, 88, 91, 101, 149, 170, 219, 244
Churches, Evangelical 152, 244
Churches, missional 175, 224, 226, 229
Community 7, 12, 16, 18–19, 23, 29, 31–2, 36–9, 41, 43–7, 55–6, 58, 60–4, 66–7, 70–2, 74–5, 80–1, 85–9, 93–4, 96, 99, 102–4, 109–10, 114, 116, 118, 122, 135, 155–60, 162–9, 172–7, 179–87, 189–96, 199–200, 204, 207–8, 214, 220–1, 223–5, 227, 232–4, 236, 238–43, 245–9
Community, British 63, 74, 80, 155, 162, 182, 199, 208, 221, 233, 240, 247–9
Community, faith 61, 64, 80, 103, 110, 114, 155, 160, 174, 176, 181, 189, 190–6, 220, 227
Consumer 91, 102–3, 105, 111, 158, 205–6
Context 1–4, 6–7, 15, 44, 50, 57, 63, 65, 73–4, 79–80, 82–3, 100, 104, 114, 117–18, 126–9, 132, 134, 137–9, 141, 146, 151, 156, 157, 162, 180, 189–90, 198, 200, 202, 204, 207–11, 216, 220, 226, 232–5, 237, 240–2, 246
Context, cultural 65, 104, 126–7, 134, 137, 207, 210–11, 233, 235, 240
Contextualization 17, 37, 64, 79, 115, 129, 136, 145, 148, 159–60, 188, 204–5, 207, 219, 221, 225, 229
Cosmology, African 4, 62, 68–9, 83, 114–15, 128, 146, 242
Cosmology, Caribbean 4–5, 62, 68, 114–15, 242
Culture 5, 7, 9–11, 13, 16, 19, 21, 23, 28–30, 37, 39–45, 47, 52, 54–7, 59–65, 68, 70, 73–5, 79, 85–9, 91–3, 102–4, 107, 111, 114–17, 121, 126–34, 136–8, 140, 144–50, 153–8, 160–1, 173–5, 177–8, 180, 182, 184–5, 188, 191, 194–5, 197–214, 216–19, 221, 223–29, 232–41, 243–9
Culture, British 9, 132–3, 137, 146, 155, 158, 197, 204, 207–8, 226, 228–9, 237

Deliverance 23, 67, 149, 181
Denominationalism 1, 42–9, 55, 57–61, 69, 72–3, 75, 78, 89–90, 92–3, 97–8, 113–14, 118, 122, 127–9, 149, 151, 156–7, 159, 168, 188, 196, 213–4, 232, 250
Development 3, 18, 47, 53, 55, 58, 61, 64, 72, 81, 83, 93–4, 96, 99, 103–4, 109, 112, 117, 126, 128, 139–40, 155–7, 159–61, 167–8, 171–3, 176, 179, 190–1, 193, 196, 198, 200, 203–4, 209, 210, 213, 215–17, 223, 228, 231, 238, 243, 245–6, 249
Diaspora 7, 19, 43–6, 49, 52, 55–6, 58–61, 64–5, 70, 83, 88, 90–1, 114, 116–17, 121, 128–9, 132–3, 136, 146, 151, 157, 159, 162, 167, 197–200, 202–3, 205, 229, 234–9, 242

308                    *Index*

Diaspora, African 56, 132–3, 162, 199, 205, 236
Diaspora, Black 61, 121
Distinctive 3, 5–6, 19–21, 27, 31, 33, 44–5, 47, 49–50, 53, 57, 63–4, 69, 73–4, 78–9, 82–4, 86, 88, 91, 94, 101, 103, 113–17, 123, 127–30, 132, 135–8, 142–3, 145, 148, 154, 156, 159, 173, 177, 187, 196–7, 202, 217, 224, 229, 234, 242
Distinctiveness 1, 3–4, 6, 30, 89, 105, 113, 124, 126, 135, 138, 219–20, 225, 230, 241, 245

Economic 7–11, 13–14, 17–8, 32, 34, 40–4, 47–9, 51–9, 61–4, 67, 69, 70, 72–5, 79–82, 87–8, 90, 95–6, 102, 116, 121, 131–2, 150–1, 154–6, 160, 162, 167, 171–2, 175, 184, 188, 199–200, 221–2, 234–9, 241, 243, 250
Education 18, 32, 40, 42, 52, 69, 73, 90–2, 110, 132, 150, 159–60, 162, 166, 168, 173–5, 177, 179, 185, 192–3, 196, 199–200, 214, 216, 220, 235, 238, 244, 247, 249
Ecumenism 5, 24, 53, 68, 94, 110, 115, 122, 135–6, 145, 168–72, 219–20, 227–8, 244, 249
Europe 12, 20, 24, 49–52, 70, 81, 115, 117–19, 128–9, 136, 144, 149, 154, 175, 178, 200–5, 209, 220, 222, 230, 234–6
Equiano, Olaudah 16, 33, 36, 140, 184
Evangelical 17, 34, 38, 46, 80, 94–7, 103, 109–10, 128, 143–4, 150, 152, 159, 161, 169, 171, 180, 189, 195, 244
Evangelical Alliance 94–7, 109–10, 152, 159, 169, 171, 244
Evangelical Alliance, African Caribbean 46, 94–5, 97–9, 108, 150, 180
Evangelicalism 169, 243–5
Evangelism 30, 36, 42, 48, 58, 60, 67, 73, 80, 84, 86, 88–9, 101, 103, 106, 113, 125, 160, 204, 214, 224, 226, 233–4, 241, 247–9

Faith 1, 4, 6–7, 10, 15–16, 19, 21, 24, 29–33, 35–7, 39, 42–5, 47–52, 54–8, 61, 63–6, 69–70, 73–4, 76–7, 80, 85, 88–92, 94, 103, 105–6, 109–12, 114, 117, 119, 128, 130–7, 140, 142, 144, 151, 153, 155–6, 160, 166–9, 172, 174, 176, 181, 183, 185, 188–98, 208, 212, 214–15, 218, 220, 223, 227, 234–5, 237, 240, 242, 244, 248–50

Gee, Donald 26–7, 29, 44, 46, 84, 231
Gerloff, Roswith 29, 46–7, 59, 83–4, 91–3, 114, 118, 120–1, 233
Goodman, Douglas 76, 106–7, 119, 211
Growth 1–4, 6, 8, 15, 20, 29–30, 41, 45–7, 49–52, 54, 56–61, 63–4, 66–7, 69, 71–7, 80, 83–4, 87–92, 95–6, 99–104, 109, 111–12, 118, 121, 129, 131, 136, 140, 148, 154–8, 168, 196, 198–201, 204–5, 208–9, 212, 215, 222–3, 226, 228–9, 230, 234–5, 237, 242, 246–7, 249

Health and Wealth 132, 149–52, 201–2, 243
Hermeneutics 5, 15, 30, 64, 82, 92, 117, 134, 136–7, 139–42, 144, 153, 203, 218, 240–2
Historic denominations 28, 44, 48, 50, 55–8, 62, 105, 114, 136, 144–5, 154, 157–8, 169, 197, 208, 213, 232, 245, 248
Historiography 3–4, 29, 55, 86, 114, 130, 161, 232–3
History 1–10, 17, 19–22, 25–6, 33–4, 37–42, 48, 49–51, 55, 59, 73–4, 84, 86, 95, 99, 106, 112, 129, 134–5, 137, 141, 143, 149–50, 153–5, 157, 175, 187, 192, 194, 197–9, 201–2, 204, 219, 226, 228–9, 230–1, 233–5, 248
Hollenweger, Walter 5, 63, 104, 117–18, 131, 213–4, 216

Immigration 39, 41–2, 54, 57, 67, 73, 90, 133, 181, 192, 199, 222, 229, 234, 236
Immigration history 39, 73
Irukwu, Agu 79, 99, 101, 106, 157–8, 170, 181, 204, 206, 211, 239

Jamaica 1, 17, 20, 37–40, 42, 44–5, 54–5, 57, 60, 70, 87, 88, 115, 121, 169, 217–18, 236
Jamaican emigrants 44
Jamaican migrants 57
Jesus House 2, 71, 80, 101–2, 106, 148–9, 159, 163–5, 167, 170, 187, 204–6, 211, 239

Kalu, Ogbu 63, 82, 114, 129, 130, 139, 144, 199, 201
KICC *see* Kingsway International Christian Centre
Kingsway International Christian Centre 70, 83, 94–6, 101, 108–9, 111, 119, 148, 162–3, 166, 186, 206, 226–7

Liberation Theological Praxis 137, 242
London 2, 7, 9, 11–3, 15, 28, 31, 34, 38, 42, 45, 47, 53, 55, 59–60, 64–5, 67, 70–1, 75, 84, 86, 92, 96, 101, 106–11, 119, 132, 146,

148, 154–7, 159, 162–4, 166–7, 170, 174, 177, 179–82, 185–7, 193, 199, 202, 211, 225, 228, 232, 234, 239–40, 243, 246

Migration 7–8, 11, 18, 23, 26, 29–31, 39–42, 49, 52–4, 57–8, 60, 64, 67–8, 73, 82, 87–90, 95–6, 102, 133, 136, 140, 144, 149, 154, 155–6, 158, 181, 191–2, 199–201, 203, 206, 222, 229, 234–9, 241, 246
Mission 21–4, 32, 45–6, 49–51, 54, 58–9, 67, 70–1, 73, 75, 84, 86–91, 112, 117, 128, 143, 151, 153, 156–7, 159, 167, 172, 196, 200, 202, 204–5, 208–10, 213–16, 222, 224–5, 228–9, 230–6, 238, 241, 243, 247–8
Missional 61, 73, 76, 93, 102–3, 157, 175, 196–7, 202, 204–9, 212–3, 219, 222–6, 229, 247–8
Missionary 17, 24, 26, 31–2, 34, 37–9, 42–3, 45–6, 48, 57–9, 63, 65–6, 70, 73, 77, 85–6, 112, 115, 121–2, 128, 143, 149, 200, 202, 214–15, 224–6, 230–4, 236, 241, 246–9
Music 12, 64, 71, 93, 96, 104, 115, 145–6, 148, 164, 175, 206
Musicians 12, 39, 96, 145, 148, 218–19

Origin 1, 3–7, 19–20, 45, 66, 69, 102, 104, 121, 123, 150, 156, 166, 225, 230–3

Pentecostalism 2, 5–6, 8, 19–21, 23, 25, 29–30, 48, 52–3, 62–3, 65, 67–72, 77, 79, 82, 84–5, 95, 101, 104, 115, 118–22, 129–31, 134, 136, 139–40, 142–5, 148–50, 153, 156, 199, 201, 216, 230–4, 238, 240–2, 244–7
Pentecostalism, African 6, 29, 79, 82, 88, 115, 118, 129–30, 143–4, 153, 242
Pentecostalism, American 21–2, 101, 115, 131, 136, 232, 234
Pentecostalism, British 3, 5, 8, 19–20, 23–6, 30, 46, 52, 84, 216, 230, 232–3, 240
Postmodernity 133, 178, 207, 209
Prayer 15, 23–4, 32, 47, 58, 60, 65, 67, 89, 104–6, 113, 118, 120, 133, 144–7, 167, 169–70, 186, 202, 213, 220, 223, 231, 248
Preaching 4, 22, 32, 34–5, 53, 55, 79, 82–3, 86, 88, 92, 104, 125, 133, 142–4, 146, 151, 233, 240–1
Prosperity gospel 69, 149–50, 153
Public policy 43, 98, 171, 183, 189, 191–2, 194, 196, 223, 245

Racism 10, 29, 32, 41, 43–5, 47–9, 51, 54–6, 61, 67–8, 84, 86–88, 118, 128, 133, 138, 160, 175, 181, 183–4, 198–9, 237–8, 241
Rastafarianism 61, 91–3, 217–19
RCCG *see* Redeemed Christian Church of God
Redeemed Christian Church of God 2, 70–2, 77–9, 80–2, 92, 96, 101, 106, 111, 119, 146, 148–9, 156, 162–3, 167, 170–2, 186, 195, 204–5, 209, 211, 213, 226, 236, 239 246
Religious 5, 7, 18–21, 25, 27, 29, 31–2, 41–4, 46, 48, 52, 56–7, 62, 64–6, 70, 74–7, 79–80, 86, 88, 91–3, 95–8, 101, 118, 121, 127, 131–2, 134–5, 145–6, 149–51, 158–60, 166, 169, 172–3, 175, 180, 184, 186, 188–96, 198, 200–1, 205–7, 215, 222, 224, 231, 234–9, 241–2, 247
Robinson 25, 96–7, 148
Robinson and Smith 210

Schism 68, 75–7, 89, 103, 120, 122, 126, 134, 143, 156, 211, 246
Slave trade 7–12, 14, 16–17, 19, 36, 41, 48, 53, 86, 115–6, 128, 184
Slavery 10–11, 14–17, 19, 28, 33, 35–7, 48, 52, 54, 115–7, 127, 137, 140, 170–1, 221, 232
Social action 33, 53, 61, 71, 80–1, 86–7, 91, 93, 121, 160–5, 167–8, 171–2, 174, 185, 190, 196, 198
Social capital 171–2, 190–1, 193, 242–6

Theology, African 64, 68, 115, 128–9
Theology, American Black 130, 149, 152–3, 197, 220
Theology, American Liberation 5, 216
Theology, Black British 2, 5, 198, 215–8, 220, 221, 229
Theology, Liberation 2, 113, 127, 133, 150, 216
Theology, Oneness 119, 121–3, 125–7, 153
Trinity 82, 123–5, 126
Trinity chapel 80, 204–5, 211, 239

Ukah, A. 77, 80, 139, 146, 148, 150, 204–6, 209

Windrush 1, 5, 8, 31–3, 39–42, 44–5, 48–50, 52, 54–6, 59, 61–2, 72, 84, 87–9, 91–3, 95, 101, 103, 111, 117, 155, 160, 178, 198–200, 204, 221, 232–3, 235–7, 243

Lightning Source UK Ltd.
Milton Keynes UK
UKOW04f1708130915

258569UK00001B/127/P